5th Workshop on Representation Learning for NLP (RepL4NLP-2020)

Online
9 July 2020

ISBN: 978-1-7138-1389-7

ACL 2020

The 5th Workshop on Representation Learning for NLP (RepL4NLP-2020)

Proceedings of the Workshop

July 9, 2020

Introduction

The 5th Workshop on Representation Learning for NLP (RepL4NLP-2020) will be hosted at ACL 2020. The workshop is being organised by Spandana Gella, Johannes Welbl, Marek Rei, Fabio Petroni, Patrick Lewis, Emma Strubell, Minjoon Seo and Hannaneh Hajishirzi; and advised by Isabelle Augenstein, Kyunghyun Cho, Edward Grefenstette, Karl Moritz Hermann, and Chris Dyer. The workshop is organised by the ACL Special Interest Group on Representation Learning (SIGREP).

The 5th Workshop on Representation Learning for NLP aims to continue the success of the 1st Workshop on Representation Learning for NLP (about 50 submissions and over 250 attendees; second most attended collocated event at ACL'16 after WMT), 2nd Workshop on Representation Learning for NLP, 3rd Workshop on Representation Learning for NLP, and 4th Workshop on Representation Learning for NLP. The workshop was introduced as a synthesis of several years of independent *CL workshops focusing on vector space models of meaning, compositionality, and the application of deep neural networks and spectral methods to NLP. It provides a forum for discussing recent advances on these topics, as well as future research directions in linguistically motivated vector-based models in NLP.

Organizers:

Spandana Gella, Amazon AI
Johannes Welbl, University College London
Marek Rei, Imperial College London
Fabio Petroni, Facebook AI Research
Patrick Lewis, University College London & FAIR
Emma Strubell, Carnegie Mellon University & FAIR
Minjoon Seo, University of Washington & Naver
Hannaneh Hajishirzi, University of Washington

Senior Advisors:

Kyunghyun Cho, NYU and Facebook AI Research
Edward Grefenstette, Facebook AI Research & University College London
Karl Moritz Hermann, DeepMind
Laura Rimell, DeepMind
Chris Dyer, DeepMind
Isabelle Augenstein, University of Copenhagen

Keynote Speakers:

Kristina Toutanova, Google Research
Ellie Pavlick, Brown University & Google
Mike Lewis, Facebook AI Research
Evelina Fedorenko, Massachusetts Institute of Technology

Program Committee:

Muhammad Abdul-Mageed
Guy Aglionby
Roee Aharoni
Arjun Akula
Julio Amador Díaz López
Mikel Artetxe
Yoav Artzi
Miguel Ballesteros
Gianni Barlacchi
Max Bartolo
Joost Bastings
Federico Bianchi
Rishi Bommasani
Samuel R. Bowman
Andrew Caines
Claire Cardie
Haw-shiuan Chang

Lin Chen
Danlu Chen
Yue Chen
Yu Cheng
Manuel R. Ciosici
William Cohen
Christopher Davis
Eliezer de Souza da Silva
Luciano Del Corro
Zhi-Hong Deng
Leon Derczynski
Shehzaad Dhuliawala
Giuseppe Antonio Di Luna
Kalpit Dixit
Aleksandr Drozd
Kevin Duh
Necati Bora Edizel
Guy Emerson
Eraldo Fernandes
Orhan Firat
Rainer Gemulla
Kevin Gimpel
Hongyu Gong
Ana Valeria González
Batool Haider
He He
Ji He
Jiaji Huang
Sung Ju Hwang
Robin Jia
Mark Johnson
Arzoo Katiyar
Santosh Kesiraju
Douwe Kiela
Ekaterina Kochmar
Julia Kreutzer
Shankar Kumar
John P. Lalor
Carolin Lawrence
Kenton Lee
Xiang Li
Shaohua Li
Tao Li
Bill Yuchen Lin
Chu-Cheng Lin
Peng Liu
Feifan Liu
Fei Liu
Suresh Manandhar
Luca Massarelli

Sneha Mehta
Todor Mihaylov
Tsvetomila Mihaylova
Swaroop Mishra
Ashutosh Modi
Lili Mou
Maximilian Mozes
Khalil Mrini
Phoebe Mulcaire
Nikita Nangia
Shashi Narayan
Thien Huu Nguyen
Tsuyoshi Okita
Ankur Padia
Ashwin Paranjape
Tom Pelsmaeker
Aleksandra Piktus
Vassilis Plachouras
Edoardo Maria Ponti
Ratish Puduppully
Leonardo Querzoni
Chris Quirk
Vipul Raheja
Muhammad Rahman
Natraj Raman
Surangika Ranathunga
Siva Reddy
Sravana Reddy
Roi Reichart
Devendra Sachan
Marzieh Saeidi
Avneesh Saluja
Hinrich Schütze
Tianze Shi
Vered Shwartz
Kyungwoo Song
Daniil Sorokin
Lucia Specia
Mark Steedman
Karl Stratos
Ming Sun
Jörg Tiedemann
Ivan Titov
Nadi Tomeh
Shubham Toshniwal
Kristina Toutanova
Lifu Tu
Lyle Ungar
Menno van Zaanen
Andrea Vanzo

Shikhar Vashishth
Eva Maria Vecchi
Elena Voita
Yogarshi Vyas
Hai Wang
Bonnie Webber
Dirk Weissenborn
Rodrigo Wilkens
Yuxiang Wu
Yadollah Yaghoobzadeh
Haiqin Yang
Majid Yazdani
Wen-tau Yih
Hong Yu
Wenxuan Zhou
Dong Zhou
Xiangyang Zhou
Imed Zitouni
Diarmuid Ó Séaghdha
Robert Östling

Table of Contents

Workshop Program

Thursday, July 9, 2020

9:30–9:45   **Welcome and Opening Remarks**

9:45–14:45   **Keynote Session**

9:45–10:30   *Invited talk 1*
Kristina Toutanova

10:30–11:00   **Coffee Break**

11:00–11:45   *Invited talk 2*
Ellie Pavlick

11:45–12:30   *Invited talk 3*
Mike Lewis

12:30–14:00   **Lunch**

14:00–14:45   *Invited talk 4*
Evelina Fedorenko

14:45–15:00   **Outstanding Papers Spotlight Presentations**

15:00–16:30   Poster Session

Zero-Resource Cross-Domain Named Entity Recognition
Zihan Liu, Genta Indra Winata and Pascale Fung

Encodings of Source Syntax: Similarities in NMT Representations Across Target Languages
Tyler A. Chang and Anna Rafferty

Learning Probabilistic Sentence Representations from Paraphrases
Mingda Chen and Kevin Gimpel

On the Ability of Self-Attention Networks to Recognize Counter Languages
Satwik Bhattamishra, Kabir Ahuja and Navin Goyal

Word Embeddings as Tuples of Feature Probabilities
Siddharth Bhat, Alok Debnath, Souvik Banerjee and Manish Shrivastava

Compositionality and Capacity in Emergent Languages
Abhinav Gupta, Cinjon Resnick, Jakob Foerster, Andrew Dai and Kyunghyun Cho

Learning Geometric Word Meta-Embeddings
Pratik Jawanpuria, Satya Dev N T V, Anoop Kunchukuttan and Bamdev Mishra

Variational Inference for Learning Representations of Natural Language Edits
Edison Marrese-Taylor, Machel Reid and Yutaka Matsuo

Improving Bilingual Lexicon Induction with Unsupervised Post-Processing of Monolingual Word Vector Spaces
Ivan Vulić, Anna Korhonen and Goran Glavaš

Adversarial Training for Commonsense Inference
Lis Pereira, Xiaodong Liu, Fei Cheng, Masayuki Asahara and Ichiro Kobayashi

Evaluating Natural Alpha Embeddings on Intrinsic and Extrinsic Tasks
Riccardo Volpi and Luigi Malagò

Enhancing Transformer with Sememe Knowledge
Yuhui Zhang, Chenghao Yang, Zhengping Zhou and Zhiyuan Liu

Evaluating Compositionality of Sentence Representation Models
Hanoz Bhathena, Angelica Willis and Nathan Dass

AI4Bharat-IndicNLP Dataset: Monolingual Corpora and Word Embeddings for Indic Languages: Monolingual Corpora and Word Embeddings for Indic Languages
Anoop Kunchukuttan, Divyanshu Kakwani, Satish Golla, Gokul N.C., Avik Bhattacharyya, Mitesh M. Khapra and Pratyush Kumar

Supertagging with CCG primitives
Aditya Bhargava and Gerald Penn

What's in a Name? Are BERT Named Entity Representations just as Good for any other Name?
Sriram Balasubramanian, Naman Jain, Gaurav Jindal, Abhijeet Awasthi and Sunita Sarawagi

16:30–17:30   **Panel Discussion**

17:30–17:40   **Closing Remarks and Best Paper Announcement**

Zero-Resource Cross-Domain Named Entity Recognition

Zihan Liu, Genta Indra Winata, Pascale Fung
Center for Artificial Intelligence Research (CAiRE)
Department of Electronic and Computer Engineering
The Hong Kong University of Science and Technology, Clear Water Bay, Hong Kong
`zihan.liu@connect.ust.hk`

Abstract

Existing models for cross-domain named entity recognition (NER) rely on numerous unlabeled corpus or labeled NER training data in target domains. However, collecting data for low-resource target domains is not only expensive but also time-consuming. Hence, we propose a cross-domain NER model that does not use any external resources. We first introduce a *Multi-Task Learning* (MTL) by adding a new objective function to detect whether tokens are named entities or not. We then introduce a framework called *Mixture of Entity Experts* (MoEE) to improve the robustness for zero-resource domain adaptation. Finally, experimental results show that our model outperforms strong unsupervised cross-domain sequence labeling models, and the performance of our model is close to that of the state-of-the-art model which leverages extensive resources.

1   Introduction

Named entity recognition (NER) is a fundamental task in text understanding and information extraction. Recently, supervised learning approaches have shown their effectiveness in detecting named entities (Ma and Hovy, 2016; Chiu and Nichols, 2016; Winata et al., 2019). However, there is a vast performance drop for low-resource target domains when massive training data are absent. To solve this data scarcity issue, a straightforward idea is to utilize the NER knowledge learned from high-resource domains and then adapt it to low-resource domains, which is called cross-domain NER.

Due to the large variances in entity names across different domains, cross-domain NER has thus far been a challenging task. Most existing methods consider a supervised setting, leveraging labeled NER data for both the source and target domains (Yang et al., 2017; Lin and Lu, 2018).

However, labeled data in target domains is not always available. Unsupervised domain adaptation naturally arises as a possible way to circumvent the usage of labeled NER data in target domains. However, the only existing method, proposed by Jia et al. (2019), requires an external unlabeled data corpus in both the source and target domains to conduct the unsupervised cross-domain NER task, and such resources are difficult to obtain, especially for low-resource target domains. Therefore, we consider unsupervised zero-resource cross-domain adaptation for NER which only utilizes the NER training samples in a single source domain.

To meet the challenge of zero-resource cross-domain adaptation, we first propose to conduct multi-task learning (MTL) by adding an objective function to detect whether tokens are named entities or not. This objective function helps the model to learn general representations of named entities and to distinguish named entities from sequences in target domains. In addition, we observe that in many cases, different entity categories could have a similar or the same context. For example, in the sentence "Arafat subsequently cancelled a meeting between Israeli and PLO officials," the person entity "Arafat", can be replaced with an organization entity within the same context, which illustrates the confusion among different entity categories and makes zero-resource adaptation much more difficult. Intuitively, when the entity type of a token is hard to be predicted based on the token itself and the token's context, we want to borrow the opinions (i.e., representations) from different experts. Hence, we propose a Mixture of Entity Experts (MoEE) framework to tackle the confusion of entity categories, and the predictions are based on the tokens and the context, as well as all entity experts.

Experimental results show that our model is able to outperform current strong unsupervised cross-domain sequence tagging approaches, and reach comparable results to the state-of-the-art unsupervised method that utilizes extensive resources.

Proceedings of the 5th Workshop on Representation Learning for NLP (RepL4NLP-2020), pages 1–6
July 9, 2020. ©2020 Association for Computational Linguistics

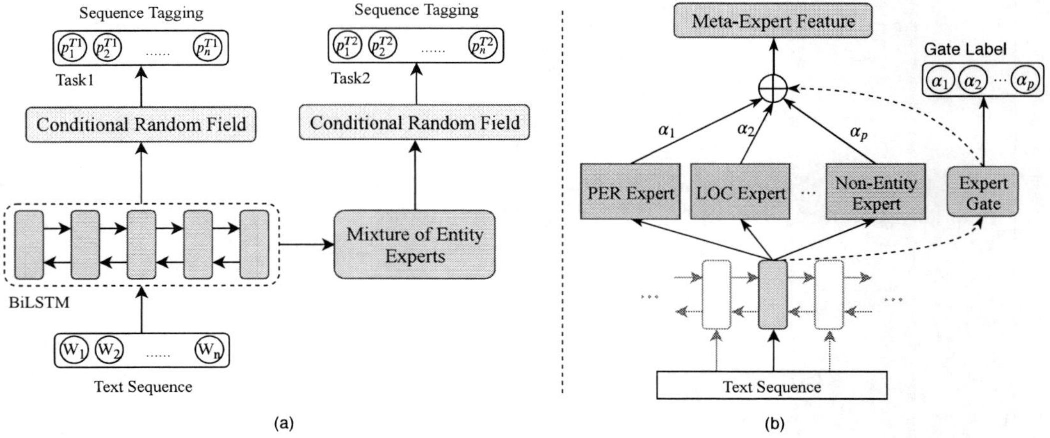

Figure 1: Model architecture (a) with multi-task learning and (b) with the Mixture of Entity Experts module.

2   Related Work

Most of the existing work on cross-domain NER has been to investigate the supervised setting, where both source and target domains have labeled data (Daume III, 2007; Obeidat et al., 2016; Yang et al., 2017; Lee et al., 2018). Yang et al. (2017) jointly trained models on the source and target domain with shared parameters. Lin and Lu (2018) added adaptation layers on top of existing models, and Wang et al. (2018) introduced label-aware feature representations for NER adaptation. Lee et al. (2018) utilized the idea of transfer learning by first initializing a target model with parameters learned from source-domain NER, and then using labeled target domain data to fine-tune the model. However, no prior work has focused on the unsupervised setting of cross-domain NER, except for Jia et al. (2019). In Jia et al. (2019), however, external unlabeled data corpora resources in both the source and target domains are required to train language models for domain adaptations. This limitation has motivated us to develop a model that doesn't need any external resources.

Tackling the low-resource scenario where there are zero or minimal existing resources has always been an interesting yet challenging task (Xie et al., 2018; Liu et al., 2019b; Lample et al., 2017; Conneau et al., 2017; Shah et al., 2019). Instead of utilizing large amounts of bilingual resources, Liu et al. (2019a,b) only utilized a few word pairs for zero-shot cross-lingual dialogue systems. Unsupervised machine translation approaches (Lample et al., 2017; Artetxe et al., 2017) have also been introduced to circumvents the need of parallel data.

Winata et al. (2020) introduced the cross-accent speech recognition task and utilized meta-learning to cope with the data scarcity issue in target accents. Bapna et al. (2017) and Shah et al. (2019) proposed to do cross-domain slot filling with minimal resources. To the best of our knowledge, we are the first to propose methods on cross-domain adaptation for NER with zero external resources.

3   Methodology

As illustrated in Fig. 1, our model combines a bidirectional LSTM and conditional random field (CRF) into a BiLSTM-CRF structure (Lample et al., 2016) with MTL and MoEE modules. The parameters of BiLSTM are shared in the multi-task learning.

3.1   Multi-Task Learning

Due to the large variations of named entities across domains, unsupervised cross-domain NER models often suffer from an inability to recognize named entities. Hence, we propose to learn general representations of named entities and enhance the robustness for adaptation by adding an objective function to predict whether tokens are named entities or not, which is represented as $Task_1$ in Fig. 1(a). To do so, based on the original named entity labels for each token in the training set, we create another label set, which represents whether tokens are named entities or not. Specifically, in this process, all non-entity tokens are consistent with the original labels, and other tokens belonging to different entity categories are classified as being in the same class representing the general named entity. $Task_2$ in

Fig. 1(a) represents the original NER task, which is to predict a concrete category for each token. Let us denote $X = [w_1, w_2, ..., w_n]$ as the input text sequence, and the MTL can be formulated as:

$$[h_1, h_2, ..., h_n] = \text{BiLSTM}([w_1, w_2, ..., w_n]),$$
$$[p_1^{T_1}, p_2^{T_1}, ..., p_n^{T_1}] = \text{CRF}_1([h_1, h_2, ..., h_n]),$$
$$[m_1, m_2, ..., m_n] = \text{MoEE}([h_1, h_2, ..., h_n]),$$
$$[p_1^{T_2}, p_2^{T_2}, ..., p_n^{T_2}] = \text{CRF}_2([m_1, m_2, ..., m_n]),$$

where CRF_1 and CRF_2 denote the CRF layers for Task_1 and Task_2, respectively, and $[p_1^{T_1}, p_2^{T_1}, ..., p_n^{T_1}]$ and $[p_1^{T_2}, p_2^{T_2}, ..., p_n^{T_2}]$ represent the corresponding predictions.

3.2 Mixture of Entity Experts

Traditional NER models make predictions based on the features of the tokens and the context. Due to the confusion among different entity categories, NER models could easily overfit to the source domain entities and lose generalization ability to the target domain. Therefore, we introduce an MoEE framework, as depicted in Fig. 1(b). It combines representations generated by experts to produce the final prediction. In this way, the knowledge from different experts is incorporated to model the inherent confusion and improve the generalization ability to target domains.

Each entity category acts as an entity expert, which consists of a linear layer. Note that we consider the non-entity as a special entity category. The *expert gate* consists of a linear layer followed by a softmax layer, which generates the confidence distribution over entity experts. We use the gold labels in Task_2 to supervise the training of the expert gate. Finally, the meta-expert feature incorporates features from all experts based on the confidential scores from the expert gate. We formulate the MoEE module as follows:

$$[\text{expt}_i^1, \cdots, \text{expt}_i^E] = [\text{L}^1(h_i), \cdots, \text{L}^E(h_i)], \quad (1)$$
$$[\alpha_1, \cdots, \alpha_E] = \text{Softmax}(\text{Linear}(h_i)), \quad (2)$$
$$m_i = \sum_{a=1}^{E} \alpha_a * \text{expt}_i^a, \quad (3)$$

where m_i is the meta-expert feature for the i-th hidden state of the BiLSTM, where expt is the feature generated from the expert, and L denotes the linear layer. We show that the MoEE has E experts following the number of entity categories plus the non-entity category. The expert features are computed based on the BiLSTM hidden states, and the predictions are conditioned on the expert features and the hidden states, which makes cross-domain adaptation more robust.

3.3 Optimization

During training, we optimize for Task_1, Task_2 and the expert gate with cross-entropy losses $\mathcal{L}^{task1}$, $\mathcal{L}^{task2}$ and $\mathcal{L}^{gate}$, respectively, as we detail below:

$$\mathcal{L}^{task1} = \sum_{j=1}^{J} \sum_{k=1}^{|Y_j|} - \log(p_{jk}^{T_1} \cdot (y_{jk}^{T_1})^T), \quad (4)$$
$$\mathcal{L}^{task2} = \sum_{j=1}^{J} \sum_{k=1}^{|Y_j|} - \log(p_{jk}^{T_2} \cdot (y_{jk}^{T_2})^T), \quad (5)$$
$$\mathcal{L}^{gate} = \sum_{j=1}^{J} \sum_{k=1}^{|Y_j|} - \log(p_{jk}^{gate} \cdot (y_{jk}^{gate})^T), \quad (6)$$

where J and $|Y_j|$ denote the number of training data and the length of the tokens for each training sample, respectively; p_{jk} and y_{jk} denote the predictions and labels for each token, respectively; and the superscripts of p_{jk} and y_{jk} represent the tasks. Hence, the final objective function is to minimize the sum of all the aforementioned loss functions.

4 Experiments

4.1 Dataset

We take the CoNLL-2003 English NER data (Sang and De Meulder, 2003) containing 15.0K/3.5K/3.7K samples for the training/validation/test sets as our source domain. We take the dataset containing 2K sentences from SciTech News provided by Jia et al. (2019) as our target domain. The datasets in the source and target domains contain the same four types of entities, namely, PER (person), LOC (location), ORG (organization), and MISC (miscellaneous).

4.2 Experimental Setup

Embeddings We test our approaches on the FastText word embeddings (Bojanowski et al., 2017) and the pre-trained model BERT (Devlin et al., 2019). Entity names in the target domain are likely to be out-of-vocabulary (OOV) words because they don't usually exist in the source domain training set. FastText word embeddings are able to leverage the subword information and avoid the OOV problem, and BERT can solve this problem by using the BPE encoding. We try both freeze and unfreeze settings

Model	BERT Fine-tune	FastText	
		unfreeze	freeze
Baseline			
Concept Tagger	67.14	62.34	66.86
Robust Sequence Tagger	67.31	63.66	68.12
Zero-Resource			
BiLSTM-CRF	67.55	63.18	68.21
w/ MTL	**68.76**	64.62	69.35
w/ MoEE	68.06	**65.24**	69.27
w/ MTL and MoEE	68.59	64.88	**69.53**
Using high-resource data in source and target domains			
Jia et al. (2019)	73.59		

Table 1: F1-scores on the target domain. Models are implemented based on the corresponding embeddings.

for FastText embeddings in the training. And for the BERT model, we add different modules (e.g., MoEE) on top to do fine-tuning.

Baselines Since we are the first to conduct zero-resource cross-domain NER, we compare our approach with strong unsupervised cross-domain sequence labeling models under minimal resources. **Concept Tagger** was proposed by Bapna et al. (2017) to utilize entity descriptions for unsupervised cross-domain utterance slot filling, and **Robust Sequence Tagger** (Shah et al., 2019) was introduced to combined both entity descriptions and a few examples from each entity category for the same unsupervised task. In addition, we also compare our approach with the following baselines **BiLSTM-CRF** (Lample et al., 2016), **BiLSTM-CRF w/ MTL**, and **BiLSTM-CRF w/ MoEE**, as well as with the state-of-the-art model of the unsupervised cross-domain NER from Jia et al. (2019) which utilizes a large corpus in both the source and target domains.

Training Details For FastText embeddings [1] based models, we use a BiLSTM with a 200-dimensional hidden state and two layers. The linear layer size for each entity expert is 200. An Adam optimizer with a learning rate of 1e-3, a batch size of 32, and a dropout rate of 0.3 are used to train our model. We utilize the binary models provided in FastText to obtain the embeddings for OOV words. For BERT-based models, given the strong textual understanding ability of the BERT model, we remove the BiLSTM from the text encoder, and only linear layer is utilized for sequence labeling (i.e., CRF layer is removed) (Devlin et al., 2019). As

[1]Available in https://fasttext.cc/docs/en/pretrained-vectors.html

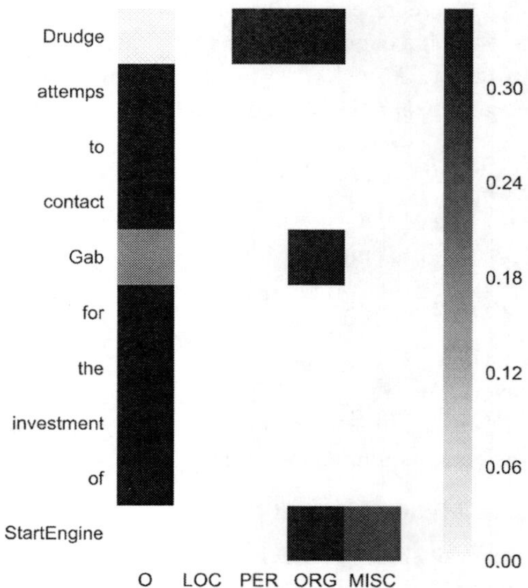

Figure 2: Confidence scores on different entity experts from the expert gate. "O" denotes non-entity expert.

for the evaluation, we use the standard IOB (in-out-begin) format to calculate the F1-score.

4.3 Results & Discussion

From Table 1, our model combined with MTL and the MoEE outperforms the strong baselines Concept Tagger and Robust Sequence Tagger on all the embedding settings that we test. We conjecture that these two baselines, which utilize slot descriptions or slot examples, are suitable for limited slot names in the slot filling task, while they fail to cope with wide variances of entity names in the NER task across different domains, while our model is more robust to the domain variations. MTL helps our model recognize named entities in the target domain, while the MoEE adds information from different entity experts and helps our model detect the specific named entity types. Surprisingly, the performance of our best model (with freezed FastText embeddings) is close to that of the state-of-the-art model that needs a large data corpus in the source and target domains, which illustrates our model's generalization ability to the target domain.

We observe that the freezed FastText embeddings bring better performance than unfreezed ones. We conjecture that the embeddings could overfit to the source domain if we unfreeze them in the training. Additionally, using freezed FastText embeddings is slightly better than BERT fine-tuning.

We speculate that the reason is that NER is a word-level sequence tagging task, while the BERT model leverages subword embeddings, which could lose part of the word-level information for the task.

We visualize the confidence scores on different entity experts for each token in Fig. 2. The expert gate can align non-entity tokens to the non-entity expert with strong confidence. For some entity tokens, e.g., "Drudge", the expert gate gives high confidence on more than one expert (e.g., "PER" and "ORG") since the model is not sure whether "Drudge" is a "PER" or "ORG". Our model is expected to learn the "PER" and "ORG" expert representations based on the hidden state of "Drudge", which contains the information of this token and its context, and then combine the expert representations for the prediction.

5 Conclusion

In this paper, we propose a zero-resource cross-domain framework for the named entity recognition task, which consists of multi-task learning and Mixture of Entity Experts modules. The former learns the general representations of named entities to cope with the model's inability to recognize named entities, while the latter learns to combine the representations of different entity experts, which are based on the BiLSTM hidden states. Experimental results show that our model outperforms strong cross-domain sequence tagging models, and the performance is close to that of the state-of-the-art model that utilizes extensive resources.

Acknowledgments

This work is partially funded by ITF/319/16FP and MRP/055/18 of the Innovation Technology Commission, the Hong Kong SAR Government.

References

Mikel Artetxe, Gorka Labaka, Eneko Agirre, and Kyunghyun Cho. 2017. Unsupervised neural machine translation. *arXiv preprint arXiv:1710.11041*.

Ankur Bapna, Gokhan Tür, Dilek Hakkani-Tür, and Larry Heck. 2017. Towards zero-shot frame semantic parsing for domain scaling. *Proc. Interspeech 2017*, pages 2476–2480.

Piotr Bojanowski, Edouard Grave, Armand Joulin, and Tomas Mikolov. 2017. Enriching word vectors with subword information. *Transactions of the Association for Computational Linguistics*, 5:135–146.

Jason Chiu and Eric Nichols. 2016. Named entity recognition with bidirectional lstm-cnns. *Transactions of the Association for Computational Linguistics*, 4(1):357–370.

Alexis Conneau, Guillaume Lample, Marc'Aurelio Ranzato, Ludovic Denoyer, and Hervé Jégou. 2017. Word translation without parallel data. *arXiv preprint arXiv:1710.04087*.

Hal Daume III. 2007. Frustratingly easy domain adaptation. In *Proceedings of the 45th Annual Meeting of the Association of Computational Linguistics*, pages 256–263.

Jacob Devlin, Ming-Wei Chang, Kenton Lee, and Kristina Toutanova. 2019. Bert: Pre-training of deep bidirectional transformers for language understanding. In *Proceedings of the 2019 Conference of the North American Chapter of the Association for Computational Linguistics: Human Language Technologies, Volume 1 (Long and Short Papers)*, pages 4171–4186.

Chen Jia, Xiaobo Liang, and Yue Zhang. 2019. Cross-domain ner using cross-domain language modeling. In *Proceedings of the 57th Annual Meeting of the Association for Computational Linguistics*, pages 2464–2474.

Guillaume Lample, Miguel Ballesteros, Sandeep Subramanian, Kazuya Kawakami, and Chris Dyer. 2016. Neural architectures for named entity recognition. In *Proceedings of the 2016 Conference of the North American Chapter of the Association for Computational Linguistics: Human Language Technologies*, pages 260–270.

Guillaume Lample, Alexis Conneau, Ludovic Denoyer, and Marc'Aurelio Ranzato. 2017. Unsupervised machine translation using monolingual corpora only. *arXiv preprint arXiv:1711.00043*.

Ji Young Lee, Franck Dernoncourt, and Peter Szolovits. 2018. Transfer learning for named-entity recognition with neural networks. In *Proceedings of the Eleventh International Conference on Language Resources and Evaluation (LREC-2018)*.

Bill Yuchen Lin and Wei Lu. 2018. Neural adaptation layers for cross-domain named entity recognition. In *Proceedings of the 2018 Conference on Empirical Methods in Natural Language Processing*, pages 2012–2022.

Zihan Liu, Jamin Shin, Yan Xu, Genta Indra Winata, Peng Xu, Andrea Madotto, and Pascale Fung. 2019a. Zero-shot cross-lingual dialogue systems with transferable latent variables. In *Proceedings of the 2019 Conference on Empirical Methods in Natural Language Processing and the 9th International Joint Conference on Natural Language Processing (EMNLP-IJCNLP)*, pages 1297–1303.

Zihan Liu, Genta Indra Winata, Zhaojiang Lin, Peng Xu, and Pascale Fung. 2019b. Attention-informed mixed-language training for zero-shot cross-lingual task-oriented dialogue systems. *arXiv preprint arXiv:1911.09273*.

Xuezhe Ma and Eduard Hovy. 2016. End-to-end sequence labeling via bi-directional lstm-cnns-crf. In *Proceedings of the 54th Annual Meeting of the Association for Computational Linguistics (Volume 1: Long Papers)*, pages 1064–1074.

Rasha Obeidat, Xiaoli Z. Fern, and Prasad Tadepalli. 2016. Label embedding approach for transfer learning. In *ICBO/BioCreative*.

Erik Tjong Kim Sang and Fien De Meulder. 2003. Introduction to the conll-2003 shared task: Language-independent named entity recognition. In *Proceedings of the Seventh Conference on Natural Language Learning at HLT-NAACL 2003*, pages 142–147.

Darsh Shah, Raghav Gupta, Amir Fayazi, and Dilek Hakkani-Tur. 2019. Robust zero-shot cross-domain slot filling with example values. In *Proceedings of the 57th Annual Meeting of the Association for Computational Linguistics*, pages 5484–5490, Florence, Italy. Association for Computational Linguistics.

Zhenghui Wang, Yanru Qu, Liheng Chen, Jian Shen, Weinan Zhang, Shaodian Zhang, Yimei Gao, Gen Gu, Ken Chen, and Yong Yu. 2018. Label-aware double transfer learning for cross-specialty medical named entity recognition. In *Proceedings of the 2018 Conference of the North American Chapter of the Association for Computational Linguistics: Human Language Technologies, Volume 1 (Long Papers)*, pages 1–15.

Genta Indra Winata, Samuel Cahyawijaya, Zihan Liu, Zhaojiang Lin, Andrea Madotto, Peng Xu, and Pascale Fung. 2020. Learning fast adaptation on cross-accented speech recognition. *arXiv preprint arXiv:2003.01901*.

Genta Indra Winata, Zhaojiang Lin, Jamin Shin, Zihan Liu, and Pascale Fung. 2019. Hierarchical meta-embeddings for code-switching named entity recognition. In *Proceedings of the 2019 Conference on Empirical Methods in Natural Language Processing and the 9th International Joint Conference on Natural Language Processing (EMNLP-IJCNLP)*, pages 3532–3538.

Jiateng Xie, Zhilin Yang, Graham Neubig, Noah A Smith, and Jaime G Carbonell. 2018. Neural cross-lingual named entity recognition with minimal resources. In *Proceedings of the 2018 Conference on Empirical Methods in Natural Language Processing*, pages 369–379.

Zhilin Yang, Ruslan Salakhutdinov, and William W. Cohen. 2017. Transfer learning for sequence tagging with hierarchical recurrent networks. In *International Conference on Learning Representations*.

Encodings of Source Syntax: Similarities in NMT Representations Across Target Languages

Tyler A. Chang
Carleton College
Northfield, MN
changt@carleton.edu

Anna N. Rafferty
Carleton College
Northfield, MN
arafferty@carleton.edu

Abstract

We train neural machine translation (NMT) models from English to six target languages, using NMT encoder representations to predict ancestor constituent labels of source language words. We find that NMT encoders learn similar source syntax regardless of NMT target language, relying on explicit morphosyntactic cues to extract syntactic features from source sentences. Furthermore, the NMT encoders outperform RNNs trained directly on several of the constituent label prediction tasks, suggesting that NMT encoder representations can be used effectively for natural language tasks involving syntax. However, both the NMT encoders and the directly-trained RNNs learn substantially different syntactic information from a probabilistic context-free grammar (PCFG) parser. Despite lower overall accuracy scores, the PCFG often performs well on sentences for which the RNN-based models perform poorly, suggesting that RNN architectures are constrained in the types of syntax they can learn.

1 Introduction

Neural machine translation (NMT) encoder representations have been used successfully for cross-task and cross-lingual transfer learning in a variety of natural language contexts (Eriguchi et al., 2018; McCann et al., 2017; Neubig and Hu, 2018). Previous work has investigated whether these representations encode syntactic information (Shi et al., 2016), as syntactic information is useful in many natural language tasks (Chen et al., 2017; Punyakanok et al., 2008). The deep recurrent neural network (RNN) architectures used by many NMT encoders can learn syntactic features, even without explicit supervision (Blevins et al., 2018; Futrell et al., 2019); NMT encoders specifically have been found to encode information about ancestor constituent labels for words (Blevins et al., 2018) and

even full syntactic parses of source language sentences (Shi et al., 2016).

Cross-linguistically, there is mixed evidence for how target language impacts the encoding of information in NMT encoder representations. Kudugunta et al. (2019) found that representations clustered based on target language family when sentence representations were aligned in a shared space. However, Belinkov et al. (2017) found only small effects of target language on the ability of NMT encoder states to predict part-of-speech (POS) tags. Because POS tags are typically reliant only on local features within sentences, these contrasting results could suggest that (1) localized encoded information is independent of NMT target language, or (2) encoded syntactic information in general is independent of NMT target language. In this work, we address the second possibility.

To evaluate more global syntactic information in NMT encoder representations, we assess the ability of NMT encoder states to predict ancestor constituent labels of words; this task is adopted from Blevins et al. (2018). Extending Blevins et al. (2018), we train NMT models towards multiple target languages and evaluate performance on individual constituent labels (e.g. noun phrases). We find that significant syntactic information is encoded regardless of target language, and target language has little impact on the syntactic information learned by NMT encoders. Furthermore, we find that NMT encoders rely on explicit morphosyntactic cues to extract syntactic information from sentences.

Finally, by training deep RNNs directly on the constituent label prediction task, we find that RNNs with explicit syntactic training data learn similar syntax to the NMT encoders. In contrast, a probabilistic context-free grammar (PCFG) parser performs significantly differently from both RNN-based models, suggesting that RNNs may be constrained by their reliance on explicit syntactic cues.

Proceedings of the 5th Workshop on Representation Learning for NLP (RepL4NLP-2020), pages 7–16
July 9, 2020. ©2020 Association for Computational Linguistics

2 Methodology

We trained NMT models from English to six different target languages, assessing the ability of NMT encoder states to predict POS, parent, grandparent, and great-grandparent constituent labels of words.

2.1 NMT Models

NMT models were trained on the United Nations (UN) Parallel Corpus, using the fully aligned subcorpus of approximately 11 million sentences translated to all six UN official languages: English, Spanish, French, Russian, Arabic, and Chinese (Ziemski et al., 2016). NMT models were trained from English to each target language using OpenNMT's PyTorch implementation (Klein et al., 2017) with byte pair encoding for subword tokenization in all languages (Sennrich et al., 2016). Each NMT encoder and decoder was a unidirectional four-layer long short-term memory (LSTM; Hochreiter and Schmidhuber, 1997) network with 500 dimensions, using dot-product global attention in the decoder (Luong et al., 2015). Each NMT model was trained for 11 epochs (approximately 2,000,000 steps) using Adam optimization (Kingma and Ba, 2014).[1] The model with the best performance on the UN evaluation dataset for each language was used to generate encoder representations in the constituent label prediction task.

2.2 Constituent Label Predictions

Dataset Constituent label predictions used tree-parsed sentences from the CoNLL-2012 dataset, containing sentences from English news and magazine articles, web data, and transcribed conversational speech (Pradhan et al., 2012).

As in Blevins et al. (2018), constituent label models were trained on the CoNLL-2012 development dataset and tested on the test dataset. A subset of the CoNLL-2012 training dataset was used as an evaluation dataset; the training, evaluation, and test datasets each contained approximately 160,000 English words.

Prediction models We trained simple feedforward neural networks to predict ancestor constituent labels (POS, parent, grandparent, and great-grandparent) of words, given the NMT encoder state after reading the word. The NMT encoders were kept fixed during constituent label training.

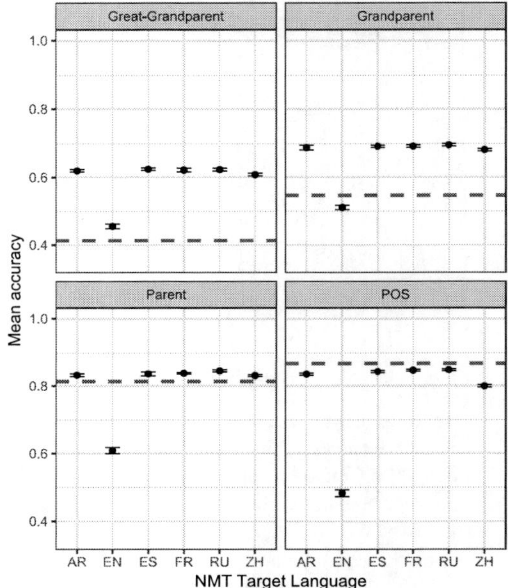

Figure 1: Results for the constituent label prediction tasks, trained from NMT encoder representations. Dots indicate mean accuracies (based on 20 feedforward models), bars indicate two standard deviations from the mean, and dashed lines represent baseline accuracies.

We used the deepest encoder layer as our encoder representation; deeper layers have been shown to perform better on constituent label prediction tasks (Blevins et al., 2018).

Each feedforward network contained one 500-dimensional hidden layer, and each model was trained until it completed 10 consecutive epochs with no improvement on the evaluation dataset. To account for variation between models based on random initialization of weights and shuffling of the training data, we trained 20 feedforward models for each combination of NMT encoder target language and constituent label (POS, parent, grandparent, or great-grandparent).

Baselines We computed a baseline accuracy for each constituent label prediction task by simply predicting the most frequent constituent label given the current input word (e.g. given the current input word "dog," the most frequent POS tag would be NN for "singular noun"). This baseline accuracy is the maximum possible accuracy for a deterministic model that only knows the current input word.

---

[1]The first 10 epochs used learning rate 0.0002; the learning rate was halved every 30,000 steps during the final epoch.

3   Results

NMT encoders learned syntax.   As shown in Figure 1, NMT encoder representations for all target languages except the autoencoder resulted in accuracy scores above the baseline for the parent, grandparent, and great-grandparent constituent label tasks (adjusted $p < 0.001$ for all comparisons, using one sample t-tests). The English autoencoder was the only target language without consistent performance above the baselines for these tasks; NMT autoencoders have been found to memorize sentences without learning syntactic information (Shi et al., 2016). These results indicate that with the exception of autoencoders, NMT encoder representations contain syntactic information regardless of target language.

Models performed poorly for POS tags.   In contrast to Blevins et al. (2018) but in line with Belinkov et al. (2017), all target languages performed slightly below the baseline for the POS prediction task (adjusted $p < 0.001$ for all comparisons, using one sample t-tests). This result may be because POS encodes less useful information than other features for machine translation tasks. For instance, Belinkov et al. (2017) found that models performed above the baseline if the task was modified to predict semantic tags.

3.1   Similarities Across Target Languages

While there were statistically significant differences in accuracy between target languages for all four constituent label tasks (one-way ANOVA, $p < 0.001$ for all tasks), these differences were quite small. The non-English target languages varied by less than 2% within each of the parent, grandparent, and great-grandparent constituent label tasks (see Figure 1).

NMT encoders learned similar syntax.   To further test the hypothesis of similar syntactic information across encoder representations, we assessed the performance of the NMT encoders on individual constituent labels (e.g. noun phrases). To do this, we considered the constituent label predictions as the results of a binary classification task for each individual label. For instance, when considering the noun POS tag, all POS tags were separated into two categories: noun and not noun. Then, we computed F1 scores for individual constituent labels for each NMT model, allowing us to quantify similarities between NMT encoders based on individual

Tokenized BLEU					
AR	EN	ES	FR	RU	ZH
37.3	99.9	56.3	44.8	37.8	24.9

Detokenized BLEU					
AR	EN	ES	FR	RU	ZH
38.0	100.0	56.3	44.5	37.4	

Table 1: BLEU scores before and after detokenizing the NMT translations for the UN test set. The detokenized BLEU score was not computed for Chinese because words were generally not separated by spaces in the Chinese dataset.

label performance.

Individual constituent label F1 scores correlated extremely highly between non-English target languages (all pairwise Pearson correlations $r > 0.93$ for the POS task; $r > 0.98$ for the parent task; $r > 0.99$ for the grandparent and great-grandparent tasks). In other words, the models performed well or poorly on the same individual labels regardless of target language. Figure 2 shows individual constituent label F1 scores for each NMT target language, displaying the three most frequent labels for each constituent label task. Similar to the overall accuracy scores, raw differences in F1 scores were small between non-English target languages.

In particular, the similar F1 scores were not simply proportional to label frequencies. For instance, all target languages performed similarly well when identifying noun grandparent constituents (25% of grandparent labels, F1 scores 0.59-0.60) and question-sentence grandparent constituents (0.6% of grandparent labels, F1 scores 0.55-0.61), despite over a 20% difference in corresponding label frequencies.[2] Similar F1 scores across non-English target languages suggest that NMT encoders encode very similar syntactic information regardless of target language.

Translation quality still varied.   Despite similar syntactic information encoded across target languages, the NMT models exhibited a wide range of BLEU scores, as shown in Table 1. This indicates that morphological and non-syntactic features have large impacts on translation performance. For instance, inflectional morphology (e.g. verb conjugation and noun pluralization) has been found

---

[2]There was a loose correlation between F1 scores and label frequencies, but this correlation could not fully account for the similarity of F1 scores across target languages.

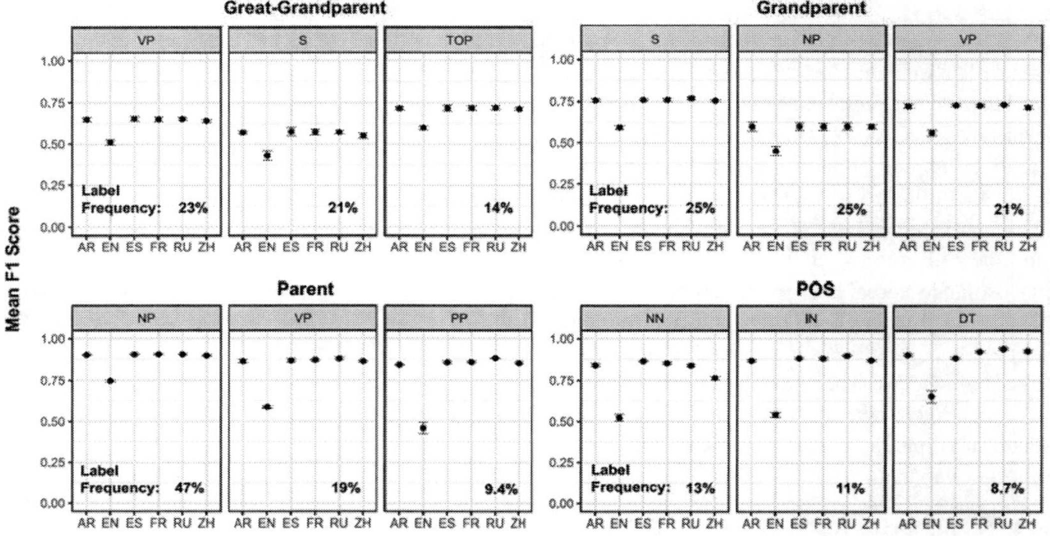

Figure 2: Mean F1 scores (based on 20 feedforward models) for individual constituent label predictions, treating each prediction task as a binary classification task. Bars indicate two standard deviations from the mean. We display the three most frequent labels for each task, comparing across all target languages. Each label's frequency in the CoNLL-2012 test set is displayed on its corresponding plot.

to account for differences in performance between languages in language modeling tasks (Cotterell et al., 2018), although these results vary depending on the metric used for morphological complexity (Mielke et al., 2019). Because differences in translation performance could not be easily explained using encoded syntactic information alone, it seems likely that the NMT models were either unable to extract more syntactic information from the training data or that the models did not find additional syntactic information to be useful.

3.2 Linguistic Analysis of Errors

To gain a better understanding of how NMT encoders extract syntax, we conducted a qualitative analysis of sentences for which the constituent label prediction models exhibited high error rates.

Selection of sentences We selected sentences based on the great-grandparent constituent label task because this task exhibited the highest accuracy scores above the baseline, indicating a large amount of learned syntax. There were high pairwise correlation scores for per-sentence great-grandparent constituent label accuracies between all non-English target languages (all Pearson correlations $r > 0.85$), so we selected sentences simply

based on their average constituent label accuracy across the five non-English target languages.

We considered the 50 complete sentences with the highest average great-grandparent constituent accuracies and the 50 complete sentences with the lowest average great-grandparent constituent accuracies.[3] The top 50 sentences all had average great-grandparent accuracies above 90%, and the bottom 50 sentences all had accuracies below 35%. Linguistic patterns found in the top and bottom 50 sentences are compiled in Table 2.

NMT encoders relied on explicit cues. The bottom 50 sentences contained a disproportionate number of null features. These features omit words or morphemes that would indicate syntactic structure in a sentence. For instance, null copulas omit forms of the verb "to be," as in the sentence "He pronounced the homework [was] finished." Appositives, where two noun phrases are placed one after another to describe the same entity (e.g. "Grant, the star baker"), serve as relative clauses with the usual explicit syntactic cues omitted (e.g. "Grant, [who is] the star baker"). Of the bottom 50 sentences, 16 contained at least one null copula or appositive; the

---

[3] Sentences were marked as "complete" by a native English speaker. We considered only sentences from text sources (e.g. not transcribed conversational speech).

Feature	Top 50 sentences	Bottom 50 sentences
Average length	9.3 words	21.7 words
Average great-grandparent constituent label accuracy	0.949	0.310
Question sentences	2	10
Infinitive phrases	26	5
Sentences with negation	13	4
Sentences containing a null copula or appositive	0	16
Embedded sentences (excluding infinitives)		
○ Head before	9	5
○ Head after	0	10

Table 2: Linguistic features in the top and bottom 50 sentences, selected based on great-grandparent constituent label accuracies per sentence.

top 50 sentences contained none of either feature. This suggests that when generating encoder representations, NMT models typically do not identify syntactic structures based on non-explicit cues.

However, the models performed well on complex syntactic structures containing explicit morphosyntactic cues. They performed well on sentences containing infinitives (e.g. "to eat" or "to pillage") and negation (e.g. "I did not eat"), exhibiting far more of these features in the top 50 sentences than in the bottom 50 sentences (see Table 2). Both infinitives and negation have clear morphosyntactic cues indicating sentence structure. The "to" in each infinitive clearly introduces the infinitized verb, and the word "not" before a verb clearly indicates a negated clause. These results suggest that NMT encoders rely on explicit morphosyntactic cues to extract syntactic structure from sentences.

NMT encoders recognized embedded sentences. In fact, the NMT encoders were able to use morphosyntactic cues to identify embedded sentences. An embedded sentence appears within another phrase (e.g. within the verb phrase "said that [sentence]"). The phrase head which introduces an embedded sentence can appear before or after the embedded sentence (e.g. "Alex said [sentence]" versus "[sentence], said Alex"). Because the NMT encoders were forward-directional RNNs, they could not be expected to recognize embedded sentences where the corresponding phrase head appeared after the embedded sentence. However, the models performed well on many sentences where the phrase head appeared before the embedded sentence, exhibiting nine such structures in the top 50 sentences (see Table 2). In many of these sentences, the head and complementizer (e.g. "said that" or "dogs that") clearly indicate the beginning of an embedded sentence.

Interestingly, the NMT encoders were often able to recognize embedded sentences even when there was a null complementizer introducing the embedded sentence, such as "that" omitted in "The dog wished [that] he was taller." Of the nine embedded sentences in the top 50 sentences, six had a null complementizer. This result may partially be explained by verb bias, the tendency for certain verbs to be followed by particular types of phrases (Garnsey et al., 1997). For instance, the verb "prove" is more often followed by a sentence complement (e.g. "proved [that] the criminal was lying") than a direct object (e.g. "proved the theorem"). People are more likely to omit complementizers when the head verb biases heavily towards a sentence complement (Ferreira and Schotter, 2013); in these cases, the verb itself serves as a syntactic cue for the upcoming embedded sentence. Of the six null complementizers in the top 50 sentences, five followed a sentence-complement-biased verb. Then, it appears that NMT encoders are able to recognize embedded sentences using a combination of verb bias and explicit complementizers.

4 NMT Syntax vs. Other Models

The similarity of syntactic information in NMT encoder representations across target languages could suggest that regardless of target language, a similar amount of syntactic information is helpful for translation. However, it is also possible that the structure of the constituent label task limited the syntactic information the encoders could represent, as predicting a label based only on a partial sentence is an inherently ambiguous task. A third alternative is that the RNN encoder architectures limited the information preserved in each representation.

To further explore how well the NMT encoders extracted syntactic information from raw sentences, we compared their constituent label prediction performance to two alternative models: an RNN trained directly for the constituent label task, and a probabilistic context-free grammar (PCFG) parser. In contrast to the NMT encoders, the RNN can learn representations that are best suited for retaining syntax; like the NMT encoders, it sees one word at a time. The PCFG is trained with complete syntactic information for partial sentences, and its prediction task is an entire hierarchical structure, rather than a single type of label. These comparisons can show whether there are syntactic features that are predictable but systematically missed by the NMT encoder representations.

4.1 Directly-Trained RNNs

RNN models We trained unidirectional four-layer LSTM models with 500 dimensions to directly predict constituent labels (POS, parent, grandparent, great-grandparent) when provided a sentence stopping at a given word. These RNNs were trained on the CoNLL-2012 development dataset (the same dataset as the feedforward models based on NMT encoder representations in Section 2.2). To account for variance in RNN training, we trained 10 RNNs for each constituent label task, and each RNN was trained until it completed 10 consecutive epochs without improvement on the evaluation dataset.

NMT representations outperformed the RNNs. Average accuracies for the RNN models in each constituent label task are shown in Figure 3, compared with the feedforward models trained from NMT encoder representations. Surprisingly, the RNN models trained directly for the constituent label tasks performed worse than the NMT encoder representation models for the parent, grandparent, and great-grandparent constituent tasks. The NMT encoder representations' improvement over the other models increased consistently as the constituent labels moved higher in the syntax tree (i.e. the NMT encoders exhibited the greatest advantage in the great-grandparent constituent task).

Because the RNNs had the same architecture as the NMT encoders, it is likely that the directly-trained RNNs were limited by the amount of training data provided (about 160,000 examples). The NMT encoder representations would be able to rely more heavily on patterns learned during NMT training and thus would be able to make better use of the limited training data for the constituent label

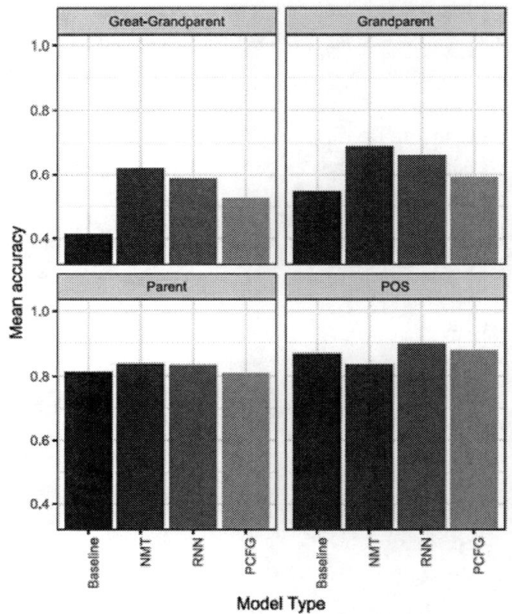

Figure 3: Average accuracies on the constituent label prediction tasks for all four types of model.

prediction tasks. It is also possible that the hyperparameters used for the NMT encoders were not optimal for the directly-trained RNNs. That said, the NMT encoder representations' high performance on the constituent label tasks supports existing literature finding that NMT encoder representations contain information useful for a variety of natural language tasks (Eriguchi et al., 2018; McCann et al., 2017).

The RNNs and NMT encoded similar syntax. Next, to assess whether the directly-trained RNNs learned different syntactic information from the NMT encoders, we compared the RNN and the NMT encoder representations' performance on individual sentences. We primarily considered great-grandparent constituent accuracies, the task for which all models performed most above the baseline.

For each sentence of length at least three, we considered the mean great-grandparent constituent label accuracy, averaging across all non-English target languages for the NMT encoder accuracies. Figure 4 shows the correlation between per-sentence accuracies from the NMT encoder representation models and the directly-trained RNN models. There was a high degree of correlation between the two types of models (Pearson correla-

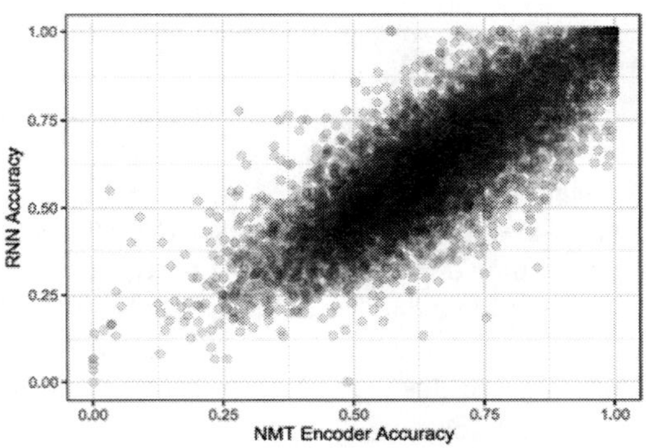

Figure 4: Mean great-grandparent constituent label accuracies per sentence for the NMT encoder-based models and the directly-trained RNNs. Each dot represents a sentence.

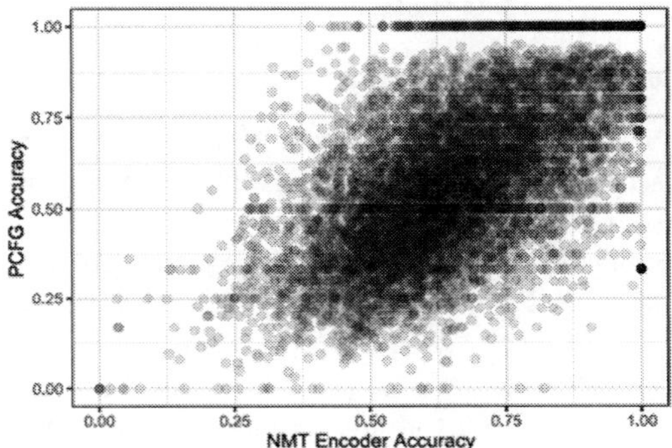

Figure 5: Mean great-grandparent constituent label accuracies per sentence for the NMT encoder-based models and the PCFG parser.

tion $r = 0.84$), indicating that the directly-trained RNNs learned similar syntactic information to the NMT encoders.

4.2 PCFG Parser

It may be that the directly-trained RNNs and the NMT encoders learned similar syntactic information because they both used the same RNN architecture. Therefore, we tested constituent label performance when using the probabilistic context-free grammar (PCFG) syntactic parser provided by Stanford NLP (Klein and Manning, 2003). We trained the PCFG on parse trees of partial sentences stopping at each word in the CoNLL-2012 development dataset, the same dataset used to train the RNN-based models. While the PCFG was not trained specifically for the constituent label prediction task, its explicit syntactic architecture (encoding a context-free grammar) provides a useful

	RNN	Baseline	PCFG
NMT	0.84	0.60	0.61
RNN		0.62	0.59
Baseline			0.42

Table 3: Pairwise Pearson correlations for per-sentence great-grandparent constituent label accuracies, computed between all four types of model.

contrast to the RNN-based models.

The PCFG encoded different syntax. The PCFG's constituent label accuracies are shown in Figure 3, along with the RNN and NMT encoder representation accuracies. As expected, because the PCFG was not trained specifically for the constituent label prediction task, the PCFG had slightly lower accuracies than the RNN-based models. However, the PCFG exhibited interesting patterns when considering its performance on individual sentences.

As with the other models, the PCFG's mean great-grandparent constituent label accuracies were considered for each sentence of length at least three. Figure 5 (comparing the PCFG with the NMT encoder representations) can then be compared to Figure 4 (comparing the directly-trained RNNs with the NMT encoder representations). The two plots indicate that the PCFG performed substantially differently from the RNN-based models. Notably, there is a set of sentences for which the PCFG obtained perfect accuracy while the NMT encoders had substantially lower accuracies (demonstrated by the horizontal line of dots at the top of Figure 5). Both RNN-based models' accuracies correlated approximately the same amount with the baseline (most-frequent tag per word) model as with the PCFG; all correlations between models are shown in Table 3.

Furthermore, for the worst 50 sentences for the NMT encoder representations (the sentences found in Section 3.2), the PCFG performed 9% better than the NMT encoder representation models and 6% better than the directly-trained RNN models, despite an overall 7-9% lower accuracy than both RNN-based models. This suggests that PCFGs can perform well on specific sentences that RNNs perform poorly on; for instance, PCFGs may be less reliant on explicit morphosyntactic cues. The PCFG's high performance on these specific sentences explains results finding that explicit syntactic information provides improvements to NMT systems even though NMT systems already implicitly encode syntax (Chen et al., 2017; Chiang et al., 2009; Li et al., 2017; Wu et al., 2017).

5 Discussion

NMT syntax is independent of target language. We found that NMT encoders learn similar source syntactic information regardless of target language, consistently outperforming RNNs trained specifically for the constituent label prediction task. These results help explain the success of NMT encoder representations in cross-task transfer learning, and they open up further questions regarding the extent of similarity between NMT encoder representations across target languages.

For instance, Schwenk and Douze (2017) found that multilingual NMT encoder representations cluster more based on semantic than syntactic similarity, indicating that semantic information may play a more prominent role than syntax in machine translation. Across target languages, Poliak et al. (2018) found inconsistencies for which target language's representations resulted in the best performance on semantic understanding tasks. This could suggest that semantic information in NMT encoder representations is also similar across target languages.

RNNs learn limited syntax. Both the NMT encoders and the directly-trained RNNs relied on explicit morphosyntactic cues to extract syntactic information from sentences. This result aligns with findings that RNNs rely on syntax heuristics to obtain high performance on tasks (McCoy et al., 2019), performing poorly on sentences requiring knowledge of complex syntactic structures (Linzen et al., 2016; Marvin and Linzen, 2018). NMT encoders specifically have been found not to encode fine-grained syntactic information (Shi et al., 2016). These limitations can be partially overcome by training an RNN model for a variety of different tasks (Enguehard et al., 2017); alternatively, we found that a PCFG syntactic parser encoded significantly different syntactic information from RNN-based models, performing well on many sentences for which RNNs performed poorly.

In some ways, the RNNs' reliance on explicit syntactic cues is similar to sentence processing in people. Many sentences are syntactically ambiguous before they are completed (notably garden-path sentences such as "The horse raced past the barn fell"), and people generally re-evaluate upon reading the disambiguating feature (Frazier and Rayner, 1982; Qian et al., 2018). Thus, it may be implausible for an online system to identify non-explicit syntactic features given only partial sentences. Compounding this problem, RNNs are unable to re-evaluate past inputs and hidden states upon reading disambiguating words. The successes of bidirectional and Transformer models (Devlin et al., 2019; Peters et al., 2018a; Vaswani et al., 2017) may be due partially to their ability to combine later information with representations of earlier words. Indeed, contextual word representations generated by these bidirectional models have been found to encode significant syntactic information (Peters et al., 2018b); future work could study whether bidirectional architectures are less reliant on explicit morphosyntactic cues.

6 Conclusion

In this work, we found that NMT encoder representations across target languages encode similar source syntax, and this syntax is comparable to the syntax learned by RNNs trained directly on syntactic tasks. However, explicit syntactic architectures may be necessary for tasks requiring fine-tuned syntactic parses. Our results have many implications in transfer learning and multilingual sentence representations: a better understanding of the information contained in sentence representations provides necessary insight into the tasks these representations can be used for.

Acknowledgments

We would like to thank Cherlon Ussery for helpful linguistic perspectives on our results, and the Carleton College Cognitive Science Department for making this work possible.

References

Yonatan Belinkov, Lluís Màrquez, Hassan Sajjad, Nadir Durrani, Fahim Dalvi, and James Glass. 2017. Evaluating layers of representation in neural machine translation on part-of-speech and semantic tagging tasks. In *Proceedings of the Eighth International Joint Conference on Natural Language Processing (Volume 1: Long Papers)*, pages 1–10, Taipei, Taiwan. Asian Federation of Natural Language Processing.

Terra Blevins, Omer Levy, and Luke Zettlemoyer. 2018. Deep RNNs encode soft hierarchical syntax. In *Proceedings of the 56th Annual Meeting of the Association for Computational Linguistics (Volume 2: Short*

Papers), pages 14–19, Melbourne, Australia. Association for Computational Linguistics.

Huadong Chen, Shujian Huang, David Chiang, and Jiajun Chen. 2017. Improved neural machine translation with a syntax-aware encoder and decoder. In *Proceedings of the 55th Annual Meeting of the Association for Computational Linguistics (Volume 1: Long Papers)*, pages 1936–1945, Vancouver, Canada. Association for Computational Linguistics.

David Chiang, Kevin Knight, and Wei Wang. 2009. 11,001 new features for statistical machine translation. In *Proceedings of Human Language Technologies: The 2009 Annual Conference of the North American Chapter of the Association for Computational Linguistics*, pages 218–226, Boulder, Colorado. Association for Computational Linguistics.

Ryan Cotterell, Sebastian J. Mielke, Jason Eisner, and Brian Roark. 2018. Are all languages equally hard to language-model? In *Proceedings of the 2018 Conference of the North American Chapter of the Association for Computational Linguistics: Human Language Technologies, Volume 2 (Short Papers)*, pages 536–541, New Orleans, Louisiana. Association for Computational Linguistics.

Jacob Devlin, Ming-Wei Chang, Kenton Lee, and Kristina Toutanova. 2019. BERT: Pre-training of deep bidirectional transformers for language understanding. In *Proceedings of the 2019 Conference of the North American Chapter of the Association for Computational Linguistics: Human Language Technologies, Volume 1 (Long and Short Papers)*, pages 4171–4186, Minneapolis, Minnesota. Association for Computational Linguistics.

Émile Enguehard, Yoav Goldberg, and Tal Linzen. 2017. Exploring the syntactic abilities of RNNs with multi-task learning. In *Proceedings of the 21st Conference on Computational Natural Language Learning (CoNLL 2017)*, pages 3–14, Vancouver, Canada. Association for Computational Linguistics.

Akiko Eriguchi, Melvin Johnson, Orhan Firat, Hideto Kazawa, and Wolfgang Macherey. 2018. Zero-shot cross-lingual classification using multilingual neural machine translation. *ArXiv*, abs/1809.04686.

Victor Ferreira and Elizabeth Schotter. 2013. Do verb bias effects on sentence production reflect sensitivity to comprehension or production factors? *The Quarterly Journal of Experimental Psychology*, 66(8):1548–1571.

Lyn Frazier and Keith Rayner. 1982. Making and correcting errors during sentence comprehension: Eye movements in the analysis of structurally ambiguous sentences. *Cognitive Psychology*, 14(2):178–210.

Richard Futrell, Ethan Wilcox, Takashi Morita, Peng Qian, Miguel Ballesteros, and Roger Levy. 2019. Neural language models as psycholinguistic subjects: Representations of syntactic state. In *Proceedings of the 2019 Conference of the North American*

Chapter of the Association for Computational Linguistics: Human Language Technologies, Volume 1 (Long and Short Papers), pages 32–42, Minneapolis, Minnesota. Association for Computational Linguistics.

Susan Garnsey, Neal Pearlmutter, Elizabeth Myers, and Melanie Lotocky. 1997. The contributions of verb bias and plausibility to the comprehension of temporarily ambiguous sentences. *Journal of Memory and Language*, 37(1):58–93.

Sepp Hochreiter and Jürgen Schmidhuber. 1997. Long short-term memory. *Neural computation*, 9:1735–80.

Diederik Kingma and Jimmy Ba. 2014. Adam: A method for stochastic optimization. *International Conference on Learning Representations*.

Dan Klein and Christopher D. Manning. 2003. Accurate unlexicalized parsing. In *Proceedings of the 41st Annual Meeting of the Association for Computational Linguistics*, pages 423–430, Sapporo, Japan. Association for Computational Linguistics.

Guillaume Klein, Yoon Kim, Yuntian Deng, Jean Senellart, and Alexander Rush. 2017. OpenNMT: Opensource toolkit for neural machine translation. In *Proceedings of ACL 2017, System Demonstrations*, pages 67–72, Vancouver, Canada. Association for Computational Linguistics.

Sneha Kudugunta, Ankur Bapna, Isaac Caswell, and Orhan Firat. 2019. Investigating multilingual nmt representations at scale. In *Proceedings of the 2019 Conference on Empirical Methods in Natural Language Processing and the 9th International Joint Conference on Natural Language Processing (EMNLP-IJCNLP)*, pages 1565–1575.

Junhui Li, Deyi Xiong, Zhaopeng Tu, Muhua Zhu, Min Zhang, and Guodong Zhou. 2017. Modeling source syntax for neural machine translation. In *Proceedings of the 55th Annual Meeting of the Association for Computational Linguistics (Volume 1: Long Papers)*, pages 688–697, Vancouver, Canada. Association for Computational Linguistics.

Tal Linzen, Emmanuel Dupoux, and Yoav Goldberg. 2016. Assessing the ability of LSTMs to learn syntax-sensitive dependencies. *Transactions of the Association for Computational Linguistics*, 4:521–535.

Thang Luong, Hieu Pham, and Christopher D. Manning. 2015. Effective approaches to attention-based neural machine translation. In *Proceedings of the 2015 Conference on Empirical Methods in Natural Language Processing*, pages 1412–1421, Lisbon, Portugal. Association for Computational Linguistics.

Rebecca Marvin and Tal Linzen. 2018. Targeted syntactic evaluation of language models. In *Proceedings of the 2018 Conference on Empirical Methods in Natural Language Processing*, pages 1192–1202, Brussels, Belgium. Association for Computational Linguistics.

Bryan McCann, James Bradbury, Caiming Xiong, and Richard Socher. 2017. Learned in translation: Contextualized word vectors. In *Advances in Neural Information Processing Systems 30*.

Tom McCoy, Ellie Pavlick, and Tal Linzen. 2019. Right for the wrong reasons: Diagnosing syntactic heuristics in natural language inference. In *Proceedings of the 57th Annual Meeting of the Association for Computational Linguistics*, pages 3428–3448, Florence, Italy. Association for Computational Linguistics.

Sebastian J. Mielke, Ryan Cotterell, Kyle Gorman, Brian Roark, and Jason Eisner. 2019. What kind of language is hard to language-model? In *Proceedings of the 57th Annual Meeting of the Association for Computational Linguistics*, pages 4975–4989, Florence, Italy. Association for Computational Linguistics.

Graham Neubig and Junjie Hu. 2018. Rapid adaptation of neural machine translation to new languages. In *Proceedings of the 2018 Conference on Empirical Methods in Natural Language Processing*, pages 875–880, Brussels, Belgium. Association for Computational Linguistics.

Matthew Peters, Mark Neumann, Mohit Iyyer, Matt Gardner, Christopher Clark, Kenton Lee, and Luke Zettlemoyer. 2018a. Deep contextualized word representations. In *Proceedings of the 2018 Conference of the North American Chapter of the Association for Computational Linguistics: Human Language Technologies, Volume 1 (Long Papers)*, pages 2227–2237, New Orleans, Louisiana. Association for Computational Linguistics.

Matthew Peters, Mark Neumann, Luke Zettlemoyer, and Wen-tau Yih. 2018b. Dissecting contextual word embeddings: Architecture and representation. In *Proceedings of the 2018 Conference on Empirical Methods in Natural Language Processing*, pages 1499–1509, Brussels, Belgium. Association for Computational Linguistics.

Adam Poliak, Yonatan Belinkov, James Glass, and Benjamin Van Durme. 2018. On the evaluation of semantic phenomena in neural machine translation using natural language inference. In *Proceedings of the 2018 Conference of the North American Chapter of the Association for Computational Linguistics: Human Language Technologies, Volume 2 (Short Papers)*, pages 513–523, New Orleans, Louisiana. Association for Computational Linguistics.

Sameer Pradhan, Alessandro Moschitti, Nianwen Xue, Olga Uryupina, and Yuchen Zhang. 2012. CoNLL-2012 shared task: Modeling multilingual unrestricted coreference in OntoNotes. In *Joint Conference on EMNLP and CoNLL - Shared Task*, pages 1–40, Jeju Island, Korea. Association for Computational Linguistics.

Vasin Punyakanok, Dan Roth, and Wen-tau Yih. 2008. The importance of syntactic parsing and inference in semantic role labeling. *Computational Linguistics*, 34(2):257–287.

Zhiying Qian, Susan Garnsey, and Kiel Christianson. 2018. A comparison of online and offline measures of good-enough processing in garden-path sentences. *Language, Cognition and Neuroscience*, 33(2):227–254.

Holger Schwenk and Matthijs Douze. 2017. Learning joint multilingual sentence representations with neural machine translation. In *Proceedings of the 2nd Workshop on Representation Learning for NLP*, pages 157–167, Vancouver, Canada. Association for Computational Linguistics.

Rico Sennrich, Barry Haddow, and Alexandra Birch. 2016. Neural machine translation of rare words with subword units. In *Proceedings of the 54th Annual Meeting of the Association for Computational Linguistics (Volume 1: Long Papers)*, pages 1715–1725, Berlin, Germany. Association for Computational Linguistics.

Xing Shi, Inkit Padhi, and Kevin Knight. 2016. Does string-based neural MT learn source syntax? In *Proceedings of the 2016 Conference on Empirical Methods in Natural Language Processing*, pages 1526–1534, Austin, Texas. Association for Computational Linguistics.

Ashish Vaswani, Noam Shazeer, Niki Parmar, Jakob Uszkoreit, Llion Jones, Aidan Gomez, Lukasz Kaiser, and Illia Polosukhin. 2017. Attention is all you need. In *Advances in neural information processing systems*, pages 5998–6008.

Shuangzhi Wu, Ming Zhou, and Dongdong Zhang. 2017. Improved neural machine translation with source syntax. In *Proceedings of the Twenty-Sixth International Joint Conference on Artificial Intelligence, IJCAI-17*, pages 4179–4185.

Michał Ziemski, Marcin Junczys-Dowmunt, and Bruno Pouliquen. 2016. The united nations parallel corpus v1.0. In *Proceedings of the Tenth International Conference on Language Resources and Evaluation (LREC 2016)*, pages 3530–3534, Portorož, Slovenia. European Language Resources Association (ELRA).

Learning Probabilistic Sentence Representations from Paraphrases

Mingda Chen   **Kevin Gimpel**

Toyota Technological Institute at Chicago, Chicago, IL, 60637, USA

`{mchen,kgimpel}@ttic.edu`

Abstract

Probabilistic word embeddings have shown effectiveness in capturing notions of generality and entailment, but there is very little work on doing the analogous type of investigation for sentences. In this paper we define probabilistic models that produce distributions for sentences. Our best-performing model treats each word as a linear transformation operator applied to a multivariate Gaussian distribution. We train our models on paraphrases and demonstrate that they naturally capture sentence specificity. While our proposed model achieves the best performance overall, we also show that specificity is represented by simpler architectures via the norm of the sentence vectors. Qualitative analysis shows that our probabilistic model captures sentential entailment and provides ways to analyze the specificity and preciseness of individual words.

1   Introduction

Probabilistic word embeddings have been shown to be useful for capturing notions of generality and entailment (Vilnis and McCallum, 2014; Athiwaratkun and Wilson, 2017; Athiwaratkun et al., 2018). In particular, researchers have found that the entropy of a word roughly encodes its generality, even though there is no training signal explicitly targeting this effect. For example, hypernyms tend to have larger variance than their corresponding hyponyms (Vilnis and McCallum, 2014). However, there is very little work on doing the analogous type of investigation for sentences.

In this paper, we define probabilistic models that produce distributions for sentences. In particular, we choose a simple and interpretable probabilistic model that treats each word as an operator that translates and scales a Gaussian random variable representing the sentence. Our models are able to capture sentence specificity as measured by the annotated datasets of Li and Nenkova

(2015) and Ko et al. (2019) by training solely on noisy paraphrase pairs. While our "word-operator" model yields the strongest performance, we also show that specificity is represented by simpler architectures via the norm of the sentence vectors. Qualitative analysis shows that our models represent sentences in ways that correspond to the entailment relationship and that individual word parameters can be analyzed to find words with varied and precise meanings.

2   Proposed Methods

We propose a model that uses ideas from flow-based variational autoencoders (VAEs) (Rezende and Mohamed, 2015; Kingma et al., 2016) by treating each word as an "operator". Intuitively, we assume there is a random variable z associated with each sentence $s = \{w_1, w_2, \cdots, w_n\}$. The random variable initially follows a standard multivariate Gaussian distribution. Then, each word in the sentence transforms the random variable sequentially, leading to a random variable that encodes its semantic information.

Our word linear operator model (WLO) has two types of parameters for each word w_i: a scaling factor $A_i \in \mathbb{R}^k$ and a translation factor $B_i \in \mathbb{R}^k$. The word operators produce a sequence of random variables $z_0, z_1, \cdots, z_n$ with $z_0 \sim \mathcal{N}(0, I_k)$, where I_k is a $k \times k$ identity matrix, and the operations are defined as

$$z_i = A_i(z_{i-1} + B_i) \tag{1}$$

The means and variances for each random variable are computed as follows:

$$\mu_i = A_i(\mu_{i-1} + B_i) \tag{2}$$
$$\Sigma_i = A_i \Sigma_{i-1} A_i^\top \tag{3}$$

For computational efficiency, we only consider diagonal covariance matrices, so the equations above can be further simplified.

17

Proceedings of the 5th Workshop on Representation Learning for NLP (RepL4NLP-2020), pages 17–23
July 9, 2020. ©2020 Association for Computational Linguistics

3 Learning

Following Wieting and Gimpel (2018), all of our models are trained with a margin-based loss on paraphrase pairs (s_1, s_2):

$$\max(0, \delta - d(s_1, s_2) + d(s_1, n_1)) +$$
$$\max(0, \delta - d(s_1, s_2) + d(s_2, n_2))$$

where δ is the margin and d is a similarity function that takes a pair of sentences and outputs a scalar denoting their similarity. The similarity function is maximized over a subset of examples (typically, the mini-batch) to choose negative examples n_1 and n_2. When doing so, we use "mega-batching" (Wieting and Gimpel, 2018) and fix the mega-batch size at 20. For deterministic models, d is cosine similarity, while for probabilistic models, we use the expected inner product of Gaussians.

3.1 Expected Inner Product of Gaussians

Let μ_1, μ_2 be mean vectors and Σ_1, Σ_2 be the variances predicted by models for a pair of input sentences. For the choice of d, following Vilnis and McCallum (2014), we use the expected inner product of Gaussian distributions:

$$\int_{x \in \mathbb{R}^k} \mathcal{N}(x; \mu_1, \Sigma_1) \mathcal{N}(x; \mu_2, \Sigma_2) dx$$
$$= \log \mathcal{N}(0; \mu_1 - \mu_2, \Sigma_1 + \Sigma_2)$$
$$= -\frac{1}{2} \log \det (\Sigma_1 + \Sigma_2) - \frac{d}{2} \log(2\pi) \tag{4}$$
$$- \frac{1}{2} (\mu_1 - \mu_2)^\top (\Sigma_1 + \Sigma_2)^{-1} (\mu_1 - \mu_2)$$

For diagonal matrices Σ_1 and Σ_2, the equation above can be computed analytically.

3.2 Regularization

To avoid the mean or variance of the Gaussian distributions from becoming unbounded during training, resulting in degenerate solutions, we impose prior constraints on the operators introduced above. We force the transformed distribution after each operator to be relatively close to $\mathcal{N}(0, I_k)$, which can be thought of as our "prior" knowledge of the operator. Then our training additionally minimizes

$$\lambda \sum_{s \in \{s_1, s_2, n_1, n_2\}} \sum_{w \in s} KL(\mathcal{N}(\mu(w), \Sigma(w)) \| \mathcal{N}(0, I))$$

where λ is a hyperparameter tuned based on the performance on the 2017 semantic textual similarity (STS; Cer et al., 2017) data. We found prior

Domain	News	Twitter	Yelp	Movie
Number of instances	900	984	845	920

Table 1: Sizes of test sets for sentence specificity.

regularization very important, as will be shown in our results. For fair comparison, we also add L2 regularization to the baseline models.

4 Experiments

4.1 Baseline Methods

We consider two baselines that have shown strong results on sentence similarity tasks (Wieting and Gimpel, 2018). The first, word averaging (WORDAVG), simply averages the word embeddings in the sentence. The second, long short-term memory (LSTM; Hochreiter and Schmidhuber, 1997) averaging (LSTMAVG), uses an LSTM to encode the sentence and averages the hidden vectors. Inspired by sentence VAEs (Bowman et al., 2016), we consider an LSTM based probabilistic baseline (LSTMGAUSSIAN) which builds upon LSTMAVG and uses separate linear transformations on the averaged hidden states to produce the mean and variance of a Gaussian distribution.

We also benchmark several pretrained models, including GloVe (Pennington et al., 2014), Skip-thought (Kiros et al., 2015), InferSent (Conneau et al., 2017), BERT (Devlin et al., 2019), and ELMo (Peters et al., 2018). When using GloVe, we either sum embeddings (GloVe SUM) or average them (GloVe AVG) to produce a sentence vector. Similarly, for ELMo, we either sum the outputs from the last layer (ELMo SUM) or average them (ELMo AVG). For BERT, we take the representation for the "[CLS]" token.

4.2 Datasets

We use the preprocessed version of ParaNMT-50M (Wieting and Gimpel, 2018) as our training set, which consists of 5 million paraphrase pairs.

For evaluating sentence specificity, we use human-annotated test sets from four domains, including news, Twitter, Yelp reviews, and movie reviews, from Li and Nenkova (2015) and Ko et al. (2019). For the news dataset, labels are either "general" or "specific" and there is additionally a training set. For the other datasets, labels are real values indicating specificity. Statistics for these datasets are shown in Table 1.

For analysis we also use the semantic textual

similarity (STS) benchmark test set (Cer et al., 2017) and the Stanford Natural Language Inference (SNLI) dataset (Bowman et al., 2015).

4.3 Specificity Prediction Setup

For predicting specificity in the news domain, we threshold the predictions either based on the entropy of Gaussian distributions produced from probabilistic models or based on the norm of vectors produced by deterministic models, which includes all of the pretrained models. The threshold is tuned based on the training set but no other training or tuning is done for this task with any of our models. For prediction in other domains, we simply compute the Spearman correlations between the entropy/norm and the labels.

Intuitively, when sentences are longer, they tend to be more specific. So, we report baselines ("Length") that predict specificity solely based on length, by thresholding the sentence length for news (choosing the threshold using the training set) or simply returning the length for the others. The latter results are reported from Ko et al. (2019). We also consider baselines that average or sum ranks of word frequencies within a sentence ("Word Freq. AVG" and "Word Freq. SUM").

5 Results

5.1 Sentence Specificity

Table 2 shows results on sentence specificity tasks. We compare to the best-performing models reported by Li and Nenkova (2015) and Ko et al. (2019). Their models are specifically designed for predicting sentence specificity and they both use labeled training data from the news domain.

Our averaging-based models (WORDAVG, LSTMAVG) failed on this task, either giving the majority class accuracy or negative correlations. So, we also evaluate WORDSUM, which sums word embeddings instead of averaging and shows strong performance compared to the other models.

While the model from Li and Nenkova (2015) performs quite well in the news domain, its performance drops on other domains, indicating some amount of overfitting. On the other hand, WORD-SUM and WLO, which are trained on a large number of paraphrases, perform consistently across the four domains and both outperform the supervised models on Yelp. Additionally, our WLO model outperforms all our other models, achieving comparable performance to the supervised methods.

	News	Twitter	Yelp	Movie
Majority baseline	54.6	-	-	-
Length	73.4	44.5	67.6	58.1
Word Freq. SUM	55.5	10.1	54.6	22.1
Word Freq. AVG	61.5	0.0	28.5	0.0
Prior work trained on labeled sentence specificity data				
Li and Nenkova (2015)	81.6	55.3	63.3	57.5
Ko et al. (2019)	-	67.9	75.0	70.6
Sentence embeddings from pretrained models				
GloVe SUM	70.4	32.2	62.8	49.0
GloVe AVG	54.6	-49.6	-59.0	-38.2
InferSent	75.0	60.5	76.6	61.2
Skip-thought	57.7	2.9	14.1	27.2
BERT	64.5	20.8	29.5	18.1
ELMo SUM	65.4	46.2	72.7	59.3
ELMo AVG	56.2	-9.4	-0.9	-22.5
Our work				
WORDAVG	54.6	-10.6	-32.3	-27.2
WORDSUM	75.8	57.9	75.4	60.0
LSTMAVG	54.6	-14.8	-41.1	-14.8
LSTMGAUSSIAN	55.5	3.2	2.2	4.1
WLO	<u>77.4</u>	<u>60.5</u>	<u>76.6</u>	<u>61.9</u>

Table 2: Sentence specificity results on test sets from four domains (accuracy (%) for News and Spearman correlations (%) for others). Highest numbers for the models described in this work are underlined.

	Full	Length norm.
Majority baseline	54.6	50.1
WORDAVG	54.6	69.0
WORDSUM	75.8	68.6
LSTMAVG	54.6	69.6
LSTMGAUSSIAN	55.5	67.0
WLO	**77.4**	**70.1**

Table 3: Accuracy (%) for the specificity News test set, in both the original and length normalized conditions. Highest numbers in each column are in bold.

Among pretrained models, BERT, Skip-thought, ELMo SUM, and GloVe SUM show slight correlations with specificity, while InferSent performs strongly across domains. InferSent uses supervised training on a large manually-annotated dataset (SNLI) while WORDSUM and WLO are trained on automatically-generated paraphrases and still show results comparable to InferSent.

To control for effects due to sentence length, we design another experiment in which sentences from News training and test are grouped by length, and thresholds are tuned on the group of length k and tested on the group of length $k - 1$, for all k, leading to a pool of 3582 test sentences.

Table 3 shows the results. In this length-normalized experiment, the averaging models demonstrate much better performance and even outperform WORDSUM, but still WLO has the best performance.

	Entailment	Neutral	Contradiction
GloVe	42.5	53.8	39.6
InferSent	78.3	57.2	55.7
Skip-thought	62.5	54.3	57.3
ELMo	78.3	58.3	63.4
BERT	65.0	55.7	56.3
WORDAVG	77.5	50.0	57.2
WORDSUM	75.0	54.7	57.7
LSTMAVG	71.7	49.5	52.4
LSTMGAUSSIAN	65.0	49.5	48.6
WLO	75.8	54.7	57.2

Table 4: Percentage of cases in which hypothesis has larger entropy (or smaller norm for non-probabilistic models) than premise for equal-length sentence pairs in the SNLI test set. In this setting, GloVe and ELMo would give the same results under either SUM or AVG.

6 Analysis

6.1 Sentence Entailment

Vilnis and McCallum (2014) explored whether their Gaussian word entropies captured the lexical entailment relationship. Here we analyze the extent to which our representations capture sentential entailment.

We test models on the SNLI test set, assuming that for a given premise p and hypothesis h, p is more specific than h for entailing sentence pairs. To avoid effects due to sentence length, we only consider $\langle p, h \rangle$ pairs with the same length. After this filtering, entailment/neural/contradiction categories have 120/192/208 instances respectively. We encode each sentence and calculate the percentage of cases in which the hypothesis has larger entropy (or smaller norm for non-probabilistic models) than the premise. Under an ideal model, this would happen with 100% of entailing pairs while showing random results (50%) for the other two types of pairs.

As shown in Table 4, our best paraphrase-trained models show similar trends to InferSent, achieving around 75% accuracy in the entailment category and around 50% accuracy in other categories. Although ELMo can also achieve similar accuracy in the entailment category, it seems to conflate entailment with contradiction, where it shows the highest percentage of all models. Other models, including BERT, GloVe, and Skip-thought, are much closer to random (50%) for entailing pairs.

6.2 Lexical Analysis

WLO associates translation and scaling parameters with each word, allowing us to analyze the

Small norm		Large norm	
small abs. ent.	small ent.	small abs. ent.	small ent.
,	addressing	staveb	cenelec
/	derived	jerusalem	ohim
by	decree	trent	placebo
an	fundamental	microwave	hydrocarbons
gon	beneficiaries	brussels	iec
as	tendency	synthetic	paras
having	detect	christians	allah
a	reservations	elephants	milan
on	remedy	seldon	madrid
for	eligibility	burger	±
from	film-coated	experimental	ukraine
'd	breach	alison	intravenous
—	exceed	63	electromagnetic
his	flashing	prophet	131
'	objectives	diego	electrons
upon	cue	mallory	northeast
under	commonly	ö	blister
towards	howling	natalie	http
's	vegetable	hornblower	renal
with	bursting	korea	asteroid

Table 5: Examples showing top-20 lists of large-norm or small-norm words ranked based on small absolute entropy or small entropy in WLO.

impact of words on sentence representations. We ranked words under several criteria based on their translation parameter norms and single-word sentence entropies. Table 5 shows the top 20 words under each criterion.

Words with small norm and small absolute entropy have little effect, both in terms of meaning and specificity; they are mostly function words. Words with large norm and small entropy have a large impact on the sentence while also making it more specific. They are organization names (*cenelec*) or technical terms found in medical or scientific literature. When they appear in a sentence, they are very likely to appear in its paraphrase.

Words with large norm and small absolute entropy contribute to the sentence semantics but do not make it more specific. Words like *microwave* and *synthetic* appear in many contexts and have multiple senses. Names (*trent, alison*) also appear in many contexts. Words like these often appear in a sentence's paraphrase, but can also appear in many other sentences in different contexts.

Words with small norm/entropy make sentences more specific but do not lend themselves to a precise characterization. They affect sentence meaning, but can be expressed in many ways. For example, when *beneficiaries* appears in a sentence, its paraphrase often has a synonym like *beneficiary*, *heirs*, or *grantees*. These words may have multiple senses, but it appears more that they correspond to

WORDSUM		WLO	
largest norm (specific)	smallest norm (general)	smallest entropy (specific)	largest entropy (general)
this regulation shall not apply to wine grape products, with the exception of wine vinegar, spirit drinks or flavoured wines.	oh, man, you're gonna... you're just gonna get it, vause[*], aren't you ?	under a light coating of dew she was a velvet study in reflected mauve with rose overtones against the indigo nightward[*] sky.	oh, man, you're gonna... you're just gonna get it, vause[*], aren't you?
operating revenue community subsidies other subsidies/revenue[*] total (a) operating expenditure staff administration operating activities total (b) operating result (c=ab)	okay, i know you don't get relationships, like, at all, but i don't need to screw anyone for an "a."	a similar influenza disease occurred in 47% of patients who received plegridy 125 micrograms every 2 weeks, and 13% of the patients were given placebo.	'authorisation' means an instrument issued in any form by the authorities by which the right to carry on the business of a credit institution is granted;

Table 6: Examples of most general and specific sentences for selected lengths (* = mapped to unknown symbol).

	With Prior		Without Prior	
	Acc.	F_1	Acc.	F_1
WLO	77.4	78.4	67.9	68.2

Table 7: Accuracy (%) and F_1 score (%) for specificity News test set with and without prior regularization.

	STS Benchmark
WORDAVG	73.4
LSTMAVG	73.6
LSTMGAUSSIAN	**74.3**
WLO	73.7

Table 8: Pearson correlation (%) for STS benchmark test set. Highest number is in bold.

concepts with many valid ways of expression.

6.3 Sentential Analysis

We subsample the ParaNMT training set and group sentences by length. For each model and length, we pick the sentence with either highest/lowest entropy or largest/smallest norm values. Table 6 shows some examples. WORDSUM tends to choose conversational sentences as general and those with many rare words as specific. WLO favors literary and technical/scientific sentences as most specific, and bureaucratic/official language as most general.

6.4 Effect of Prior Regularization

As shown in Table 7, there is a large performance improvement after adding prior regularization for avoiding degenerate solutions.

6.5 Semantic Textual Similarity

Although semantic textual similarity is not our target task, we still include the performance of our models on the STS benchmark test set in Table 8 to show that our models are competitive with standard strong baselines. When using probabilistic models to predict sentence similarity during test time, we let $v_1 = concat(\mu_1, \Sigma_1)$, $v_2 = concat(\mu_2, \Sigma_2)$, where $concat$ is a concatenation operation, and predict sentence similarity via $cosine(v_1, v_2)$, since we find it performs better than solely using the mean vectors. The two probabilistic models, LSTMGAUSSIAN and WLO, are able to outperform the baselines slightly.

7 Related Work

Our models are related to work in learning probabilistic word embeddings (Vilnis and McCallum, 2014; Athiwaratkun and Wilson, 2017; Athiwaratkun et al., 2018) and text-based VAEs (Miao et al., 2016; Bowman et al., 2016; Yang et al., 2017; Kim et al., 2018; Xu and Durrett, 2018, *inter alia*). The WLO is also related to flow-based VAEs (Rezende and Mohamed, 2015; Kingma et al., 2016), where hidden layers are viewed as operators over the density function of latent variables.

Previous work on sentence specificity relies on hand-crafted features or direct training on annotated data (Louis and Nenkova, 2011; Li and Nenkova, 2015). Recently, Ko et al. (2019) used domain adaptation for this problem when only the source domain has annotations. Our work also relates to learning sentence embeddings from paraphrase pairs (Wieting et al., 2016; Wieting and Gimpel, 2018).

8 Conclusion

We trained sentence models on paraphrase pairs and showed that they naturally capture specificity and entailment. Our proposed WLO model, which treats each word as a linear transformation operator, achieves the best performance and lends itself to analysis.

Acknowledgments

We would like to thank the anonymous reviewers, NVIDIA for donating GPUs used in this research, Jessy Li for clarifying the experimental setup used in Li and Nenkova (2015), and Google for a faculty research award to K. Gimpel that partially supported this research.

References

Ben Athiwaratkun and Andrew Wilson. 2017. Multimodal word distributions. In *Proceedings of the 55th Annual Meeting of the Association for Computational Linguistics (Volume 1: Long Papers)*, pages 1645–1656. Association for Computational Linguistics.

Ben Athiwaratkun, Andrew Wilson, and Anima Anandkumar. 2018. Probabilistic FastText for multi-sense word embeddings. In *Proceedings of the 56th Annual Meeting of the Association for Computational Linguistics (Volume 1: Long Papers)*, pages 1–11, Melbourne, Australia. Association for Computational Linguistics.

Samuel R. Bowman, Gabor Angeli, Christopher Potts, and Christopher D. Manning. 2015. A large annotated corpus for learning natural language inference. In *Proceedings of the 2015 Conference on Empirical Methods in Natural Language Processing*, pages 632–642. Association for Computational Linguistics.

Samuel R. Bowman, Luke Vilnis, Oriol Vinyals, Andrew Dai, Rafal Jozefowicz, and Samy Bengio. 2016. Generating sentences from a continuous space. In *Proceedings of The 20th SIGNLL Conference on Computational Natural Language Learning*, pages 10–21. Association for Computational Linguistics.

Daniel Cer, Mona Diab, Eneko Agirre, Inigo Lopez-Gazpio, and Lucia Specia. 2017. Semeval-2017 task 1: Semantic textual similarity multilingual and crosslingual focused evaluation. In *Proceedings of the 11th International Workshop on Semantic Evaluation (SemEval-2017)*, pages 1–14. Association for Computational Linguistics.

Alexis Conneau, Douwe Kiela, Holger Schwenk, Loïc Barrault, and Antoine Bordes. 2017. Supervised learning of universal sentence representations from natural language inference data. In *Proceedings of the 2017 Conference on Empirical Methods in Natural Language Processing*, pages 670–680. Association for Computational Linguistics.

Jacob Devlin, Ming-Wei Chang, Kenton Lee, and Kristina Toutanova. 2019. BERT: Pre-training of deep bidirectional transformers for language understanding. In *Proceedings of the 2019 Conference of the North American Chapter of the Association for Computational Linguistics: Human Language Technologies, Volume 1 (Long and Short Papers)*, pages 4171–4186, Minneapolis, Minnesota. Association for Computational Linguistics.

Sepp Hochreiter and Jürgen Schmidhuber. 1997. Long short-term memory. *Neural computation*, 9(8):1735–1780.

Yoon Kim, Sam Wiseman, Andrew Miller, David Sontag, and Alexander Rush. 2018. Semi-amortized variational autoencoders. In *Proceedings of the 35th International Conference on Machine Learning*, volume 80 of *Proceedings of Machine Learning Research*, pages 2678–2687, Stockholmsmssan, Stockholm Sweden. PMLR.

Diederik P Kingma and Jimmy Ba. 2014. Adam: A method for stochastic optimization. *arXiv preprint arXiv:1412.6980*.

Diederik P Kingma, Tim Salimans, Rafal Jozefowicz, Xi Chen, Ilya Sutskever, and Max Welling. 2016. Improved variational inference with inverse autoregressive flow. In D. D. Lee, M. Sugiyama, U. V. Luxburg, I. Guyon, and R. Garnett, editors, *Advances in Neural Information Processing Systems 29*, pages 4743–4751. Curran Associates, Inc.

Ryan Kiros, Yukun Zhu, Ruslan Salakhutdinov, Richard S. Zemel, Antonio Torralba, Raquel Urtasun, and Sanja Fidler. 2015. Skip-thought vectors. In *Proceedings of the 28th International Conference on Neural Information Processing Systems - Volume 2*, NIPS'15, pages 3294–3302, Cambridge, MA, USA. MIT Press.

Wei-Jen Ko, Greg Durrett, and Junyi Jessy Li. 2019. Domain agnostic real-valued specificity prediction. In *Proceedings of the Thirty-Third AAAI Conference on Artificial Intelligence*, pages 6610–6617. AAAI Press.

Junyi Jessy Li and Ani Nenkova. 2015. Fast and accurate prediction of sentence specificity. In *Proceedings of the Twenty-Ninth AAAI Conference on Artificial Intelligence*, pages 2281–2287. AAAI Press.

Annie Louis and Ani Nenkova. 2011. Automatic identification of general and specific sentences by leveraging discourse annotations. In *Proceedings of 5th International Joint Conference on Natural Language Processing*, pages 605–613. Asian Federation of Natural Language Processing.

Yishu Miao, Lei Yu, and Phil Blunsom. 2016. Neural variational inference for text processing. In *Proceedings of the 33rd International Conference on International Conference on Machine Learning - Volume 48*, ICML'16, pages 1727–1736. JMLR.

Jeffrey Pennington, Richard Socher, and Christopher Manning. 2014. Glove: Global vectors for word representation. In *Proceedings of the 2014 Conference on Empirical Methods in Natural Language Processing (EMNLP)*, pages 1532–1543. Association for Computational Linguistics.

Matthew Peters, Mark Neumann, Mohit Iyyer, Matt Gardner, Christopher Clark, Kenton Lee, and Luke Zettlemoyer. 2018. Deep contextualized word representations. In *Proceedings of the 2018 Conference of the North American Chapter of the Association for Computational Linguistics: Human Language Technologies, Volume 1 (Long Papers)*, pages 2227–2237, New Orleans, Louisiana. Association for Computational Linguistics.

Danilo Rezende and Shakir Mohamed. 2015. Variational inference with normalizing flows. In *Proceedings of the 32nd International Conference on Machine Learning*, volume 37 of *Proceedings of Machine Learning Research*, pages 1530–1538, Lille, France. PMLR.

Luke Vilnis and Andrew McCallum. 2014. Word representations via Gaussian embedding. *arXiv preprint arXiv:1412.6623*.

John Wieting, Mohit Bansal, Kevin Gimpel, and Karen Livescu. 2016. Towards universal paraphrastic sentence embeddings. In *Proceedings of International Conference on Learning Representations*.

John Wieting and Kevin Gimpel. 2018. ParaNMT-50M: Pushing the limits of paraphrastic sentence embeddings with millions of machine translations. In *Proceedings of the 56th Annual Meeting of the Association for Computational Linguistics (Volume 1: Long Papers)*, pages 451–462. Association for Computational Linguistics.

Jiacheng Xu and Greg Durrett. 2018. Spherical latent spaces for stable variational autoencoders. In *Proceedings of the 2018 Conference on Empirical Methods in Natural Language Processing*, pages 4503–4513. Association for Computational Linguistics.

Zichao Yang, Zhiting Hu, Ruslan Salakhutdinov, and Taylor Berg-Kirkpatrick. 2017. Improved variational autoencoders for text modeling using dilated convolutions. In *Proceedings of the 34th International Conference on Machine Learning*, volume 70 of *Proceedings of Machine Learning Research*, pages 3881–3890, International Convention Centre, Sydney, Australia. PMLR.

A Supplementary Material

A.1 Hyperparameters

For all experiments, the dimension of word embeddings and word operator is 50. The dimension of LSTM is 100. The dimension of Gaussian distribution for LSTMGAUSSIAN is 100. Mini-batch size is 100. For LSTM, LSTMGAUSSIAN, and WLO, we scramble training sentences with a probability of 0.4. For baseline models, the margin δ is 0.4. For other models, δ is 1. All models are randomly initialized and trained with Adam (Kingma and Ba, 2014) using learning rate of 0.001.

Word Embeddings as Tuples of Feature Probabilities

Siddharth Bhat[1]**, Alok Debnath**[2]**, Souvik Bannerjee**[2] and **Manish Shrivastava**[2]
[1]Center for Security, Theory & Algorithmic Research (C-STAR)
[2]Language Technologies Research Center (LTRC)
Kohli Center on Intelligent Systems
International Institute of Information Technology, Hyderabad
{siddharth.bhat, alok.debnath, souvik.bannerjee}@research.iiit.ac.in
m.shrivastava@iiit.ac.in

Abstract

In this paper, we provide an alternate perspective on word representations, by reinterpreting the dimensions of the vector space of a word embedding as a collection of features. In this reinterpretation, every component of the word vector is normalized against all the word vectors in the vocabulary. This idea now allows us to view each vector as an n-tuple (akin to a fuzzy set), where n is the dimensionality of the word representation and each element represents the probability of the word possessing a feature. Indeed, this representation enables the use fuzzy set theoretic operations, such as union, intersection and difference. Unlike previous attempts, we show that this representation of words provides a notion of similarity which is inherently asymmetric and hence closer to human similarity judgements. We compare the performance of this representation with various benchmarks, and explore some of the unique properties including function word detection, detection of polysemous words, and some insight into the interpretability provided by set theoretic operations.

1 Introduction

Word embedding is one of the most crucial facets of Natural Language Processing (NLP) research. Most non-contextualized word representations aim to provide a distributional view of lexical semantics, known popularly by the adage *"a word is known by the company it keeps"* (Firth, 1957). Popular implementations of word embeddings such as word2vec (Mikolov et al., 2013a) and GloVe (Pennington et al., 2014) aim to represent words as embeddings in a vector space. These embeddings are trained to be oriented such that vectors with higher similarities have higher dot products when normalized. Some of the most common methods of intrinsic evaluation of word embeddings include similarity, analogy and compositionality. While similarity is computed using the notion of dot product, analogy and compositionality use vector addition.

However, distributional representations of words over vector spaces have an inherent lack of interpretablity (Goldberg and Levy, 2014). Furthermore, due to the symmetric nature of the vector space operations for similarity and analogy, which are far from human similarity judgements (Tversky, 1977). Other word representations tried to provide asymmetric notions of similarity in a non-contextualized setting, including Gaussian embeddings (Vilnis and McCallum, 2014) and word similarity by dependency (Gawron, 2014). However, these models could not account for the inherent compositionality of word embeddings (Mikolov et al., 2013b). Moreover, while work has been done on providing entailment for vector space models by entirely reinterpreting word2vec as an entailment based semantic model (Henderson and Popa, 2016), it requires an external notion of compositionality. Finally, word2vec and GloVe, as such, are meaning conflation deficient, meaning that a single word with all its possible meanings is represented by a single vector (Camacho-Collados and Pilehvar, 2018). Sense representation models in non-contextualized representations such as multi-sense skip gram, by performing joint clustering for local word neighbourhood. However, these sense representations are conditioned on non-disambiguated senses in the context and require additional conditioning on the intended senses (Li and Jurafsky, 2015).

In this paper, we aim to answer the question: *Can a single word representation mechanism account for lexical similarity and analogy, compositionality, lexical entailment **and be used to detect and resolve polysemy?*** We find that by performing column-wise normalization of word vectors trained using the word2vec skip-gram negative sampling

Proceedings of the 5th Workshop on Representation Learning for NLP (RepL4NLP-2020), pages 24–33
July 9, 2020. ©2020 Association for Computational Linguistics

regime, we can indeed represent all the above characteristics in a single representation. We interpret a column wise normalized word representation. We now treat these representations as fuzzy sets and can therefore use fuzzy set theoretic operations such as union, intersection, difference, etc. while also being able to succinctly use asymmetric notions of similarity such as K-L divergence and cross entropy. Finally, we show that this representation can highlight syntactic features such as function words, use their properties to detect polysemy, and resolve it qualitatively using the inherent compositionality of this representation.

In order to make these experiments and their results observable in general, we have provided the code which can be used to run these operations. The code can be found at `https://github.com/AlokDebnath/fuzzy_embeddings`. The code also has a working command line interface where users can perform qualitative assessments on the set theoretic operations, similarity, analogy and compositionality which are discussed in the paper.

2   Related Work

The representation of words using logical paradigms such as fuzzy logic, tensorial representations and other probabilistic approaches have been attempted before. In this section, we uncover some of these representations in detail.

Lee (1999) introduced measures of distributional similarity to improve the probability estimation for unseen occurrences. The measure of similarity of distributional word clusters was based on multiple measures including Euclidian distance, cosine distance, Jaccard's Coefficient, and asymmetric measures like α-skew divergence.

Bergmair (2011) used a fuzzy set theoretic view of features associated with word representations. While these features were not adopted from the vector space directly, it presents a unique perspective of entailment chains for reasoning tasks. Their analysis of inference using fuzzy representations provides interpretability in reasoning tasks.

Grefenstette (2013) presents a tenosrial calculus for word embeddings, which is based on compositional operators *which uses* vector representation of words to create a compositional distributional model of meaning. By providing a category-theoretic framework, the model creates an inherently compositional structure based on distributional word representations. However, they showed that in this framework, quantifiers could not be expressed.

Herbelot and Vecchi (2015) refers to a notion of general formal semantics inferred from a distributional representation by creating relevant ontology based on the existing distribution. This mapping is therefore from a standard distributional model to a set-theoretic model, where dimensions are predicates and weights are generalised quantifiers.

Emerson and Copestake (2016, 2017) developed functional distributional semantics, which is a probabilistic framework based on model theory. The framework relies on differentiating and learning entities and predicates and their relations, on which Bayesian inference is performed. This representation is inherently compositional, context dependent representation.

3   Background: Fuzzy Sets and Fuzzy Logic

In this section, we provide a basic background of fuzzy sets including some fuzzy set operations, reinterpreting sets as tuples in a universe of finite elements and showing some set operations. We also cover the computation of fuzzy entropy as a Bernoulli random variable.

A fuzzy set is defined as a set with probabilistic set membership. Therefore, a fuzzy set is denoted as $A = \{(x, \mu_A(x)), x \in \Omega\}$, where x is an element of set A with a probability $\mu_A(x)$ such that $0 \leq \mu_A \leq 1$, and Ω is the universal set.

If our universe Ω is finite and of cardinality n, our notion of probabilistic set membership is constrained to a maximum n values. Therefore, each fuzzy set A can be represented as an n-tuple, with each member of the tuple $A[i]$ being the probability of the ith member of Ω. We can rewrite a fuzzy set as an n-tuple $A' = (\mu_{A'}(x), \forall x \in \Omega)$, such that $|A'| = |\Omega|$. In this representation, $A[i]$ is the probability of the ith member of the tuple A. We define some common set operations in terms of this representation as follows.

$$(A \cap B)[i] \equiv A[i] \times B[i] \quad \text{(set intersection)}$$
$$(A \cup B)[i] \equiv A[i] + B[i] - A[i] \times B[i] \ \text{(set union)}$$
$$(A \sqcup B)[i] \equiv \max(1, \min(0, A[i] + B[i])) \ \text{(disjoint union)}$$
$$(\neg A)[i] \equiv 1 - A[i] \quad \text{(complement)}$$
$$(A \setminus B)[i] \equiv A[i] - \min(A[i], B[i]) \quad \text{(set difference)}$$
$$(A \subseteq B) \equiv \forall x \in \Omega : \mu_A(x) \leq \mu_B(x) \ \text{(set inclusion)}$$
$$|A| \equiv \sum_{i \in \Omega} \mu_A(i) \quad \text{(cardinality)}$$

The notion of entropy in fuzzy sets is an extrapolation of Shannon entropy from a single variable on the entire set. Formally, the fuzzy entropy of a set S is a measure of the uncertainty of the elements belonging to the set. The possibility of a member x belonging to the set S is a random variable X_i^S which is *true* with probability (p_i^S) and *false* with probability $(1 - p_i^S)$. Therefore, X_i^S is a Bernoulli random variable. In order to compute the entropy of a fuzzy set, we sum the entropy values of each X_i^S:

$$H(A) \equiv \sum_i H(X_i^A)$$
$$\equiv \sum_i -p_i^A \ln p_i^A - (1 - p_i^A) \ln(1 - p_i^A)$$
$$\equiv \sum_i -A[i] \ln A[i] - (1 - A[i]) \ln(1 - A[i])$$

This formulation will be useful in section 4.4 where we discuss two asymmetric measures of similarity, cross-entropy and K-L divergence, which can be seen as a natural extension of this formulation of fuzzy entropy.

4 Representation and Operations

In this section, we use the mathematical formulation above to reinterpret word embeddings. We first show how these word representations are created, then detail the interpretation of each of the set operations with some examples. We also look into some measures of similarity and their formulation in this framework. All examples in this section have been taken using the Google News Negative 300 vectors[1]. We used these gold standard vectors

[1] https://code.google.com/archive/p/word2vec/

4.1 Constructing the Tuple of Feature Probabilities

We start by converting the skip-gram negative sample word vectors into a tuple of feature probabilities. In order to construct a tuple of features representation in $\mathbb{R}^n$, we consider that the projection of a vector $\vec{v}$ onto a dimension i is a function of its probability of possessing the feature associated with that dimension. We compute the conversion from a word vector to a tuple of features by first exponentiating the projection of each vector along each direction, then averaging it over that feature for the entire vocabulary size, i.e. column-wise.

$$v_{exp}[i] \equiv \exp \vec{v}[i]$$
$$\hat{v}[i] \equiv \frac{v_{\exp}[i]}{\sum_{w \in \text{VOCAB}} \exp w_{\exp}[i]}$$

This normalization then produces a tuple of probabilities associated with each feature (corresponding to the dimensions of $\mathbb{R}^n$).

In line with our discussion from 3, this tuple of probabilities is akin to our representation of a fuzzy set. Let us consider the word v, and its corresponding n-dimensional word vector $\vec{v}$. The projection of $\vec{v}$ on a dimension i normalized (as shown above) to be interpreted as *if this dimension i were a property, what is probability that v would possess that property?*

In word2vec, words are distributed in a vector space of a particular dimensionality. Our representation attempts to provide some insight into how the arrangement of vectors provides insight into the properties they share. We do so by considering a function of the projection of a word vector onto a dimension and interpreting as a probability. This allows us an avenue to explore the relation between words in relation to the properties they share. It also allows us access to the entire arsenal of set operations, which are described below in section 4.2.

4.2 Operations on Feature Probabilities

Now that word vectors can be represented as tuples of feature probabilities, we can apply fuzzy set theoretic operations in order to ascertain the veracity of the implementation. We show qualitative examples of the set operations in this subsection, and the information they capture. Throughout this subsection, we follow the following notation: For any two words $w_1, w_2 \in$ VOCAB, $\hat{w}_1$ and $\hat{w}_2$ represents

$\hat{R}$	$\vec{R}$	$\hat{V}$	$\vec{V}$	$\hat{R} \cup \hat{V}$
risen	cashew	wavelengths	yellowish	flower
capita	risen	ultraviolet	whitish	red
peaked	soared	purple	aquamarine	stripes
declined	acuff	infrared	roans	flowers
increased	rafters	yellowish	bluish	green
rises	equalled	pigment	greenish	garlands

Table 1: An example of feature union. `Rose` is represented by R and `Violet` by V. We see here that while the word rose and violet have different meanings and senses, the union $R \cup V$ captures the sense of the flower as well as of colours, which are the senses common to these two words. We list words closest to the given word in the table. Closeness measured by cosine similarity for word2vec and cross-entropy-similarity for our vectors.

those words using our representation, while $\vec{w}_1$ and $\vec{w}_2$ are the word2vec vectors of those words.

Feature Union, Intersection and Difference In section 3, we showed the formulation of fuzzy set operations, assuming a finite universe of elements. As we saw in section 4.1, considering each dimension as a feature allows us to reinterpret word vectors as tuples of feature probabilities. Therefore, we can use the fuzzy set theoretic operations on this reinterpretation of fuzzy sets. For convenience, these operations have been called feature union, intersection and difference.

Intuitively, the feature intersection of words $\hat{w}_1$ and $\hat{w}_2$ should give us that word $\hat{w}_{1 \cap 2}$ which has the features common between the two words; an example of which is given in table 1. Similarly, the feature union $\hat{w}_{1 \cup 2} \simeq \hat{w}_1 \cup \hat{w}_2$ which has the properties of both the words, normalized for those properties which are common between the two, and feature difference $\hat{w}_{1 \setminus 2} \simeq \hat{w}_1 \setminus \hat{w}_2$ is that word which is similar to w_1 without the features of w_2. Examples of feature intersection and feature difference are shown in table 2 and 3 respectively.

While feature union does not seem to have a word2vec analogue, we consider that feature intersection is analogous to vector addition, and feature difference as analogous to vector difference.

Feature Inclusion Feature inclusion is based on the subset relation of fuzzy sets. We aim to capture feature inclusion by determining if there exist two words w_1 and w_2 such that *all* the feature probabilities of $\hat{w}_1$ are less than that of $\hat{w}_2$, then $\hat{w}_2 \subseteq \hat{w}_1$. We find that feature inclusion is closely linked to hyponymy, which we will show in 5.3.

$\hat{C}$	$\hat{P}$	$\hat{C} \cap \hat{P}$
hardware	vested	cpu
graphics	purchasing	hardware
multitasking	capita	powerpc
console	exercise	machine
firewire	parity	multitasking
mainframe	veto	microcode
$\vec{C}$	$\vec{P}$	$\vec{C} + \vec{P}$
bioses	centralize	expandability
scummvm	veto	writable
hardware	decembrist	cpcs
imovie	exercised	reconfigure
writable	redistribution	backplane
console	devolving	oem

Table 2: An example of feature intersection with the possible word2vec analogue (vector addition). The word `computer` is represented by C and `power` by P. Note that power is also a decent example of polysemy, and we see that in the context of computers, the connotations of hardware and the CPU are the most accessible. We list words closest to the given word in the table. Closeness measured by cosine similarity for word2vec and cross-entropy-similarity for our vectors.

4.3 Interpreting Entropy

For a word represented using a tuple of feature probabilities, the notion of entropy is strongly tied to the notion of certainty (Xuecheng, 1992), i.e. with what certainty does this word possess or not possess this set of features? Formally, the fuzzy entropy of a set S is a measure of the uncertainty of elements belonging to the set. The possibility a member x_i belonging to S is a random variable X_i^S, which is `true` with probability p_i^S, `false` with probability $(1 - p_i^S)$. Thus, X_i^S is a Bernoulli random variable. So, to measure the fuzzy entropy of a set, we add up the entropy values of each of the X_i^S (MacKay and Mac Kay, 2003).

Intuitively, words with the highest entropy are those which have features which are equally likely to belong to them and to their complement, i.e. $\forall i \in \Omega, A[i] \simeq 1 - A[i]$. So words with high fuzzy entropy can occur only in two scenarios: (1) The words occur with very low frequency so their random initialization remained, or (2) The words occur around so many different word groups that their corresponding fuzzy sets have some probability of possessing most of the features.

Therefore, our representation of words as tuples of features can be used to isolate function words better than the more commonly considered notion of simply using frequency, as it identifies the information theoretic distribution of features based on the context the function word occurs in. Table

$\hat{F}$	$\hat{B}$	$\hat{F} \setminus \hat{B}$
french	isles	communaut
english	colonial	aise
france	subcontinent	langue
german	cinema	monet
spanish	boer	dictionnaire
british	canadians	gascon

$\vec{F}$	$\vec{B}$	$\vec{F} - \vec{B}$
french	scottish	ranjit
english	american	privatised
france	thatcherism	tardis
german	netherlands	molloy
spanish	hillier	isaacs
british	cukcs	raj

Table 3: An example of feature difference, along with a possible word2vec analogue (vector difference). `French` is represented by F and `British` by B. We see here that set difference capture french words from the dataset, while there does not seem to be any such correlation in the vector difference. We list words closest to the given word in the table. Closeness measured by cosine similarity for word2vec and cross-entropy-similarity for our vectors.

4 provides the top 15 function words by entropy, and the correspodingly ranked words by frequency. We see that frequency is clearly not a good enough measure to identify function words.

4.4 Similarity Measures

One of the most important notions in presenting a distributional word representation is its ability to capture similarity (Van der Plas and Tiedemann, 2006). Since we use and modify vector based word representations, we aim to preserve the "distribution" of the vector embeddings, while providing a more robust interpretation of similarity measures. With respect to similarity, we make two strong claims:

1. Representing words as a tuple of feature probabilities lends us an inherent notion of similarity. Feature difference provides this notion, as it estimates the difference between two words along each feature probability.

2. Our representation allows for an easy adoption of known similarity measures such as K-L divergence and cross-entropy.

Note that feature difference (based on fuzzy set difference), K-L divergence and cross-entropy are all asymmetric measures of similarity. As Nematzadeh et al. (2017) points out, human similarity judgements are inherently asymmetric in nature.

We would like to point out that while most methods of introducing asymmetric similarity measures in word2vec account for both the focus and context vector Asr et al. (2018) and provide the asymmetry by querying on this combination of focus and context representations of each word. Our representation, on the other hand, uses only the focus representations (which are a part of the word representations used for downstream task as well as any other intrinsic evaluation), and still provides an innately asymmetric notion of similarity.

K-L Divergence From a fuzzy set perspective, we measure similarity as an overlap of features. For this purpose, we exploit the notion of fuzzy information theory by comparing how close the probability distributions of the similar words are using a standard measure, Kullback-Leibler (K-L) divergence. K-L divergence is an asymmetric measure of similarity.

The K-L divergence of a distribution P from another distribution Q is defined in terms of loss of compression. Given data d which follows distribution P, the extra bits need to store it under the false assumption that the data d follows distribution Q is the K-L divergence between the distributions P and Q. In the fuzzy case, we can compute the KL divergence as:

$$D(S \parallel T) \equiv D\left(X_i^S \,\middle\|\, X_i^T\right) = \sum_i p_i^S \log\left(p_i^S / p_i^T\right)$$

We see in table 5 some qualitative examples of how K-L divergence shows the relation between two words (or phrases when composed using feature intersection as in the case of `north korea`). We exemplify Nematzadeh et al. (2017)'s human annotator judgement of the distance between China and North Korea, where human annotators considered "North Korea" to be very similar to "China," while the reverse relationship was rated as significantly less strong ("China" is not very similar to "North Korea").

Cross Entropy We also calculate the cross entropy between two words, as it can be used to determine the entropy associated with the similarity between two words. Ideally, by determining the "spread" of the similarity of features between two words, we can determine the features that allow two words to be similar, allowing a more interpretable notion of feature-wise relation.

28

and	the	in	one	which	to	however	_two_	for	_eight_
this	of	of	in	the	_zero_	to		is	a	for
as	and	only	a	also	_nine_	it		as	but	_s_

Table 4: On the left: Top 15 words with highest entropy with frequency ≥ 100 (note that all of them are function words). On the right: Top 15 words with the highest frequency. The non-function words have been emphasized for comparison.

Example 1	$D(ganges \parallel delta)$	6.3105
	$D(delta \parallel ganges)$	6.3040
Example 2	$D(north \cap korea \parallel china)$	1.02923
	$D(china \parallel north \cap korea)$	10.60665

Table 5: Examples of KL-divergence as an asymmetric measure of similarity. Lower is closer. We see here that the evaluation of North Korea as a concept being closer to China than vice versa can be observed by the use of K-L Divergence on column-wise normalization.

$\hat{N}$	$\hat{M}$	$\hat{G}$	$\hat{N} \cap \hat{M}$	$\hat{N} \cap \hat{G}$
nobility	metal	bad	fusible	good
isotope	fusible	manners	unreactive	dharma
fujwara	ductility	happiness	metalloids	morals
feudal	with	evil	ductility	virtue
clan	alnico	excellent	heavy	righteous
$\vec{N}$	$\vec{M}$	$\vec{G}$	$\vec{N} + \vec{M}$	$\vec{N} + \vec{G}$
noblest	trivalent	bad	fusible	gracious
auctoritas	carbides	natured	metals	virtuous
abies	metallic	humoured	sulfides	believeth
eightfold	corrodes	selfless	finntroll	savages
vojt	alloying	gracious	rhodium	hedonist

Table 6: Polysemy of the word `noble`, in the context of the words `good` and `metal`. `noble` is represented by N, `metal` by M and `good` by G. We also provide the word2vec analogues of the same.

The cross-entropy of two distributions P and Q is a sum of the entropy of P and the K-L divergence between P and Q. In this sense, in captures both the _uncertainty in_ P, as well as the distance from P to Q, to give us a general sense of the information theoretic difference between the concepts of P and Q. We use a generalized version of cross-entropy to fuzzy sets (Li, 2015), which is:

$$H(S, T) \equiv \sum_i H(X_i^S) + D(X_i^S \parallel X_i^T)$$

Feature representations which on comparison provide high cross entropy imply a more distributed feature space. Therefore, provided the right words to compute cross entropy, it could be possible to extract various features common (or associated) with a large group of words, lending some insight into how a single surface form (and its representation) can capture the distribution associated with different senses. Here, we use cross-entropy as a measure of polysemy, and isolate polysemous words based on context. We provide an example of capturing polysemy using composition by feature intersection in table 6.

We can see that the words which are most similar to `noble` are a combination of words from many senses, which provides some perspective into its distribution, . Indeed, it has an entropy value of 6.2765^2.

4.5 Constructing Analogy

Finally, we construct the notion of analogy in our representation of a word as a tuple of features. Word analogy is usually represented as a problem

---

[2]For reference, the word `the` has an entropy of 6.2934.

where given a pairing $(a : b)$, and a prior x, we are asked to compute an unknown word $y_?$ such that $a : b :: x : y_?$. In the vector space model, analogy is computed based on vector distances. We find that this training mechanism does not have a consistent interpretation beyond evaluation. This is because normalization of vectors _performed only during inference, not during training_. Thus, computing analogy in terms of vector distances provides little insight into the distribution of vectors or to the notion of the length of the word vectors, which seems to be essential to analogy computation using vector operations

In using a fuzzy set theoretic representation, vector projections are inherently normalized, making them feature dense. This allows us to compute analogies much better in lower dimension spaces. We consider analogy to be an operation involving union and set difference. Word analogy is computed as follows:

$$a : b :: x : y_?$$

$$y_? = b - a + x \implies y_? = (b + x) - a$$

$$y = (b \sqcup x) \setminus a \quad \text{(Set-theoretic interpretation)}$$

Notice that this form of word analogy can be "derived" from the vector formula by re-arrangement. We use non-disjoint set union so that the common features are not eliminated, but the values

Word 1	Word 2	Word 3	word2vec	Our representation
bacteria	tuberculosis	virus	polio	hiv
cold	freezing	hot	evaporates	boiling
ds	nintendo	dreamcast	playstation	sega
pool	billiards	karate	taekwondo	judo

Table 7: Examples of analogy compared to the analogy in word2vec. We see here that the comparisons constructed by feature representations are similar to those given by the standard word vectors.

Dims.	word2vec	Our Representation	
		K-L Divergence	Cross-Entropy
20	0.2478	0.2690	**0.2744**
50	0.2916	0.2966	**0.2981**
100	0.2960	0.3124	**0.3206**
200	0.3259	0.3253	**0.3298**

Table 8: Similarity scores on the SimLex-999 dataset (Hill et al., 2015), for various dimension sizes (Dims.). The scores are provided according to the Spearman Correlation to incorporate higher precision.

are clipped at $(0, 1]$ so that the fuzzy representation is consistent. Analogical reasoning is based on the common features between the word representations, and conflates multiple types of relations such as synonymy, hypernymy and causal relations (Chen et al., 2017). Using fuzzy set theoretic representations, we can also provide a context for the analogy, effectively reconstructing analogous reasoning to account for the type of relation from a lexical semantic perspective.

Some examples of word analogy based are presented in table 7.

5 Experiments and Results

In this section, we present our experiments and their results in various domains including similarity, analogy, function word detection, polysemy detection, lexical entailment and compositionality. All the experiments have been conducted on established datasets.

5.1 Similarity and Analogy

Similarity and analogy are the most popular intrinsic evaluation mechanisms for word representations (Mikolov et al., 2013a). Therefore, to evaluate our representations, the first tasks we show are similarity and analogy. For similarity computations, we use the SimLex corpus (Hill et al., 2015) for training and testing at different dimensions For word analogy, we use the MSR Word Relatedness Test (Mikolov et al., 2013c). We compare it to the vector representation of words for different dimensions.

5.1.1 Similarity

Our scores our compared to the word2vec scores of similarity using the Spearman rank correlation coefficient (Spearman, 1987), which is a ratio of the covariances and standard deviations of the inputs being compared.

As shown in table 8, using our representation, similarity is *slightly* better represented according to the SimLex corpus. We show similarity on both the asymmetric measures of similarity for our repre-

Category		word2vec		Our representation	
		50	100	50	100
Capital Common Countries		21.94	37.55	**39.13**	**47.23**
Capital World		13.02	20.10	**27.30**	**26.54**
Currency		12.24	18.60	**25.27**	**24.90**
City-State		10.38	16.70	**23.24**	**23.51**
Family		10.61	17.34	**23.67**	**23.88**
Adjective-Adverb	Syntactic	4.74	3.23	**7.26**	**3.83**
	Semantic	10.61	17.34	**23.67**	**23.88**
	Overall	9.92	15.68	**21.73**	**21.52**
Opposite	Syntactic	4.06	3.66	**7.61**	**4.92**
	Semantic	10.61	17.34	**23.67**	**23.88**
	Overall	9.36	14.73	**20.60**	**20.26**
Comparative	Syntactic	8.86	12.63	**16.88**	**15.39**
	Semantic	10.61	17.34	**23.67**	**23.88**
	Overall	10.10	15.96	**21.67**	**21.39**
Superlative	Syntactic	7.59	11.30	**14.32**	**13.36**
	Semantic	10.61	17.34	**23.67**	**23.88**
	Overall	9.54	15.20	**20.35**	**20.15**
Present-Participle	Syntactic	7.51	10.96	**14.31**	**13.14**
	Semantic	10.61	17.34	**23.67**	**23.88**
	Overall	9.34	14.73	**19.84**	**19.49**
Nationality	Syntactic	12.51	19.07	**21.64**	**21.96**
	Semantic	10.61	17.34	**23.67**	**23.88**
	Overall	11.51	18.16	**22.71**	**22.97**
Past Tense	Syntactic	11.65	17.09	**20.43**	**19.76**
	Semantic	10.61	17.34	**23.67**	**23.88**
	Overall	11.16	17.21	**21.96**	**27.72**
Plural	Syntactic	11.76	17.23	**20.53**	**19.89**
	Semantic	10.61	17.34	**23.67**	**23.88**
	Overall	11.26	17.28	**21.90**	**21.64**
Plural Verbs	Syntactic	11.36	16.60	**19.88**	**19.46**
	Semantic	10.61	17.34	**23.67**	**23.88**
	Overall	11.05	16.91	**21.46**	**21.30**

Table 9: Comparison of Analogies between word2vec and our representation for 50 and 100 dimensions (Dims.). For the first five, only overall accuracy is shown as overall accuracy is the same as semantic accuracy (as there is no syntactic accuracy measure). For all the others, we present, syntactic, semantic and overall accuracy as well. We see here that we outperform word2vec on every single metric.

sentation, K-L divergence as well as cross-entropy. We see that cross-entropy performs better than K-L Divergence. While the similarity scores are generally higher, we see a reduction in the degree of similarity beyond 100 dimension vectors (features).

5.1.2 Analogy

For analogy, we see that our model outperforms word2vec at both 50 and 100 dimensions. We see that at lower dimension sizes, our normalized feature representation captures significantly more syntactic and semantic information than its vector counterpart. We conjecture that this can primarily be attributed to the fact that constructing feature probabilities provides more information about the

top n words	word2vec	Our Representation
15	10	**15**
30	21	**30**
50	39	**47**

Table 10: Function word detection using entropy (in our representation) and by frequency in word2vec. We see that we consistently detect more function words than word2vec, based on the 176 function word list released by Nation (2016). The metric is *number of words*, i.e. the number of words chosen by frequency for word2vec and entropy for our representation

common (and distinct) "concepts" which are shared between two words.

Since feature representations are inherently fuzzy sets, lower dimension sizes provide a more reliable probability distribution, which becomes more and more sparse as the dimensionality of the vectors increases (i.e. number of features rise). Therefore, we notice that the increase in feature probabilities is a lot more for 50 dimensions than it is for 100.

5.2 Function Word Detection

As mentioned in section 4.3, we use entropy as a measure of detecting function words for the standard GoogleNews-300 negative sampling dataset[3]. In order to quantitatively evaluate the detection of function words, we choose the top n words in our representation ordered by entropy with a frequency ≥ 100, and compare it to the top n words ordered by frequency from word2vec; n being 15, 30 and 50. We compare the number of function words in both in table 10. The list of function words is derived from Nation (2016).

5.3 Compositionality

Finally, we evaluate the compositionality of word embeddings. Mikolov et al. (2013b) claims that word embeddings in vector spaces possess additive compositionality, i.e. by vector addition, semantic phrases such as compounds can be well represented. We claim that our representation in fact captures the semantics of phrases by performing a literal combination of the features of the head and modifier word, therefore providing a more robust representation of phrases.

We use the English nominal compound phrases from Ramisch et al. (2016). An initial set of experiments on nominal compounds using word2vec have been done before (Cordeiro et al., 2016), where it

---

[3]https://code.google.com/archive/p/word2vec/

Dims.	Metric	word2vec	Our Representation
50	Spearman	0.3946	**0.4117**
	Pearson	0.4058	**0.4081**
100	Spearman	0.4646	**0.4912**
	Pearson	0.4457	**0.4803**
200	Spearman	0.4479	**0.4549**
	Pearson	**0.4163**	0.4091

Table 11: Results for compositionality of word embeddings for nominal compounds for various dimensions (Dims.). We see that almost across the board, we perform better, however, for the Pearson correlation metric, at 200 dimensions, we find that word2vec has a better representation of rank by frequency for nominal compounds.

was shown to be a fairly difficult task for modern non-contextual word embeddings. In order to analyse nominal compounds, we adjust our similarity metric to account for asymmetry in the similarity between the head-word and the modifier, and vice versa. We report performance on two metrics, the Spearman correlation (Spearman, 1987) and Pearson correlation (Pearson, 1920).

The results are shown in table 11. The difference in scores for the Pearson and Spearman rank correlation show that word2vec at higher dimensions better represents the rank of words (by frequency), but at lower dimensions, the feature probability representation has a better analysis of both rank by frequency, and its correlation with similarity of words with a nominal compound. Despite this, we show a higher Spearman correlation coefficient at 200 dimensions as well, as we capture non-linear relations.

5.4 Dimensionality Analysis and Feature Representations

In this subsection, we provide some interpretation of the results above, and examine the effect of scaling dimensions to the feature representation. As seen here, the evaluation has been done on smaller dimension sizes of 50 and 100, and we see that our representation can be used for a slightly larger range of tasks from the perspective of intrinsic evaluations. However, the results of quantitative analogy for higher dimensions have been observed to be lower for fuzzy representations rather than the word2vec negative-sampling word vectors.

We see that the representation we propose does not scale well as dimensions increase. This is because our representation relies on the distribution of probability mass per feature (dimension) across all the words. Therefore, increasing the dimensionality of the word vectors used makes the representation that much more sparse.

6 Conclusion

In this paper, we presented a reinterpretation of distributional semantics. We performed a column-wise normalization on word vectors, such that each value in this normalized representation represented the probability of the word possessing a feature that corresponded to each dimension. This provides us a representation of each word as a tuple of feature probabilities. We find that this representation can be seen as a fuzzy set, with each probability being the function of the projection of the original word vector on a dimension.

Considering word vectors as fuzzy sets allows us access to set operations such as union, intersection and difference. In our modification, these operations provide the product, disjoint sum and difference of the word representations, feature wise. Using qualitative examples, we show that our representation naturally captures an asymmetric notion of similarity using feature difference, from which known asymmetric measures can be easily constructed, such as Cross Entropy and K-L Divergence.

We qualitatively show how our model accounts for polysemy, while showing quantitative proofs of our representation's performance at lower dimensions in similarity, analogy, compositionality and function word detection. We hypothesize that lower dimensions are more suited for our representation as sparsity increases with higher dimensions, so the significance of feature probabilities reduces. This sparsity causes a diffusion of the probabilities across multiple features.

Through this work, we aim to provide some insights into interpreting word representations by showing one possible perspective and explanation of the lengths and projections of word embeddings in the vector space. These feature representations can be adapted for basic neural models, allowing the use of feature based representations at lower dimensions for downstream tasks.

Acknowledgements

We would like to thank the anonymous reviewers for their time and comments which have helped make this paper and its contribution better.

References

Fatemeh Torabi Asr, Robert Zinkov, and Michael Jones. 2018. Querying word embeddings for similarity and relatedness. In *Proceedings of the 2018 Conference of the North American Chapter of the Association for Computational Linguistics: Human Language Technologies, Volume 1 (Long Papers)*, pages 675–684.

Richard Bergmair. 2011. *Monte Carlo Semantics: Robust inference and logical pattern processing with Natural Language text*. Ph.D. thesis, University of Cambridge.

Jose Camacho-Collados and Mohammad Taher Pilehvar. 2018. From word to sense embeddings: A survey on vector representations of meaning. *Journal of Artificial Intelligence Research*, 63:743–788.

Dawn Chen, Joshua C Peterson, and Thomas L Griffiths. 2017. Evaluating vector-space models of analogy. *arXiv preprint arXiv:1705.04416*.

Silvio Cordeiro, Carlos Ramisch, Marco Idiart, and Aline Villavicencio. 2016. Predicting the compositionality of nominal compounds: Giving word embeddings a hard time. In *Proceedings of the 54th Annual Meeting of the Association for Computational Linguistics (Volume 1: Long Papers)*, pages 1986–1997, Berlin, Germany. Association for Computational Linguistics.

Guy Emerson and Ann Copestake. 2016. Functional distributional semantics. In *Proceedings of the 1st Workshop on Representation Learning for NLP*, pages 40–52.

Guy Emerson and Ann Copestake. 2017. Semantic composition via probabilistic model theory. In *IWCS 2017-12th International Conference on Computational Semantics-Long papers*.

John R Firth. 1957. A synopsis of linguistic theory, 1930-1955. *Studies in linguistic analysis*.

Jean Mark Gawron. 2014. Improving sparse word similarity models with asymmetric measures. In *Proceedings of the 52nd Annual Meeting of the Association for Computational Linguistics (Volume 2: Short Papers)*, pages 296–301.

Yoav Goldberg and Omer Levy. 2014. word2vec explained: deriving mikolov et al.'s negative-sampling word-embedding method. *arXiv preprint arXiv:1402.3722*.

Edward Grefenstette. 2013. Towards a formal distributional semantics: Simulating logical calculi with tensors. *arXiv preprint arXiv:1304.5823*.

James Henderson and Diana Nicoleta Popa. 2016. A vector space for distributional semantics for entailment. *arXiv preprint arXiv:1607.03780*.

Aurélie Herbelot and Eva Maria Vecchi. 2015. Building a shared world: Mapping distributional to model-theoretic semantic spaces. In *Proceedings of the 2015 Conference on Empirical Methods in Natural Language Processing*, pages 22–32.

Felix Hill, Roi Reichart, and Anna Korhonen. 2015. Simlex-999: Evaluating semantic models with (genuine) similarity estimation. *Computational Linguistics*, 41(4):665–695.

Lillian Lee. 1999. Measures of distributional similarity. In *Proceedings of the 37th Annual Meeting of the Association for Computational Linguistics*, pages 25–32.

Jiwei Li and Dan Jurafsky. 2015. Do multi-sense embeddings improve natural language understanding? *arXiv preprint arXiv:1506.01070*.

Xiang Li. 2015. Fuzzy cross-entropy. *Journal of Uncertainty Analysis and Applications*, 3(1):2.

David JC MacKay and David JC Mac Kay. 2003. *Information theory, inference and learning algorithms*. Cambridge university press.

Tomas Mikolov, Kai Chen, Greg Corrado, and Jeffrey Dean. 2013a. Efficient estimation of word representations in vector space. *arXiv preprint arXiv:1301.3781*.

Tomas Mikolov, Ilya Sutskever, Kai Chen, Greg S Corrado, and Jeff Dean. 2013b. Distributed representations of words and phrases and their compositionality. In *Advances in neural information processing systems*, pages 3111–3119.

Tomáš Mikolov, Wen-tau Yih, and Geoffrey Zweig. 2013c. Linguistic regularities in continuous space word representations. In *Proceedings of the 2013 conference of the north american chapter of the association for computational linguistics: Human language technologies*, pages 746–751.

Ian Stephen Paul Nation. 2016. *Making and using word lists for language learning and testing*. John Benjamins Publishing Company.

Aida Nematzadeh, Stephan C Meylan, and Thomas L Griffiths. 2017. Evaluating vector-space models of word representation, or, the unreasonable effectiveness of counting words near other words. In *CogSci*.

Karl Pearson. 1920. Notes on the history of correlation. *Biometrika*, 13(1):25–45.

Jeffrey Pennington, Richard Socher, and Christopher D Manning. 2014. Glove: Global vectors for word representation. In *Proceedings of the 2014 conference on empirical methods in natural language processing (EMNLP)*, pages 1532–1543.

Lonneke Van der Plas and Jörg Tiedemann. 2006. Finding synonyms using automatic word alignment and measures of distributional similarity. In *Proceedings of the COLING/ACL on Main conference poster sessions*, pages 866–873. Association for Computational Linguistics.

Carlos Ramisch, Silvio Cordeiro, Leonardo Zilio, Marco Idiart, and Aline Villavicencio. 2016. How naked is the naked truth? a multilingual lexicon of nominal compound compositionality. In *Proceedings of the 54th Annual Meeting of the Association for Computational Linguistics (Volume 2: Short Papers)*, pages 156–161, Berlin, Germany. Association for Computational Linguistics.

Charles Spearman. 1987. The proof and measurement of association between two things. *The American journal of psychology*, 100(3/4):441–471.

Amos Tversky. 1977. Features of similarity. *Psychological review*, 84(4):327.

Luke Vilnis and Andrew McCallum. 2014. Word representations via gaussian embedding. *arXiv preprint arXiv:1412.6623*.

Liu Xuecheng. 1992. Entropy, distance measure and similarity measure of fuzzy sets and their relations. *Fuzzy sets and systems*, 52(3):305–318.

Compositionality and Capacity in Emergent Languages

Abhinav Gupta[*]
MILA
abhinavg@nyu.edu

Cinjon Resnick[*]
New York University
cinjon@nyu.edu

Jakob Foerster
Facebook AI Research
jnf@fb.com

Andrew M. Dai
Google AI
adai@google.com

Kyunghyun Cho
New York University
Facebook AI Research
kyunghyun.cho@nyu.edu

Abstract

Recent works have discussed the extent to which emergent languages can exhibit properties of natural languages particularly learning compositionality. In this paper, we investigate the learning biases that affect the efficacy and compositionality in multi-agent communication in addition to the communicative bandwidth. Our foremost contribution is to explore how the capacity of a neural network impacts its ability to learn a compositional language. We additionally introduce a set of evaluation metrics with which we analyze the learned languages. Our hypothesis is that there should be a specific range of model capacity and channel bandwidth that induces compositional structure in the resulting language and consequently encourages systematic generalization. While we empirically see evidence for the bottom of this range, we curiously do not find evidence for the top part of the range and believe that this is an open question for the community.

1 Introduction

Compositional language learning in the context of multi agent emergent communication has been extensively studied (Foerster et al., 2016; Lazaridou et al., 2017; Baroni, 2020). These works have found that while most emergent languages do not tend to be compositional, they can be guided towards this attribute through artificial task-specific constraints (Harding Graesser et al., 2019; Lee et al., 2018; Gupta* et al., 2020).

In this paper, we focus on how a neural network, specifically a generative one, can learn a compositional language. Moreover, we ask how this can occur without task-specific constraints. To accomplish this, we first define what is a language and what we mean by compositionality. In tandem, we introduce *precision* and *recall*, two metrics that help us measure how well a generative model at

large has learned a grammar from a finite set of training instances. We then use a variational autoencoder with a discrete sequence bottleneck to investigate how well the model learns a compositional language, in addition to what affects that learning. This allows us to derive *residual entropy*, a third metric that reliably measures compositionality in our particular environment. We use this metric to cross-validate precision and recall.

Our paper is most similar to Kottur et al. (2017), which showed that compositional language arose only when certain constraints on the agents are satisfied. While the constraints they examined were either making their models memoryless or having a minimal vocabulary in the language, we hypothesized about the importance for agents to have small capacity relative to the number of concepts to which they are exposed. Each of Verhoef et al. (2016); Kirby et al. (2015); Zaslavsky et al. (2018) examine the trade-off between expression and compression in both emergent and natural languages, in addition to how that trade-off affects the learners. We differ in that we target a specific aspect of the agent (capacity) and ask how that aspect biases the learning.

2 Compositional Language and Learning

We consider the problem of learning an underlying language $L^\star$ from a finite set of training strings randomly drawn from it: $D = \{s|s \sim G^\star\}$ where $G^\star$ is the minimal length generator associated with $L^\star$. We assume $|D| \ll |L^\star|$ and our goal is to use D to learn a language L that approximates $L^\star$ as well as possible. We know that there exists an equivalent generator G for L, and so our problem becomes estimating a generator from this finite set rather than reconstructing an entire set of strings belonging to the original language L^*. We cast the problem of estimating a generator G as density modeling, in which case the goal is to estimate a distribution $p(s)$. Sampling from $p(s)$ is equivalent

---

These two authors contributed equally.

Proceedings of the 5th Workshop on Representation Learning for NLP (RepL4NLP-2020), pages 34–38
July 9, 2020. ©2020 Association for Computational Linguistics

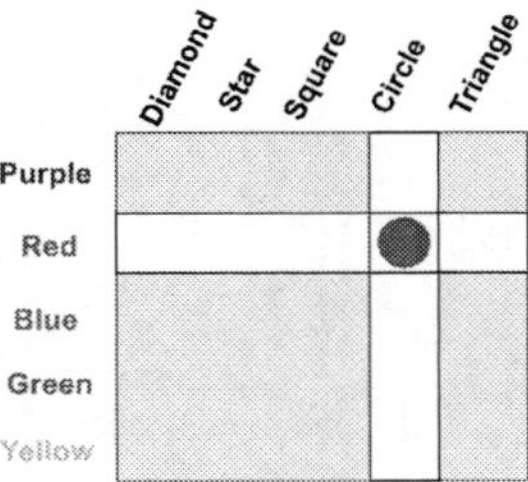

Figure 1: The grid above shows five shapes and five colors. Agents with a non-compositional language can use this shared map to communicate "Red Circle" with only $\lceil \log_2 5^2 \rceil = 5$ bits. If they instead used a compositional language, it would require $\lceil \log_2 5 \rceil = 3$ bits for each concept for a total of 6 bits to convey the string. On the other hand, the agent needs 25 memory slots to store the concepts in the former case but only 10 slots in the compositional case. This trade-off exemplifies the motivation for our investigation because it suggests that a key driver of compositionality in language is the capacity of an agent relative to the total number of objects in its environment.

to generating a string from the generator G.

Evaluation metrics When the language was learned perfectly, any string sampled from the learned distribution $p(s)$ must belong to $L^\star$. Also, any string in $L^\star$ must be assigned a non-zero probability under $p(s)$. Otherwise, the set of strings generated from this generator, implicitly defined via $p(s)$, is not identical to the original language $L^\star$. This observation leads to two metrics for evaluating the quality of the estimated language with the distribution $p(s)$, *precision* and *recall*:

$$\text{Precision}(L^\star, p) = \frac{1}{|L^\star|} \sum_{s \in L} \mathbb{I}(s \in L^\star) \quad (1)$$

$$\text{Recall}(L^\star, p) = \sum_{s \in L^\star} \log p(s) \quad (2)$$

where $\mathbb{I}(x)$ is the indicator function. These metrics are designed to be fit for any compositional structure rather than one-off evaluation approaches.

Our setup We simplify and assume that each of the characters in the string $s \in L^\star$ correspond to underlying concepts. While the inputs are ordered according to the sequential concepts, our model encodes them using a bag of words (BoW) representation.

The speaker f_θ is parameterized using a recurrent policy which receives the sequence of concatenated one-hot input tokens of s and converts each of

them to an embedding. It then runs an LSTM non-autoregressively for l timesteps taking the flattened representation of the input embeddings as its input and linearly projecting each result to a probability distribution over $\{0, 1\}$. This results in a sequential Bernoulli distribution over l latent variables: $f_\theta(z|s) = \prod_{t=1}^{l} p(z_t|s; \theta)$. From this distribution, we can sample a latent string $z = (z_1, \ldots, z_l)$.

The listener g_ϕ receives z and uses a BoW representation to encode them into its own embedding space. Taking the flattened representation of these embeddings as input, we run an LSTM for $|\mathcal{N}|$ time steps, each time outputting a probability distribution over the full alphabet Σ: $g_\phi(s|z) = \prod_{j=1}^{|\mathcal{N}|} p(s_j|z; \phi)$.

To train the whole system end-to-end (Sukhbaatar et al., 2016; Mordatch and Abbeel, 2018) via backpropogation, we apply a continuous approximation to z_t that depends on a learned temperature parameter τ. We use the 'straight-through' version of Gumbel-Softmax (Jang et al., 2017; Maddison et al., 2017) to convert the continuous distribution to a discrete distribution for each z_t. The final sequence of one hot vectors encoding z is our *message*, which is passed to the listener g_ϕ.

The prior p_λ encodes the *message* z using a BoW representation. It gives the probability of z according to the prior (binary) distribution for each z_t and is defined as: $p_\lambda(z) = \prod_{t=1}^{l} p(z_t|\lambda)$.

This can be used both to compute the prior probability of a latent string and also to efficiently sample from p_λ using ancestral sampling. Penalizing the KL divergence between the speaker's distribution and the prior distribution encourages the emergent protocol to use latent strings that are as diverse as possible.

Hypotheses on compositionality Under this framework for language learning, we can make the following observations. If the length of the latent sequence $l < \log_2 |L^\star|$, it is impossible for the model to avoid the failure case because there will be $|L^\star| - 2^l$ strings in $L^\star$ that cannot be generated from the trained model. Consequently, recall cannot be maximized. However, this may be difficult to check using the sample-based estimate as the chance of sampling $s \in L^\star \setminus \int g_\phi(s|z)p_\lambda(z)\mathrm{d}z$ decreases proportionally to the size of $L^\star$. This is especially true when the gap $|L^\star| - 2^l$ is narrow.

When $l \geq \log_2 |L^\star|$, there are three cases. The first is when there are not enough parameters θ to learn the underlying compositional grammar, in

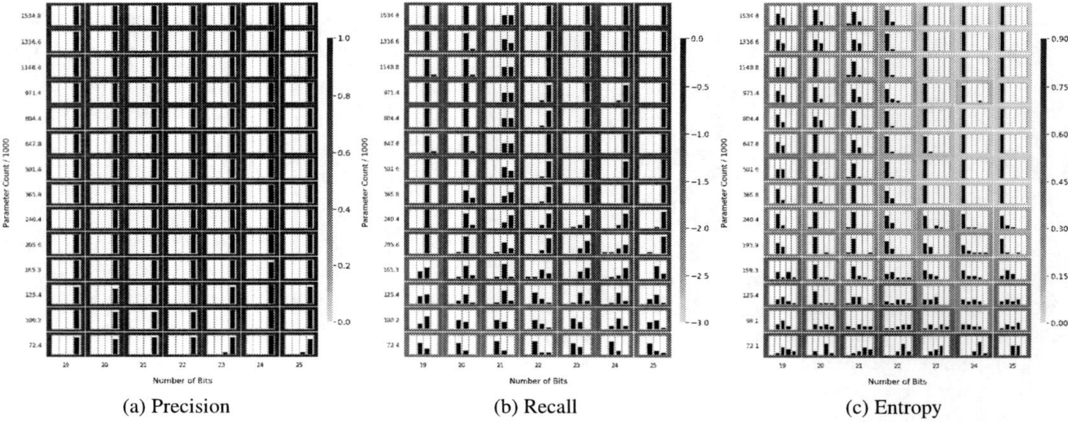

(a) Precision   (b) Recall   (c) Entropy

Figure 2: Histograms showing precision, recall (defined in § 2), and entropy (defined in § 3) over the test set. We show results for bits 19 to 25 and parameter range $72k$ to $1534k$ (details in § 3). Each bit/parameter combination is trained for 10 seeds over $200k$ steps.

which case $L^\star$ cannot be learned. The second case is when the number of parameters $|\theta|$ is greater than that required to store all the training strings, i.e., $|\theta| = O(l|D|)$. Here, it is highly likely for the model to overfit as it can map each training string with a unique latent string without having to learn any of $L^\star$'s compositional structure. Lastly, when the number of parameters lies in between these two poles, we hypothesize that the model will capture the underlying compositional structure and exhibit systematic generalization (Bahdanau et al., 2019).

3 Experiments

Models and Learning The task is to communicate 6 concepts, each of which have 10 possible values with a total dataset size of 10^6. We train the proposed VAE We gradually decrease the number of LSTM units from the base model by a factor $\alpha \in (0, 1]$. This is how we control the number of parameters ($|\theta|$ and $|\phi|$). We obtain seven models from each of these by varying the length of the latent sequence l from $\{19, 20, 21, 22, 23, 24, 25\}$. These were chosen because we both wanted to show a range of bits and because we need at least 20 bits to cover the 10^6 strings in L^* ($\lceil \log_2 10^6 \rceil = 20$).

Evaluation: Residual Entropy Our setup allows us to design a metric by which we can check the compositionality of the learned language L by examining how the underlying concepts are described by a string. Let p be a sequence of partitions of $\{1, 2, \ldots, l\}$. We define the degree of compositionality as the ratio between the variabil-

ity of each concept C_i and the variability explained by a latent subsequence $z[p_i]$ indexed by an associated partition p_i. More formally, the degree of compositionality given the partition sequence p is defined as a residual entropy

$$\mathrm{re}(p, L, L^\star) = \frac{1}{|\mathcal{N}|} \sum_{i=1}^{|\mathcal{N}|} \mathcal{H}_L(C_i | z[p_i]) / \mathcal{H}_{L^\star}(C_i)$$

where there are $|\mathcal{N}|$ concepts by the definition of our language. When each term inside the summation is close to zero, it implies that a subsequence $z[p_i]$ explains most of the variability of the specific concept C_i, and we consider this situation compositional. The residual entropy of a trained model is then the smallest $\mathrm{re}(p)$ over all possible sequences of partitions $\mathcal{P}$ and spans from 0 (compositional) to 1 (non-compositional) where $\mathrm{re}(L, L^\star) = \min_{p \in \mathcal{P}} \mathrm{re}(p, L, L^\star)$.

3.1 Results

Fig. 3 shows the main findings of our research. In plot (a), we see the parameter counts at the threshold. Below these values, the model cannot solve the task but above these, it can solve it. Further, observe the curve delineated by the lower left corner of the shift from unsuccessful to successful models. This inverse relationship between bits and parameters shows that the more parameters in the model, the fewer bits it needs to solve the task. Note however that it could only solve the task with fewer bits if it was forming a non-compositional code, suggesting that higher parameter models are able to do so while lower parameter ones cannot.

36

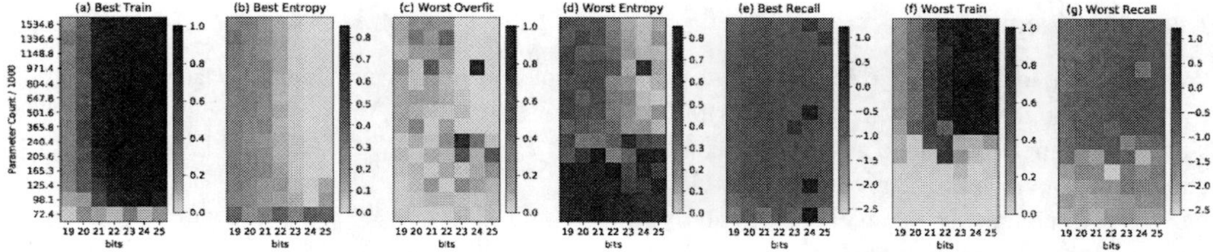

Figure 3: Main results showing best and worst performances of the proposed metrics over 10 seeds. See Section 3.1 for detailed analysis. Panels (a) and (f) show the accuracy of the training data, (b) and (d) show entropy, (e) and (g) show recall over the test data, and (c) plots the max difference in accuracy between training and test.

Observe further that all of our models above the minimum threshold (72,400) have the capacity to learn a compositional code. This is shown by the perfect training accuracy achieved by all of those models in plot (a) for 24 bits and by the perfect compositionality (zero entropy) in plot (b) for 24 bits. Together with the above, this validates that learning compositional codes requires less capacity than learning non-compositional codes. Plot (c) confirms our hypothesis that large models can memorize the entire dataset. The 24 bit model with 971,400 parameters achieves a train accuracy of 1.0 and a validation accuracy of 0.0. Cross-validating this with plots (d) and (g), we find that a member of the same parameter class is non-compositional and that there is one that achieves unusually low recall. We verified that these are all the same seed, which shows that the agents in this model are memorizing the dataset.

Plots (b) and (e) show that our compositionality metrics pass two sanity checks - high recall and perfect entropy can only be achieved with a channel that is sufficiently large (i.e. 24 bits) to allow for a compositional latent representation. Plot (f) shows that while the capacity does not affect the ability to learn a compositional language across the model range, it does change the *learnability*. Here we find that smaller models can fail to solve the task for any bandwidth, which coincides with literature suggesting a link between overparameterization and learnability (Li and Liang, 2018; Du et al., 2019). Finally, as expected, we find that no model learns to solve the task with < 20 bits, validating that the minimum required number of bits for learning a language of size $|L|$ is $\lceil \log(|L|) \rceil$. We also see that no model learns to solve it for 20 bits, which is likely due to optimization difficulties.

We first confirm the effectiveness of training by observing that almost all the models achieve perfect precision (Fig. 2 (a)), implying that $L \subseteq L^\star$, where L is the language learned by the model. This occurs even with our learning which encouraging the model to capture all training strings rather than to focus on only a few training strings. A natural follow-up question is how large is $L^\star \backslash L$. We measure this with recall in Fig. 2 (b), which shows a clear phase transition according to the model capacity when $l \geq 22$. This agrees with what we saw in Fig. 3 and is equivalent to saying $|L^\star \backslash L| \gg 0$ at a value that is close to our predicted boundary of $l = \lceil \log_2 10^6 \rceil = 20$. We attribute this gap to the difficulty in learning a perfectly-parameterized neural network.

These results clearly confirm the first part of our hypothesis - the latent sequence length must be at least as large as $\log |L^\star|$. They also confirm that there is a lowerbound on the number of parameters over which this model can successfully learn the underlying language. We have not been able to verify the upper bound in our experiments, which may require either a more (computationally) extensive set of experiments with even more parameters or a better theoretical understanding of the inherent biases behind learning with this architecture, such as from recent work on overparameterized models (Belkin et al., 2019; Nakkiran et al., 2020).

4 Conclusion

This paper opens the door for a vast amount of follow-up research. All our models were sufficiently large to represent the compositional structure of the language when given sufficient bandwidth. Furthermore, while large models did overfit, this was an exception rather than the rule. We hypothesize that this is due to the large number of examples in our language, which forces the model to generalize, but note that there are likely additional biases at play that warrant further investigation.

Acknowledgements

We would like to thank Marco Baroni and Angeliki Lazaridou for their comments on an earlier version of the paper. We would also like to thank the anonymous reviewers for giving insightful feedback in turn enhancing this work, particularly reviewer two for their thoroughness. Special thanks to Adam Roberts, Doug Eck, Mohammad Norouzi, and Jesse Engel.

References

Dzmitry Bahdanau, Shikhar Murty, Michael Noukhovitch, Thien Huu Nguyen, Harm de Vries, and Aaron Courville. 2019. Systematic generalization: What is required and can it be learned? In *International Conference on Learning Representations*.

Marco Baroni. 2020. Linguistic generalization and compositionality in modern artificial neural networks. *Philosophical Transactions of the Royal Society B: Biological Sciences*, 375:20190307.

Mikhail Belkin, Daniel Hsu, Siyuan Ma, and Soumik Mandal. 2019. Reconciling modern machine-learning practice and the classical bias–variance trade-off. *Proceedings of the National Academy of Sciences*, 116(32):15849–15854.

Simon S. Du, Xiyu Zhai, Barnabas Poczos, and Aarti Singh. 2019. Gradient descent provably optimizes over-parameterized neural networks. In *International Conference on Learning Representations*.

Jakob Foerster, Ioannis Alexandros Assael, Nando de Freitas, and Shimon Whiteson. 2016. Learning to communicate with deep multi-agent reinforcement learning. In D. D. Lee, M. Sugiyama, U. V. Luxburg, I. Guyon, and R. Garnett, editors, *Advances in Neural Information Processing Systems 29*, pages 2137–2145. Curran Associates, Inc.

Abhinav Gupta*, Agnieszka Słowik*, William Hamilton, Mateja Jamnik, Sean Holden, and Christopher Pal. 2020. Analyzing structural prios in multi-agent communication. *Adaptive and Learning Agents Workshop (ALA) @ AAMAS*.

Laura Harding Graesser, Kyunghyun Cho, and Douwe Kiela. 2019. Emergent linguistic phenomena in multi-agent communication games. In *EMNLP-IJCNLP*, pages 3691–3701, Hong Kong, China. Association for Computational Linguistics.

Eric Jang, Shixiang Gu, and Ben Poole. 2017. Categorical reparameterization with gumbel-softmax. In *International Conference on Learning Representations*.

Simon Kirby, Monica Tamariz, Hannah Cornish, and Kenny Smith. 2015. Compression and communication in the cultural evolution of linguistic structure. *Cognition*, 141:87–102.

Satwik Kottur, José Moura, Stefan Lee, and Dhruv Batra. 2017. Natural language does not emerge 'naturally' in multi-agent dialog. In *Proceedings of the 2017 Conference on Empirical Methods in Natural Language Processing*, pages 2962–2967. Association for Computational Linguistics.

Angeliki Lazaridou, Alexander Peysakhovich, and Marco Baroni. 2017. Multi-Agent Cooperation and the Emergence of (Natural) Language. In *International Conference on Learning Representations*.

Jason Lee, Kyunghyun Cho, Jason Weston, and Douwe Kiela. 2018. Emergent translation in multi-agent communication. In *International Conference on Learning Representations*.

Yuanzhi Li and Yingyu Liang. 2018. Learning over-parameterized neural networks via stochastic gradient descent on structured data. In *Advances in Neural Information Processing Systems 31*, pages 8157–8166. Curran Associates, Inc.

Chris J. Maddison, Andriy Mnih, and Yee Whye Teh. 2017. The concrete distribution: A continuous relaxation of discrete random variables. In *International Conference on Learning Representations*.

Igor Mordatch and Pieter Abbeel. 2018. Emergence of grounded compositional language in multi-agent populations. In *AAAI Conference on Artificial Intelligence*.

Preetum Nakkiran, Gal Kaplun, Yamini Bansal, Tristan Yang, Boaz Barak, and Ilya Sutskever. 2020. Deep double descent: Where bigger models and more data hurt. In *International Conference on Learning Representations*.

Sainbayar Sukhbaatar, Arthur Szlam, and Rob Fergus. 2016. Learning multiagent communication with backpropagation. In D. D. Lee, M. Sugiyama, U. V. Luxburg, I. Guyon, and R. Garnett, editors, *NeurIPS*, pages 2244–2252. Curran Associates, Inc.

Tessa Verhoef, Simon Kirby, and Bart de Boer. 2016. Iconicity and the emergence of combinatorial structure in language. *Cognitive Science*, 40(8):1969–1994.

Noga Zaslavsky, Charles Kemp, Terry Regier, and Naftali Tishby. 2018. Efficient compression in color naming and its evolution. *Proceedings of the National Academy of Sciences*, 115(31):7937–7942.

Learning Geometric Word Meta-Embeddings

Pratik Jawanpuria[1], N T V Satya Dev[2], Anoop Kunchukuttan[1], Bamdev Mishra[1]
[1]Microsoft, India   [2]Vayve Technologies, India
[1]{pratik.jawanpuria,ankunchu,bamdevm}@microsoft.com
[2]tvsatyadev@gmail.com

Abstract

We propose a geometric framework for learning meta-embeddings of words from different embedding sources. Our framework transforms the embeddings into a common latent space, where, for example, simple averaging or concatenation of different embeddings (of a given word) is more amenable. The proposed latent space arises from two particular geometric transformations - source embedding specific orthogonal rotations and a common Mahalanobis metric scaling. Empirical results on several word similarity and word analogy benchmarks illustrate the efficacy of the proposed framework.

1 Introduction

Word embeddings have become an integral part of modern NLP. They capture semantic and syntactic similarities and are typically used as features in training NLP models for diverse tasks like named entity tagging, sentiment analysis, and classification, to name a few. Word embeddings are learned in an unsupervised manner from large text corpora and a number of pre-trained embeddings are readily available. The quality of the word embeddings, however, depends on various factors like the size and genre of training corpora as well as the training method used. This has led to ensemble approaches for creating meta-embeddings from different original embeddings (Yin and Shutze, 2016; Coates and Bollegala, 2018; Bao and Bollegala, 2018; O'Neill and Bollegala, 2020). Meta-embeddings are appealing because they can improve quality of embeddings on account of noise cancellation and diversity of data sources and algorithms.

Various approaches have been proposed to learn meta-embeddings and can be broadly classified into two categories: (a) simple linear methods like averaging or concatenation, or a low-dimensional projection via singular value projection (Yin and Shutze, 2016; Coates and Bollegala, 2018) and (b) non-linear methods that aim to learn meta-embeddings as shared representation using auto-encoding or transformation between common representation and each embedding set (Muromägi et al., 2017; Bollegala et al., 2018; Bao and Bollegala, 2018; O'Neill and Bollegala, 2020).

In this work, we focus on simple linear methods such as averaging and concatenation for computing meta-embeddings, which are very easy to implement and have shown highly competitive performance (Yin and Shutze, 2016; Coates and Bollegala, 2018). Due to the nature of the underlying embedding generation algorithms (Mikolov et al., 2013; Pennington et al., 2014), correspondences between dimensions, e.g., of two embeddings $x \in \mathbb{R}^d$ and $z \in \mathbb{R}^d$ of the same word, are usually not known. Hence, averaging may be detrimental in cases where the dimensions are negatively correlated. Consider the scenario where $z := -x$. Here, simple averaging of x and z would result in the zero vector. Similarly, when z is a (dimension-wise) permutation of x, simple averaging would result in a sub-optimal meta-embedding vector compared to averaging of *aligned* embeddings. Therefore, we propose to align the embeddings (of a given word) as an important first step towards generating meta-embeddings.

To this end, we develop a geometric framework for learning meta-embeddings, by aligning different embeddings in a common latent space, where the dimensions of different embeddings (of a given word) are in coherence. Mathematically, we perform different orthogonal transformations of the source embeddings to learn a latent space along with a Mahalanobis metric that scales different features appropriately. The meta-embeddings are, subsequently, learned in the latent space, e.g., using averaging or concatenation. Empirical results on the word similarity and the word analogy tasks

39

Proceedings of the 5th Workshop on Representation Learning for NLP (RepL4NLP-2020), pages 39–44
July 9, 2020. ©2020 Association for Computational Linguistics

show that the proposed geometrically aligned meta-embeddings outperform strong baselines such as the plain averaging and the plain concatenation models.

2   Proposed Geometric Modeling

Consider two (monolingual) embeddings $x_i \in \mathbb{R}^d$ and $z_i \in \mathbb{R}^d$ of a given word i in a d-dimensional space. As discussed earlier, embeddings generated from different algorithms (Turian et al., 2010; Mikolov et al., 2013; Pennington et al., 2014; Dhillon et al., 2015; Bojanowski et al., 2017) may express different characteristics (of the same word). Hence, the goal of learning a meta-embedding w_i (corresponding to word i) is to generate a representation that inherits the properties of the different source embeddings (e.g., x_i and z_i).

Our framework imposes orthogonal transformations on the given source embeddings to enable alignment. To allow a more effective model for comparing similarity between different embeddings of a given word, we additionally induce this latent space with the Mahalanobis metric. The Mahalanobis similarity generalizes the cosine similarity measure, which is commonly used for evaluating the relatedness between word embeddings. Unlike cosine similarity, the Mahalanobis metric does not assume uncorrelated feature and it incorporates the feature correlation information from the training data (Jawanpuria et al., 2019). The combination of orthogonal transformation and Mahalanobis metric learning allows to capture any *affine* relationship that may exist between word embeddings. Mathematically, this relates to the singular value decomposition of a matrix (Bonnabel and Sepulchre, 2009; Mishra et al., 2014).

Overall, we formulate the problem of learning geometric transformations – the orthogonal rotations and the metric scaling – via a binary classification problem (discussed later). The meta-embeddings are subsequently computed using these transformations. The following sections formalize the proposed latent space and meta-embedding models.

2.1   Learning the Latent Space

In this section, we learn the latent space using geometric transformations.

Let $\mathbf{U} \in \mathcal{M}^d$ and $\mathbf{V} \in \mathcal{M}^d$ be orthogonal transformations for embeddings x_i and z_i, respectively, for all words $i = 1, \ldots, n$. Here $\mathcal{M}^d$ represents the set of $d \times d$ orthogonal matrices. The aligned embeddings in the latent space corresponding to x_i and z_i can then be expressed as $\mathbf{U}x_i$ and $\mathbf{V}z_i$, respectively. We next induce the Mahalanobis metric $\mathbf{B}$ in this (aligned) latent space, where $\mathbf{B}$ is a $d \times d$ symmetric positive-definite matrix. In this latent space, the similarity between the two embeddings x_i and z_i can be obtained by the following expression of their dot product: $(\mathbf{U}x_i)^\top \mathbf{B}(\mathbf{V}z_i)$. This expression may also be interpreted as the standard dot product (cosine similarity) between $\mathbf{B}^{\frac{1}{2}}\mathbf{U}x_i$ and $\mathbf{B}^{\frac{1}{2}}\mathbf{V}z_i$, where $\mathbf{B}^{\frac{1}{2}}$ denotes the matrix square root of the symmetric positive definite matrix $\mathbf{B}$.

The orthogonal transformations as well as the Mahalanobis metric are learned via the following binary classification problem: pairs of word embeddings $\{x_i, z_i\}$ of the same word i belong to the positive class while pairs $\{x_i, z_j\}$ belong to the negative class (for $i \neq j$). We consider the similarity between the two embeddings in the latent space as the decision function of the proposed binary classification problem. Let $\mathbf{X} = [x_1, \ldots, x_n] \in \mathbb{R}^{d \times n}$ and $\mathbf{Z} = [z_1, \ldots, z_n] \in \mathbb{R}^{d \times n}$ be the word embedding matrices for n words, where the columns correspond to different words. In addition, let $\mathbf{Y}$ denote the label matrix, where $\mathbf{Y}_{ii} = 1$ for $i = 1, \ldots, n$ and $\mathbf{Y}_{ij} = 0$ for $i \neq j$. The proposed optimization problem employs the simple to optimize square loss function:

$$\min_{\substack{\mathbf{U},\mathbf{V} \in \mathcal{M}^d, \\ \mathbf{B} \succ 0}} \left\| \mathbf{X}^\top \mathbf{U}^\top \mathbf{B} \mathbf{V} \mathbf{Z} - \mathbf{Y} \right\|^2 + C \left\| \mathbf{B} \right\|^2, \quad (1)$$

where $\| \cdot \|$ is the Frobenius norm (which generalizes the 2-norm to matrices) and $C > 0$ is the regularization parameter.

2.2   Averaging and Concatenation in Latent Space

Meta-embeddings constructed by averaging or concatenating the given word embeddings have been shown to obtain highly competitive performance (Yin and Shutze, 2016; Coates and Bollegala, 2018). Hence, we propose to learn meta-embeddings as averaging or concatenation in the learned latent space.

Geometry-Aware Averaging

The meta-embedding w_i of a word i is generated as an average of the (aligned) word embeddings in the latent space. The latent space representation of x_i, as a function of orthogonal transformation $\mathbf{U}$ and metric $\mathbf{B}$, is $\mathbf{B}^{\frac{1}{2}}\mathbf{U}x_i$

(Jawanpuria et al., 2019). Hence, we obtain $w_i = \mathtt{average}(\mathbf{B}^{\frac{1}{2}}\mathbf{U}x_i, \mathbf{B}^{\frac{1}{2}}\mathbf{V}z_i) = (\mathbf{B}^{\frac{1}{2}}\mathbf{U}x_i + \mathbf{B}^{\frac{1}{2}}\mathbf{V}z_i)/2$.

It should be noted that the proposed geometry-aware averaging approach generalizes the *plain averaging* method proposed in (Coates and Bollegala, 2018), which is now a particular case in our framework by choosing $\mathbf{U}$, $\mathbf{V}$, and $\mathbf{B}$ as identity matrices.

Geometry-Aware Concatenation

We next propose to concatenate the aligned embeddings in the learned latent space. For a given word i, with x_i and z_i as different source embeddings, the meta-embeddings w_i learned by the proposed geometry-aware concatenation model is $w_i = \mathtt{concatenation}(\mathbf{B}^{\frac{1}{2}}\mathbf{U}x_i, \mathbf{B}^{\frac{1}{2}}\mathbf{V}z_i) = [(\mathbf{B}^{\frac{1}{2}}\mathbf{U}x_i)^\top, (\mathbf{B}^{\frac{1}{2}}\mathbf{V}z_i)^\top]^\top$. The plain concatenation method studied in (Yin and Shutze, 2016) is a special case of the proposed geometry-aware concatenation (by setting $\mathbf{U}$, $\mathbf{V}$, and $\mathbf{B}$ as identity matrices).

2.3 Optimization

The proposed optimization problem (1) employs square loss function and ℓ_2-norm regularization, both of which are well-studied in the literature. The search space is the Cartesian product of the set of d-dimensional symmetric positive definite matrices and the set of d-dimensional orthogonal matrices, both of which are smooth spaces. Such sets have well-known Riemannian manifold structure (Lee, 2003) that allows to propose computationally efficient iterative optimization algorithms. A manifold may be viewed as a generalization of the notion of surface to higher dimensions. We employ the popular Riemannian optimization framework (Absil et al., 2008) to solve (1). Recently, Jawanpuria et al. (2019) have studied a similar optimization problem in the context of learning cross-lingual word embeddings.

Our implementation is done using the Pymanopt toolbox (Townsend et al., 2016), which is a publicly available Python toolbox for Riemannian optimization algorithms. In particular, we use the conjugate gradient algorithm of Pymanopt. For this, we just need to supply the objective function of (1). This can be done efficiently as the numerical cost of computing the objective function is $O(nd^2)$. The overall computational cost of our implementation scales linearly with the number of words in the vocabulary sets. Our code is available at `https://github.com/SatyadevNtv/geo-meta-emb`.

3 Experiments

In this section, we evaluate the performance of the proposed meta-embedding models.

3.1 Evaluation Tasks and Datasets

We consider the following standard evaluation tasks (Yin and Shutze, 2016; Coates and Bollegala, 2018):

- **Word similarity**: in this task, we compare the human-annotated similarity scores between pairs of words with the corresponding cosine similarity computed via the constructed meta-embeddings. We report results on the following benchmark datasets: **RG** (Rubenstein and Goodenough, 1965), **MC** (Miller and Charles, 1991), **WS** (Finkelstein et al., 2001), **MTurk** (Halawi et al., 2012), **RW** (Luong et al., 2013), and **SL** (Hill et al., 2015). Following previous works (Yin and Shutze, 2016; Coates and Bollegala, 2018; O'Neill and Bollegala, 2020), we report the Spearman correlation score (higher is better) between the cosine similarity (computed via meta-embeddings) and the human scores.

- **Word analogy**: in this task, the aim is to answer questions which have the form "*A is to B as C is to ?*" (Mikolov et al., 2013). After generating the meta-embeddings a, b, and c (corresponding to terms A, B, and C, respectively), the answer is chosen to be the term whose meta-embedding has the maximum cosine similarity with $(b - a + c)$ (Mikolov et al., 2013). The benchmark datasets include **MSR** (Gao et al., 2014), **GL** (Mikolov et al., 2013), and **SemEval** (Jurgens et al., 2012). Following previous works (Yin and Shutze, 2016; Coates and Bollegala, 2018; O'Neill and Bollegala, 2020), we report the percentage of correct answers for MSR and GL datasets, and the Spearman correlation score for SemEval. In both cases, a higher score implies better performance.

We learn the meta-embeddings from the following publicly available 300-dimensional pre-trained word embeddings for English.

- **CBOW** (Mikolov et al., 2013): has 929 023 word embeddings trained on Google News.
- **GloVe** (Pennington et al., 2014): has

Model	RG	MC	WS	MTurk	RW	SL	Avg.(WS)	MSR	GL	SemEvaL	Avg.(WA)
CBOW	76.1	80.0	77.2	68.4	53.4	44.2	66.5	71.7	55.4	**20.4**	49.2
GloVe	82.9	84.0	79.6	70.0	48.7	45.3	68.4	69.3	**75.2**	18.6	54.4
CONC	81.1	84.6	**81.4**	71.9	54.6	46.0	69.9	76.6	69.9	20.1	55.5
AVG	81.5	83.7	79.4	**72.1**	52.9	46.2	69.3	73.7	66.9	19.7	53.4
Geo-CONC	**86.0**	**85.0**	81.2	70.5	55.6	**48.2**	**71.1**	**78.1**	73.3	19.9	**57.1**
Geo-AVG	85.8	83.5	81.2	69.1	**55.7**	**48.2**	70.6	77.3	72.3	19.5	56.3

Table 1: Generalization performance of the meta-embedding algorithms on the word similarity and the word analogy tasks with GloVe and CBOW source embeddings. The columns 'Avg.(WS)' and 'Avg.(WA)' correspond to the average performance on the word similarity and the word analogy tasks, respectively.

Model	RG	MC	WS	MTurk	RW	SL	Avg.(WS)	MSR	GL	SemEvaL	Avg.(WA)
GloVe	82.9	**84.0**	79.6	70.0	48.7	45.3	68.4	69.3	75.2	18.6	54.4
fastText	**83.8**	82.5	**83.5**	73.3	**58.0**	46.4	71.2	78.7	71.0	22.5	57.4
CONC	**83.8**	82.5	83.4	73.3	57.9	46.4	71.2	79.8	71.7	22.5	58.0
AVG	83.4	82.1	**83.5**	73.3	**58.0**	46.5	71.1	79.7	71.7	22.4	57.9
Geo-CONC	83.7	**84.0**	82.6	**74.6**	55.1	**48.4**	**71.4**	**80.4**	**79.3**	21.5	**60.4**
Geo-AVG	83.6	82.0	82.7	74.3	57.0	**48.4**	71.3	79.1	71.1	**23.1**	57.8

Table 2: Generalization performance of the meta-embedding algorithms on the word similarity and the word analogy tasks with GloVe and fastText source embeddings. The columns 'Avg.(WS)' and 'Avg.(WA)' correspond to the average performance on the word similarity and the word analogy tasks, respectively.

1 917 494 word embeddings trained on 42B tokens of web data from the common crawl.

- **fastText** (Bojanowski et al., 2017): has 2 000 000 word embeddings trained on common crawl.

The meta-embeddings are learned on the common set of words from different pairs of the source embeddings. The number of common words between various source embeddings pairs are as follows: 154 077 (GloVe ∩ CBOW), 552 168 (GloVe ∩ fastText), and 641 885 (CBOW ∩ fastText).

3.2 Results and Discussion

The performance of our geometry-aware averaging and concatenation models, henceforth termed as Geo-AVG and Geo-CONC, respectively, are reported in Tables 1-3. Each table corresponds to a pair of source embeddings (from CBOW, GloVe, and fastText) and the meta-embeddings generated from the source embeddings. We report the performance of the following:

- the proposed models Geo-AVG and Geo-CONC
- the meta-embeddings models AVG (Coates and Bollegala, 2018) and CONC (Yin and Shutze, 2016), which perform plain averaging and concatenation, respectively
- the source embeddings, which serve as a benchmark the meta-embeddings algorithms should ideally surpass in order to justify their usage

We observe that the proposed geometry-aware models (Geo-AVG and Geo-CONC) outperform the individual source embeddings in most datasets. Among the source embeddings, fastText performs better than CBOW and GloVe. Interestingly, we observe that the performance of the meta-embeddings generated by the proposed Geo-CONC with CBOW and GloVe (results in Table 1) is at par with the fastText embeddings (results in Table 2).

The proposed models also easily surpass the AVG and CONC models in both the word similarity and the word analogy tasks. In all the three tables, the proposed models obtain the best overall performance in both the tasks. This shows that the alignment of word embedding spaces with orthogonal rotations and the Mahalanobis metric improves the overall quality of the meta-embeddings.

Model	RG	MC	WS	MTurk	RW	SL	Avg.(WS)	MSR	GL	SemEvaL	Avg.(WA)
CBOW	76.1	80.0	77.2	68.4	53.4	44.2	66.5	71.7	55.4	20.4	49.2
fastText	83.8	82.5	**83.5**	73.3	58.0	46.4	71.2	78.7	71.0	**22.5**	57.4
CONC	83.8	82.5	**83.5**	73.6	**59.9**	46.4	71.6	79.9	75.8	**22.5**	59.4
AVG	83.7	82.5	83.4	**73.7**	59.8	46.4	71.6	79.9	75.8	**22.5**	59.4
Geo-CONC	85.3	84.3	82.9	73.6	59.7	**47.4**	72.2	**80.1**	76.9	22.1	**59.7**
Geo-AVG	**85.5**	**84.6**	82.9	73.6	59.7	**47.4**	**72.3**	79.9	**76.9**	22.0	59.6

Table 3: Generalization performance of the meta-embedding algorithms on the word similarity and the word analogy tasks with CBOW and fastText source embeddings. The columns 'Avg.(WS)' and 'Avg.(WA)' correspond to the average performance on the word similarity and the word analogy tasks, respectively.

4 Conclusion

We propose a geometric framework for learning meta-embeddings of words from various sources of word embeddings. Our framework aligns the embeddings in a common latent space. The importance of learning the latent space is shown in several benchmark datasets, where the proposed algorithms (Geo-AVG and Geo-CONC) outperforms the plain averaging and the plain concatenation models.

Extending the proposed geometric framework to non-linear word meta-embedding approaches and for generating sentence meta-embeddings are promising directions of future research.

References

P.-A. Absil, R. Mahony, and R. Sepulchre. 2008. *Optimization Algorithms on Matrix Manifolds*. Princeton University Press, Princeton, NJ.

C. Bao and D. Bollegala. 2018. Learning word meta-embeddings by autoencoding. In *Proceedings of the 27th International Conference on Computational Linguistics*, pages 1650–1661.

P. Bojanowski, E. Grave, A. Joulin, and T. Mikolov. 2017. Enriching word vectors with subword information. *Transactions of the Association for Computational Linguistics*, 5:135–146. https://fasttext.cc/docs/en/english-vectors.html.

D. Bollegala, K. Hayashi, and K. Kawarabayashi. 2018. Think globally, embed locally—locally linear meta-embedding of words. In *Proceedings of the International Joint Conference on Artificial Intelligence (IJCAI)*.

S. Bonnabel and R. Sepulchre. 2009. Riemannian metric and geometric mean for positive semidefinite matrices of fixed rank. *SIAM Journal on Matrix Analysis and Applications*, 31(3):1055–1070.

J. N. Coates and D. Bollegala. 2018. Frustratingly easy meta-embedding – computing meta-embeddings by averaging source word embeddings. In *Proceedings of NAACL-HLT 2018*, pages 194–198.

P. S. Dhillon, D. P. Foster, and L. H. Ungar. 2015. Eigenwords: Spectral word embeddings. *Journal of Machine Learning Research*, 16:3035–3078.

L. Finkelstein, E. Gabrilovich, Y. Matias, E. Rivlin, Z. Solan, G. Wolfman, and E. Ruppin. 2001. Placing search in context: The concept revisited. In *Proceedings of the 10th international conference on World Wide Web. ACM*, pages 406–414.

B. Gao, J. Bian, and T.-Y. Liu. 2014. Wordrep: A benchmark for research on learning word representation. Technical report, arXiv preprint arXiv:1407.1640.

G. Halawi, G. Dror, E. Gabrilovich, and Y. Koren. 2012. Large-scale learning of word relatedness with constraint. In *Proceedings of the 18th ACM SIGKDD international conference on Knowledge discovery and data mining*, pages 1406–1414.

F. Hill, R. Reichart, and A. Korhonen. 2015. Simlex-999: Evaluating semantic models with (genuine) similarity estimation. *Computational Linguistics*, pages 665–695.

P. Jawanpuria, A. Balgovind, A. Kunchukuttan, and B. Mishra. 2019. Learning multilingual word embeddings in latent metric space: A geometric approach. *Transactions of the Association for Computational Linguistics*, 7:107–120.

D. A. Jurgens, P. D. Turney, S. M. Mohammad, and K. J. Holyoak. 2012. Semeval-2012 task 2: Measuring degrees of relational similarity. In *Proceedings of the First Joint Conference on Lexical and Computational Semantics-Volume 1: Proceedings of the main conference and the shared task, and Volume 2: Proceedings of the Sixth International Workshop on Semantic Evaluation*, pages 356–364.

J. M. Lee. 2003. *Introduction to smooth manifolds*, second edition, volume 218 of *Graduate Texts in Mathematics*. Springer-Verlag, New York.

T. Luong, R. Socher, and C. D. Manning. 2013. Better word representations with recursive neural networks for morphology. In *Proceedings of the Seventeenth Conference on Computational Natural Language Learning (CoNLL)*, pages 104–113.

T. Mikolov, I. Sutskever, K. Chen, G. S. Corrado, and J. Dean. 2013. Distributed representations of words and phrases and their compositionality. In *Advances in neural information processing systems (NeurIPS)*, pages 3111–3119.

G. A. Miller and W. G. Charles. 1991. Contextual correlates of semantic similarity. *Language and congnitive processes*, pages 1–28.

B. Mishra, G. Meyer, S. Bonnabel, and R. Sepulchre. 2014. Fixed-rank matrix factorizations and Riemannian low-rank optimization. *Computational Statistics*, 29(3):591–621.

A. Muromägi, K. Sirts, and S. Laur. 2017. Linear ensembles of word embedding models. In *Proceedings of the 21st Nordic Conference on Computational Linguistics*, pages 96–104.

J. O'Neill and D. Bollegala. 2020. Meta-embedding as auxiliary task regularization. In *Proceedings of the European Conference on Artificial Intelligence (ECAI)*.

J. Pennington, R. Socher, and C. D. Manning. 2014. Glove: Global vectors for word representation. *Proceedings of the 2014 conference on empirical methods in natural language processing (EMNLP)*, 14:1532–1543.

H. Rubenstein and J. B. Goodenough. 1965. Contextual correlates of synonymy. *Communications of ACM*, pages 627–633.

J. Townsend, N. Koep, and S. Weichwald. 2016. Pymanopt: A python toolbox for optimization on manifolds using automatic differentiation. *Journal of Machine Learning Research*, 17(137):1–5.

J. Turian, L. Ratinov, and B. Bengio. 2010. Word representations: a simple and general method for semi-supervised learning. In *Proceedings of the Annual Meeting of the Association of Computational Linguistics (ACL)*, pages 384–394.

W. Yin and H. Shutze. 2016. Learning word meta-embeddings. In *Proceedings of the 54th Annual Meeting of the Association of Computational Linguistics (ACL)*, pages 1351–1360.

Improving Bilingual Lexicon Induction with Unsupervised Post-Processing of Monolingual Word Vector Spaces

Ivan Vulić[◇]   Anna Korhonen[◇]   Goran Glavaš[♣]

[◇] Language Technology Lab, TAL, University of Cambridge
[♣] Data and Web Science Group, University of Mannheim
{iv250,alk23}@cam.ac.uk   goran@informatik.uni-mannheim.de

Abstract

Work on projection-based induction of cross-lingual word embedding spaces (CLWEs) predominantly focuses on the improvement of the projection (i.e., mapping) mechanisms. In this work, in contrast, we show that a simple method for post-processing monolingual embedding spaces facilitates learning of the cross-lingual alignment and, in turn, substantially improves bilingual lexicon induction (BLI). The post-processing method we examine is grounded in the generalisation of first- and second-order monolingual similarities to the nth-order similarity. By post-processing monolingual spaces before the cross-lingual alignment, the method can be coupled with any projection-based method for inducing CLWE spaces. We demonstrate the effectiveness of this simple monolingual post-processing across a set of 15 typologically diverse languages (i.e., 15×14 BLI setups), and in combination with two different projection methods.

1   Introduction

Cross-lingual word embeddings (CLWEs) are a mainstay of modern cross-lingual NLP (Ruder et al., 2019b). CLWE models induce a *shared cross-lingual vector space* in which words with similar meanings obtain similar vectors regardless of their language. Their usefulness has been attested in tasks such as bilingual lexicon induction (BLI) (Gouws et al., 2015; Heyman et al., 2017), information retrieval (Litschko et al., 2018), machine translation (Artetxe et al., 2018b; Lample et al., 2018), document classification (Klementiev et al., 2012), and many others (Ruder et al., 2019b).

Importantly, CLWEs are one of the central mechanisms for facilitating transfer of language technologies for low-resource languages, which often lack sufficient bilingual signal for obvious transfer via machine translation. Lack of language resources is the main reason for popularity of the so-called *projection-based* CLWE methods (Mikolov et al., 2013a; Artetxe et al., 2016, 2018a). These models align two independently trained monolingual word vector spaces post-hoc, using limited bilingual supervision in the form of several hundred to several thousand word translation pairs (Mikolov et al., 2013a; Vulić and Korhonen, 2016; Joulin et al., 2018; Ruder et al., 2018). Some models even align the monolingual spaces using only identical strings (Smith et al., 2017; Søgaard et al., 2018) or numerals (Artetxe et al., 2017). The most recent work focused on fully unsupervised CLWE induction: they extract seed translation lexicons relying on topological similarities between monolingual spaces (Conneau et al., 2018; Artetxe et al., 2018a; Hoshen and Wolf, 2018; Alaux et al., 2019).

In this work, we do not focus on projection itself: rather, we investigate a transformation of *input monolingual word vector spaces* that facilitates the projection and leads to higher quality CLWEs. Regardless of the actual projection method, the quality of the input monolingual spaces has a profound impact on the induced shared cross-lingual space, and, in turn, on the quality of induced bilingual lexicons. We demonstrate that simple *unsupervised post-processing* of monolingual embedding spaces leads to substantial BLI performance gains across a large number of language pairs. Our work is inspired by observations that monolingual *"embeddings capture more information than what is immediately obvious"* (Artetxe et al., 2018c). In other words, the information surfaced in the pretrained monolingual vector spaces may not be optimal for an application such as word-level translation (BLI).

We rely on a monolingual post-processing method of Artetxe et al. (2018c): a linear transformation controlled by a single parameter that adjusts the similarity order of the input embedding spaces. We demonstrate that applying this trans-

45

Proceedings of the 5th Workshop on Representation Learning for NLP (RepL4NLP-2020), pages 45–54
July 9, 2020. ©2020 Association for Computational Linguistics

formation on both monolingual spaces before any standard projection-based CLWE framework yields consistent BLI gains for a wide array of languages. We run a large-scale BLI evaluation with 15 typologically diverse languages (i.e., $15 \times 14 = 210$ BLI setups) and show that this simple monolingual post-processing yields gains in 183/210 setups over the current state-of-the-art BLI models which combine self-learning (Artetxe et al., 2018a) with (weak) word-level supervision (Vulić et al., 2019). We further show that this monolingual post-processing yields improvements on other BLI datasets (Glavaš et al., 2019), for different projection-based CLWE models, and also for BLI with 210 similar (major European) languages (Dubossarsky et al., 2020), indicating the importance and robustness of monolingual post-processing for BLI.

2 Methodology

Projection-Based CLWEs: Preliminaries. Projection-based CLWE models learn a linear projection between two independently trained monolingual spaces – X (source language L_s) and Z (target language L_t) – using a word translation dictionary D to guide the alignment. $X_D \subset X$ and $Z_D \subset Z$ denote the row-aligned subsets of X and Z containing vectors of aligned words from D. X_D and Z_D are used to learn orthogonal projections W_x and W_z defining the bilingual space: $Y = XW_x \cup ZW_z$. While (weakly) supervised methods start from a readily available dictionary D, fully unsupervised models automatically induce the seed dictionary D (i.e., from monolingual data).[1]

Furthermore, it has been empirically validated (Artetxe et al., 2017; Vulić et al., 2019) that applying an *iterative self-learning* procedure leads to consistent BLI improvements, especially for distant languages and in low-data regimes. In a nutshell, at each self-learning iteration k, a dictionary $D^{(k)}$ is first used to learn the joint space $Y^{(k)} = XW_x^{(k)} \cup ZW_z^{(k)}$. The mutual cross-lingual nearest neighbours in $Y^{(k)}$ are then used to extract the new dictionary $D^{(k+1)}$. Relying on mutual nearest neighbours partially removes the noise, leading to better performance. For more technical

details on self-learning, we refer the reader to prior work (Ruder et al., 2019a; Vulić et al., 2019).

Motivation. Most existing CLWE models ignore the properties of the initial monolingual spaces X and Z (i.e., they are taken "as-is") and focus on improving the projection. However, monolingual post-processing of X and Z prior to learning the projections may facilitate the projection and be beneficial for iterative setups such as self-learning. This intuition is already confirmed by a number of monolingual transformations, e.g., ℓ_2-normalisation, mean centering, or whitening/dewhitening, that are "by default" performed by toolkits such as MUSE (Conneau et al., 2018) and VecMap (Artetxe et al., 2018b; Zhang et al., 2019). In this work, however, we investigate a transformation to the monolingual spaces which is applied before they undergo the series of standard normalisation and centering steps.

Further, we investigate a line of research that leverages unsupervised post-processing of monolingual word vectors (Mu et al., 2018; Wang et al., 2018; Raunak et al., 2019; Tang et al., 2019) to emphasise semantic properties over syntactic aspects, typically with small gains reported on intrinsic word similarity (e.g., SimLex-999 (Hill et al., 2015)). In this work, we empirically validate that these unsupervised post-processing techniques can also be effective in cross-lingual scenarios for low-resource BLI, even when coupled with the current state-of-the-art CLWE frameworks that rely on "all the bells and whistles", such as self-learning and additional vector space preprocessing.

Unsupervised Monolingual Post-processing. We now outline the simple post-processing method of Artetxe et al. (2018c) used in this work, and then extend it to the bilingual setup. The core idea is to generalise the notion of first-and second-order similarity (Schütze, 1998)[2] to nth-order similarity. Let us define the (standard, first-order) similarity matrix of the source language space X as $M_1(X) = XX^T$ (similar for Z). The second-order similarity can then be defined as $M_2(X) = XX^TXX^T$, where it holds $M_2(X) = M_1(M_1(X))$; the nth-order similarity is then $M_n(X) = (XX^T)^n$. The embeddings of words w_i and w_j are given by the rows i and j of each M_n matrix.

We are then looking for a general linear transformation that adjusts the similarity order of input

---

[1] Recent empirical studies (Glavaš et al., 2019; Vulić et al., 2019) show that, under fair evaluation, (weakly) supervised methods always outperform their unsupervised counterparts. We thus base all our experiments in §4 on the weakly supervised setup; nonetheless, we observe substantial relative gains for the fully unsupervised setup as well.

[2] With second-order similarity, the similarity of two words is captured in terms of how similar they are to other words.

Language	Family	Type	ISO 639-1
Bulgarian	IE: Slavic	fusional	BG
Catalan	IE: Romance	fusional	CA
Esperanto	– (constructed)	agglutinative	EO
Estonian	Uralic	agglutinative	ET
Basque	– (isolate)	agglutinative	EU
Finnish	Uralic	agglutinative	FI
Hebrew	Afro-Asiatic	introflexive	HE
Hungarian	Uralic	agglutinative	HU
Indonesian	Austronesian	isolating	ID
Georgian	Kartvelian	agglutinative	KA
Korean	Koreanic	agglutinative	KO
Lithuanian	IE: Baltic	fusional	LT
Bokmål	IE: Germanic	fusional	NO
Thai	Kra-Dai	isolating	TH
Turkish	Turkic	agglutinative	TR

Table 1: Languages used in the main BLI experiments (Vulić et al., 2019), along with family (IE=Indo-European), morphological type, and ISO 639-1 code.

matrices X and Z. As proven by Artetxe et al. (2018c), the nth-order similarity transformation can be obtained as $M_n(X) = M_1(X R_{(n-1)/2})$, with $R_\alpha = Q\Delta^\alpha$, where Q and Δ are the matrices obtained via eigendecomposition of $X^T X$ ($X^T X = Q\Delta Q^T$): Δ is a diagonal matrix containing eigenvalues of $X^T X$; Q is an orthogonal matrix with eigenvectors of $X^T X$ as columns.[3]

Finally, we apply the above post-processing on both monolingual vector spaces X and Z. This results in adjusted vector spaces $X'_{\alpha_s} = X R_{\alpha_s}$ and $Z'_{\alpha_t} = Z R_{\alpha_t}$. Transformed spaces X'_{α_s} and Z'_{α_t} then replace the original spaces X and Z as input to any standard projection-based CLWE method.

3 Experimental Setup

We evaluate the impact of unsupervised monolingual post-processing described in §2 on BLI, focusing on pairs of typologically diverse languages.[4] Mean reciprocal rank (MRR) is used as the main evaluation metric, reported as MRR$\times 100\%$.[5]

Training and Test Data. We exploit the training and test dictionaries compiled from PanLex (Kamholz et al., 2014) by Vulić et al. (2019): the data encompasses 15 diverse languages listed in Table 1 and a total of 210 distinct $L_s \rightarrow L_t$ BLI

setups.[6] In addition, we evaluate on 15 European languages (i.e., 210 pairs) from Dubossarsky et al. (2020).[7], and on diverse language pairs from the BLI evaluation suite of Glavaš et al. (2019). Training and test dictionaries in all setups contain $5K$ and $2K$ word translation pairs, respectively. We create smaller training dictionaries (e.g., spanning 1K training translation pairs) by taking the most frequent pairs from the 5K dictionaries.

Monolingual Embeddings. We use the 300-dim vectors of Grave et al. (2018) for all languages, pretrained on Common Crawl and Wikipedia with fastText (Bojanowski et al., 2017).[8] All vocabularies are trimmed to the 200K most frequent words.

Projection-Based Framework. We base the induction of projection-based CLWEs on the well-known VecMap framework (Artetxe et al., 2018b);[9] it shows very competitive and robust BLI performance, especially for distant pairs, according to the recent comparative studies (Glavaš et al., 2019; Vulić et al., 2019; Doval et al., 2019). We analyse the impact of unsupervised monolingual postprocessing from §2 by (1) feeding the original vectors X and Y to VecMap (BASELINE), and then by (2) feeding their post-processed variants X'_{α_s} and Y'_{α_t} (POSTPROC). We experiment with projection model variants without and with self-learning, and with different initial dictionary sizes (5K and 1K).

Note that the POSTPROC variant requires tuning of two hyper-parameters: α_s and α_t. Due to a lack of development sets for BLI experiments, we tune the two α-parameters on a single language pair (BG–CA) via cross-validation; we grid-search over the following values: $[-0.5, -0.25, -0.15, 0, 0.15, 0.25, 0.5]$. We then keep them fixed to the following values: $\alpha_s = -0.25$, $\alpha_t = 0.15$ in all subsequent experiments.

4 Results and Discussion

Main BLI results averaged over each source language (L_s) are provided in Table 2, while additional results per language pair are available in

---

[3]Although the post-processing motivation stems from the desire to adjust discrete similarity orders, note that α is in fact a continuous parameter which can be carefully fine-tuned (negative values are also allowed). The code is available at: https://github.com/artetxem/uncovec.

[4]The focus of this work is on the standard BLI task; however, it has recently shown (Glavaš et al., 2019) that some downstream tasks strongly correlate with BLI.

[5]Our findings also hold for *Precision@M*, for $M \in \{1, 5\}$

[6]github.com/cambridgeltl/panlex-bli. For a detailed procedure on how the lexicons were obtained from PanLex, we refer the reader to the work of Vulić et al. (2019).

[7]The languages are English, German, Dutch, Swedish, Danish, Italian, Portuguese, Spanish, French, Romanian, Croatian, Polish, Russian, Czech, Bulgarian.

[8]Experiments with other monolingual vectors such as the original fastText and skip-gram (Mikolov et al., 2013b) trained on Wikipedia show the same trends in the final results.

[9]https://github.com/artetxem/vecmap

	BG-*	CA-*	EO-*	ET-*	EU-*	FI-*	HE-*	HU-*
BASELINE (supervised, 5k)	34.3	33.5	30.4	30.1	22.8	32.4	28.7	35.4
BASELINE (self-learning, 5k)	36.1	35.6	33.6	31.6	24.4	34.8	29.4	37.4
POSTPROC (self-learning, 5k)	**37.6**	**36.9**	**34.8**	**33.5**	**25.7**	**37.4**	**31.2**	**39.5**
BASELINE (supervised, 1k)	14.6	12.9	9.8	11.7	6.5	11.7	9.6	14.3
BASELINE (self-learning, 1k)	34.1	32.7	30.2	29.3	21.2	32.9	26.8	35.4
POSTPROC (self-learning, 1k)	**35.3**	**34.0**	**30.6**	**31.1**	**21.3**	**35.3**	**27.9**	**37.5**
Improves for... (5k)	*13/14*	*12/14*	*13/14*	*13/14*	*10/14*	*14/14*	*11/14*	*14/14*
Improves for... (1k)	*13/14*	*13/14*	*9/14*	*13/14*	*7/14*	*14/14*	*11/14*	*14/14*

	ID-*	KA-*	KO-*	LT-*	NO-*	TH-*	TR-*	**Avg**
BASELINE (supervised, 5k)	26.1	25.0	23.9	30.2	33.2	15.4	28.3	28.6
BASELINE (self-learning, 5k)	27.2	26.3	25.1	31.0	35.6	14.8	29.9	30.2
POSTPROC (self-learning, 5k)	**28.1**	**28.2**	**26.6**	**33.3**	**37.3**	**15.6**	**32.3**	**31.9**
BASELINE (supervised, 1k)	8.9	7.9	6.1	11.1	12.7	4.4	9.1	10.1
BASELINE (self-learning, 1k)	24.3	23.7	20.3	28.4	33.7	10.3	27.4	27.4
POSTPROC (self-learning, 1k)	**25.1**	**25.0**	**21.3**	**30.4**	**35.1**	**11.1**	**29.8**	**28.7**
Improves for... (5k)	*11/14*	*13/14*	*12/14*	*11/14*	*14/14*	*8/14*	*14/14*	*183/210*
Improves for... (1k)	*11/14*	*12/14*	*13/14*	*13/14*	*13/14*	*11/14*	*14/14*	*181/210*

Table 2: BLI results (MRR×100%) for main models in comparison. We report the results with the supervised BASELINE model based on the VecMap framework (Artetxe et al., 2018b), *without* any self-learning (i.e., supervised only), and *with* the most robust self-learning setup according to the comparative analysis of Vulić et al. (2019). The scores are averaged over experimental setups where each of the 15 languages is used as the source language L_s (e.g., BG-* averages scores over 14 setups in which Bulgarian (BG) is the source language). 5k and 1k denote seed dictionary sizes. The **Avg** column shows averaged MRR scores for each model over all 15×14=210 BLI setups and we also report the number of BLI setups in which the POSTPROC method improves over both BASELINE models.

	RCSLS		VecMap	
Pair	BASELINE (SUP)	POSTPROC (SUP)	BASELINE (SUP+SL)	POSTPROC (SUP+SL)
DE–HR	17.2	21.2	40.9	42.5
DE–TR	21.4	23.6	38.5	39.1
FI–FR	37.8	40.3	47.5	48.9
FI–HR	18.9	23.5	38.1	39.9
HR–IT	30.2	31.4	47.8	49.1
TR–FI	23.6	26.1	37.5	39.0

Table 3: BLI scores on 6 distant language pairs from the evaluation sets of Glavaš et al. (2019). Supervised models without (SUP) and with self-learning (SUP+SL).

the supplemental material. We also observe performance gains with a "pure" supervised model variant (i.e., without self-learning), but for clarity, we focus our analysis on the more powerful baseline, with self-learning. We note improvements in 183/210 (seed dictionary size 5K) and 181/210 BLI setups (size: 1K) over the projection-based baselines that held previous peak scores using the same data (Vulić et al., 2019). This validates our intuition that monolingual vectors store more information which needs to be "uncovered" via monolingual post-processing. The effect of monolingual post-processing pertains after applying other perturbations such as ℓ_2-norm or mean centering. For some languages – e.g., FI, TR, NO – we achieve gains in all BLI setups with those languages as sources.

What is more, we have not carefully fine-tuned α_s and α_t: we note that even higher scores can be achieved by finer-grained fine-tuning in the future. For instance, setting $(\alpha_s, \alpha_t) = (-0.5, 0.25)$ instead of $(-0.25, 0.15)$ for TR–BG increases BLI score from 37.8 to 39.5; the previous peak score with BASELINE was 35.1. The baseline mapping is simply obtained by setting $(\alpha_s, \alpha_t) = (0, 0)$, and we note that the tuned post-processing validated in our work should be considered as a tunable option for any projection-based CLWE method.

We further probe the robustness of unsupervised post-processing by running experiments on additional BLI evaluation set of Glavaš et al. (2019) and with another mapping model: RCSLS (Joulin et al., 2018). While we again observe gains across a range of different model variants and with different seed dictionary sizes, we summarise a selection of results in Table 3. Finally, small but consistent improvements extend also to a set of 15 European languages from Dubossarsky et al. (2020) (see Footnote 6): POSTPROC yields gains on average for all 15/15 source languages, and across 173/210 setups (5K seed dictionary); the global average improves from 43.9 (the strongest BASELINE) to 44.7. In summary, these results further underline the usefulness of the monolingual post-processing method.

5 Conclusion and Future Work

We have demonstrated a simple and effective method for improving bilingual lexicon induction (BLI) with projection-based cross-lingual word embeddings. The method is based on standalone unsupervised post-processing of initial monolingual word embeddings before mapping, and as such applicable to any projection-based CLWE method. We have verified the importance and robustness of this monolingual post-processing with a wide range of (dis)similar language pairs as well as in different BLI setups and with different CLWE methods.

In future work, we will test other unsupervised post-processors, and also probe similar methods that inject external lexical knowledge into monolingual word vectors towards improved BLI. We also plan to probe if similar gains still hold with recently proposed more sophisticated self-learning methods (Karan et al., 2020), non-linear mapping-based CLWE methods (Glavaš and Vulić, 2020; Mohiuddin and Joty, 2020). Another idea is to also apply a similar principle to contextualised word representations in cross-lingual settings (Schuster et al., 2019; Liu et al., 2019).

Acknowledgments

This work is supported by the ERC Consolidator Grant LEXICAL (no 648909) awarded to Anna Korhonen. Goran Glavaš is supported by the Eliteprogramm of the Baden-Württemberg Stiftung (AGREE grant). We thank the reviewers for their insightful suggestions.

References

Jean Alaux, Edouard Grave, Marco Cuturi, and Armand Joulin. 2019. Unsupervised hyperalignment for multilingual word embeddings. In *Proceedings of ICLR*.

Mikel Artetxe, Gorka Labaka, and Eneko Agirre. 2016. Learning principled bilingual mappings of word embeddings while preserving monolingual invariance. In *Proceedings of EMNLP*, pages 2289–2294.

Mikel Artetxe, Gorka Labaka, and Eneko Agirre. 2017. Learning bilingual word embeddings with (almost) no bilingual data. In *Proceedings of ACL*, pages 451–462.

Mikel Artetxe, Gorka Labaka, and Eneko Agirre. 2018a. A robust self-learning method for fully unsupervised cross-lingual mappings of word embeddings. In *Proceedings of ACL*, pages 789–798.

Mikel Artetxe, Gorka Labaka, Eneko Agirre, and Kyunghyun Cho. 2018b. Unsupervised neural machine translation. In *Proceedings of ICLR*.

Mikel Artetxe, Gorka Labaka, Iñigo Lopez-Gazpio, and Eneko Agirre. 2018c. Uncovering divergent linguistic information in word embeddings with lessons for intrinsic and extrinsic evaluation. In *Proceedings of CoNLL*, pages 282–291.

Piotr Bojanowski, Edouard Grave, Armand Joulin, and Tomas Mikolov. 2017. Enriching word vectors with subword information. *Transactions of the ACL*, 5:135–146.

Alexis Conneau, Guillaume Lample, Marc'Aurelio Ranzato, Ludovic Denoyer, and Hervé Jégou. 2018. Word translation without parallel data. In *Proceedings of ICLR*.

Yerai Doval, Jose Camacho-Collados, Luis Espinosa-Anke, and Steven Schockaert. 2019. On the robustness of unsupervised and semi-supervised cross-lingual word embedding learning. *CoRR*, abs/1908.07742.

Haim Dubossarsky, Ivan Vulić, Roi Reichart, and Anna Korhonen. 2020. Lost in embedding space: Explaining cross-lingual task performance with eigenvalue divergence. *CoRR*, abs/2001.11136.

Goran Glavaš, Robert Litschko, Sebastian Ruder, and Ivan Vulić. 2019. How to (properly) evaluate cross-lingual word embeddings: On strong baselines, comparative analyses, and some misconceptions. In *Proceedings of ACL*, pages 710–721.

Goran Glavaš and Ivan Vulić. 2020. Non-linear instance-based cross-lingual mapping for non-isomorphic embedding spaces. In *Proceedings of ACL*.

Stephan Gouws, Yoshua Bengio, and Greg Corrado. 2015. BilBOWA: Fast bilingual distributed representations without word alignments. In *Proceedings of ICML*, pages 748–756.

Edouard Grave, Piotr Bojanowski, Prakhar Gupta, Armand Joulin, and Tomas Mikolov. 2018. Learning word vectors for 157 languages. In *Proceedings of LREC*, pages 3483–3487.

Geert Heyman, Ivan Vulić, and Marie-Francine Moens. 2017. Bilingual lexicon induction by learning to combine word-level and character-level representations. In *Proceedings of EACL*, pages 1085–1095.

Felix Hill, Roi Reichart, and Anna Korhonen. 2015. SimLex-999: Evaluating semantic models with (genuine) similarity estimation. *Computational Linguistics*, 41(4):665–695.

Yedid Hoshen and Lior Wolf. 2018. Non-adversarial unsupervised word translation. In *Proceedings of EMNLP*, pages 469–478.

Armand Joulin, Piotr Bojanowski, Tomas Mikolov, Hervé Jégou, and Edouard Grave. 2018. Loss in translation: Learning bilingual word mapping with a retrieval criterion. In *Proceedings of EMNLP*, pages 2979–2984.

David Kamholz, Jonathan Pool, and Susan M. Colowick. 2014. Panlex: Building a resource for panlingual lexical translation. In *Proceedings of LREC*, pages 3145–3150.

Mladen Karan, Ivan Vulić, Anna Korhonen, and Goran Glavaš. 2020. Classification-based self-learning for weakly supervised bilingual lexicon induction. In *Proceedings of ACL*.

Alexandre Klementiev, Ivan Titov, and Binod Bhattarai. 2012. Inducing crosslingual distributed representations of words. In *Proceedings of COLING*, pages 1459–1474.

Guillaume Lample, Myle Ott, Alexis Conneau, Ludovic Denoyer, and Marc'Aurelio Ranzato. 2018. Phrase-based & neural unsupervised machine translation. In *Proceedings of EMNLP*, pages 5039–5049.

Robert Litschko, Goran Glavaš, Simone Paolo Ponzetto, and Ivan Vulić. 2018. Unsupervised cross-lingual information retrieval using monolingual data only. In *Proceedings of SIGIR*, pages 1253–1256.

Qianchu Liu, Diana McCarthy, Ivan Vulić, and Anna Korhonen. 2019. Investigating cross-lingual alignment methods for contextualized embeddings with token-level evaluation. In *Proceedings of CoNLL*, pages 33–43.

Tomas Mikolov, Quoc V Le, and Ilya Sutskever. 2013a. Exploiting similarities among languages for machine translation. *CoRR, abs/1309.4168*.

Tomas Mikolov, Ilya Sutskever, Kai Chen, Gregory S Corrado, and Jeffrey Dean. 2013b. Distributed Representations of Words and Phrases and their Compositionality. In *Proceedings of NIPS*, pages 3111–3119.

Bari Saiful M. Mohiuddin, Tasnim and Shafiq Joty. 2020. Lnmap: Departures from isomorphic assumption in bilingual lexicon induction through non-linear mapping in latent space. *CoRR, abs/1309.4168*.

Jiaqi Mu, Suma Bhat, and Pramod Viswanath. 2018. All-but-the-top: Simple and effective postprocessing for word representations. In *Proceedings of ICLR*.

Vikas Raunak, Vivek Gupta, and Florian Metze. 2019. Effective dimensionality reduction for word embeddings. In *Proceedings of the 4th Workshop on Representation Learning for NLP*, pages 235–243.

Sebastian Ruder, Ryan Cotterell, Yova Kementchedjhieva, and Anders Søgaard. 2018. A discriminative latent-variable model for bilingual lexicon induction. In *Proceedings of EMNLP*, pages 458–468.

Sebastian Ruder, Anders Søgaard, and Ivan Vulić. 2019a. Unsupervised cross-lingual representation learning. In *Proceedings of ACL: Tutorial Abstracts*, pages 31–38.

Sebastian Ruder, Ivan Vulić, and Anders Søgaard. 2019b. A survey of cross-lingual word embedding models. *Journal of Artificial Intelligence Research*, 65:569–631.

Tal Schuster, Ori Ram, Regina Barzilay, and Amir Globerson. 2019. Cross-lingual alignment of contextual word embeddings, with applications to zero-shot dependency parsing. In *Proceedings of NAACL-HLT*, pages 1599–1613.

Hinrich Schütze. 1998. Automatic word sense discrimination. *Computational Linguistics*, 24(1):97–123.

Samuel L. Smith, David H.P. Turban, Steven Hamblin, and Nils Y. Hammerla. 2017. Offline bilingual word vectors, orthogonal transformations and the inverted softmax. In *Proceedings of ICLR*.

Anders Søgaard, Sebastian Ruder, and Ivan Vulić. 2018. On the limitations of unsupervised bilingual dictionary induction. In *Proceedings of ACL*, pages 778–788.

Shuai Tang, Mahta Mousavi, and Virginia R. de Sa. 2019. An empirical study on post-processing methods for word embeddings. *CoRR*, abs/1905.10971.

Ivan Vulić, Goran Glavaš, Roi Reichart, and Anna Korhonen. 2019. Do we really need fully unsupervised cross-lingual embeddings? In *Proceedings of EMNLP*, pages 4406–4417.

Ivan Vulić and Anna Korhonen. 2016. On the role of seed lexicons in learning bilingual word embeddings. In *Proceedings of ACL*, pages 247–257.

Bin Wang, Fenxiao Chen, Angela Wang, and C.-C. Jay Kuo. 2018. Post-processing of word representations via variance normalization and dynamic embedding. *CoRR*, abs/1808.06305.

Mozhi Zhang, Keyulu Xu, Ken-ichi Kawarabayashi, Stefanie Jegelka, and Jordan Boyd-Graber. 2019. Are girls neko or shōjo? Cross-lingual alignment of non-isomorphic embeddings with iterative normalization. In *Proceedings of ACL*, pages 3180–3189.

A Supplemental Material

We report main BLI results for all $15 \times 14 = 210$ language pairs based on PanLex training and test data in the supplemental material, grouped by the source language, and for two dictionary sizes: $|D| = 1,000$ and $|D| = 5,000$ (while similar relative performance is also observed with other dictionary sizes, e.g., $|D| = 500$). The results are provided in Table 4–Table 18, and they are the basis of the results reported in the main paper. The language codes are available in Table 1 (in the main paper). As mentioned in the main paper, all results are obtained with the two α-hyperparameters fixed to the following values: $\alpha_S = -0.25$, $\alpha_T = 0.15$, without any further fine-tuning. A more careful language pair-specific fine-tuning results in even higher performance for many language pairs.

In all tables, BASELINE refers to the best-performing weakly supervised projection-based approach *without* and *with* self-learning, as reported in a recent comparative study of Vulić et al. (2019); $5k$ and $1k$ denote the seed dictionary D size. The scores in bold indicate improvements over the BASELINE methods. All results are reported as MRR scores: the MRR score of $.xyz$ should be read as $xy.z\%$ (e.g., the score of .432 can be read as 43.2%).

(The actual tables with the full results in all BLI setups start on the next page.)

	Bulgarian: BG-													
	-CA	-EO	-ET	-EU	-FI	-HE	-HU	-ID	-KA	-KO	-LT	-NO	-TH	-TR
BASELINE (supervised, 5k)	.432	.327	.407	.250	.357	.361	.460	.283	.364	.205	.405	.398	.169	.349
BASELINE (self-learning, 5k)	.456	.370	.405	.296	.374	.368	.475	.325	.367	.215	.407	.446	.179	.374
POSTPROC (self-learning, 5k)	**.473**	**.419**	**.420**	**.302**	**.386**	**.392**	**.489**	**.330**	**.371**	.211	**.419**	**.462**	**.203**	**.379**
BASELINE (supervised, 1k)	.229	.147	.211	.070	.129	.112	.254	.116	.157	.054	.230	.163	.044	.133
BASELINE (self-learning, 1k)	.444	.357	.388	.279	.361	.345	.467	.314	.333	.186	.369	.441	.128	.357
POSTPROC (self-learning, 1k)	**.458**	**.408**	**.398**	**.286**	**.377**	**.376**	**.478**	**.321**	.329	**.188**	**.375**	**.458**	**.133**	**.362**

Table 4: All BLI scores (MRR) with Bulgarian (BG) as the source language.

	Catalan: CA-													
	-BG	-EO	-ET	-EU	-FI	-HE	-HU	-ID	-KA	-KO	-LT	-NO	-TH	-TR
BASELINE (supervised, 5k)	.396	.395	.356	.338	.329	.336	.431	.286	.309	.217	.366	.396	.196	.337
BASELINE (self-learning, 5k)	.414	.456	.352	.391	.356	.357	.449	.322	.302	.245	.343	.433	.218	.348
POSTPROC (self-learning, 5k)	**.434**	**.510**	**.359**	**.409**	**.359**	**.373**	**.454**	**.326**	**.322**	.242	.347	**.448**	**.234**	**.351**
BASELINE (supervised, 1k)	.212	.167	.165	.116	.110	.103	.210	.126	.101	.046	.144	.138	.035	.133
BASELINE (self-learning, 1k)	.395	.446	.300	.370	.319	.335	.435	.320	.253	.202	.295	.424	.142	.334
POSTPROC (self-learning, 1k)	**.413**	**.508**	**.309**	**.393**	**.321**	**.351**	**.439**	**.326**	**.274**	**.204**	**.306**	**.438**	**.146**	.332

Table 5: All BLI scores (MRR) with Catalan (CA) as the source language.

	Esperanto: EO-													
	-BG	-CA	-ET	-EU	-FI	-HE	-HU	-ID	-KA	-KO	-LT	-NO	-TH	-TR
BASELINE (supervised, 5k)	.367	.491	.334	.294	.329	.258	.400	.267	.281	.171	.343	.337	.107	.285
BASELINE (self-learning, 5k)	.410	.533	.342	.354	.363	.288	.426	.315	.296	.184	.384	.390	.117	.299
POSTPROC (self-learning, 5k)	**.428**	**.546**	**.353**	**.369**	**.372**	**.299**	**.432**	**.342**	**.311**	.186	**.404**	**.405**	**.124**	.292
BASELINE (supervised, 1k)	.152	.221	.136	.083	.080	.044	.145	.099	.078	.024	.120	.083	.017	.087
BASELINE (self-learning, 1k)	.385	.521	.314	.315	.328	.241	.411	.298	.255	.111	.358	.376	.056	.259
POSTPROC (self-learning, 1k)	**.404**	**.535**	**.318**	**.317**	.316	.235	.404	**.316**	**.271**	.092	**.368**	**.389**	**.061**	.251

Table 6: All BLI scores (MRR) with Esperanto (EO) as the source language.

	Estonian: ET-													
	-BG	-CA	-EO	-EU	-FI	-HE	-HU	-ID	-KA	-KO	-LT	-NO	-TH	-TR
BASELINE (supervised, 5k)	.393	.333	.271	.238	.430	.287	.432	.212	.258	.191	.360	.328	.168	.307
BASELINE (self-learning, 5k)	.404	.357	.307	.238	.443	.301	.459	.223	.251	.185	.358	.383	.178	.331
POSTPROC (self-learning, 5k)	**.433**	**.401**	**.352**	**.239**	**.447**	**.320**	**.471**	**.253**	.253	**.192**	**.380**	**.407**	**.205**	**.334**
BASELINE (supervised, 1k)	.200	.121	.116	.099	.200	.069	.188	.065	.095	.052	.179	.112	.041	.102
BASELINE (self-learning, 1k)	.381	.346	.297	.208	.437	.277	.449	.204	.215	.148	.337	.377	.108	.313
POSTPROC (self-learning, 1k)	**.415**	**.392**	**.337**	.200	**.446**	**.289**	**.461**	**.227**	**.224**	**.150**	**.356**	**.408**	.108	**.319**

Table 7: All BLI scores (MRR) with Estonian (ET) as the source language.

	Basque: EU-													
	-BG	-CA	-EO	-ET	-FI	-HE	-HU	-ID	-KA	-KO	-LT	-NO	-TH	-TR
BASELINE (supervised, 5k)	.292	.391	.245	.250	.233	.211	.259	.183	.197	.109	.242	.240	.095	.240
BASELINE (self-learning, 5k)	.310	.441	.277	.248	.270	.206	.283	.225	.189	.106	.237	.287	.094	.248
POSTPROC (self-learning, 5k)	**.332**	**.453**	**.324**	**.255**	**.276**	.207	**.302**	**.238**	.188	.108	.229	**.309**	**.119**	**.254**
BASELINE (supervised, 1k)	.120	.142	.077	.088	.048	.037	.077	.049	.059	.021	.071	.053	.018	.055
BASELINE (self-learning, 1k)	.276	.428	.253	.213	.247	.166	.266	.213	.147	.060	.169	.261	.056	.212
POSTPROC (self-learning, 1k)	**.294**	**.440**	**.292**	.209	.232	.144	.263	**.214**	.136	**.069**	.157	**.272**	**.059**	.201

Table 8: All BLI scores (MRR) with Basque (EU) as the source language.

	Finnish: FI-													
	-BG	-CA	-EO	-ET	-EU	-HE	-HU	-ID	-KA	-KO	-LT	-NO	-TH	-TR
BASELINE (supervised, 5k)	.379	.377	.284	.409	.220	.323	.456	.263	.275	.222	.390	.419	.171	.346
BASELINE (self-learning, 5k)	.397	.404	.320	.424	.271	.351	.474	.298	.289	.243	.405	.460	.168	.365
POSTPROC (self-learning, 5k)	**.423**	**.430**	**.386**	**.456**	**.302**	**.386**	**.477**	**.311**	**.329**	**.258**	**.434**	**.481**	**.196**	**.370**
BASELINE (supervised, 1k)	.174	.142	.077	.167	.054	.071	.226	.098	.084	.052	.158	.161	.028	.149
BASELINE (self-learning, 1k)	.381	.396	.304	.416	.235	.331	.463	.300	.270	.211	.389	.455	.107	.353
POSTPROC (self-learning, 1k)	**.409**	**.413**	**.372**	**.447**	**.259**	**.369**	**.466**	**.307**	**.303**	**.228**	**.424**	**.477**	**.112**	**.360**

Table 9: All BLI scores (MRR) with Finnish (FI) as the source language.

	Hebrew: HE-													
	-BG	-CA	-EO	-ET	-EU	-FI	-HU	-ID	-KA	-KO	-LT	-NO	-TH	-TR
BASELINE (supervised, 5k)	.397	.376	.248	.288	.225	.329	.375	.239	.213	.204	.309	.316	.173	.328
BASELINE (self-learning, 5k)	.378	.384	.278	.278	.211	.320	.393	.266	.217	.218	.301	.349	.192	.337
POSTPROC (self-learning, 5k)	**.401**	**.418**	**.307**	**.298**	.212	**.333**	**.402**	**.293**	.213	**.219**	.308	**.379**	**.238**	**.342**
BASELINE (supervised, 1k)	.180	.148	.087	.106	.065	.077	.135	.076	.067	.054	.105	.086	.042	.111
BASELINE (self-learning, 1k)	.360	.371	.252	.250	.182	.293	.383	.251	.188	.187	.254	.343	.114	.321
POSTPROC (self-learning, 1k)	**.381**	**.401**	**.280**	**.255**	.174	**.311**	**.388**	**.274**	.174	.184	**.255**	**.366**	**.131**	**.326**

Table 10: All BLI scores (MRR) with Hebrew (HE) as the source language.

	Hungarian: HU-													
	-BG	-CA	-EO	-ET	-EU	-FI	-HE	-ID	-KA	-KO	-LT	-NO	-TH	-TR
BASELINE (supervised, 5k)	.431	.443	.344	.423	.282	.397	.349	.338	.326	.259	.411	.406	.173	.372
BASELINE (self-learning, 5k)	.438	.477	.392	.433	.305	.407	.376	.374	.332	.285	.419	.441	.176	.380
POSTPROC (self-learning, 5k)	**.466**	**.495**	**.453**	**.457**	**.310**	**.418**	**.405**	**.403**	**.353**	**.293**	**.436**	**.457**	**.194**	**.387**
BASELINE (supervised, 1k)	.241	.221	.125	.196	.094	.168	.098	.147	.112	.063	.183	.149	.026	.184
BASELINE (self-learning, 1k)	.427	.467	.369	.413	.274	.400	.356	.377	.306	.268	.381	.423	.113	.374
POSTPROC (self-learning, 1k)	**.458**	**.484**	**.431**	**.443**	**.276**	**.410**	**.385**	**.406**	**.331**	**.270**	**.401**	**.447**	**.126**	**.377**

Table 11: All BLI scores (MRR) with Hungarian (HU) as the source language.

	Indonesian: ID-													
	-BG	-CA	-EO	-ET	-EU	-FI	-HE	-HU	-KA	-KO	-LT	-NO	-TH	-TR
BASELINE (supervised, 5k)	.281	.300	.247	.281	.173	.233	.290	.349	.222	.193	.260	.294	.218	.316
BASELINE (self-learning, 5k)	.287	.323	.274	.266	.220	.269	.295	.345	.200	.197	.242	.320	.241	.326
POSTPROC (self-learning, 5k)	**.307**	**.333**	**.303**	.273	**.225**	**.270**	**.298**	**.360**	.205	**.203**	.242	**.335**	**.256**	**.328**
BASELINE (supervised, 1k)	.121	.114	.092	.115	.038	.053	.093	.129	.063	.062	.086	.081	.052	.152
BASELINE (self-learning, 1k)	.258	.316	.254	.213	.187	.250	.264	.337	.140	.175	.152	.309	.226	.319
POSTPROC (self-learning, 1k)	**.280**	**.327**	**.282**	**.221**	**.197**	**.252**	**.271**	**.346**	.131	**.184**	.149	**.325**	.225	**.322**

Table 12: All BLI scores (MRR) with Indonesian (ID) as the source language.

	Georgian: KA-													
	-BG	-CA	-EO	-ET	-EU	-FI	-HE	-HU	-ID	-KO	-LT	-NO	-TH	-TR
BASELINE (supervised, 5k)	.372	.297	.243	.282	.217	.292	.245	.308	.169	.154	.327	.214	.127	.257
BASELINE (self-learning, 5k)	.376	.320	.265	.293	.216	.318	.251	.326	.172	.143	.340	.253	.139	.275
POSTPROC (self-learning, 5k)	**.412**	**.355**	**.307**	**.300**	**.218**	**.331**	**.270**	**.343**	**.200**	.154	**.342**	**.281**	**.153**	**.280**
BASELINE (supervised, 1k)	.153	.088	.083	.112	.068	.065	.046	.103	.048	.036	.138	.048	.025	.091
BASELINE (self-learning, 1k)	.352	.305	.248	.271	.172	.306	.213	.308	.155	.103	.317	.238	.077	.255
POSTPROC (self-learning, 1k)	**.378**	**.341**	**.283**	**.279**	**.174**	**.308**	**.233**	**.323**	**.177**	.098	**.321**	**.260**	**.078**	.249

Table 13: All BLI scores (MRR) with Georgian (KA) as the source language.

| | Korean: KO- | | | | | | | | | | | | | |
	-BG	-CA	-EO	-ET	-EU	-FI	-HE	-HU	-ID	-KA	-LT	-NO	-TH	-TR
BASELINE (supervised, 5k)	.190	.183	.083	.145	.102	.206	.166	.238	.142	.112	.156	.150	.076	.213
BASELINE (self-learning, 5k)	.289	.283	.176	.242	.170	.273	.257	.326	.210	.178	.241	.256	.174	.278
POSTPROC (self-learning, 5k)	**.324**	**.330**	**.217**	**.247**	.153	**.310**	**.281**	**.367**	**.264**	**.180**	.239	**.313**	**.199**	**.301**
BASELINE (supervised, 1k)	.093	.078	.045	.059	.045	.066	.048	.096	.060	.039	.053	.047	.038	.085
BASELINE (self-learning, 1k)	.245	.253	.110	.191	.108	.266	.232	.343	.206	.122	.150	.244	.089	.279
POSTPROC (self-learning, 1k)	**.268**	**.274**	**.134**	**.193**	.106	**.271**	**.239**	**.348**	**.236**	**.117**	**.152**	**.264**	**.102**	**.284**

Table 14: All BLI scores (MRR) with Korean (KO) as the source language.

| | Lithuanian: LT- | | | | | | | | | | | | | |
	-BG	-CA	-EO	-ET	-EU	-FI	-HE	-HU	-ID	-KA	-KO	-NO	-TH	-TR
BASELINE (supervised, 5k)	.462	.353	.317	.394	.236	.368	.299	.395	.184	.284	.168	.304	.162	.296
BASELINE (self-learning, 5k)	.437	.363	.348	.383	.222	.385	.316	.413	.191	.304	.160	.336	.168	.319
POSTPROC (self-learning, 5k)	**.470**	**.408**	**.406**	**.400**	**.233**	**.394**	**.338**	**.426**	**.220**	.300	.160	**.372**	**.205**	**.326**
BASELINE (supervised, 1k)	.256	.138	.102	.190	.085	.143	.073	.159	.058	.097	.040	.081	.030	.097
BASELINE (self-learning, 1k)	.408	.345	.332	.361	.181	.380	.286	.399	.168	.288	.109	.322	.094	.302
POSTPROC (self-learning, 1k)	**.438**	**.387**	**.388**	**.382**	**.191**	**.390**	**.306**	**.412**	**.195**	.282	**.117**	**.355**	**.109**	**.305**

Table 15: All BLI scores (MRR) with Lithuanian (LT) as the source language.

| | Norwegian: NO- | | | | | | | | | | | | | |
	-BG	-CA	-EO	-ET	-EU	-FI	-HE	-HU	-ID	-KA	-KO	-LT	-TH	-TR
BASELINE (supervised, 5k)	.394	.424	.323	.389	.261	.396	.319	.441	.306	.291	.220	.366	.188	.325
BASELINE (self-learning, 5k)	.422	.457	.377	.395	.328	.419	.353	.452	.340	.298	.250	.351	.197	.341
POSTPROC (self-learning, 5k)	**.441**	**.474**	**.425**	**.411**	**.345**	**.424**	**.381**	**.455**	**.354**	**.315**	**.257**	**.367**	**.227**	**.346**
BASELINE (supervised, 1k)	.203	.198	.128	.172	.075	.153	.078	.206	.132	.088	.057	.132	.032	.123
BASELINE (self-learning, 1k)	.411	.444	.374	.371	.300	.412	.336	.443	.339	.268	.228	.315	.140	.332
POSTPROC (self-learning, 1k)	**.433**	**.466**	**.419**	**.389**	**.313**	**.417**	**.366**	**.445**	**.352**	**.279**	**.236**	**.332**	.136	**.336**

Table 16: All BLI scores (MRR) with Norwegian (NO) as the source language.

| | Thai: TH- | | | | | | | | | | | | | |
	-BG	-CA	-EO	-ET	-EU	-FI	-HE	-HU	-ID	-KA	-KO	-LT	-NO	-TR
BASELINE (supervised, 5k)	.210	.134	.087	.186	.094	.173	.173	.178	.141	.116	.112	.214	.162	.177
BASELINE (self-learning, 5k)	.174	.123	.073	.164	.093	.167	.203	.160	.170	.126	.097	.215	.147	.160
POSTPROC (self-learning, 5k)	.176	**.145**	.068	.168	**.098**	**.178**	.176	**.188**	**.203**	**.136**	**.118**	**.218**	.143	.170
BASELINE (supervised, 1k)	.049	.027	.021	.070	.029	.032	.057	.044	.044	.034	.040	.084	.029	.052
BASELINE (self-learning, 1k)	.108	.084	.036	.128	.057	.094	.152	.111	.168	.073	.065	.145	.098	.121
POSTPROC (self-learning, 1k)	**.112**	**.104**	**.049**	.120	.049	**.104**	.150	**.127**	**.192**	**.079**	**.078**	.151	**.107**	**.125**

Table 17: All BLI scores (MRR) with Thai (TH) as the source language.

| | Turkish: TR- | | | | | | | | | | | | | |
	-BG	-CA	-EO	-ET	-EU	-FI	-HE	-HU	-ID	-KA	-KO	-LT	-NO	-TH
BASELINE (supervised, 5k)	.344	.360	.215	.307	.230	.294	.319	.378	.336	.205	.196	.295	.311	.170
BASELINE (self-learning, 5k)	.351	.376	.238	.309	.244	.322	.323	.397	.370	.229	.214	.280	.346	.183
POSTPROC (self-learning, 5k)	**.378**	**.405**	**.291**	**.328**	**.252**	**.338**	**.361**	**.413**	**.395**	**.261**	**.226**	**.298**	**.369**	**.210**
BASELINE (supervised, 1k)	.150	.133	.052	.112	.062	.093	.076	.167	.131	.053	.050	.099	.073	.028
BASELINE (self-learning, 1k)	.327	.364	.204	.274	.209	.310	.301	.398	.363	.201	.194	.215	.344	.137
POSTPROC (self-learning, 1k)	**.361**	**.394**	**.259**	**.289**	**.217**	**.326**	**.336**	**.411**	**.390**	**.245**	**.200**	**.234**	**.368**	**.142**

Table 18: All BLI scores (MRR) with Turkish (TR) as the source language.

Adversarial Training for Commonsense Inference

Lis Pereira[1], Xiaodong Liu[2], Fei Cheng[3], Masayuki Asahara[4], Ichiro Kobayashi[1]
[1] Ochanomizu University [2] Microsoft Research [3] Kyoto University
[4] The National Institute for Japanese Language and Linguistics (NINJAL)
kanashiro.pereira@ocha.ac.jp, xiaodl@microsoft.com, feicheng@i.kyoto-u.ac.jp
masayu-a@ninjal.ac.jp, koba@is.ocha.ac.jp

Abstract

We propose an AdversariaL training algorithm for commonsense InferenCE (ALICE). We apply small perturbations to word embeddings and minimize the resultant adversarial risk to regularize the model. We exploit a novel combination of two different approaches to estimate these perturbations: 1) using the true label and 2) using the model prediction. Without relying on any human-crafted features, knowledge bases or additional datasets other than the target datasets, our model boosts the fine-tuning performance of RoBERTa, achieving competitive results on multiple reading comprehension datasets that require commonsense inference.

1 Introduction

Commonsense knowledge is often necessary for natural language understanding. As shown in Table 1, we can understand that the writer needs help to get dressed and seems upset with this situation, indicating that he or she is probably not a child. Thus, we can infer that a possible reason that the writer needs to be dressed by other people is that he or she may have a physical disability (Huang et al., 2019). Although a simple task for humans, it is still challenging for computers to understand and reason about commonsense.

Commonsense inference in natural language processing (NLP) is generally evaluated via machine reading comprehension task, in the format of selecting plausible responses with respect to natural language queries. Recent approaches are based on the use of pre-trained Transformer-based language models such as BERT (Devlin et al., 2019). Some approaches rely solely on these models by adopting either a single or multi-stage fine-tuning approach (by fine-tuning using additional datasets in a stepwise manner) (Li and Xie, 2019; Sharma and Roychowdhury, 2019; Liu and Yu, 2019; Huang et al.,

---

Paragraph: It's a very humbling experience when you need someone to dress you every morning, tie your shoes, and put your hair up. Every menial task takes an unprecedented amount of effort. It made me appreciate Dan even more. But anyway I shan't dwell on this (I'm not dying after all) and not let it detract from my lovely 5 days with my friends visiting from Jersey.

Question: What's a possible reason the writer needed someone to dress him every morning?

Option1: The writer doesn't like putting effort into these tasks.
Option2: **The writer has a physical disability.**
Option3: The writer is bad at doing his own hair.
Option4: None of the above choices.

Table 1: Example from the CosmosQA dataset (Huang et al., 2019). The task is to identify the correct answer option. The correct answer is in **bold.**

2019; Zhou et al., 2019), while others further enhance their word representations with knowledge bases such as ConceptNet (Jain and Singh, 2019; Da, 2019; Wang et al., 2020). However, due to the often limited data from the downstream tasks and the extremely high complexity of the pre-trained model, aggressive fine-tuning can easily make the adapted model overfit the data of the target task, making it unable to generalize well on unseen data (Jiang et al., 2019). Moreover, some researchers have shown that such pre-trained models are vulnerable to adversarial attacks (Jin et al., 2020).

Inspired by the recent success of adversarial training in NLP (Zhu et al., 2020; Jiang et al., 2019), our AdversariaL training algorithm for commonsense InferenCE (ALICE) focuses on improving the generalization of pre-trained language mod-

Proceedings of the 5th Workshop on Representation Learning for NLP (RepL4NLP-2020), pages 55–60
July 9, 2020. ©2020 Association for Computational Linguistics

els on downstream tasks by enhancing their robustness in the embedding space. More specifically, during the fine-tuning stage of Transformer-based models, e.g. RoBERTa (Liu et al., 2019b), random perturbations are added to the embedding layer to regularize the model by updating the parameters on these adversarial embeddings. ALICE exploits a novel way of combining two different approaches to estimate these perturbations: 1) using the true label and 2) using the model prediction. Experiments show that we were able to boost the performance of RoBERTa on multiple reading comprehension datasets that require commonsense inference, achieving competitive results with state-of-the-art approaches.

2 ALICE

Given a dataset D of N training examples, $D = \{(x_1, y_1), (x_2, y_2), ..., (x_N, y_N)\}$, the objective of supervised learning is to learn a function $f(x; \theta)$ that minimizes the empirical risk, which is defined by $\min_\theta E_{(x,y)\sim D}[l(f(x; \theta), y)]$. Here, the function $f(x; \theta)$ maps input sentences x to an output space y, and θ are learnable parameters. While this objective is effective to train a neural network, it usually suffers from overfitting and poor generalization to unseen cases (Goodfellow et al., 2015; Madry et al., 2018). To alleviate these issues, one can use adversarial training, which has been primarily explored in computer vision (Goodfellow et al., 2015; Madry et al., 2018). The idea is to perturb the data distribution in the embedding space by performing adversarial attacks. Specifically, its objective is defined by:

$$\min_\theta E_{(x,y)\sim D}[\max_\delta l(f(x + \delta; \theta), y)], \quad (1)$$

where δ is the perturbation added to the embeddings. One challenge of adversarial training is how to estimate this perturbation δ, which is to solve the inner maximization, $\max_\delta l(f(x + \delta; \theta), y)$. A feasible solution is to approximate it by a fixed number of steps of a gradient-based optimization approach (Madry et al., 2018).

Based on recent successful cases that applied adversarial training to NLP (Jiang et al., 2019; Miyato et al., 2018), the approaches to estimate δ can be divided into two categories: adversarial training that uses the label y (Zhu et al., 2020) and adversarial training that uses the model prediction $f(x; \theta)$, i.e. a "virtual" label (Miyato et al., 2018; Jiang et al., 2019). We hypothesize that these two categories

complement each other: the first one is to improve the robustness of our target label, by avoiding an increase in the error of the unperturbed inputs, while the second term enforces the smoothness of the model, encouraging the output of the model not to change much, when injecting a small perturbation to the input. Thus, ALICE proposes a novel algorithm by combining these two approaches, which is defined by:

$$\min_\theta E_{(x,y)\sim D}[\max_{\delta_1} l(f(x + \delta_1; \theta), y) + \\ \alpha \max_{\delta_2} l(f(x + \delta_2; \theta), f(x; \theta))], \quad (2)$$

where δ_1 and δ_2 are two perturbations, bounded by a general l_p norm ball, estimated by a fixed K steps of the gradient-based optimization approach. In our experiments, we set $p = \infty$. It has been shown that a larger K can lead to a better estimation of δ (Qin et al., 2019; Madry et al., 2018). However, this can be expensive, especially in large models, e.g. BERT and RoBERTa. Thus, K is set to 1 for a better trade-off between speed and performance. Note that α is a hyperparameter balancing these two loss terms. In our experiments, we set α to 1.

3 Experiments

3.1 Datasets and Evaluation Metrics

We evaluate ALICE on three reading comprehension benchmarks that require commonsense inference:

CosmosQA (Huang et al., 2019): a large-scale dataset that focuses on people's everyday narratives, asking questions about the likely causes or effects of events that require reasoning beyond the exact text spans in the context. It has 35,888 questions on 21,886 distinct contexts taken from blogs of personal narratives. Each question has four answer candidates, one of which is correct. 93.8% of the dataset requires contextual commonsense reasoning.

MCScript2.0 (Ostermann et al., 2019b): a dataset focused on short narrations on different everyday activities (e.g. baking a cake, taking a bus, etc.). It has 19,821 questions on 3,487 texts. Each question has two answer candidates, one of which is correct. Roughly half of the questions require inferences over commonsense knowledge.

MC-TACO (Zhou et al., 2019): a dataset that entirely focuses on a specific reasoning capablity: temporal commonsense. It considers five temporal properties, (1) duration (how long an event takes), (2) temporal ordering (typical order of events), (3)

Dataset	#Train	#Dev	#Test	#Label	Task	Metrics
CosmosQA	25,262	2,985	6,963	4	Relevance Ranking	Accuracy
MCScript2.0	14,191	2,020	3,610	2	Relevance Ranking	Accuracy
MCTACO	-	3,783	9,442	2	Pairwise Text Classification	Exact Match (EM)/F1

Table 2: Summary of the three datasets: CosmosQA, MCScript2.0 and MCTACO.

typical time (when an event occurs), (4) frequency (how often an event occurs), and (5) stationarity (whether a state is maintained for a very long time or indefinitely). It contains 13k tuples, each consisting of a sentence, a question, and a candidate answer, that should be judged as plausible or not. The sentences are taken from different sources such as news, Wikipedia and textbooks.

The summary of the datasets is in Table 2. For the MCTACO dataset, no training set is available. Following (Zhou et al., 2019), we use the dev set for fine-tuning the model. We perform 5-fold cross-validation for fine-tuning the parameters.

We evaluate CosmosQA and MCScript2.0 in terms of accuracy. Following (Ostermann et al., 2019a), we also report for the MCScript2.0 accuracy on the commonsense based questions and accuracy on the questions that are not commonsense based. For the MCTACO, we report the exact match (EM) and F1 scores, following (Zhou et al., 2019). EM measures how many questions a system correctly labeled all candidate answers, while F1 measures the average overlap between one's predictions and the ground truth. Our implementation for pairwise text classification and relevance ranking tasks are based on the MT-DNN framework[1] (Liu et al., 2019a, 2020).

3.2 Implementation Details

The RoBERTa$_{\text{LARGE}}$ model (Liu et al., 2019b) was used as the text encoder. We used ADAM (Kingma and Ba, 2015) as our optimizer with a learning rate in the range $\in \{1 \times 10^{-5}, 2 \times 10^{-5}, 3 \times 10^{-5}, 5 \times 10^{-5}, 5 \times 10^{-5}\}$ and a batch size $\in \{16, 32, 64\}$. The maximum number of epochs was set to 10. A linear learning rate decay schedule with warm-up over 0.1 was used, unless stated otherwise. We also set the dropout rate of all the task specific layers as 0.1, except 0.3 for MCTACO. To avoid gradient exploding, we clipped the gradient norm within 1. All the texts were tokenized using wordpieces and were chopped to spans no longer than 512 tokens.

3.3 Baselines

We compare ALICE to a list of state-of-the-art models, as shown in Table 3. **BERT + unit normalization** (Zhou et al., 2019) is the BERT base model. The authors further add unit normalization to temporal expressions in candidate answers and fine-tune on the MC-TACO dataset. **RoBERTa$_{\text{LARGE}}$** is our re-implementation of the large RoBERTa model by (Liu et al., 2019b). **PSH-SJTU** (Li and Xie, 2019) is based on multi-stage fine-tuning XL-NET (Yang et al., 2019) on RACE (Lai et al., 2017), SWAG (Zellers et al., 2018) and MC-Script2.0 datasets. **K-ADAPTER** (Wang et al., 2020) further enhances RoBERTa word representations with multiple knowledge sources, such as factual knowledge obtained through Wikipedia and Wikidata and linguistic knowledge obtained through dependency parsing web texts. **SMART** (Jiang et al., 2019) is an adversarial training model for fine-tuning pre-trained language models through regularization. SMART uses the model prediction, $f(x; \theta)$, for estimating the perturbation δ. This model recently obtained state-of-the-art results on a bunch of NLP tasks on the GLUE benchmark (Wang et al., 2018). We also compare ALICE with a baseline that uses only the label y for estimating the perturbation δ (called model **ADV** hereafter) (Madry et al., 2018).

3.4 Results

The results are summarized in Table 3. Overall, we observed that adversarial methods, i.e. ADV, SMART and ALICE, were able to achieve competitive results over the baselines, without using any additional knowledge source, and without using any additional dataset other than the target task datasets. These results suggest that adversarial training lead to a more robust model and help generalize better on unseen data.

ALICE consistently outperformed SMART (which overall outperformed ADV) across all three datasets on both dev and test sets, indicating that adversarial training that uses the label y and adversarial training that uses the model prediction

---

[1]https://github.com/namisan/mt-dnn

Model	CosmosQA	MCScript2.0			MCTACO	
	Acc	Acc	Acc_{cs}	Acc_{ood}	EM	F1
Development Set Results						
RoBERTa$_{LARGE}$ (Liu et al., 2019b)	80.60	90.0	87.7	92.1	44.12	64.85
ADV	81.14	92.1	89.8	94.3	52.70	78.12
SMART (Jiang et al., 2019)	82.00	93.6	**91.8**	95.2	53.79	78.31
ALICE	**83.60**	**93.8**	91.7	**95.7**	**58.02**	**78.64**
Test Set Results						
Human Performance	94.00	97.0	-	-	75.80	87.10
BERT + unit normalization (Zhou et al., 2019)	-	-	-	-	42.70	69.90
T5-3B fine-tuned + number normalization[*]	-	-	-	-	**59.08**	79.46
PSH-SJTU (Li and Xie, 2019)	-	90.6	90.3	91.5	-	-
K-ADAPTER (Wang et al., 2020)	81.83	-	-	-	-	-
GB-KSI(v2)[*]	83.97	-	-	-	-	-
RoBERTa$_{LARGE}$ (Liu et al., 2019b)	-	88.8	87.0	90.7	51.05	76.85
ADV	-	91.1	90.3	92.0	54.27	77.23
SMART (Jiang et al., 2019)	81.90	91.8	90.5	93.4	54.80	78.03
ALICE	**84.57**	**92.5**	**91.6**	**93.5**	56.45	**79.50**

Table 3: Development and test results of CosmosQA, MCScript 2.0 and MCTACO. The best results are in **bold**. Note that RoBERTa$_{LARGE}$, SMART and ALICE models use RoBERTa$_{LARGE}$ as the text encoder, and for a fair comparison, all these results are produced by ourselves. On the test results, note that CosmosQA and MCTACO are scored by using the official evaluation server (https://leaderboard.allenai.org/). * denotes unpublished work and scores were obtained from the evaluation server on April 16, 2020. Acc_{cs} denotes the accuracy on commonsense based questions and Acc_{ood} denotes the accuracy on questions that are not commonsense based, i.e. out-of-domain questions.

$f(x; \theta)$ are complementary, leading to better results. For example, on the CosmosQA dataset, we obtained a dev-set accuracy of 83.6% with ALICE, a 1.6% and 3.0% absolute gains over SMART and RoBERTa$_{LARGE}$, respectively. On the blind test-set, ALICE outperforms by a large margin K-ADAPTER, a model that enhances RoBERTa word representations with multiple knowledge sources. Our submission to the CosmosQA leaderboard achieved a test-set accuracy of 84.57%, ranking first place among all submissions (as of April 16, 2020). On the MCScript2.0 dataset, ALICE obtained a dev-set accuracy of 93.8% in total, a 0.2% and 3.8% absolute gains over SMART and RoBERTa$_{LARGE}$, respectively. On the commonsense based questions, ALICE underperformed SMART by 0.1% and outperformed RoBERTa$_{LARGE}$ by 4.0%. On the out-of-domain questions, ALICE obtained 0.5% and 3.6% absolute gains over SMART and RoBERTa$_{LARGE}$, respectively. On the MCScript2.0 test-set, ALICE outperformed all baselines (on all types of questions), including SMART, indicating that it can generalize better to unseen cases. Moreover, ALICE outperformed PSH-SJTU, which is based on

XLNET, and used additional datasets other than MCScript2.0, while ALICE does not use any additional dataset. On the MCTACO dataset, ALICE obtained on the dev-set 56.20% EM score, a 2.41% and 12.8% absolute gains over SMART and RoBERTa$_{LARGE}$, respectively, and 79.06% F1 score, a 0.75% and 14.21% absolute gains over SMART and RoBERTa$_{LARGE}$, respectively. On the test-set, ALICE outperformed SMART obtaining absolute gains of 1.65% and 1.47% on EM and F1 scores, respectively. Compared to the T5-3B fine-tuned + number normalization model, which uses T5, a much larger model (with 3B parameters) than RoBERTa (300M parameters), ALICE obtained competitive results, outperforming by 0.04 on F1 score and obtaining 2.63% lower score on EM. Regarding the training time, ALICE takes on average 4X more time to train compared to standard fine-tuning.

4 Conclusion

We proposed ALICE, a simple and efficient adversarial training algorithm for fine-tuning large scale pre-trained language models. Our experiments demonstrated that it achieves competitive results on multiple machine reading comprehension datasets, without relying on any additional resource other than the target task dataset. Although in this paper we focused on the machine reading comprehension task, ALICE can be generalized to solve other downstream tasks as well, and we will explore this direction as future work.

Acknowledgments

We thank the reviewers for their helpful feedback. This work has been supported by the project KAKENHI ID: 18H05521.

References

Jeff Da. 2019. Jeff da at coin-shared task. In *Proceedings of the First Workshop on Commonsense Inference in Natural Language Processing*, pages 85–92.

Jacob Devlin, Ming-Wei Chang, Kenton Lee, and Kristina Toutanova. 2019. Bert: Pre-training of deep bidirectional transformers for language understanding. *Proceedings of NAACL-HLT 2019*, pages 4171–4186.

Ian J Goodfellow, Jonathon Shlens, and Christian Szegedy. 2015. Explaining and harnessing adversarial examples. *ICLR 2015*.

Lifu Huang, Ronan Le Bras, Chandra Bhagavatula, and Yejin Choi. 2019. Cosmos qa: Machine reading comprehension with contextual commonsense reasoning. *Proceedings of the 2019 Conference on Empirical Methods in Natural Language Processing and the 9th International Joint Conference on Natural Language Processing*, pages 2391–2401.

Yash Jain and Chinmay Singh. 2019. Karna at coin shared task 1: Bidirectional encoder representations from transformers with relational knowledge for machine comprehension with common sense. In *Proceedings of the First Workshop on Commonsense Inference in Natural Language Processing*, pages 75–79.

Haoming Jiang, Pengcheng He, Weizhu Chen, Xiaodong Liu, Jianfeng Gao, and Tuo Zhao. 2019. Smart: Robust and efficient fine-tuning for pretrained natural language models through principled regularized optimization. *arXiv preprint arXiv:1911.03437*.

Di Jin, Zhijing Jin, Joey Tianyi Zhou, and Peter Szolovits. 2020. Is bert really robust? natural language attack on text classification and entailment. *AAAI 2020*.

Diederik P Kingma and Jimmy Ba. 2015. Adam: A method for stochastic optimization. *ICLR (Poster) 2015*.

Guokun Lai, Qizhe Xie, Hanxiao Liu, Yiming Yang, and Eduard Hovy. 2017. Race: Large-scale reading comprehension dataset from examinations. *Proceedings of the 2017 Conference on Empirical Methods in Natural Language Processing*, pages 785–794.

Zhexi Zhang Wei Zhu Zheng Li Yuan Ni Peng Gao Junchi Yan Li, Xiepeng and Guotong Xie. 2019. Pingan smart health and sjtu at coin-shared task: utilizing pre-trained language models and common-sense knowledge in machine reading tasks. In *In Proceedings of the First Workshop on Commonsense Inference in Natural Language Processing*, pages 93–98, Hong Kong.

Chunhua Liu and Dong Yu. 2019. Blcu-nlp at coin-shared task1: Stagewise fine-tuning bert for commonsense inference in everyday narrations. In *Proceedings of the First Workshop on Commonsense Inference in Natural Language Processing*, pages 99–103.

Xiaodong Liu, Pengcheng He, Weizhu Chen, and Jianfeng Gao. 2019a. Multi-task deep neural networks for natural language understanding. *Proceedings of the 57th Annual Meeting of the Association for Computational Linguistics*, pages 4487–4496.

Xiaodong Liu, Yu Wang, Jianshu Ji, Hao Cheng, Xueyun Zhu, Emmanuel Awa, Pengcheng He, Weizhu Chen, Hoifung Poon, Guihong Cao, and Jianfeng Gao. 2020. The microsoft toolkit of multi-task deep neural networks for natural language understanding. *arXiv preprint arXiv:2002.07972*.

Yinhan Liu, Myle Ott, Naman Goyal, Jingfei Du, Mandar Joshi, Danqi Chen, Omer Levy, Mike Lewis, Luke Zettlemoyer, and Veselin Stoyanov. 2019b. Roberta: A robustly optimized bert pretraining approach. *arXiv preprint arXiv:1907.11692*.

Aleksander Madry, Aleksandar Makelov, Ludwig Schmidt, Dimitris Tsipras, and Adrian Vladu. 2018. Towards deep learning models resistant to adversarial attacks. *ICLR 2018*.

Takeru Miyato, Shin-ichi Maeda, Masanori Koyama, and Shin Ishii. 2018. Virtual adversarial training: a regularization method for supervised and semi-supervised learning. *IEEE transactions on pattern analysis and machine intelligence*, 41(8):1979–1993.

Simon Ostermann, Michael Roth, and Manfred Pinkal. 2019a. Mcscript2. 0: A machine comprehension corpus focused on script events and participants. *Proceedings of the Eighth Joint Conference on Lexical and Computational Semantics (*SEM 2019)*, pages 103–117.

Simon Ostermann, Sheng Zhang, Michael Roth, and Peter Clark. 2019b. Commonsense inference in natural language processing (coin)-shared task report. In *Proceedings of the First Workshop on Commonsense Inference in Natural Language Processing*, pages 66–74.

Chongli Qin, James Martens, Sven Gowal, Dilip Krishnan, Alhussein Fawzi, Soham De, Robert Stanforth, Pushmeet Kohli, et al. 2019. Adversarial robustness through local linearization. *33rd Conference on Neural Information Processing Systems (NeurIPS 2019)*.

Prakhar Sharma and Sumegh Roychowdhury. 2019. Iitkgp at coin 2019: Using pre-trained language models for modeling machine comprehension. In *Proceedings of the First Workshop on Commonsense Inference in Natural Language Processing*, pages 80–84.

Alex Wang, Amanpreet Singh, Julian Michael, Felix Hill, Omer Levy, and Samuel R Bowman. 2018. Glue: A multi-task benchmark and analysis platform for natural language understanding. *Proceedings of the 2018 EMNLP Workshop BlackboxNLP: Analyzing and Interpreting Neural Networks for NLP*, pages 353–355.

Ruize Wang, Duyu Tang, Nan Duan, Zhongyu Wei, Xuanjing Huang, Cuihong Cao, Daxin Jiang, Ming Zhou, et al. 2020. K-adapter: Infusing knowledge into pre-trained models with adapters. *arXiv preprint arXiv:2002.01808*.

Zhilin Yang, Zihang Dai, Yiming Yang, Jaime Carbonell, Russ R Salakhutdinov, and Quoc V Le. 2019. Xlnet: Generalized autoregressive pretraining for language understanding. In *Advances in neural information processing systems*, pages 5754–5764.

Rowan Zellers, Yonatan Bisk, Roy Schwartz, and Yejin Choi. 2018. Swag: A large-scale adversarial dataset for grounded commonsense inference. *Proceedings of the 2018 Conference on Empirical Methods in Natural Language Processing*, pages 93–104.

Ben Zhou, Daniel Khashabi, Qiang Ning, and Dan Roth. 2019. "going on a vacation" takes longer than" going for a walk": A study of temporal commonsense understanding. *Proceedings of the 2019 Conference on Empirical Methods in Natural Language Processing and the 9th International Joint Conference on Natural Language Processing (EMNLP-IJCNLP)*, pages 3363–3369.

Chen Zhu, Yu Cheng, Zhe Gan, Siqi Sun, Thomas Goldstein, and Jingjing Liu. 2020. Freelb: Enhanced adversarial training for language understanding. *ICLR 2020*.

Evaluating Natural Alpha Embeddings on Intrinsic and Extrinsic Tasks

Riccardo Volpi
Machine Learning and Optimization,
Romanian Institute of
Science and Technology (RIST),
Cluj-Napoca, Romania
volpi@rist.ro

Luigi Malagò
Machine Learning and Optimization,
Romanian Institute of
Science and Technology (RIST),
Cluj-Napoca, Romania
malago@rist.ro

Abstract

Skip-Gram is a simple, but effective, model to learn a word embedding mapping by estimating a conditional probability distribution for each word of the dictionary. In the context of Information Geometry, these distributions form a Riemannian statistical manifold, where word embeddings are interpreted as vectors in the tangent bundle of the manifold. In this paper we show how the choice of the geometry on the manifold allows impacts on the performances both on intrinsic and extrinsic tasks, in function of a deformation parameter alpha.

1 Introduction

Word embeddings are compact representations for the words of a dictionary. Rumelhart et al. (1986) first introduced the idea of using the internal representation of a neural network to construct a word embedding. Bengio et al. (2003) employ a neural network to predict the probability of the next word given the previous ones. Mikolov et al. (2010) proposed the use of a recurrency language model based on RNN, to learn the vector representations. More recently, this approach has been exploited further, with great success by means of bidirectional LSTM (Peters et al., 2018) and transformers (Radford et al., 2018; Devlin et al., 2018; Yang et al., 2019). In this paper we focus on Skip-Gram (SG), a well-known model for the conditional probability of the context of a given central word, which it has been shown to work well at efficiently capturing syntactic and semantic information. SG is at the basis of many popular word embeddings algorithms, such as Word2Vec (Mikolov et al., 2013a,b), the contpdfinfoinuous bag of words (Mikolov et al., 2013a,b), and models based on weighted matrix factorization of the global co-occurrences as GloVe (Pennington et al., 2014), cf. Levy and Goldberg (2014). These methods are

deeply related, Levy and Goldberg showed how Word2Vec SG with negative sampling is effectively performing a matrix factorization of the Shifted Positive PMI (Levy and Goldberg, 2014).

It has been noted (Mikolov et al., 2013c) how, once the embedding space has been learned, syntactic and semantic analogies between words translate in linear relations between the respective word vectors. There have been numerous works investigating the reason of the correspondence between linear properties and word relations. Pennington et al. gave a very intuitive explanation in their paper on GloVe (Pennington et al., 2014). More recently Arora et al. (Arora et al., 2016) tried to study this property by introducing a hidden Markov model, under some regularity assumptions on the distribution of the word embedding vectors, cf. (Mu et al., 2017). Word embeddings are also often used as input for another computational model, to solve more complex inference tasks. The evaluation of the quality of a word embedding, which ideally should encode syntactic and semantic information, is not easy to be determined and different approaches have been proposed in the literature. This evaluation can be in terms of performance on intrinsic tasks like word similarity (Bullinaria and Levy, 2007, 2012; Pennington et al., 2014; Levy et al., 2015), or by solving word analogies (Mikolov et al., 2013c,a), however several authors (Tsvetkov et al., 2015; Schnabel et al., 2015) has showed a low degree of correlation between the quality of an embedding for word similarities and analogies on one side, and on downstream (extrinsic) tasks, for instance on classification or prediction, to which the embedding is given in input.

Several works have highlighted the effectiveness of post-processing techniques (Bullinaria and Levy, 2007, 2012), such as PCA (Raunak, 2017; Mu et al., 2017), focusing on the fact that certain dominant components are not carriers of semantic nor syn-

61

Proceedings of the 5th Workshop on Representation Learning for NLP (RepL4NLP-2020), pages 61–71
July 9, 2020. ©2020 Association for Computational Linguistics

tactic information and thus act like noise for determinate tasks of interest. A different approach which still acts on the learned vectors after training has been recently proposed by Volpi and Malagò (2019). The authors present a geometrical framework in which word embeddings are represented as vectors in the tangent space of a probability simplex. A family of word embeddings called natural alpha embeddings is introduced, where α is a deformation parameter for the geometry of the probability simplex, known in Information Geometry in the context of α-connections (Amari and Nagaoka, 2000; Amari, 2016). Noticeably, alpha word embeddings include the classical word embeddings as a special case. In this paper we provide an experimental evaluation of natural alpha embeddings over different tasks, both intrinsic and extrinsic, including word similarities and analogies, as well as downstream tasks, such as document classification and sentiment analysis, in order to study the impact of the geometry on performances.

2 Conditional Models and the Embeddings Structure

The Skip-Gram conditional model (Mikolov et al., 2013b; Pennington et al., 2014) allows the unsupervised training of a set of word-embeddings, by predicting the conditional probability of any word χ to be in the context of a central word w

$$p(\chi|w) = p_w(\chi) = \frac{\exp(u_w^{\mathrm{T}} v_\chi)}{Z_w} \qquad (1)$$

with $Z_w = \sum_{\chi' \in \mathscr{D}} \exp(u_w^{\mathrm{T}} v_{\chi'})$ partition function. The conditional model represents an exponential family in the simplex, parameterized by two matrices U and V of size $n \times d$, where n is the cardinality of the dictionary $\mathscr{D}$, and d is the size of the embeddings. We will refer to the rows of a matrix V as v_χ or V^χ, and to its columns as V_k. It is common practice in the literature of word embedding to consider u_w or alternatively $u_w + v_w$ as embedding vectors for w (Bullinaria and Levy, 2012; Mikolov et al., 2013a,b; Pennington et al., 2014; Raunak, 2017). In the remaining part of this section we briefly review the natural alpha embeddings and limit embeddings, based on Information Geometry framework. We refer the reader to Volpi and Malagò (2019) for more details and mathematical derivations.

2.1 Alpha Embeddings

After training, the matrices U and V are fixed. For each w, the conditional model $p_w(\chi)$ is an exponential family $\mathcal{E}$ in the $n-1$ dimensional simplex, where n is the size of the dictionary. This models the probability of a word χ in the context, when w is the central word. The sufficient statistics of this model are determined by the columns of V, while each row u_w of U can be seen as an assignment for the natural parameters, i.e., each row identifies a probability distribution.

According to the language of Information Geometry, a statistical model can be modelled as a Riemannian manifold endowed with the Fisher information matrix and with a family of α-connections (Amari, 1985; Shun-Ichi and Hiroshi, 2000; Amari, 2016). The alpha embeddings are defined up to the choice of a reference distribution p_0. The natural alpha embedding of a given word w is defined as the projection of the logarithmic map $\mathrm{Log}_{p_0}^\alpha \, w$ onto the tangent space of the submodel $\mathrm{T}_{p_0} \mathcal{E}$. The main intuition is that a word embedding for w corresponds to the vector in the tangent space which allows to reach the distribution of the context of w from p_0. Deforming the simplex continuously with a family of isometries depending from a parameter alpha, and by considering a family of α-logarithmic maps, depending on the choice of the α-connection, a family of natural alpha embeddings $W_{p_0}^\alpha(w)$ can be defined as a function of the deformation parameter α

$$W_{p_0}^\alpha(w) = \Pi_0^\alpha \left(\mathrm{Log}_{p_0}^\alpha \, p_w \right)$$
$$= I(p_0)^{-1} \sum_\chi l_{p_0 \, w}^\alpha(\chi) \, \Delta V(p_0)^\chi \qquad (2)$$

where $\Delta V(p_0) = V - \mathrm{E}_{p_0}[V]$ is the matrix of centered sufficient statistics in p_0 and

$$l_{p_0 \, w}^\alpha(\chi) = \begin{cases} p_0(\chi)(\ln p_w(\chi) - \ln p_0(\chi)) & \alpha = 1 \\ p_0(\chi)\frac{2}{1-\alpha} \left(\left(\frac{p_w(\chi)}{p_0(\chi)} \right)^{\frac{1-\alpha}{2}} - 1 \right) & \alpha \neq 1 \end{cases}.$$
$$(3)$$

The Fisher metric is simply computed as the metric for an exponential family (Amari and Nagaoka, 2000)

$$I(p_0) = \mathrm{E}_{p_0} \left[\Delta V(p_0)^{\mathrm{T}} \Delta V(p_0) \right] , \qquad (4)$$

and it does not depend on alpha since the family of alpha divergences induces the same Fisher information metric for any value of alpha.

The notion of alpha embeddings can be used both for downstream tasks and also to evaluate similarities and analogies in the tangent space of the manifold (Volpi and Malagò, 2019). Given two words a and b, a measure of similarity is defined by

$$\text{sim}_{p_0}^\alpha(a, b) = \frac{\langle W_{p_0}^\alpha(a), W_{p_0}^\alpha(b) \rangle_{I(p_0)}}{||W_{p_0}^\alpha(a)||_{I(p_0)} ||W_{p_0}^\alpha(b)||_{I(p_0)}}, \tag{5}$$

while analogies of the form $a : b = c : d$ can be solved by minimizing an analogy measure $\kappa_{p_0}^{(\alpha)}(p_a, p_b, p_c, p_d)$ defined as

$$\left\| W_{p_0}^\alpha(b) - W_{p_0}^\alpha(a) - W_{p_0}^\alpha(d) + W_{p_0}^\alpha(c) \right\|_{I(p_0)}. \tag{6}$$

It is possible to show that for $\alpha = 1$ and choosing p_0 equal to the uniform distribution, the embeddings of Eq. (2) reduce to the standard vectors u_w. Furthermore, by substituting the Fisher Information matrix $I(p_0)$ with the identity[1], Eqs. (5) and (6) reduce to the standard formulas used in the literature for similarities and analogies.

The embedding vectors $u + v$ have been shown to provide better results (Pennington et al., 2014) than simply u. In the context of natural alpha embeddings, the vectors $u + v$ can be interpreted as a recentering of the natural parameters u of the exponential family. This corresponds to a reweighting of the probabilities in Eq. (1)

$$p^{(+)}(\chi|w) = N_w \exp(v_w v_\chi) p(\chi|w) \tag{7}$$

based on a change of reference measure proportional to $\exp(v_w v_\chi)$, i.e., by weighting more those words χ in the context whose outer vectors are aligned to the outer vector of the central word w.

2.2 Limit Embeddings

The behavior of the alpha embeddings for α progressively approaching minus infinity turns out to be particularly interesting. In this case, $l_{p_0\,w}^\alpha(\chi)$ is progressively more and more peaked on

$$\chi_w^* = \arg\max_\chi \frac{p_w(\chi)}{p_0(\chi)}, \tag{8}$$

and presents a growing norm, see Eq. (3). By normalizing these alpha embeddings to preserve the direction of the tangent vector, a simple formula

can be obtained depending only on the χ_w^* row of the matrix of sufficient statistics $\Delta V(p_0)$. The normalized limit embeddings then simplify to

$$\begin{aligned} LW_{p_0}^\alpha(w) &= \lim_{\alpha \to -\infty} W_0^\alpha(w) \\ &= I(p_0)^{-1} \Delta V(p_0)^{\chi_w^*}, \end{aligned} \tag{9}$$

leading to simple geometrical methods in the limit. Let us notice that the same row ΔV^a can be associated to multiple words, thus limit embeddings are also naturally inducing a clustering in the embedding space.

3 Experiments

We considered two corpora: English Wikipedia dump October 2017 (enwiki), with 1.5B words, and its augmented version composed by Gutenberg (Gutenberg), English Wikipedia and BookCorpus (Zhu et al., 2015; BookCorpus; Kobayashi) (geb), with 1.8B words. For each corpus we trained a set of GloVe word embeddings (Pennington et al., 2014) with vector sizes of 300 and 50, window size of 10, until convergence for a maximum of 1,000 epochs (more details in Appendix A).

The embeddings in Eq. (2) will be denoted with 'E' in figures and tables, while the limit embeddings in Eq. (9) will be denoted with 'LE'. Embeddings have been normalized either with the Fisher Information matrix (F) or with the Identity (I). Similarly after normalization, the scalar products can be computed with the respective metric (on the tasks that requires scalar product calculation). In this study, normalization and scalar product are always using the same metric. For the reference distribution needed for the computation of the alpha embeddings we have chosen the uniform distribution (0), the unigram distribution of the model (u) - obtained by marginalization of the joint distribution learned by the model, or the unigram distribution estimated from the corpus data (ud). Embeddings are denoted by 'U', if in the computation of Eqs. (2) and (9), the formula used for p_w is Eq. (1), while they will be denoted by 'U+V' if Eq. (7) is used instead.

We evaluated the alpha embeddings on intrinsic (similarities, analogies, concept categorization) and extrinsic (document classification, sentiment analysis) tasks.

3.1 Intrinsic Tasks

In Fig. 1 we report results for similarities and analogies with embedding size 300. For similarities we use: ws353 (Finkelstein et al., 2001),

---

[1] Proposition 3 in Volpi and Malagò (2019) provides conditions under which Fisher Information matrix is isotropic, i.e., proportional to the identity.

Table 1: Spearman correlations for similarities tasks. WG5 inside the enwiki and geb section are the wikigiga5 pretrained vectors on 6B words (Pennington et al., 2014) tested for comparison on the dictionary of the smaller corpora enwiki and geb. Lastly, U and U+V are the standard methods with the word embeddings vectors. PM are the accuracies reported by Pennington et al. (2014) on enwiki, BDK is the best setup across tasks (varying hyperparameters) reported by Baroni et al. (2014) and LGD are the best methods in cross-validation with fixed window size of 10 and 5 (for varying hyperparameters) reported by Levy et al. (2015).

	method	ws353	mc	rg	scws	ws353sim	ws353rel	men	mturk287	rw	simlex999	all
enwiki	LE-U+V-ud-F	**75.5**	**83.4**	**81.5**	**63.5**	**77.8**	**69.2**	75.6	60.1	**55.6**	41.6	**62.6**
	WG5-U+V	65.1	73.8	77.6	62.2	71.3	60.7	**77.2**	65.7	51.5	41.0	61.3
	U	60.2	69.3	69.8	58.3	67.1	56.4	69.2	67.2	47.1	31.4	53.6
	U+V	63.8	74.5	75.2	58.7	69.5	60.9	71.6	**67.3**	45.5	32.2	55.1
geb	LE-U+V-ud-F	**77.0**	**81.2**	**83.5**	**65.0**	**80.3**	**68.7**	**79.6**	62.4	**59.3**	**46.9**	**65.2**
	WG5-U+V	65.1	73.8	77.9	61.8	71.3	60.7	77.2	65.7	53.2	40.6	60.4
	U	61.3	73.0	76.3	58.7	68.6	54.0	68.7	**68.1**	48.9	30.6	51.9
	U+V	64.9	77.4	79.9	59.1	71.5	58.8	71.4	**68.1**	48.5	32.5	53.7
	PM 6B	65.8	72.7	77.8	53.9	-	-	-	-	38.1	-	-
	BDK	73	-	83	-	78	68	80	-	-	-	-
	LGD win5	-	-	-	-	74.5	61.7	74.6	63.1	41.6	38.9	-
	LGD win10	-	-	-	-	74.6	64.3	75.4	61.6	26.6	37.5	-

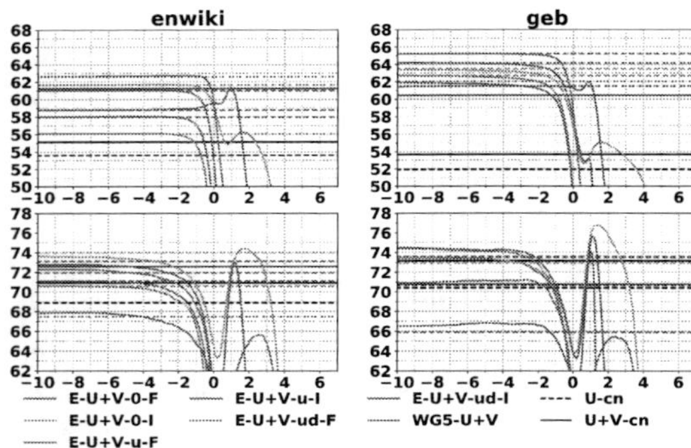

Figure 1: Word similarities (top) and word analogies (bottom) for different values of α.

mc (Miller and Charles, 1991), rg (Rubenstein and Goodenough, 1965), scws (Huang et al., 2012), men (Bruni et al., 2014), mturk287 (Radinsky et al., 2011), rw (Luong et al., 2013) and simlex999 (Hill et al., 2015). For analogies we use the Google analogy dataset (Mikolov et al., 2013a). The limit embeddings (colored dotted lines) achieve good performances on both tasks, above the competitor methods from the literature U and U+V centered and normalized by column, as described in Pennington et al. (2014). Comparison with baseline methods from literature on word similarity is presented in Tables 1, we compare with the limit embeddings since they usually seem to be the best performing on the similarity task, see Fig. 1 top row. The limit embedding methods reported in the table outperform Wiki Giga 5 pretrained vectors (Pennington et al., 2014) (6B words corpus)

and other comparable baselines from the literature with similar window size. In Table 2 we report

Table 2: Analogy tasks for the different methods on enwiki and geb. The best alpha is selected with a 3-fold cross validation (α between -10 and 10), unless the limit embedding is the best performing. PM are the accuracies reported by Pennington et al. (2014) on enwiki, BDK is the best setup across tasks (varying hyperparameters) reported by Baroni et al. (2014).

	method	sem	syn	tot
enwiki	E-U+V-0-I	**84.5** ± 0.4	67.33 ± 0.6	**74.4** ± 0.1
	WG5-U+V	79.4	**67.5**	72.6
	U	77.8	62.1	68.9
	U+V	80.9	63.4	70.9
geb	E-U+V-0-I	**83.8** ± 0.4	**72.2** ± 0.4	**76.7** ± 0.3
	WG5-U+V	78.7	65.2	70.7
	U	75.7	66.8	70.4
	U+V	80.0	68.5	73.2
	PM 1.6B	80.8	61.5	70.3
	PM 6B	77.4	67.0	71.7
	BDK	80.0	68.5	73.2

best performances on analogy task on alpha embeddings, where alpha is selected with cross-validation (Table 3). For enwiki syn, the limit embedding has been found to work better instead. The errors reported are obtained averaging the performances on test of the top three alpha selected based on best performances on validation. The errors obtained are relatively small which indicates that tuning alpha is easy also on tasks with small amount of data in cross-validation. The best tuned alpha on the geb dataset completely outperform the baselines.

The last intrinsic tasks considered are cluster purity for concept categorization datasets AP (Almuhareb, 2006) and BLESS (Baroni and Lenci, 2011). The purity curves (Fig. 2) are more noisy, this is because the datasets available for this task are quite limited in size. Almost all the curves exhibit a peak which is relatively more pronounced for smaller embedding sizes, while the limit behaviour for very negative alphas is better performing for larger embedding size. This points to the fact that the natural clustering performed by the limit embeddings of Eq. 9 is better behaved when the dimension of the embedding grows. Increasing the embedding size, increases the number of sufficient statistics, thus allowing more flexibility for the limit clustering during training.

Table 3: Best cross-validated alphas for methods of Table 2 (enwiki and geb).

	method	sem	syn	tot
en	E-U+V-0-I	1.8 ± 0.1	$-\infty$	1.7 ± 0.1
geb	E-U+V-0-I	1.7 ± 0.1	1.3 ± 0.1	1.3 ± 0.1

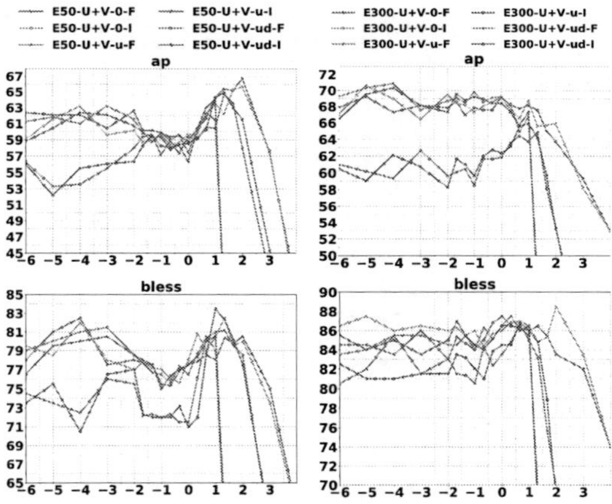

Figure 2: Cluster purity on concept categorization task.

3.2 Extrinsic Tasks

As extrinsic tasks we choose 20 Newsgroup multi classification (Lang, 1995) and IMDBReviews sentiment analysis (Maas et al., 2011). Embeddings are normalized before training either with I or F. We use a linear architecture (BatchNorm+Dense) for both tasks, while for sentiment analysis we also use a recurrent architecture (Bidirectional LSTM 32 channels, GlobalMaxPool1D, Dense 20 + Dropout 0.05, Dense). In Tables 4 and 5 we report the best methods chosen with respect to the validation set and the best limit embedding performances for embedding size 300. A more complete set of

experiments can be found in Appendix. Limit Embeddings have been generalized, instead of considering only the max row χ^* (see Sec. 2.2), by considered the top k rows from ΔV. Limit embeddings are evaluated with respect to top 1, 3, and 5, denoted -t1/3/5. Furthermore we denote by -w if a weighted average (with weights $p_w(\chi)/p_0(\chi)$) is performed for the top rows of ΔV. The improvements reported in the Tables are small but consistent, of above 0.5% accuracy on both Newsgroups and IMDBReviews, furthermore the improvement persist also with increased complexity of the network architecture (bidirectional LSTM). Fig. 3

Table 4: AUC and accuracy on test of 20 Newsgroups multiclass classification, compared to baseline vectors. Best alpha and best limit method (on validation) are reported in parenthesis.

method	20 Newsgroups	
	AUC	acc
U+V	96.34	65.06
E-U+V-0-F	96.76 (0.2)	65.86 (0.4)
E-U+V-u-F	96.79 (0.2)	66.30 (0.2)
E-U+V-ud-F	96.79 (0.4)	65.24 (0.6)
LE-U+V-0-F	96.65 (t3-w)	64.47 (t1)
LE-U+V-u-F	96.65 (t3-w)	64.54 (t1)
LE-U+V-ud-F	96.38 (t5-w)	64.76 (t3-w)

Table 5: Accuracy on test of IMDBReviews sentiment analysis binary classification, with linear and with BiLSTM architecture, compared to baseline vectors. Best alpha and best limit method (on validation), are reported in parenthesis.

method	IMDB Reviews	
	acc lin	acc BiLSTM
U+V	83.76	88.00
E-U+V-0-F	83.58 (2.4)	88.12 (-4.0)
E-U+V-u-F	83.72 (-3.0)	88.56 (-4.0)
E-U+V-ud-F	84.23 (-3.0)	88.48 (-2.2)
LE-U+V-0-F	84.00 (t1)	88.36 (t1)
LE-U+V-u-F	84.29 (t1)	88.66 (t1)
LE-U+V-ud-F	84.00 (t3-w)	88.49 (t3-w)

reports curves for the values on test with early stopping based on validation for embedding sizes of 50 and 300. The improvements for tuning alpha are higher on size 50 exhibiting a more evident peak. For size 300 improvements are smaller but consistent. In particular a peak performance for alpha can be always easily identified for a chosen reference distribution and a chosen normalization.

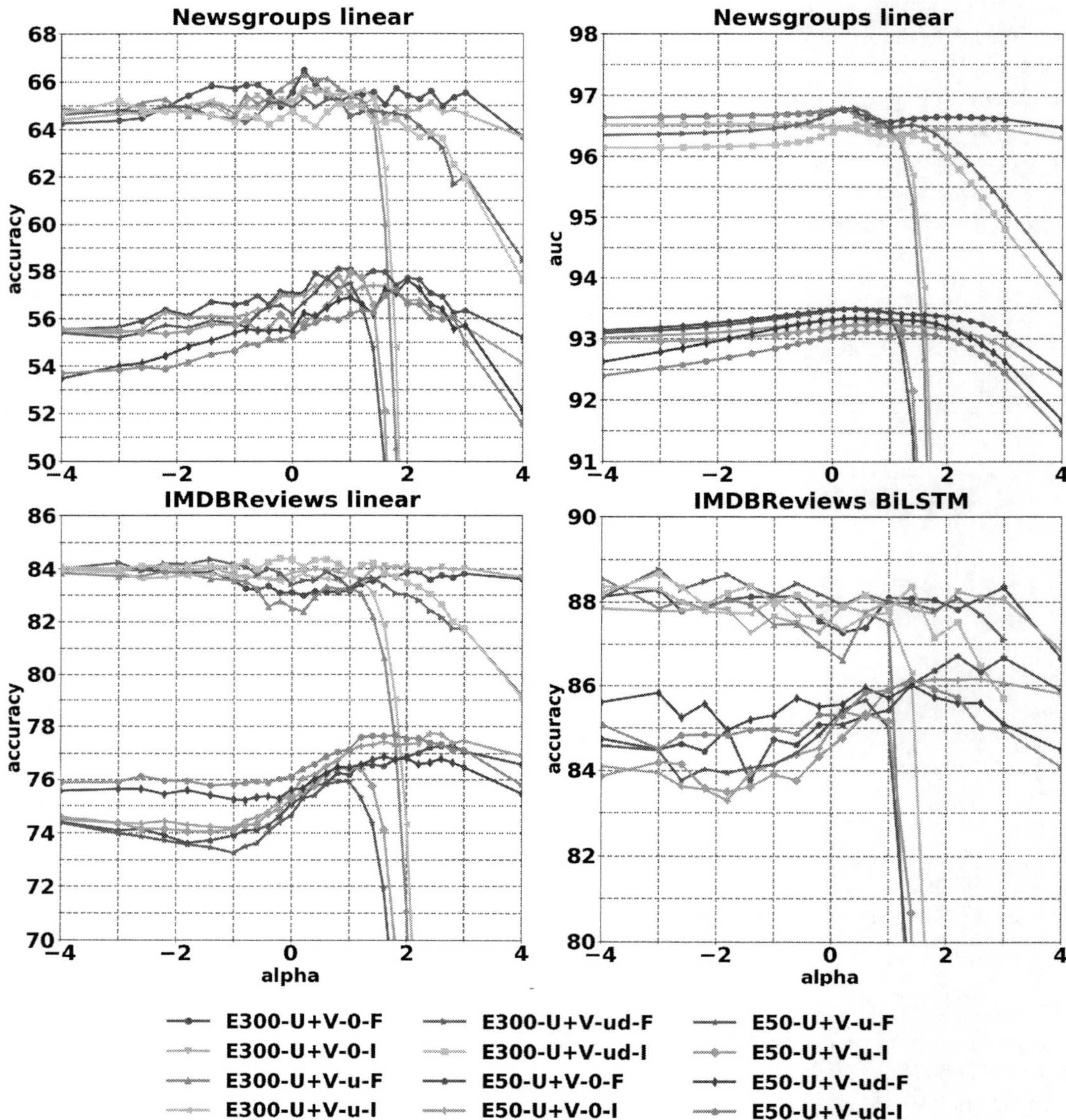

Figure 3: Performances on 20 Newsgroups and IMDB Reviews for varying alphas. Metrics I and F refers to embeddings normalization before training.

4 Conclusions

For word similarities and analogies alpha embeddings provide significant improvements over baseline methods (corresponding to $\alpha = 1$). For the other tasks the improvements are smaller but consistent, depending on the value of α, the chosen reference distribution (0, u, ud) and the chosen normalization method (I, F). The improvements persist also when increasing the complexity of the networks used (linear vs BiLSTM). This motivates further studies on more complex architectures, for example on models employing transformers with the aim to close the experimental gap with the state of the art.

The best value of alpha depends both on the task and on the dataset. Alpha embeddings thus provide an extra handle on the optimization problem, allowing to choose the deformation parameter based on data. Alpha values lower than 1 and negative seems to be preferred across most tasks. Limit embeddings provide a simple method which does not require validation over alpha, but can still offer an improvement on several tasks of interest. Furthermore limit embeddings can be interpreted as a natural clustering in space learned by the SG model itself during training. Performances of the limit embeddings grow with increasing dimension, pointing to the possibility to have a consistent improvement in higher embedding dimensions without tuning alpha.

Acknowledgments

R. Volpi and L. Malagò are supported by the Deep-Riemann project, co-funded by the European Regional Development Fund and the Romanian Government through the Competitiveness Operational Programme 2014-2020, Action 1.1.4, project ID P_37_714, contract no. 136/27.09.2016.

References

Abdulrahman Almuhareb. 2006. *Attributes in lexical acquisition*. Ph.D. thesis, University of Essex.

Shun-ichi Amari. 1985. *Differential-geometrical methods in statistics*, volume 28 of *Lecture Notes in Statistics*. Springer-Verlag, New York.

Shun-ichi Amari. 2016. *Information Geometry and Its Applications*, volume 194 of *Applied Mathematical Sciences*. Springer Japan, Tokyo.

Shun-ichi Amari and Hiroshi Nagaoka. 2000. *Methods of information geometry*. American Mathematical Society, Providence, RI. Translated from the 1993 Japanese original by Daishi Harada.

Sanjeev Arora, Yuanzhi Li, Yingyu Liang, Tengyu Ma, and Andrej Risteski. 2016. Rand-walk: A latent variable model approach to word embeddings. *arXiv preprint arXiv:1502.03520*.

Attardi. Wikiextractor: A tool for extracting plain text from wikipedia dumps. https://github.com/attardi/wikiextractor. Accessed: 2017-10.

Marco Baroni, Georgiana Dinu, and Germán Kruszewski. 2014. Don't count, predict! a systematic comparison of context-counting vs. context-predicting semantic vectors. In *Proceedings of the 52nd Annual Meeting of the Association for Computational Linguistics (Volume 1: Long Papers)*, pages 238–247.

Marco Baroni and Alessandro Lenci. 2011. How we blessed distributional semantic evaluation. In *Proceedings of the GEMS 2011 Workshop on GEometrical Models of Natural Language Semantics*, pages 1–10. Association for Computational Linguistics.

Yoshua Bengio, Réjean Ducharme, Pascal Vincent, and Christian Jauvin. 2003. A neural probabilistic language model. *Journal of machine learning research*, 3(Feb):1137–1155.

BookCorpus. Aligning books and movie: Towards story-like visual explanations by watching movies and reading books. https://yknzhu.wixsite.com/mbweb. Accessed: 2019-09.

Elia Bruni, Nam-Khanh Tran, and Marco Baroni. 2014. Multimodal distributional semantics. *Journal of artificial intelligence research*, 49:1–47.

John A. Bullinaria and Joseph P. Levy. 2007. Extracting semantic representations from word co-occurrence statistics: A computational study. *Behavior Research Methods*, 39(3):510–526.

John A. Bullinaria and Joseph P. Levy. 2012. Extracting semantic representations from word co-occurrence statistics: stop-lists, stemming, and SVD. *Behavior Research Methods*, 44(3):890–907.

Jacob Devlin, Ming-Wei Chang, Kenton Lee, and Kristina Toutanova. 2018. BERT: Pre-training of Deep Bidirectional Transformers for Language Understanding. *arXiv:1810.04805 [cs]*. ArXiv: 1810.04805.

Lev Finkelstein, Evgeniy Gabrilovich, Yossi Matias, Ehud Rivlin, Zach Solan, Gadi Wolfman, and Eytan Ruppin. 2001. Placing search in context: The concept revisited. In *Proceedings of the 10th international conference on World Wide Web*, pages 406–414.

Gutenberg. Free ebooks - project gutenberg. https://www.gutenberg.org. Accessed: 2019-09.

Felix Hill, Roi Reichart, and Anna Korhonen. 2015. Simlex-999: Evaluating semantic models with (genuine) similarity estimation. *Computational Linguistics*, 41(4):665–695.

Eric H Huang, Richard Socher, Christopher D Manning, and Andrew Y Ng. 2012. Improving word representations via global context and multiple word prototypes. In *Proceedings of the 50th Annual Meeting of the Association for Computational Linguistics: Long Papers-Volume 1*, pages 873–882. Association for Computational Linguistics.

Sosuke Kobayashi. Homemade bookcorpus. https://github.com/soskek/bookcorpus. Accessed: 2019.

Ken Lang. 1995. Newsweeder: Learning to filter netnews. In *Machine Learning Proceedings 1995*, pages 331–339. Elsevier.

Omer Levy and Yoav Goldberg. 2014. Neural word embedding as implicit matrix factorization. In *Advances in neural information processing systems*, pages 2177–2185.

Omer Levy, Yoav Goldberg, and Ido Dagan. 2015. Improving distributional similarity with lessons learned from word embeddings. *Transactions of the Association for Computational Linguistics*, 3:211–225.

Minh-Thang Luong, Richard Socher, and Christopher D Manning. 2013. Better word representations with recursive neural networks for morphology. In *Proceedings of the Seventeenth Conference on Computational Natural Language Learning*, pages 104–113.

Andrew L Maas, Raymond E Daly, Peter T Pham, Dan Huang, Andrew Y Ng, and Christopher Potts. 2011. Learning word vectors for sentiment analysis. In *Proceedings of the 49th annual meeting of the association for computational linguistics: Human language technologies-volume 1*, pages 142–150. Association for Computational Linguistics.

Tomas Mikolov, Kai Chen, Greg Corrado, and Jeffrey Dean. 2013a. Efficient estimation of word representations in vector space. *arXiv preprint arXiv:1301.3781*.

Tomáš Mikolov, Martin Karafiát, Lukáš Burget, Jan Černocký, and Sanjeev Khudanpur. 2010. Recurrent neural network based language model. In *Eleventh annual conference of the international speech communication association*.

Tomas Mikolov, Ilya Sutskever, Kai Chen, Greg S. Corrado, and Jeff Dean. 2013b. Distributed representations of words and phrases and their compositionality. In *Advances in neural information processing systems*, pages 3111–3119.

Tomas Mikolov, Wen-tau Yih, and Geoffrey Zweig. 2013c. Linguistic regularities in continuous space word representations. In *NAACL-HLT*, pages 746–751.

George A Miller and Walter G Charles. 1991. Contextual correlates of semantic similarity. *Language and cognitive processes*, 6(1):1–28.

Jiaqi Mu, Suma Bhat, and Pramod Viswanath. 2017. All-but-the-Top: Simple and Effective Postprocessing for Word Representations. *arXiv:1702.01417 [cs, stat]*. ArXiv: 1702.01417.

Jeffrey Pennington, Richard Socher, and Christopher Manning. 2014. Glove: Global vectors for word representation. In *Proceedings of the 2014 conference on empirical methods in natural language processing (EMNLP)*, pages 1532–1543.

Matthew E. Peters, Mark Neumann, Mohit Iyyer, Matt Gardner, Christopher Clark, Kenton Lee, and Luke Zettlemoyer. 2018. Deep contextualized word representations. *arXiv:1802.05365 [cs]*. ArXiv: 1802.05365.

Alec Radford, Karthik Narasimhan, Tim Salimans, and Ilya Sutskever. 2018. Improving language understanding by generative pre-training. *URL https://s3-us-west-2. amazonaws. com/openai-assets/researchcovers/languageunsupervised/language understanding paper. pdf*.

Kira Radinsky, Eugene Agichtein, Evgeniy Gabrilovich, and Shaul Markovitch. 2011. A word at a time: computing word relatedness using temporal semantic analysis. In *Proceedings of the 20th international conference on World wide web*, pages 337–346.

Vikas Raunak. 2017. Simple and Effective Dimensionality Reduction for Word Embeddings. *arXiv:1708.03629 [cs]*. ArXiv: 1708.03629.

Herbert Rubenstein and John B Goodenough. 1965. Contextual correlates of synonymy. *Communications of the ACM*, 8(10):627–633.

David E. Rumelhart, Geoffrey E. Hinton, and Ronald J. Williams. 1986. Learning representations by back-propagating errors. *Nature*, 323(6088):533–536.

Tobias Schnabel, Igor Labutov, David Mimno, and Thorsten Joachims. 2015. Evaluation methods for unsupervised word embeddings. In *Proceedings of the 2015 Conference on Empirical Methods in Natural Language Processing*, pages 298–307, Lisbon, Portugal. Association for Computational Linguistics.

Amari Shun-Ichi and Nagaoka Hiroshi. 2000. *(Translations of mathematical monographs 191) Methods of information geometry*. American Mathematical Society.

Yulia Tsvetkov, Manaal Faruqui, Wang Ling, Guillaume Lample, and Chris Dyer. 2015. Evaluation of word vector representations by subspace alignment. In *Proceedings of the 2015 Conference on Empirical Methods in Natural Language Processing*, pages 2049–2054, Lisbon, Portugal. Association for Computational Linguistics.

Riccardo Volpi and Luigi Malagò. 2019. Natural alpha embeddings. ArXiv:1912.02280.

Zhilin Yang, Zihang Dai, Yiming Yang, Jaime G. Carbonell, Ruslan Salakhutdinov, and Quoc V. Le. 2019. Xlnet: Generalized autoregressive pretraining for language understanding. *ArXiv*, abs/1906.08237.

Yukun Zhu, Ryan Kiros, Rich Zemel, Ruslan Salakhutdinov, Raquel Urtasun, Antonio Torralba, and Sanja Fidler. 2015. Aligning books and movies: Towards story-like visual explanations by watching movies and reading books. In *Proceedings of the IEEE international conference on computer vision*, pages 19–27.

A   Additional Details

We have performed experiments using two corpora: english Wikipedia dump October 2017 (enwiki) and also we augmented this last one with Guthenberg(Gutenberg) and BookCorpus(BookCorpus; Kobayashi) calling this geb (guthenberg, enwiki, bookcorpus). We used the wikiextractor python script(Attardi) to parse the Wikipedia dump xml file. A minimal preprocessing have been used: lower case all the letters, remove stop-words and remove punctuation. We use a cut-off minimum frequency ($m0$) of 1000 during GloVe training (Pennington et al., 2014). We obtained a dictionary of about 67k words for both enwiki and geb. The window size was set to be 10 as in (Pennington et al., 2014), with decaying weighting rate from the center of $1/d$ for the calculation of cooccurrences. We trained the models for a maximum of 1000 epochs. Embedding sizes used are 50 and 300.

Table 6: AUC on Newsgroups with linear architecture (BatchNorm + Dense). We use geb embeddings, fixed during the classifiers training. The alpha for which to report performances on test is chosen based on the best measure on the validation set and we report both performances on validation and on test (α between -4 and 4 with adaptive step: 0.2 between [-1, 1] and 0.4 in between [-3, 3] and 1 between [-4, 4]). We also report limit embedding performances.

method	AUC val	AUC test
E-U+V-0-I ($\alpha = 1.0$)	0.96347	0.96342
E-U+V-0-F ($\alpha = 0.2$)	0.96765	0.9676
E-U+V-u-F ($\alpha = 0.2$)	0.96792	0.96787
E-U+V-ud-F ($\alpha = 0.4$)	0.96798	0.96792
LE-U+V-0-F-t3-w	0.9666	0.96654
LE-U+V-u-F-t3-w	0.96662	0.96655
LE-U+V-ud-F-t5-w	0.96388	0.96381

Table 7: Accuracy on Newsgroups (BatchNorm + Dense).

method	accuracy val	accuracy test
E-U+V-0-I ($\alpha = 1.0$)	0.66846	0.65056
E-U+V-0-F ($\alpha = 0.4$)	0.67708	0.65858
E-U+V-u-F ($\alpha = 0.2$)	0.68068	0.66298
E-U+V-ud-F ($\alpha = 0.6$)	0.67744	0.65242
LE-U+V-0-F-t1	0.66739	0.64472
LE-U+V-u-F-t1	0.66954	0.64545
LE-U+V-ud-F-t3-w	0.6602	0.64763

Table 8: Accuracy on IMDBReviews with linear architecture (BatchNorm + Dense).

method	accuracy val	accuracy test
E-U+V-0-I ($\alpha = 1.0$)	0.83426	0.83758
E-U+V-0-F ($\alpha = 2.4$)	0.83574	0.83582
E-U+V-u-F ($\alpha = -3.0$)	0.83434	0.83721
E-U+V-ud-F ($\alpha = -3.0$)	0.8360	0.8423
LE-U+V-0-F-t1-f	0.8351	0.84001
LE-U+V-u-F-t1-wf	0.83724	0.84293
LE-U+V-ud-F-t3-wf	0.83493	0.84001

Table 9: Accuracy on IMDBReviews with BiLSTM-pool architecture (Bidirectional LSTM 32 channels, GlobalMaxPool1D, Dense 20 + Dropout 0.05, Dense).

method	accuracy val	accuracy test
E-U+V-0-I ($\alpha = 1.0$)	0.87813	0.88002
E-U+V-0-F ($\alpha = -4.0$)	0.88066	0.88117
E-U+V-u-F ($\alpha = -4.0$)	0.88173	0.88565
E-U+V-ud-F ($\alpha = -2.2$)	0.88366	0.88481
LE-U+V-0-F-t1	0.88258	0.88365
LE-U+V-u-F-t1	0.87761	0.88656
LE-U+V-ud-F-t1	0.88117	0.8825

Table 10: Spearman correlations for similarities tasks for the different methods on enwiki and geb. LE represents the cos product between limit embeddings on the exponential family model. WG5 inside the enwiki and geb section are the wikigiga5 pretrained vectors on 6B words (Pennington et al., 2014) tested for comparison on the dictionary of the smaller corpora enwiki and geb. Lastly, U and U+V are the non-geometric methods with the word embeddings vectors.

	method	ws353	mc	rg	scws	ws353sim	ws353rel	men	mturk287	rw	simlex999	all
enwiki	LE-U+V-0-F	70.7	77.2	77.3	64.0	75.7	66.6	74.7	68.7	54.2	37.7	61.0
	LE-U+V-0-I	72.1	82.7	81.3	64.2	76.5	67.1	74.8	65.9	54.8	40.0	61.7
	LE-U+V-u-F	69.6	77.1	77.5	63.6	74.7	65.2	74.5	**69.1**	54.1	36.7	60.5
	LE-U+V-u-I	72.5	81.9	**81.7**	**64.3**	76.7	67.8	75.6	67.7	**55.9**	39.1	62.1
	LE-U+V-ud-F	**75.5**	**83.4**	81.5	63.5	**77.8**	**69.2**	75.6	60.1	55.6	**41.6**	**62.6**
	LE-U+V-ud-I	68.6	82.9	78.9	59.3	73.6	57.2	71.3	50.3	53.8	**41.6**	58.8
	WG5-U+V	65.1	73.8	77.6	62.2	71.3	60.7	**77.2**	65.7	51.5	41.0	61.3
	U	60.2	69.3	69.8	58.3	67.1	56.4	69.2	67.2	47.1	31.4	53.6
	U+V	63.8	74.5	75.2	58.7	69.5	60.9	71.6	67.3	45.5	32.2	55.1
geb	LE-U+V-0-F	72.9	80.5	83.9	65.4	78.6	66.3	77.2	**70.7**	57.6	39.6	62.0
	LE-U+V-0-I	74.3	**82.2**	84.6	**66.0**	79.3	67.1	78.0	67.3	58.6	43.4	63.5
	LE-U+V-u-F	74.1	81.4	84.6	65.8	79.9	67.5	78.2	70.4	57.7	40.4	62.7
	LE-U+V-u-I	75.7	82.1	**84.8**	**66.0**	**80.5**	68.2	79.2	67.0	58.8	44.1	64.1
	LE-U+V-ud-F	**77.0**	81.2	83.5	65.0	80.3	**68.7**	**79.6**	62.4	**59.3**	46.9	**65.2**
	LE-U+V-ud-I	71.5	78.2	79.9	60.9	76.8	58.9	74.7	52.4	57.2	**48.1**	61.5
	WG5-U+V	65.1	73.8	77.9	61.8	71.3	60.7	77.2	65.7	53.2	40.6	60.4
	U	61.3	73.0	76.3	58.7	68.6	54.0	68.7	68.1	48.9	30.6	51.9
	U+V	64.9	77.4	79.9	59.1	71.5	58.8	71.4	68.1	48.5	32.5	53.7

Table 11: Analogy tasks for the different methods on enwiki and geb. The best alpha is selected with a 3-fold cross validation (α between -10 and 10). The methods reported are implementing either euclidean normalization (I) or normalization with the Fisher (F) in different points on the manifold (0, u). Scalar products (-p) are always calculated with respect to the Identity in this table (I).

corpus	method	semantic		syntactic		total	
		alpha	acc	alpha	acc	alpha	acc
enwiki 1.5B	E-U+V-0-nF-pI	1.7 ± 0.1	**85.7 ± 0.3**	-9.5 ± 0.5	65.9 ± 0.4	-9.5 ± 0.5	73.6 ± 0.4
	E-U+V-0-nI-pI	1.8 ± 0.0	84.6 ± 0.4	-2.2 ± 5.5	66.6 ± 0.3	1.7 ± 0.1	**74.4 ± 0.1**
	E-U+V-u-nF-pI	-7.2 ± 3.3	81.8 ± 0.2	-9.5 ± 0.7	65.7 ± 0.5	-9.5 ± 0.7	72.7 ± 0.4
	E-U+V-u-nI-pI	-8.5 ± 0.3	82.3 ± 0.4	-9.1 ± 1.2	67.1 ± 0.4	-8.5 ± 1.1	73.6 ± 0.4
	LE-U+V-0-nF-pI	$-\infty$	83.4	$-\infty$	66.9	$-\infty$	74.0
	LE-U+V-0-nI-pI	$-\infty$	82.8	$-\infty$	67.3	$-\infty$	74.0
	LE-U+V-u-nF-pI	$-\infty$	81.6	$-\infty$	66.2	$-\infty$	72.8
	LE-U+V-u-nI-pI	$-\infty$	82.0	$-\infty$	**67.5**	$-\infty$	73.7
	WG5-U+V	n/a	79.4	n/a	**67.5**	n/a	72.6
	U	n/a	77.8	n/a	62.1	n/a	68.9
	U+V	n/a	80.9	n/a	63.4	n/a	70.9
geb 1.8B	E-U+V-0-nF-pI	1.9 ± 0.2	**84.6 ± 0.3**	-8.5 ± 2.0	68.1 ± 0.2	-9.9 ± 0.1	73.8 ± 0.3
	E-U+V-0-nI-pI	1.7 ± 0.1	83.8 ± 0.4	1.3 ± 0.1	**72.2 ± 0.4**	1.3 ± 0.1	**76.7 ± 0.3**
	E-U+V-u-nF-pI	-9.1 ± 1.3	80.0 ± 0.2	-9.7 ± 0.4	69.7 ± 0.4	-9.7 ± 0.4	73.9 ± 0.3
	E-U+V-u-nI-pI	1.0 ± 0.0	81.8 ± 0.3	-2.1 ± 4.4	70.3 ± 0.8	1.0 ± 0.0	75.2 ± 0.2
	LE-U+V-0-nF-pI	$-\infty$	82.1	$-\infty$	67.1	$-\infty$	73.2
	LE-U+V-0-nI-pI	$-\infty$	81.2	$-\infty$	67.3	$-\infty$	72.9
	LE-U+V-u-nF-pI	$-\infty$	80.1	$-\infty$	68.0	$-\infty$	72.9
	LE-U+V-u-nI-pI	$-\infty$	80.9	$-\infty$	68.5	$-\infty$	73.5
	WG5-U+V	n/a	78.7	n/a	65.2	n/a	70.7
	U	n/a	75.7	n/a	66.8	n/a	70.4
	U+V	n/a	80.0	n/a	68.5	n/a	73.2

Exploring the Limits of Simple Learners in Knowledge Distillation for Document Classification with DocBERT

Ashutosh Adhikari[†], Achyudh Ram[†], Raphael Tang[†],
William L. Hamilton[‡], Jimmy Lin[†]

[†]David R. Cheriton School of Computer Science, University of Waterloo
[‡] Mila, McGill University
{adadhika, arkeshav, r33tang, jimmylin}@uwaterloo.ca
wlh@cs.mcgill.ca

Abstract

Fine-tuned variants of BERT are able to achieve state-of-the-art accuracy on many natural language processing tasks, although at significant computational costs. In this paper, we verify BERT's effectiveness for document classification and investigate the extent to which BERT-level effectiveness can be obtained by different baselines, combined with knowledge distillation—a popular model compression method. The results show that BERT-level effectiveness can be achieved by a single-layer LSTM with at least $40\times$ fewer FLOPS and only $\sim 3\%$ parameters. More importantly, this study analyzes the limits of knowledge distillation as we distill BERT's knowledge all the way down to linear models—a relevant baseline for the task. We report substantial improvement in effectiveness for even the simplest models, as they capture the knowledge learnt by BERT.

1 Introduction

Transformer-based (Vaswani et al., 2017) pretrained contextual word embedding models such as BERT (Devlin et al., 2019) and XLNet (Yang et al., 2019) currently power many of the state-of-the-art models across various natural language processing (NLP) tasks. However, these models consume immense computational resources (Strubell et al., 2019). With the surge of such pre-trained models being developed in quick succession, there is a need for effective compression techniques for their inexpensive deployment.

Knowledge distillation (KD; Hinton et al. 2015; Ba and Caruana 2014) has been shown to be a fairly straightforward and effective model-agnostic compression method, which transfers knowledge learnt by huge models into more efficient models. In this work, we investigate if BERT-level effectiveness can be achieved by more efficient models using KD. And more importantly, if so, *how simple* can these models be?

We investigate these questions through the lens of document classification—a setting where these computational concerns are particularly relevant due to potentially long document lengths. Further, in previous work, neural networks as an architectural choice have been questioned owing to the effectiveness of simple bag-of-words baselines (Adhikari et al., 2019).

We first confirm that a fine-tuned BERT model leads to state-of-the-art model quality by a substantial margin on standard document classification benchmarks. Following this, we investigate the extent to which BERT-level effectiveness can be obtained by various different baselines, combined with KD. We demonstrate, quite surprisingly, that it is possible to apply KD successfully on impoverished student models, such as a single-layer convolutional neural network (CNN) (Kim, 2014) and even linear models. The key contributions of this work are as follows:

1. We develop and release[*] a fine-tuned BERT model (DocBERT), which achieves state-of-the-art model quality for document classification. While this finding is perhaps obvious, we carefully document experimental results.

2. We explore the limits of KD from BERT by distilling to substantially simpler and more efficient baselines than previous work (e.g., logistic regression). We are the first, to our knowledge, to demonstrate the working of KD all the way down to linear models.

3. We show that an LSTM baseline ($40\times$ faster than $BERT_{base}$), combined with KD can achieve BERT-level model quality.

---

[*] https://github.com/castorini/hedwig

Proceedings of the 5th Workshop on Representation Learning for NLP (RepL4NLP-2020), pages 72–77
July 9, 2020. ©2020 Association for Computational Linguistics

2 Background and Methods

Typically, the task of document classification deals with classifying long texts (documents). More often than not, a document may be associated with more than one label, thus exposing the classifiers to multi-label classification and class imbalance. Here, we review a subset of approaches developed to solve the task and highlight the methods that we compare and build upon in this work.

2.1 Document Classification Models

Neural network-based models. In recent years neural network-based architectures have dominated the task of document classification. Many researchers (Kim, 2014; Conneau et al., 2017; Johnson and Zhang, 2017) show convolutional neural networks to be effective for classifying single-label short texts. Furthermore, Liu et al. (2017) develop a variant of the popular KimCNN (Kim, 2014), XML-CNN, for addressing the multi-label nature of document classification, which they call extreme classification. Alternatively, others (Yang et al., 2016; Adhikari et al., 2019; Yang et al., 2018) show effective use of recurrent neural networks to exploit semantic representations by treating documents as a sequence of words or sentences for classification. In this work, we explore several neural baseline models and use both LSTM (Hochreiter and Schmidhuber, 1997) and KimCNN architectures for knowledge distillation experiments.

Non-neural models. Logistic regression (LR) and support vector machines (SVM) trained on tf–idf vectors form efficient and effective baselines for document classification. Adhikari et al. (2019) show LR and SVM surpass most of the neural baselines on multiple datasets, questioning the need for employing neural networks to model syntactic structure for document classification. Here, we explore both LR and SVMs, and we perform knowledge distillation experiments using an LR model.

Large-scale pre-training. Recent work (Howard and Ruder, 2018; Devlin et al., 2019; Yang et al., 2019) has demonstrated the effectiveness of large-scale pre-training for NLP tasks. In this work, we use BERT as a representative of this approach and demonstrate the power of fine-tuned BERT on document classification (termed DocBERT).

2.2 Knowledge Distillation

Knowledge distillation (KD; Hinton et al., 2015; Ba and Caruana, 2014) is an effective model-agnostic approach to model compression, where an efficient *student* model captures the knowledge learnt by privileged but cumbersome *teacher* model(s). The knowledge transfer takes place by forcing the *student* to mimic the soft target probabilities of the teacher. Hinton et al. (2015) highlight that it is in the interest of the generalizability of the *student* model to capture the exact class probabilities from a better model, the *teacher*. In supervised settings, the *student* is trained using a distillation objective in combination with the classification objective:

$$\mathcal{L} = \mathcal{L}_{classification} + \lambda \cdot \mathcal{L}_{distill} \qquad (1)$$

where λ is a hyperparameter chosen to weigh the two different optimization objectives. The $\mathcal{L}_{classification}$ term is the task-specific classification loss, which is most often the cross-entropy loss between the logits of the *student* model and the target labels, while the distillation term $\mathcal{L}_{distill}$ quantifies the difference between the student predictions and the teacher. In this work, we use a fine-tuned BERT model as the teacher and experiment with various baseline architectures for the students. Following Hinton et al. (2015), we set $\mathcal{L}_{distill}$ to be equal to the Kullback–Leibler divergence between the class probabilities output by the *student* and the *teacher* BERT model.

3 Datasets

We use the following four datasets to evaluate BERT: Reuters-21578 (Reuters; Apté et al., 1994), arXiv Academic Paper dataset (AAPD; Yang et al., 2018), IMDB reviews, and Yelp 2014 reviews. Reuters and AAPD are multi-label datasets while documents in IMDB and Yelp '14 contain only a single label per document. Table 1 summarizes the statistics of these datasets.

For Reuters, we use the standard ModApté splits (Apté et al., 1994); for AAPD, we use the

Dataset	C	N	W	S
Reuters	90	10,789	144.3	6.6
AAPD	54	55,840	167.3	1.0
IMDB	10	135,669	393.8	14.4
Yelp 2014	5	1,125,386	148.8	9.1

Table 1: Summary of the datasets. C denotes the number of classes in the dataset, N the number of samples, and W and S the average number of words and sentences per document, respectively.

splits provided by Yang et al. (2018); for IMDB and Yelp, following Yang et al. (2016), we randomly sample 80% of the data for training and 10% each for validation and test.

4 Training and Hyperparameters

As a simple and straightforward adaptation of BERT models (Devlin et al., 2019) for document classification, we introduce a fully-connected layer over the final hidden state corresponding to the [CLS] input token. During fine-tuning, we optimize the entire model end-to-end, with the additional softmax classifier parameters $W \in \mathbf{R}^{K \times H}$, where H is the dimension of the hidden state vectors and K is the number of classes. We minimize the cross-entropy and binary cross-entropy loss for single-label and multi-label tasks, respectively. While fine-tuning BERT, we optimize the number of epochs, batch size, learning rate, and maximum sequence length (MSL; i.e., the number of tokens that documents are truncated to).

For knowledge distillation, we train the LSTM, KimCNN, and LR to capture the learnt representations from $BERT_{large}$ using the objective of the type shown in Equation (1). Depending upon the dataset, we use cross-entropy or binary cross-entropy loss as $\mathcal{L}_{classification}$, Equation (1). For $\mathcal{L}_{distill}$, following Hinton et al. (2015), we minimize the Kullback–Leibler (KL) divergence $KL(p||q)$ where p and q are the class probabilities produced by the student and the teacher models, respectively.

To build an effective transfer set for distillation as suggested by Ba and Caruana (2014), we augment the training splits of the datasets by applying POS-guided word swapping and random masking, as in Tang et al. (2019), along with randomizing the order of the sentences of documents in the training set. The transfer set sizes for Reuters, IMDB and AAPD are 3×, 4×, and 4× their training splits, respectively; for Yelp2014, no data augmentation was performed due to computational restrictions. Refer to the appendix for further details regarding the training hyperparameters.

5 Results and Discussion

In Table 2, which shows our main results, we report the mean F_1 scores for multi-label datasets and accuracy for single-label datasets, along with the corresponding standard deviation across five runs. Due to their higher computational costs, we report the scores from only a single run per task for $BERT_{base}$ and $BERT_{large}$.

Rows 1–7 report the model quality of pre-BERT models (that do not take advantage of pre-training). As observed by Adhikari et al. (2019), LR and SVM trained with tf–idf vectors form effective baselines as they challenge many neural network-based baselines (e.g., HAN) on multiple datasets. This raises the question whether neural networks are a suitable architectural choice for document classification. However, at a much higher computational cost, the regularized LSTM (Adhikari et al., 2019) (row 7) achieves the best numbers for the class of models that do not exploit pre-training.

Consistent with Devlin et al. (2019), the BERT-based models achieve state-of-the-art results on all four datasets (see Table 2, rows 8 and 9), with the $BERT_{large}$ model consistently achieving the highest model quality (compared to $BERT_{base}$).

Surprisingly, distilled LSTM (KD-LSTM, row 10) achieves parity with $BERT_{base}$ on average for Reuters, AAPD, and IMDB. In fact, it outperforms $BERT_{base}$ (on both dev and test) in at least one of the five runs. For Yelp, we see that KD-LSTM reduces the difference between $BERT_{base}$ and LSTM, but not to the same extent as in the other datasets.

Next, we explore the limits of KD by further distilling $BERT_{base}$ all the way down to KimCNN (Kim, 2014) (a single-layer CNN) and LR. It is not surprising that these models don't come close to $BERT_{base}$ owing to their limited expressivity. However, interestingly, we see massive leaps in model quality of these models after distillation (rows 1–3; 11–12). Specifically for multi-label datasets, both these models beat or come close to HAN and SGM, which are far more complex models. To put things in perspective, LR is a simple fully-connected layer and KimCNN contains merely $\sim 0.4\%$ parameters of $BERT_{base}$. These results demonstrate that KD can yield a broad spectrum of baselines for varying computational costs, all of which can be useful depending on the requirements.

Table 3 emphasizes the scale of compression achieved during inference with the help of KD, yielding over 4000× faster LR to 40× faster but effective LSTM compared to $BERT_{base}$. We calculate the number of parameters (# params) of models and floating-point operations (# FLOPS) during inference on average for Reuters. Additionally, Figure 1 shows the comparison between the number of parameters and prediction quality on the vali-

#	Model	Reuters		AAPD		IMDB		Yelp '14	
		Val. F_1	Test F_1	Val. F_1	Test F_1	Val. Acc.	Test Acc.	Val. Acc.	Test Acc.
1	LR	77.0	74.8	67.1	64.9	43.1	43.4	61.1	60.9
2	SVM	89.1	86.1	71.1	69.1	42.5	42.4	59.7	59.6
3	KimCNN	83.5 ±0.4	80.8 ±0.3	54.5 ±1.4	51.4 ±1.3	42.9 ±0.3	42.7 ±0.4	66.5 ±0.1	66.1 ±0.6
4	XML-CNN	88.8 ±0.5	86.2 ±0.3	70.2 ±0.7	68.7 ±0.4	–	–	–	–
5	HAN	87.6 ±0.5	85.2 ±0.6	70.2 ±0.2	68.0 ±0.6	51.8 ±0.3	51.2 ±0.3	68.2 ±0.1	67.9 ±0.1
6	SGM	82.5 ±0.4	78.8 ±0.9	–	71.0†	–	–	–	–
7	LSTM	89.1 ±0.8	87.0 ±0.5	73.1 ±0.4	70.5 ±0.5	53.4 ±0.2	52.8 ±0.3	69.0 ±0.1	68.7 ±0.1
8	BERT$_{base}$	90.5	89.0	75.3	73.4	54.4	54.2	72.1	72.0
9	BERT$_{large}$	**92.3**	**90.7**	**76.6**	**75.2**	**56.0**	**55.6**	**72.6**	**72.5**
10	KD-LSTM	91.0 ±0.2	88.9 ±0.2	75.4 ±0.2	72.9 ±0.3	54.5 ±0.1	53.7 ±0.3	69.7 ±0.1	69.4 ±0.1
11	KD-KimCNN	90.0 ±0.3	87.0 ±0.2	72.7 ±0.4	70.6 ±0.1	49.0 ±0.2	48.3 ±0.3	66.5 ±0.1	66.2 ±0.0
12	KD-LR	87.0	83.7	73.1	71.3	43.8	43.3	62.7	62.3

Table 2: Results for each model on the validation and test sets. Best values are bolded. Rows 1–7 have been taken from Adhikari et al. (2019). Model names of type "KD-X" (rows 10-12) refer to X trained using knowledge distillation from the fine-tuned BERT$_{large}$ (row 9).

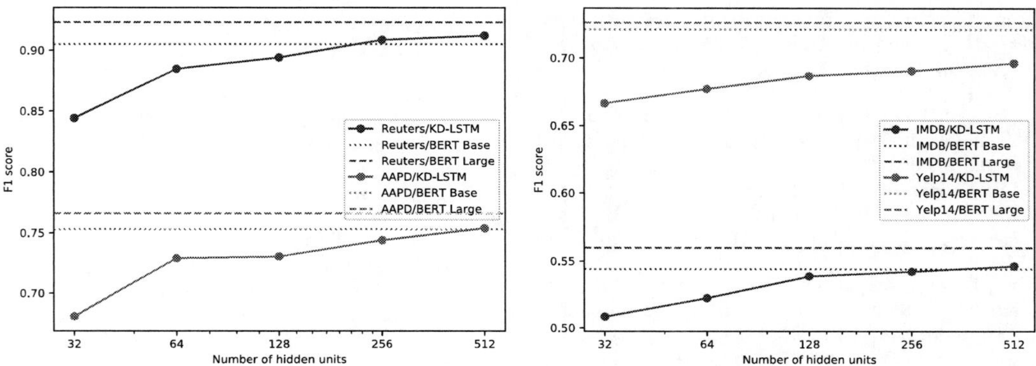

Figure 1: Effectiveness of KD-LSTM vs. BERT$_{base}$ and BERT$_{large}$

Model	# Params	# FLOPS
LR	3.3 (3%)	6.5 (4620×)
KimCNN	0.4 (0.4%)	26.0 (1150×)
LSTM	3.3 (3%)	780.9 (40×)
BERT$_{base}$	110	∼30000

Table 3: # params for the models and # FLOPS for a single inference pass. Values are in millions. Figures in brackets are relative comparisons to BERT$_{base}$.

dation sets. These plots convey the effectiveness of the KD-LSTM model with different numbers of hidden units: 32, 64, 128, 256, and 512. We find that KD-LSTM, with just 256 hidden units (i.e., $\sim 1\%$ parameters of BERT$_{base}$) attains parity with BERT$_{base}$ on Reuters and IMDB, while for AAPD, 512 hidden units ($\sim 3\%$ of BERT$_{base}$) are enough.

6 Conclusion and Future Work

In this paper we improve baselines for document classification by fine-tuning BERT (DocBERT). Using DocBERT, we show the effectiveness of KD over a range of efficient models—a single-layer LSTM model, a single layer CNN, and a logistic regression trained on tf–idf. This provides us with a spectrum of baselines for varying tradeoffs in classification accuracy and complexity. In fact, we show that the distilled LSTM model achieves BERT$_{base}$ parity on a majority of datasets, using only $\sim 3\%$ parameters of the latter.

While distillation is an effective way to reduce computational cost during inference, it doesn't aid in reducing resources needed for training. Thus, methods for reducing the computational resources required while training deserve attention in future.

7 Acknowledgements

This research was supported in part by the Natural Sciences and Engineering Research Council (NSERC) of Canada.

References

Ashutosh Adhikari, Achyudh Ram, Raphael Tang, and Jimmy Lin. 2019. Rethinking complex neural network architectures for document classification. In *Proceedings of the 2019 Conference of the North American Chapter of the Association for Computational Linguistics: Human Language Technologies, Volume 1 (Long and Short Papers)*, pages 4046–4051.

Chidanand Apté, Fred Damerau, and Sholom M. Weiss. 1994. Automated learning of decision rules for text categorization. *ACM Transactions on Information Systems*, 12(3):233–251.

Jimmy Ba and Rich Caruana. 2014. Do deep nets really need to be deep? In *Advances in Neural Information Processing Systems 27*, pages 2654–2662.

Alexis Conneau, Holger Schwenk, Loïc Barrault, and Yann Lecun. 2017. Very deep convolutional networks for text classification. In *Proceedings of the 15th Conference of the European Chapter of the Association for Computational Linguistics: Volume 1, Long Papers*, pages 1107–1116.

Jacob Devlin, Ming-Wei Chang, Kenton Lee, and Kristina Toutanova. 2019. BERT: pre-training of deep bidirectional transformers for language understanding. In *Proceedings of the 2019 Conference of the North American Chapter of the Association for Computational Linguistics: Human Language Technologies, Volume 1 (Long and Short Papers)*, pages 4171–4186.

Geoffrey E. Hinton, Oriol Vinyals, and Jeffrey Dean. 2015. Distilling the knowledge in a neural network. *arxiv/1503.02531*.

Sepp Hochreiter and Jürgen Schmidhuber. 1997. Long short-term memory. *Neural Comput.*, 9(8):1735–1780.

Jeremy Howard and Sebastian Ruder. 2018. Universal language model fine-tuning for text classification. In *Proceedings of the 56th Annual Meeting of the Association for Computational Linguistics (Volume 1: Long Papers)*, pages 328–339.

Rie Johnson and Tong Zhang. 2017. Deep pyramid convolutional neural networks for text categorization. In *Proceedings of the 55th Annual Meeting of the Association for Computational Linguistics (Volume 1: Long Papers)*, pages 562–570.

Yoon Kim. 2014. Convolutional neural networks for sentence classification. In *Proceedings of the 2014 Conference on Empirical Methods in Natural Language Processing*, pages 1746–1751.

Jingzhou Liu, Wei-Cheng Chang, Yuexin Wu, and Yiming Yang. 2017. Deep learning for extreme multi-label text classification. In *Proceedings of the 40th International ACM SIGIR Conference on Research and Development in Information Retrieval*, pages 115–124.

Emma Strubell, Ananya Ganesh, and Andrew McCallum. 2019. Energy and policy considerations for deep learning in NLP. In *Proceedings of the 57th Annual Meeting of the Association for Computational Linguistics*, pages 3645–3650.

Raphael Tang, Yao Lu, Linqing Liu, Lili Mou, Olga Vechtomova, and Jimmy Lin. 2019. Distilling task-specific knowledge from BERT into simple neural networks. *arxiv/1903.12136*.

Ashish Vaswani, Noam Shazeer, Niki Parmar, Jakob Uszkoreit, Llion Jones, Aidan N. Gomez, Łukasz Kaiser, and Illia Polosukhin. 2017. Attention is all you need. In *Advances in Neural Information Processing Systems*, pages 5998–6008.

Pengcheng Yang, Xu Sun, Wei Li, Shuming Ma, Wei Wu, and Houfeng Wang. 2018. SGM: sequence generation model for multi-label classification. In *Proceedings of the 27th International Conference on Computational Linguistics*, pages 3915–3926.

Zhilin Yang, Zihang Dai, Yiming Yang, Jaime Carbonell, Russ R. Salakhutdinov, and Quoc V. Le. 2019. XLNet: Generalized autoregressive pretraining for language understanding. In *Advances in Neural Information Processing Systems 32*, pages 5753–5763.

Zichao Yang, Diyi Yang, Chris Dyer, Xiaodong He, Alex Smola, and Eduard Hovy. 2016. Hierarchical attention networks for document classification. In *Proceedings of the 2016 Conference of the North American Chapter of the Association for Computational Linguistics: Human Language Technologies*, pages 1480–1489.

A Appendix

A.1 Training Hyperparameters

While fine-tuning BERT, we optimize the number of epochs, batch size, learning rate, and maximum sequence length (MSL), the number of tokens that documents are truncated to. We observe that model quality is quite sensitive to the number of epochs, and thus the number must be tailored for each dataset. We train on Reuters, AAPD, and IMDB for 30, 20, and 4 epochs, respectively. Due to resource constraints, we train on Yelp for only one epoch. As is the case with Devlin et al. (2019), we find that choosing a batch size of 16, learning rate of 2×10^{-5}, and MSL of 512 tokens yields optimal model quality on the validation sets for all the datasets.

For distillation, we train an LSTM to capture the learnt representations from BERT_{large} using the objective shown in Equation (1). We use a batch size of 128 for the multi-label tasks and 64 for the single-label tasks. We find the learning rates and dropout rates used in Adhikari et al. (2019) to be optimal even for the distillation process.

To build an effective transfer set for distillation as suggested by Hinton et al. (2015), we augment the training splits of the datasets by applying POS-guided word swapping and random masking for data augmentation, similar to Tang et al. (2019). For the distillation objective given in Equation (1), we use a λ of 1 for multi-label datasets and 4 for single-label datasets.

A.2 Hyperparameter Analysis for DocBERT

MSL analysis. A decrease in the maximum sequence length (MSL) corresponds to only a minor loss in F_1 on Reuters (see top-left subplot in Figure 2), possibly due to Reuters having shorter documents. On IMDB (top-right subplot in Figure 2), lowering the MSL corresponds to a drastic fall in accuracy, suggesting that the entire document is necessary for this dataset.

On the one hand, these results appear obvious. Alternatively, one can argue that, since IMDB contains longer documents, truncating tokens may hurt less. The top two subplots in Figure 2 show that this is *not* the case, since truncating to even 256 tokens causes accuracy to fall lower than that of the much smaller LSTM_{reg} (see Table 2). From these results, we conclude that any amount of truncation is detrimental in document classification, but the level of degradation may differ.

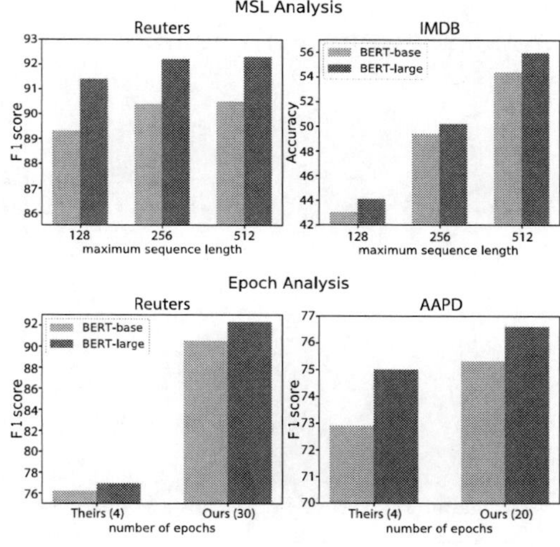

Figure 2: Results on the validation set from varying the MSL and the number of epochs.

Epoch analysis. The bottom two subplots in Figure 2 illustrate the F_1 score of BERT fine-tuned using different numbers of epochs for AAPD and Reuters. Contrary to Devlin et al. (2019), who achieve the state of the art on small datasets with only a few epochs of fine-tuning, we find that smaller datasets require many more epochs to converge. On both the datasets (see Figure 2), we see a significant drop in model quality when the BERT models are fine-tuned for only four epochs, as suggested in the original paper. On Reuters, using four epochs result in an F_1 worse than even logistic regression (Table 2, row 1).

Joint Training with Semantic Role Labeling for Better Generalization in Natural Language Inference

Cemil Cengiz   **Deniz Yuret**
KUIS AI Lab
Koç University, İstanbul, Turkey
`ccengiz17,dyuret@ku.edu.tr`

Abstract

End-to-end models trained on natural language inference (NLI) datasets show low generalization on out-of-distribution evaluation sets. The models tend to learn shallow heuristics due to dataset biases. The performance decreases dramatically on diagnostic sets measuring compositionality or robustness against simple heuristics. Existing solutions for this problem employ dataset augmentation which has the drawbacks of being applicable to only a limited set of adversaries and at worst hurting the model performance on other adversaries not included in the augmentation set. Our proposed solution is to improve sentence understanding (hence out-of-distribution generalization) with joint learning of explicit semantics. We show that a BERT based model trained jointly on English semantic role labeling (SRL) and NLI achieves significantly higher performance on external evaluation sets measuring generalization performance.

1 Introduction

NLI is the task of determining the inference relationship between a premise and a hypothesis sentence which is usually formulated as a three-class classification task with *entailment*, *contradiction* and *neutral* labels. It has been regarded as a central problem in natural language understanding and found its place in benchmarks such as GLUE (Wang et al., 2018). Contemporary neural network based models achieve state-of-the-art (SOTA) results on these benchmarks. However, scoring high on test sets that have a similar distribution to the training sets does not guarantee wider generalization. Models that top the leaderboards on standard test sets may perform poorly on specifically constructed evaluation sets targeting dataset biases. For instance, the HANS challenge dataset (McCoy et al., 2019b) showed that models trained on NLI get fooled easily by heuristics when the input sentence pairs have high lexical similarity. The following example from HANS can explain how this might happen.

Premise: *The judge by the actor stopped the banker.*

Hypothesis: *The banker stopped the actor.*

A human reading this sentence pair carefully can conclude that the hypothesis can not be inferred from the premise. However, models relying on the lexical overlap heuristic will be fooled and predict the label as *entailment* since the premise contains all words of the hypothesis. Existing approaches commonly tackle such adversaries by training the model with a dataset augmented with similar adversarial examples. As detailed in Section 5, the problem with this approach is that it might lead to overfitting to the adversaries on the augmentation set. Therefore, it can decrease the performance on other possible adversaries and hurt generalization (Nie et al., 2018).

Semantic Role Labeling (SRL) asks the *"who did what to whom, when and where etc."* questions to find the semantic roles of words or phrases in a sentence (He et al., 2017). We hypothesize that using the SRL task as a joint objective should improve the semantic knowledge of the models, thus making them less prone to dataset biases. Consider the semantic roles in the previous example sentence pair, which are shown in Table 1. We can see that the role of *"the banker"* differs between the sentences. Since *"stop"* is not a reciprocal verb, a model that is aware of the semantic roles can find out that the inference relation is *non-entailment* although the premise contains all words in the hypothesis, albeit with a different order. In contrast, if a model pays too much attention to lexical similarity, it might falsely predict the relation as *entailment* as the SOTA models analyzed on HANS such as BERT (Devlin et al., 2018) do. SRL informs the model directly about the semantic roles of words

Proceedings of the 5th Workshop on Representation Learning for NLP (RepL4NLP-2020), pages 78–88
July 9, 2020. ©2020 Association for Computational Linguistics

Premise	The judge by the actor stopped the banker.
VERB	stopped
ARG0	The judge by the actor
ARG1	the banker

Hypoth.	The banker stopped the actor.
VERB	stopped
ARG0	The banker
ARG1	the actor

Table 1: An example pair from HANS, including the semantic roles of the words in each sentence. *ARG0* represents the proto-agent, i.e. the thing that stops, *ARG1* represents the proto-patient, i.e. the object being stopped, in this example.

which makes it easier for the model to rely on more than just shallow lexical cues.

Our contribution in this work is threefold:

- We propose a BERT based multi-task learning (MTL) model jointly trained on English SRL and NLI (Section 3), and show that this model achieves scores comparable to the single-task BERT on both tasks (Section 4).

- We evaluate the proposed model on out-of-distribution test sets such as HANS (McCoy et al., 2019b) and Comparisons (Dasgupta et al., 2018) and demonstrate that it exceeds the single-task BERT performance significantly. Specifically, when trained on MultiNLI, the multi-task model exceeds the single-task model accuracy by 4% on HANS and 5.3% on Comparisons without using data augmentation. (Section 4.1.2 and 4.2)

- We compare the proposed MTL approach to the sequential transfer learning and show that the MTL is more helpful. (Section 4.1.3)

2 Datasets

In this section, we describe the datasets used in the experiments. We explain the shortcomings of the NLI datasets and describe an SRL dataset that can be used to alleviate these shortcomings.

2.1 Large-scale NLI Datasets

In this work, we consider two open-domain, large-scale NLI datasets in English, SNLI (Bowman et al., 2015) and MultiNLI (Williams et al., 2018). SNLI is created using image captions written by humans whereas MultiNLI includes five different genres of written and spoken English such as travel guides and telephone conversations. Both datasets have been used for training general NLI models, or as an intermediate training resource for transfer learning to a domain-specific dataset, possibly with smaller size (Cengiz et al., 2019). Recently, deep neural network models achieved human-level performance on NLI tasks in benchmarks such as GLUE (Wang et al., 2018) and SuperGLUE (Wang et al., 2019). However, as McCoy et al. (2019b) and Dasgupta et al. (2018) showed, these results do not reflect the performance of the models on out-of-distribution test sets. They proposed such adversarial test sets targeting specific biases apparent in the original NLI datasets to show that SOTA models are vulnerable to these superficial patterns.

2.2 Adversarial NLI Datasets

HANS is an extensive evaluation set proposed by McCoy et al. (2019b), that consists of three types of adversarial examples: *lexical overlap, subsequence* and *constituent. Lexical overlap* is the most general category, indicating all the words in the hypothesis sentence are present in the premise as well. An example from this category with *entailment* gold label is the following: *"The banker near the judge saw the actor.* ⇒ *The banker saw the actor." Subsequence* is a special case of *lexical overlap*, indicating that the hypothesis is a contiguous subsequence of the premise. The following pair is an example from this category with *entailment* gold label: *"The artist and the student called the judge.* ⇒ *The student called the judge."* Lastly, *constituent* is a special case of the *subsequence*, denoting that the hypothesis is a complete subtree of the premise's constituency parse tree. An instance from *constituent* category with *non-entailment* gold label is as following: *"If the actor slept, the judge saw the artist.* ⇒ *The actor slept."* It is worth noting that although there is a hierarchical relation between the categories, their instances do not overlap. Therefore, they will be treated as distinct categories throughout the paper. The sentences included in this dataset were created using templates and ensured to be plausible. Moreover, the verbs were chosen from the frequently used verbs in MultiNLI so that the models trained on MultiNLI are familiar with them. Differently than MultiNLI, this dataset has binary labels, a label is either *entailment* or *non-entailment*. Finally, this dataset has two parti-

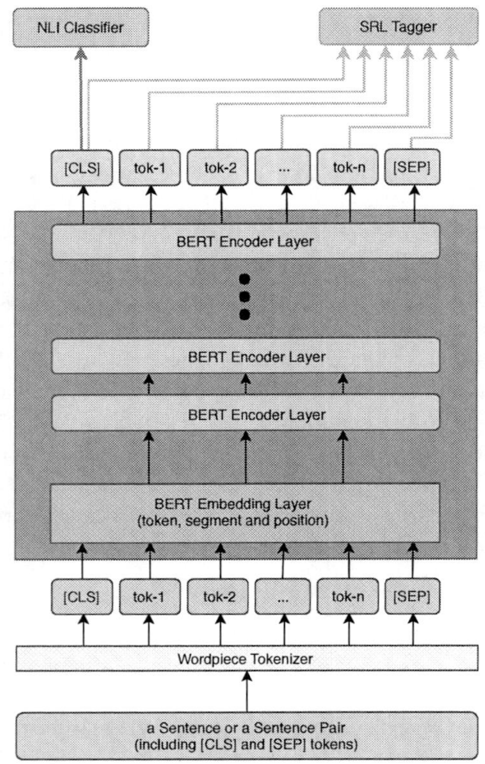

Figure 1: Multi-task BERT model for SRL and NLI. Each task-specific head contains a linear layer to transform the embeddings into the task's label space.

tions with identical size, a test set to evaluate the models and an augmentation set to augment the MultiNLI training set. In our experiments, we treat the augmentation set as a validation set and do not use it for training.

The Comparisons dataset (Dasgupta et al., 2018) attempts to evaluate the models trained on SNLI for three types of adversarial examples: *same, more-less, not*. The *same* category consists of hypothesis-premise pairs having exactly the same words in a different order. An example with *contradiction* gold label is as following: *"The woman is more cheerful than the man. ⇒ The man is more cheerful than the woman."* The *more-less* type contains instances whose sentence pair differ by including the word *"more"* or the word *"less"*, and possibly in word order. The following pair is an example from this category with *entailment* label: *"The woman is more cheerful than the man. ⇒ The man is less cheerful than the woman."* The third category is the *not* type, representing the instances having the negation word *"not"* either in the hypothesis or in

the premise, but not in both. The word order of the sentences might differ as well. A sentence pair from this category with *entailment* gold label is the following: *"The woman is more cheerful than the man. ⇒ The man is not more cheerful than the woman."* The authors created this dataset by automatically generating examples fitting into one of the described categories using a vocabulary similar to SNLI's. Moreover, they analyzed SNLI and showed that it has many examples fitting into the examined categories with labels mostly supporting the heuristic choice. Unlike SNLI, this dataset does not have the *neutral* label. It has the *entailment* label for the positive examples and the *contradiction* label for the negative examples.

2.3 Semantic Role Labeling as an Auxiliary Objective for Sentence Understanding

In this work, we use the English Ontonotes v5.0 SRL dataset with the CONLL-2012 shared task format (Pradhan et al., 2013) which gives the predicate-argument structure for each sentence. The auxiliary task we used is formulated as prediction of the arguments for a given predicate in a sentence. Therefore, each predicate in a sentence together with the semantic role label spans associated with it yield a different training instance. The number of training instances in the whole dataset is around 280,000.

3 Model Description

We propose a multi-task BERT model to jointly predict semantic roles and perform natural language inference. BERT is used as the shared encoder module and two separate decoder heads are appended on top of it to perform task-specific operations. The overall picture of the model can be seen from Figure 1. Following Liu et al. (2019), the tasks share the encoder part of the model including the lexicon encoder and all BERT layers.

We follow the original sentence pair classification formulation for BERT while training it for NLI task. On the input side, we concatenate the premise and hypothesis tokens, add a [SEP] token at the end of both sentences, and finally add a [CLS] token at the beginning of the whole sequence. Figure 2 shows the token embedding for an example sentence pair. While processing an NLI input, we take the [CLS] token embedding at the BERT's output and treat it as the summary of the whole sequence. The dimension of this embedding is reduced to

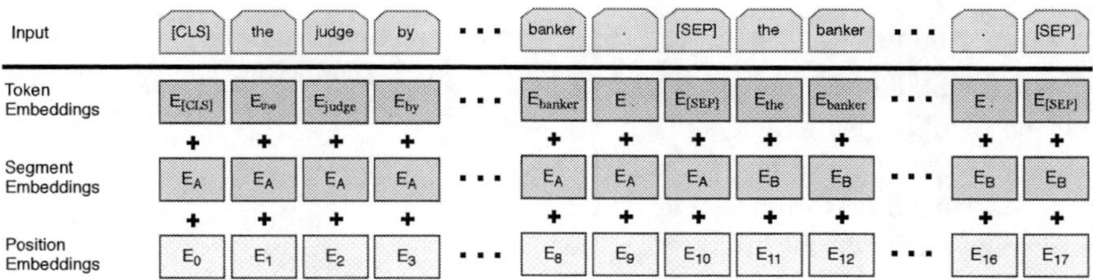

Figure 2: Input representation of *"The judge by the actor stopped the banker. ⇒ The banker stopped the actor."* sentence pair for NLI task.

three after passing through a two-layer MLP since there are three labels in MultiNLI and SNLI. Finally, a softmax is applied to get the probability for each label class. Following McCoy et al. (2019b), when we evaluate the model on HANS or Comparisons, we collapse the predicted *contradiction* and *neutral* labels into a single negative label to output binary labels.

For the SRL training, we adapt an architecture similar to the one proposed by Shi and Lin (2019). In our implementation, we indicate the predicate using the segment embeddings by assigning 1 to the predicate word pieces and 0 to the other tokens. Figure 3 denotes the embeddings used for the SRL. We opt for a simple decoder and rely purely on the self attention to capture contextual information. The embedding of each token is directly passed through a two-layer MLP independently, and the SRL tag is determined by a final softmax layer. We use the Inside Outside Beginning (IOB)[1] tagging for spans, and a Viterbi decoder to ensure prediction of valid spans during testing. As Figure 2 and 3 show, the segment embeddings represent different things for SRL and NLI inputs. In NLI, segment embeddings separate the sentences whereas they indicate the target verb in SRL. Moreover, how the

BERT outputs are processed is also different between the tasks. In spite of these differences, the training is expected to optimize the BERT weights so that it can generate embeddings suitable for both tasks. Intuitively, this representation will be less prone to dataset biases in the NLI thanks to explicitly forcing the model to pay attention to the semantic roles of the words.

4 Experiments and Results

In this section, we present the experiments we conducted by training the BERT based model in single-task and multi-task learning setups. MultiNLI and SNLI datasets are used to train the models whereas HANS and Comparisons are used for evaluation. For the multi-task learning experiments, we used the SRL dataset for joint training with NLI. In both of the HANS and Comparisons experiments, we tuned the hyperparameters using a validation set from the same distribution as the adversarial test set. Nevertheless, we also tested our highest performing models on the original MultiNLI and SNLI validation sets to make sure our multi-task BERT model performs well on those as well. Indeed, the multi-task model performance on the original validation sets turned out to be similar (accuracy difference is around $\pm 0.5\%$, depending on the hyperparameters) to the single-task BERT performance.

---

[1] In IOB style tagging, each span begins with a *B-* tag and continues with *I-* tags except for *Other* tokens, which takes *O* tags.

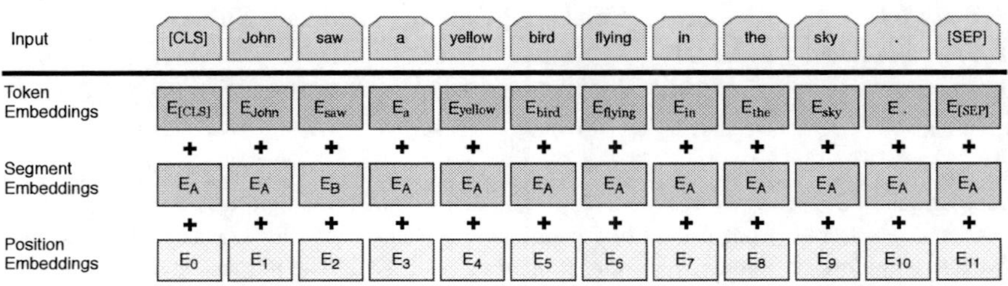

Figure 3: Input representation of *"John saw a yellow bird flying in the sky."* sentence for SRL task when the predicate is *saw*.

4.1 HANS Experiments

We experimented with direct training on NLI, sequential transfer learning using SRL, and a multi-task learning approach to train on the NLI and SRL tasks jointly. As HANS was proposed as an adversarial evaluation set for the NLI models trained on MultiNLI, we use it as the NLI training dataset. Following McCoy et al. (2019b), we output *non-entailment* label when a model predicts *contradiction* or *neutral*.

4.1.1 Single-task MultiNLI Training

We trained a single-task BERT model on the MultiNLI dataset to be used as the baseline for the HANS evaluation. The BERT weights are initialized with the pre-trained weights from Devlin et al. (2018) whereas the classifier head is randomly initialized. During training, all weights are updated. We used the HANS augmentation dataset as the development set for hyperparameter tuning.

As reported by McCoy et al. (2019b), BERT performs poorly on HANS although better than bag-of-words or LSTM (Hochreiter and Schmidhuber, 1997) based models. However, the follow-up work by McCoy et al. (2019a) showed BERT's performance on HANS varied dramatically depending on the order of instances fed during training and the initial weights of the classifier head, both of which can be varied by changing the random seeds. To further investigate that, they repeated the training of BERT 100 times with the same settings except that randomness and compared the results. The largest variance was encountered on the *lexical overlap* category when the gold label is *non-entailment* whereas the other results were close among different runs. In our experiment, we got a 51% accuracy on *lexical overlap*, which is close to the upper limit of the range $(6\% - 54\%)$ reported by McCoy et al. (2019a). Table 2 includes

the comparison of the original results (McCoy et al., 2019b) with our run. Our results are comparable so we use this model as the baseline for single-task BERT.

4.1.2 Multi-task Training for SRL and MultiNLI

In this part, we present the result of training BERT on SRL and MultiNLI jointly with the multi-task approach described in Section 3. We used the HANS augmentation dataset as the validation set for MultiNLI, and CoNLL-2012 development set for SRL validation. We validated the trained model against both validation set separately at the end of each epoch. Then, the model performed highest on the HANS augmentation set was evaluated on the HANS test set. The results are shown in Table 2, together with the single-task results for comparison. The multi-task approach improved the overall accuracy by 4%. Although there is a slight decrease in the results when the correct label is *entailment*, this is an expected drop. The accuracy of the single-task model reaches 100% on the *subsequence* category, and is at least 96% on the remaining two categories when the correct label is *entailment*. Since the MultiNLI instances involving a heuristic examined by HANS are mostly labeled with *entailment*, the models tend to assign *entailment* labels to such examples in the HANS dataset. Because our multi-task model is less severely affected by the heuristics, it is less likely to output *entailment* when these heuristics are encountered. As one would expect, the gains come from the instances whose correct label is *non-entailment*. Noticeably, the multi-task training improved the accuracy for this label in all three categories dramatically.

To examine the improvements in more detail, we present the results broken down into subcategories in Table 3. We refer the readers to McCoy

| | **Correct: Entailment** | | | **Correct: Non-entailment** | | | |
BERT model	**Lexical**	**Subseq.**	**Const.**	**Lexical**	**Subseq.**	**Const.**	**Avg.**
McCoy et al. (2019b)	0.95	0.99	**1.00**	0.16	0.04	0.16	0.55
Single-task	**0.96**	**1.00**	0.99	0.51	0.05	0.18	0.62
Multi-task	0.91	0.98	0.95	**0.71**	**0.13**	**0.25**	**0.66**

Table 2: Comparison of the previous work (McCoy et al., 2019b) and our single-task and multi-task BERT models on HANS. All models started from pre-trained weights. The multi-task model was jointly trained on SRL and MultiNLI whereas single-task models were only trained on MultiNLI. The highest accuracy for each category is indicated with bold. Note that (McCoy et al., 2019b) results on the *entailment* and *non-entailment* categories were obtained by averaging the subcases using the BERT column of Table 7 and Table 8 respectively in their paper. (**Lexical**: lexical overlap, **Subseq.**: subsequence, **Const.**: constituent)

Category	Single-Task	Multi-Task
Lexical Overlap		
Subject-object swap	0.68	0.83
Preposition	0.68	0.79
Relative clause	0.60	0.73
Conjunction	0.55	0.70
Passive	0.01	0.51
Subsequence		
NP/S ambiguity	0.00	0.03
Prepositional phrase on subject	0.14	0.20
Relative clause on subject	0.10	0.24
Past participle	0.00	0.06
NP/Z ambiguity	0.02	0.15
Constituent		
Embedded under if	0.46	0.71
After if clause	0.00	0.00
Embedded under verb	0.31	0.47
Disjunction	0.07	0.02
Adverb	0.08	0.06

Table 3: Fine-grained comparison of single-task and multi-task BERT on HANS's three different categories when the correct label is *non-entailment*. The rows denote the heuristic type found in the sentences.

et al. (2019b) for details and examples of the subcategories. The top part of the Table 3 shows the fine-grained results for the *lexical overlap* category with the *non-entailment* gold labels. Although all subcategories improved, the largest gain comes from the *passive* examples. The *passive* case with *non-entailment* labels includes examples with sentence pairs almost identical to each other, only one of them has an active verb while the other has the passive form of it. An example sentence pair is the following: *"The senators were helped by the managers. ⇒ The senators helped the managers."* The single-task model misclassified almost all *non-entailment* examples involving passive sentences whereas the multi-task model could predict them correctly half of the time. This is a significant improvement, the multi-task model has begun to identify the meaning changes when a verb is switched from passive to active while the word order is kept unchanged.

The middle section of Table 3 shows the results on the *subsequence* category for the *non-entailment* gold labels. All subcategories improved although the degree is less than *lexical overlap*. The largest improvement is found on *relative clause on subject*, which represents the sentence pairs differing by their subjects such that the premise's subject is a relative clause and the hypothesis's subject is a particular segment of that clause that leads to *non-entailment*. An example sentence pair from this category is the following: *"The secretary that admired the senator saw the actor. ⇒ The senator saw the actor."*. When trained with a multi-task approach, the model makes some progress on recognizing that the overall meaning of a relative clause does not necessarily entail a part of it.

The last category we investigated is *constituents* with *non-entailment* gold labels, whose results are given in the bottom part of Table 3. There are significant improvements in two subcategories whereas the remaining three did not improve or very slightly dropped. The largest improvement (25% accuracy) is on *embedded under if* subcategory, which denotes the examples with a premise having an *if* (or *unless*) clause whereas the hypothesis has the result part of the *if* clause. An example from this subcategory is: *"Unless the authors saw the students, the doctors resigned. ⇒ The doctors resigned."* The second largest gain (16% accuracy) comes from *embedded under verb* subcategory, which is similar to the previous one, except that the embedding is achieved using a verb. An example is: *"The tourists said that the lawyer saw the banker. ⇒ The lawyer saw the banker."*.

As shown by the HANS results, there are solid improvements on NLI evaluation after switching to the multi-task training. However one needs to ask if the joint training hurts the other task, SRL. In the multi-task experiment, the F1 score on SRL test dataset is 86.0 which is comparable to the single model SOTA results noted by Shi and Lin (2019). Therefore, the joint training did not harm the SRL performance, while improving the out-of-distribution performance on NLI.

4.1.3 Sequential Transfer Learning from SRL to MultiNLI

We experimented with sequential transfer learning to test if a simple transfer learning strategy is

Model	same	more /less	not	Avg.
BOW-MLP	50.0	50.0	49.9	50.0
InferSent	51.4	**50.1**	47.8	49.8
BERT	**85.3**	47.9	44.5	59.2
MTL-BERT	80.5	47.9	**51.3**	**59.9**

Table 4: Percent accuracy of the models on Comparisons dataset. BERT based models are our implementations while the others are from Dasgupta et al. (2018). Multi-task (MTL) BERT is trained on SRL and SNLI. The highest accuracy for each category is indicated with bold. Note that the BOW-MLP and InferSent rows are obtained by merging the *neutral* and *contradiction* labels in Figure 2 and 3 from Dasgupta et al. (2018).

enough to carry information from the SRL task so that the model is more robust to the biases in the NLI dataset. First, an SRL tagger head with random weights is appended on top of the pre-trained BERT encoder. This model is fine-tuned on SRL until the F1 score on the SRL validation set is maximized. The model weights from the epoch resulting in the highest SRL development set score is stored. Then, its SRL head is stripped, and an NLI classifier head with random weights is appended on top of the [CLS] token. Finally, the model is trained on MultiNLI and validated against HANS augmentation set. After training, the model is evaluated on HANS test set. The result is within the accuracy range for the single-task training results reported by McCoy et al. (2019a). This shows that our transfer learning strategy did not improve HANS results over the BERT trained only on MultiNLI. We anticipate that this is because the model forgets most of the knowledge about the SRL task during NLI training. To avoid that, we switched to multi-task setup presented in Section 3 to learn SRL and NLI jointly so that the semantic role knowledge is not forgotten.

4.2 Comparisons Dataset Results

We trained BERT with single-task and multi-task learning approaches and compared them on the Comparisons dataset. First, we used the SNLI dataset as the NLI training source following Dasgupta et al. (2018). We used the validation set released with the Comparisons dataset for hyperparameter optimization during training of both the single-task and multi-task models. Unlike SNLI, this dataset contains only two labels, *entailment* and *contradiction*. Therefore, differently than Dasgupta et al. (2018), we converted the predicted *neutral* labels to *contradiction* to have a unified negative label. Table 4 compares the overall performance of our BERT based models and the previously examined models on the test set. InferSent (Conneau et al., 2017) is a sentence encoding based NLI model that uses LSTM as the encoder. Although it is more complex than the bag-of-words (BOW-MLP) model, their performances are similar on this set. We see that the performance of BERT models on the *same* category are much better than the simpler models. The high performance of BERT models on this category can be attributed to the fact that the BERT was pre-trained on a large corpus with missing word prediction and next sentence prediction tasks, making it more aware of the word order. However, in the remaining two categories, both the single-task and multi-task BERT perform relatively close to the remaining models.

MultiNLI is a more diverse dataset compared to SNLI, including examples from several genres. Therefore, we also tried MultiNLI as the NLI training source and replicated the experiments to see how the single-task and multi-task BERT performance will change. The results are given in Table 5 together with the SNLI based results for comparison. We see that switching to MultiNLI improved both models substantially. However, the increase in the multi-task model is significantly more prominent, showing the advantage of the joint training with SRL. The multi-task model correctly classifies almost all test examples in the *more/less* category and most of the *not* category. However, the trend of observing better performance on the *same* category from the single-task model holds here as well. This result is surprising and needs further investigation.

BERT Model	Training set: SNLI				Training set: MultiNLI			
	same	more/less	not	Avg.	same	more/less	not	Avg.
Single-task	85.3	47.9	44.5	59.2	74.1	88.3	74.3	78.9
Multi-task	80.5	47.9	51.3	59.9	63.3	97.3	91.9	84.2

Table 5: Percent accuracy of the BERT models on Comparisons dataset.

4.3 Training Details

We used the PyTorch (Paszke et al., 2017) framework and the AllenNLP (Gardner et al., 2018) library for implementation. We adapted some code to implement the multi-task training logic from Sanh et al. (2019)'s hierarchical multi-task learning project[2]. In all experiments, we used the base version of BERT by initializing it with the weights released by Devlin et al. (2018).

We use uniform mini-batches, i.e. a mini-batch contains instances from a single-task. Each dataset is divided into mini-batches with the same size and an iterator for each of them is created that can cycle through a dataset and provide batches indefinitely. In a training step, we decide which task to train with a probabilistic sampling, get a mini-batch from the iterator for that task, and perform a forward pass on it and back-propagate the loss. During the back-propagation, we update the task-specific head of the chosen task, as well as the BERT encoder. Following Sanh et al. (2019), we use proportional sampling to decide on the task type at the beginning of each training step.

Recent studies generally use a single global optimizer for all tasks (Sanh et al., 2019; Liu et al., 2019). In this work, we tried both this approach and using a different optimizer for each task. The advantage of using multiple optimizers is that the learning rates of the individual tasks can be set to different values, and each task can have its own learning rate scheduler. We used *BertAdam* optimizer from HuggingFace, and set its maximum learning rate to 2e-5 or 5e-5 according to the validation accuracy on the NLI evaluation task. Moreover, we employed a slanted triangular learning rate scheduler (Howard and Ruder, 2018) with a cut fraction of 0.1 and decay factor of 0.38. In all experiments the maximum sequence length is set to 256, and longer sequences are truncated. In all training experiments, 4 GPUs were used in parallel and the datasets were divided into mini-batches of size 12 based on GPU memory limitations.

5   Related Work

In this section, we discuss various solution approaches proposed for the NLI task. We start with a sentence embedding based approach and continue with a data augmentation method targeting the generalization problem of NLI models. Then,

we discuss some models benefiting from syntax or semantic roles and touch on multi-task models.

Some previous studies used sentence embedding based approaches to solve NLI. Noticeably, InferSent (Conneau et al., 2017) uses an LSTM to encode the premise and hypothesis sentences independently. Then, it concatenates the premise, hypothesis embeddings and two feature vectors obtained by their element-wise multiplication and absolute difference to get the overall sentence pair representation. Finally, an MLP layer followed by a softmax is used to calculate the class scores. Being trained on SNLI, this model suffers from the biases in its training data and performed close to the BOW model on the Comparisons evaluation set.

There are a number of studies that use data augmentation to address the generalization problem revealed by NLI challenge datasets like HANS and Comparisons. McCoy et al. (2019b); Dasgupta et al. (2018); Nie et al. (2018) created augmentation sets consisting of training instances with properties similar to the proposed adversarial evaluation set. The augmentation set is focused on the examined phenomena and considerably smaller than the original training set in general. Nevertheless, the models are shown to achieve very strong results, even close to %100 accuracy on the evaluation sets after training with augmented datasets. However, there are some problems with an augmentation approach performed this way, i.e. using a new dataset targeting the inspected phenomena in the proposed evaluation set. First of all, it is not clear if they do result in improvement on the language understanding of the model in general. Rather, the model at hand is patched so that it can excel on some specific cases that the new evaluation dataset examines. However, one can presumably find other adversarial example classes for a given training dataset, so creating an augmentation set for each possible adversarial class may not be feasible. Moreover, Nie et al. (2018) showed that augmenting the training dataset by targeting some specific category of adversarial examples might be harmful to other types of adversarial examples. In other words, dataset augmentation with such limited focus might lead to overfitting to the targeted adversaries and hurt the overall robustness. Therefore, in this work, we took a different approach and introduced an inductive bias on the model by explicitly enforcing it to produce representations suitable to extract semantic

---

[2]`https://github.com/huggingface/hmtl`

role information.

Some recent studies have investigated the benefits of semantic role labeling on the performance of natural language inference models. Noticeably, Zhang et al. (2020, 2018) used SRL as a supplementary task for text comprehension tasks such as textual entailment and question answering. Similar to our work, they used PropBank (Palmer et al., 2005) style role annotations and treated SRL as a sequence tagging problem. Zhang et al. (2020)'s approach is different from ours in that they use a pre-trained, SOTA SRL model to provide semantic embeddings to enrich the contextual embeddings from BERT. They kept the SRL model frozen and trained other parts of the model including the BERT encoder. Similarly, Zhang et al. (2018) employed two different networks where one of them is an SRL model responsible for generating the semantic embeddings to support the other network which is trained to solve the downstream task at hand. Moreover, both networks in this model use pre-trained word embeddings such as ELMo (Peters et al., 2018) or GloVe (Pennington et al., 2014). The main difference of our approach from these is that we use a single network and train it in a multi-task fashion by sharing encoder representations among different tasks. Moreover, unlike our work, they evaluated their models on the original datasets e.g. MultiNLI, so their focus was not to improve the model performance on the adversarial evaluation sets.

Instead of semantic role information, some recent works investigated the benefits of syntax to support the natural language inference models. Noticeably, Pang et al. (2019) used the hidden word representations of an externally trained, high performing dependency parser to enrich the BERT based NLI models. With this approach, the models achieved some modest increase on the overall HANS results.

Multi-task models powered with pre-trained language model based encoders have achieved SOTA performance on natural language understanding benchmarks such as GLUE (Wang et al., 2018), and SuperGLUE (Wang et al., 2019). However, there is not much work focusing on simultaneously solving both a word-level semantics task such as SRL and a sentence-level understanding such as NLI which requires higher level reasoning. Instead, the existing approaches such as Liu et al. (2019); Clark et al. (2019) combine multiple sentence-level

understanding tasks to solve them jointly without any aid from lower level tasks focusing on syntax or word-level semantics. Our approach differs from them in that we hypothesize using both word-level semantics and high level reasoning tasks might be a more suitable approach to learn deeper understanding of the sentences, thereby suffering less from the dataset biases in reasoning tasks such as NLI.

Some previous work attempted to cast NLI to a different natural language understanding task such as question answering. Particularly, McCann et al. (2018) suggested a collection of various tasks including NLI for a benchmark and proposed a novel approach to solve all those tasks using a single multi-task model. They casted each task to the question answering problem and trained a model to solve all of them jointly.

6 Conclusion and Future Work

This work presents a multi-task learning approach using SRL task to apply an inductive bias on a BERT based NLI model. Our experiments show that joint training with SRL makes the model more robust to the superficial patterns in the NLI training data. As opposed to the augmentation based solutions focused on specific adversarial classes, this approach has the advantage of being applicable to a variety of adversaries without overfitting to some of them. Having access to the semantic role information improves the sentence understanding of the model, hence making it generalize better to the unseen dataset distributions including the adversarial ones such as HANS and Comparisons. The SRL task utilized in this work processes a single predicate per data instance. The future work might incorporate joint prediction of all predicates and corresponding roles to analyze its effect on adversarial NLI evaluation performance.

Acknowledgments

The authors would like to thank Ulaş Sert and Ceyda Özler for their help in creating the figures and the anonymous reviewers for their valuable feedback. Cemil Cengiz is supported by Huawei Turkey R&D Center through the Huawei Graduate Research Support Scholarship.

References

Samuel R. Bowman, Gabor Angeli, Christopher Potts, and Christopher D. Manning. 2015. A large annotated corpus for learning natural language inference.

In *Proceedings of the 2015 Conference on Empirical Methods in Natural Language Processing*. Association for Computational Linguistics.

Cemil Cengiz, Ulaş Sert, and Deniz Yuret. 2019. KU_ai at MEDIQA 2019: Domain-specific pre-training and transfer learning for medical NLI. In *Proceedings of the 18th BioNLP Workshop and Shared Task*, pages 427–436, Florence, Italy. Association for Computational Linguistics.

Kevin Clark, Minh-Thang Luong, Urvashi Khandelwal, Christopher D. Manning, and Quoc V. Le. 2019. BAM! born-again multi-task networks for natural language understanding. In *Proceedings of the 57th Annual Meeting of the Association for Computational Linguistics*, pages 5931–5937, Florence, Italy. Association for Computational Linguistics.

Alexis Conneau, Douwe Kiela, Holger Schwenk, Loïc Barrault, and Antoine Bordes. 2017. Supervised learning of universal sentence representations from natural language inference data. In *Proceedings of the 2017 Conference on Empirical Methods in Natural Language Processing*, pages 670–680, Copenhagen, Denmark. Association for Computational Linguistics.

Ishita Dasgupta, Demi Guo, Andreas Stuhlmüller, Samuel J Gershman, and Noah D Goodman. 2018. Evaluating compositionality in sentence embeddings. *arXiv preprint arXiv:1802.04302*.

Jacob Devlin, Ming-Wei Chang, Kenton Lee, and Kristina Toutanova. 2018. Bert: Pre-training of deep bidirectional transformers for language understanding. *arXiv preprint arXiv:1810.04805*.

Matt Gardner, Joel Grus, Mark Neumann, Oyvind Tafjord, Pradeep Dasigi, Nelson F. Liu, Matthew Peters, Michael Schmitz, and Luke Zettlemoyer. 2018. AllenNLP: A deep semantic natural language processing platform. In *Proceedings of Workshop for NLP Open Source Software (NLP-OSS)*, pages 1–6, Melbourne, Australia. Association for Computational Linguistics.

Luheng He, Kenton Lee, Mike Lewis, and Luke Zettlemoyer. 2017. Deep semantic role labeling: What works and what's next. In *Proceedings of the 55th Annual Meeting of the Association for Computational Linguistics (Volume 1: Long Papers)*, pages 473–483, Vancouver, Canada. Association for Computational Linguistics.

Sepp Hochreiter and Jürgen Schmidhuber. 1997. Long short-term memory. *Neural Computation*, 9(8):1735–1780.

Jeremy Howard and Sebastian Ruder. 2018. Universal language model fine-tuning for text classification. In *Proceedings of the 56th Annual Meeting of the Association for Computational Linguistics (Volume 1: Long Papers)*, pages 328–339, Melbourne, Australia. Association for Computational Linguistics.

Xiaodong Liu, Pengcheng He, Weizhu Chen, and Jianfeng Gao. 2019. Multi-task deep neural networks for natural language understanding. In *Proceedings of the 57th Annual Meeting of the Association for Computational Linguistics*, pages 4487–4496, Florence, Italy. Association for Computational Linguistics.

Bryan McCann, Nitish Shirish Keskar, Caiming Xiong, and Richard Socher. 2018. The natural language decathlon: Multitask learning as question answering. *arXiv preprint arXiv:1806.08730*.

R. Thomas McCoy, Junghyun Min, and Tal Linzen. 2019a. Berts of a feather do not generalize together: Large variability in generalization across models with similar test set performance.

Tom McCoy, Ellie Pavlick, and Tal Linzen. 2019b. Right for the wrong reasons: Diagnosing syntactic heuristics in natural language inference. In *Proceedings of the 57th Annual Meeting of the Association for Computational Linguistics*, pages 3428–3448, Florence, Italy. Association for Computational Linguistics.

Yixin Nie, Yicheng Wang, and Mohit Bansal. 2018. Analyzing compositionality-sensitivity of NLI models. *CoRR*, abs/1811.07033.

Martha Palmer, Daniel Gildea, and Paul Kingsbury. 2005. The proposition bank: An annotated corpus of semantic roles. *Computational Linguistics*, 31(1):71–106.

Deric Pang, Lucy H. Lin, and Noah A. Smith. 2019. Improving natural language inference with a pretrained parser.

Adam Paszke, Sam Gross, Soumith Chintala, Gregory Chanan, Edward Yang, Zachary DeVito, Zeming Lin, Alban Desmaison, Luca Antiga, and Adam Lerer. 2017. Automatic differentiation in pytorch. In *NIPS-W*.

Jeffrey Pennington, Richard Socher, and Christopher Manning. 2014. Glove: Global vectors for word representation. In *Proceedings of the 2014 Conference on Empirical Methods in Natural Language Processing (EMNLP)*, pages 1532–1543, Doha, Qatar. Association for Computational Linguistics.

Matthew E. Peters, Mark Neumann, Mohit Iyyer, Matt Gardner, Christopher Clark, Kenton Lee, and Luke Zettlemoyer. 2018. Deep contextualized word representations. In *Proc. of NAACL*.

Sameer Pradhan, Alessandro Moschitti, Nianwen Xue, Hwee Tou Ng, Anders Björkelund, Olga Uryupina, Yuchen Zhang, and Zhi Zhong. 2013. Towards robust linguistic analysis using OntoNotes. In *Proceedings of the Seventeenth Conference on Computational Natural Language Learning*, pages 143–152, Sofia, Bulgaria. Association for Computational Linguistics.

Victor Sanh, Thomas Wolf, and Sebastian Ruder. 2019. A hierarchical multi-task approach for learning embeddings from semantic tasks. *Proceedings of the AAAI Conference on Artificial Intelligence*, 33:6949–6956.

Peng Shi and Jimmy Lin. 2019. Simple bert models for relation extraction and semantic role labeling. *CoRR*, abs/1904.05255.

Alex Wang, Yada Pruksachatkun, Nikita Nangia, Amanpreet Singh, Julian Michael, Felix Hill, Omer Levy, and Samuel R. Bowman. 2019. Superglue: A stickier benchmark for general-purpose language understanding systems. In *NeurIPS*.

Alex Wang, Amanpreet Singh, Julian Michael, Felix Hill, Omer Levy, and Samuel Bowman. 2018. GLUE: A multi-task benchmark and analysis platform for natural language understanding. In *Proceedings of the 2018 EMNLP Workshop BlackboxNLP: Analyzing and Interpreting Neural Networks for NLP*, pages 353–355, Brussels, Belgium. Association for Computational Linguistics.

Adina Williams, Nikita Nangia, and Samuel Bowman. 2018. A broad-coverage challenge corpus for sentence understanding through inference. In *Proceedings of the 2018 Conference of the North American Chapter of the Association for Computational Linguistics: Human Language Technologies, Volume 1 (Long Papers)*, pages 1112–1122, New Orleans, Louisiana. Association for Computational Linguistics.

Zhuosheng Zhang, Yuwei Wu, Zuchao Li, and Hai Zhao. 2018. Explicit contextual semantics for text comprehension.

Zhuosheng Zhang, Yuwei Wu, Hai Zhao, Zuchao Li, Shuailiang Zhang, Xi Zhou, and Xiang Zhou. 2020. Semantics-aware BERT for language understanding. In *the Thirty-Fourth AAAI Conference on Artificial Intelligence (AAAI-2020)*.

A Metric Learning Approach to Misogyny Categorization

Juan M. Coria and **Sahar Ghannay** and **Sophie Rosset** and **Hervé Bredin**

Université Paris-Saclay, CNRS, LIMSI

`{coria, ghannay, rosset, bredin}@limsi.fr`

Abstract

The task of automatic misogyny identification and categorization has not received as much attention as other natural language tasks have, even though it is crucial for identifying hate speech in social Internet interactions. In this work, we address this sentence classification task from a representation learning perspective, using both a bidirectional LSTM and BERT optimized with the following metric learning loss functions: contrastive loss, triplet loss, center loss, congenerous cosine loss and additive angular margin loss. We set new state-of-the-art for the task with our fine-tuned BERT, whose sentence embeddings can be compared with a simple cosine distance, and we release all our code as open source for easy reproducibility. Moreover, we find that almost every loss function performs equally well in this setting, matching the regular cross entropy loss.

1 Introduction

Whether it is at the word or at the sentence level, learning robust representations allows neural networks to consolidate knowledge that can later be transferred to other tasks and domains. Many approaches have dealt with this problem in different ways, for instance with CBOW or skip-gram from word2vec (Mikolov et al., 2013) for context-independent word embeddings, or more recently with BERT's (Devlin et al., 2019) sentence embeddings and contextual word embeddings.

In order to learn sentence representations, a neural encoder enc needs to learn a mapping from an initial representation x_i to a target vector space. In a metric learning approach, the distances between each pair of sentence embeddings $(\mathrm{enc}(x_i), \mathrm{enc}(x_j))$ should be low if classes $y_i = y_j$ (intra-class compactness) and high if $y_i \neq y_j$ (inter-class separability). To achieve this objective, the angle θ_{ij} separating a pair of embeddings (as depicted

in Figure 1) can be used to redefine the model's loss function.

In the domain of face recognition, many loss functions (Schroff et al., 2015; Wen et al., 2016; Liu et al., 2017; Wang et al., 2018; Deng et al., 2019) have been proposed to learn better face representations, motivated by high intra-class variability due to lighting, position or background. Other studies have experimented with these methods in different domains with similar characteristics, like speaker verification (Bredin, 2017; Chung et al., 2018; Yadav and Rai, 2018), and even as an enhancement of BERT's sentence representations (Reimers and Gurevych, 2019) for semantic textual similarity. A recent study (Srivastava et al., 2019) has also focused on comparing these methods on face verification, showing that angular margin losses achieve superior performance.

On the other hand, the automatic misogyny identification (AMI) evaluation campaign (Fersini et al., 2018a) was proposed to address misogyny on tweets. Included tasks were identification (i.e. misogynous or not), categorization over five different misogyny types, and target identification (to an individual or a group). However, no participant has proposed a metric learning model. The best system (Ahluwalia et al., 2018) uses a bidirectional LSTM with word embeddings of size 100 for the identification task, and ensemble methods with feature engineering for category and target classification. They achieve a macro F1 score of 36.1 on the misogyny categorization part of sub-task B, which is the one we address as well. A different architecture (Caselli et al., 2018) uses a multi-layer character bidirectional LSTM for categorization, obtaining a macro F1 score of 14.1.

In this paper, we focus on five metric learning losses for the task of misogyny categorization, using the AMI (Fersini et al., 2018a) dataset. Our hypothesis was that metric learning might reduce

89

Proceedings of the 5th Workshop on Representation Learning for NLP (RepL4NLP-2020), pages 89–94

July 9, 2020. ©2020 Association for Computational Linguistics

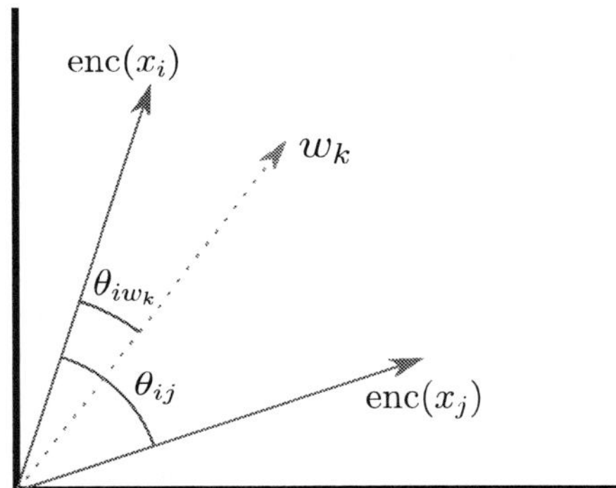

Figure 1: Depiction of embeddings in two dimensions. The dotted vector w_k represents a centroid for some class k, while the other vectors are sentence embeddings. θ values are angles separating two vectors.

the natural intra-class variability within misogyny categories, making representations robust to writing styles, irony, insults, etc. The loss functions we experiment with are contrastive loss (Hadsell et al., 2006), triplet loss (Schroff et al., 2015), center loss (Wen et al., 2016), congenerous cosine loss (Liu et al., 2017) and additive angular margin loss (Deng et al., 2019), as well as cross entropy loss. We optimize these loss functions with two different architectures: a bidirectional LSTM (Hochreiter and Schmidhuber, 1997) and BERT (Devlin et al., 2019), and we evaluate their performance using a simple K-nearest neighbors (KNN) classifier to better measure representation quality.

Our main contributions consist of new state-of-the-art performance for the misogyny categorization task, as well as empirical evidence that these methods do not perform better than cross entropy loss on closed-set sentence classification. Moreover, our code is released as open source for easy reproducibility.

2 Loss Functions

In this section, we present the loss functions chosen for our study, which can be separated into contrast-based and classification-based, according to how they are computed.

2.1 Contrast-based losses

The contrastive loss (Hadsell et al., 2006) uses pairs annotated as similar/dissimilar (also called positive/negative). It brings representations from similar examples closer together, while separating dissimilar ones explicitly:

$$\mathcal{L} = \sum_{i=1}^{P_+} (D_i)^2 + \sum_{i=1}^{P_-} \max(m - D_i, 0)^2 \quad (1)$$

where P_+ is the number of similar pairs, P_- the number of dissimilar pairs, $D_i = 1 - \cos \theta_i$ the distance between embeddings of the ith pair, and m a margin.

The triplet loss (Schroff et al., 2015) is calculated over triplets composed of a reference example known as the anchor, a positive and a negative, both the latter with respect to the anchor. Following the idea introduced by Gelly and Gauvain (2017), we define this loss using the sigmoid function:

$$\mathcal{L} = \sum_{i=0}^{T} \text{sigmoid}(\alpha \left(\cos \theta_i^n - \cos \theta_i^p\right)) \quad (2)$$

where T is the number of triplets, α a scaling hyper-parameter, θ_i^p the angle separating the anchor and the positive embeddings, and θ_i^n the angle separating the anchor and the negative ones.

Taking Figure 1 as an example, contrast-based losses encourage the cosine distance between embeddings i and j to be larger if $y_i \neq y_j$, and smaller if $y_i = y_j$. This is achieved a single pair at a time with contrastive loss, while triplet loss does it jointly using both the positive and negative inside the triplet.

2.2 Classification-based losses

These loss functions derive from the cross entropy loss, either by modifying how the classification layer output is calculated or working as a penalization term. The cross entropy loss is defined as:

$$\mathcal{L}_{\text{CE}} = -\frac{1}{N} \sum_{i=1}^{N} \log \text{softmax}(\sigma_i, y_i) \quad (3)$$

where N is the number of training examples, σ_i the output of the classification layer, and y_i the class of the ith example.

The congenerous cosine (CoCo) loss (Liu et al., 2017) interprets the weights w_k of the classification layer as class centroids, learning to maximize the cosine similarity between a representation and its centroid. The classification layer output σ_i is redefined as:

$$\forall k \quad \sigma_{ik} = \alpha \cdot \cos \theta_{iw_k} \quad (4)$$

where θ_{iw_k} is the angle separating the ith representation and w_k, and α a scaling hyper-parameter.

The additive angular margin (AAM) loss (Deng et al., 2019) goes one step further adding a margin in angular space to penalize the distance between a representation and its centroid:

$$\forall k \quad \sigma_{ik} = \alpha \cdot \cos(\theta_{iw_k} + \delta_{ik}\, m) \qquad (5)$$

where m is a margin, and $\delta_{ik} = 1$ if $k = y_i$ and 0 otherwise.

Finally, the center loss (Wen et al., 2016) penalizes the cross entropy loss with the distance to jointly learned centroids c_k external to the classification layer:

$$\mathcal{L} = \mathcal{L}_{\mathrm{CE}} + \frac{\lambda}{2} \sum_{i=1}^{N} (1 - \cos\theta_{ic_{y_i}})^2 \qquad (6)$$

where λ is a hyper-parameter controlling the effect of penalization.

To see the effect of classification-based losses more intuitively, consider embeddings and centers in Figure 1. If $y_i = k$, then both congenerous cosine loss and center loss will penalize the loss value with the distance from embedding i to w_k (or c_k in the case of center loss), hence bringing all vectors from class k close to the centroid k. The additive angular margin loss follows the same principle, but penalizing further by artificially augmenting the distance of embedding i to w_k with the angular margin.

3 Task

The term misogyny is defined as hatred towards women. Hate speech of this nature is unfortunately common in social Internet interactions, and current language models are generally unable to accurately detect and classify it. The AMI task and corpus were proposed in the context of the IberEval 2018 (Fersini et al., 2018b) and Evalita 2018 (Fersini et al., 2018a) evaluation campaigns, allowing researchers to train models focused specifically on misogyny. The corpus consists of an ensemble of tweets with three different types of annotations: misogyny (binary), misogyny category and target (active or passive).

We use the same dataset as in Fersini et al. (2018a) and we focus exclusively on misogyny categorization, using an additional class for non misogynous tweets. Our results are thus compared to the categorization part of sub-task B. An explanation of misogyny categories according to the definitions given in Fersini et al. (2018a) can be found in Table 2.

Class	Train	Dev	Test
derailing	74	18	11
discredit	811	203	141
dominance	118	30	124
sexual harassment	282	70	44
stereotype	143	36	140
non misogynous	1,772	443	540
total	3,200	800	1,000

Table 1: Number of sentences per class for each partition of the AMI dataset. Note that classes are greatly imbalanced.

As the corpus does not provide a development set, one was constructed from the training set following the same class distribution. The final Train set is composed of 3200 tweets, and the Dev and Test sets of 800 and 1000 tweets respectively. Class distribution is described in detail in Table 1. The task is evaluated using the macro F1 score.

4 Experiments

4.1 Experimental protocol

As different losses rely on different hyper-parameters, we perform a hyper-parameter search including learning rates, margins m, scalings α, and λ. The values we have experimented with are shown in Table 3. Each configuration is trained on Train for 60 epochs and validated using a KNN classifier on Dev. As we deal with a rather small dataset, the best configuration for each loss and each architecture is then trained and validated from scratch 10 times to reduce the effect of randomness. Reported results are the mean macro F1 score and standard deviation on Test over these 10 runs.

In all experiments we use the cosine distance to compare embeddings, as congenerous cosine loss and additive angular margin loss can only be optimized in this way. Additionally, a linear classification layer is jointly trained with the sentence encoder when optimizing classification-based loss functions.

4.2 Architecture

We experiment with two different encoder architectures. The first one is a one-layer bidirectional LSTM (Hochreiter and Schmidhuber, 1997) with output size 768 (to match BERT) and word embeddings of size 300 obtained from a word2vec CBOW model (Mikolov et al., 2013) trained on 2-billion-word Wikipedia dumps. The second one is

Category	Description	Example
derailing	"to justify women abuse, rejecting male responsibility"	"if rape is real why aren't more people reporting it? just another feminist lie"
discredit	"slurring over women with no other larger intention"	"this b*** is a s***"
dominance	"to assert the superiority of men over women to highlight gender inequality"	"#didyouknow the male brain is 3.4 times larger than the female brain? #maledominance"
sexual harassment	"sexual advances, harassment of a sexual nature, etc."	"come on box I show you my c*** darling"
stereotype	"a widely held but fixed and oversimplified image or idea of a woman"	"these people are hysterical. it's like a commercial for why men should never marry [...]"

Table 2: Misogyny categories as described by the corpus authors (Fersini et al., 2018a) along with examples found in the training set.

Parameter	Values
LR	$\{10^{-2}, 10^{-3}, 10^{-4}, 10^{-5}, 10^{-6}\}$• $\{10^{-4}, 10^{-5}, 10^{-6}, 10^{-7}\}$°
m	$\{0.02, 0.05, 0.25, 0.5, 0.75\}$
α and λ	$\{0.01, 0.1, 1, 10, 100, 1000\}$

Table 3: Values tested during initial hyper-parameter search, totaling 486 configurations. LR stands for learning rate, and m, α and λ are loss parameters (see Section 2). Values with • are LSTM only and values with ° are BERT only.

the standard monolingual uncased BERT (Devlin et al., 2019) from the huggingface library (Wolf et al., 2019) pretrained on Wikipedia.

To obtain a sentence embedding from an encoder, we perform a max pooling over the hidden states of the last layer, leaving us with sentence embeddings of size 768 on both models.

4.3 Implementation details

All sentences are pre-tokenized using the `TweetTokenizer` from the NLTK toolkit (Bird et al., 2009) in order to correctly deal with Twitter-specific tokens like hashtags, mentions, and even emojis. During this process we remove handles and URLs. When training BERT, we do a second pass of tokenization with BERT's pretrained tokenizer. We use a batch size of 32 sentences and RMSprop as optimizer, reducing the learning rate by half every 5 epochs of no improvement. The best configurations found during hyper-parameter search for each architecture and loss function are shown in Table 4.

Our code is released as open source, available at `github.com/juanmc2005/MetricAMI`.

4.4 Evaluation

We evaluate each model with the macro F1 score of a KNN classifier with $K = 10$ fit with all sentence embeddings from Train. However, given the high class imbalance, the a priori probability of a random embedding being closer to a *non-misogynous* embedding is higher than for a *discredit* one (see Table 1). To circumvent this issue, we penalize the vote for class k by the number of examples from k in Train. We believe this simple classifier to be a better measure for representation quality, as it relates to the separability and compactness properties that we expect from a metric learning model.

5 Results

The results are summarized in Figure 2. With a fixed architecture, it is clear that all loss functions perform equally, with the exception of LSTM with contrastive and triplet loss. As the LSTM encoder is rather shallow (4.4M parameters) in comparison to BERT (110M parameters), it is possible that contrast-based losses need bigger models to perform competitively.

The fact that almost all losses perform equally well shows that, contrary to what we thought, metric learning models perform no better than cross entropy, in contrast to other findings (Srivastava et al., 2019) on face verification. One possible explanation is that the AMI dataset may not contain enough examples or classes for these models to exploit. However, another factor might be responsible for this behavior. One of the key differences of AMI with respect to face verification is the closed-set nature of the problem. An open-set task is evaluated with unseen *classes*, while a closed-set task is evaluated with unseen *instances* of the train-

Loss	Hyper-parameters
Cross entropy	$LR = 10^{-3}$ • $LR = 10^{-5}$ ○
AAM	$LR = 10^{-3}, m = 0.05, \alpha = 100$ • $LR = 10^{-5}, m = 0.05, \alpha = 100$ ○
Center	$LR = 10^{-4}, \lambda = 1000$ • $LR = 10^{-5}, \lambda = 0.1$ ○
Congenerous cosine	$LR = 10^{-3}, \alpha = 10$ • $LR = 10^{-5}, \alpha = 100$ ○
Contrastive	$LR = 10^{-4}, m = 0.25$ • $LR = 10^{-6}, m = 0.25$ ○
Triplet	$LR = 10^{-4}, \alpha = 1000$ • $LR = 10^{-6}, \alpha = 1000$ ○

Table 4: Best hyper-parameter configurations found per loss function. LR stands for learning rate, and m, α and λ are loss parameters (see Section 2). Rows with • correspond to LSTM and rows with ○ to BERT.

ing classes. It is possible that open-set verification tasks are more suitable for metric learning than closed-set tasks, meaning that the power of metric learning might in fact lie in generalizing to unseen classes rather than unseen class instances. The fact that verification tasks more closely resemble the training objective than exact class prediction could provide an explanation for this.

On the other hand, our fine-tuned BERT outperforms the Evalita winner baseline (Ahluwalia et al., 2018), setting new state-of-the-art for misogyny categorization, with the added benefit of having comparable embeddings with a simple cosine distance.

As a final note, results in Table 4 suggest that congenerous cosine loss and center loss hyper-parameters could be more sensitive to architecture changes than other losses, as they are the only ones whose best configurations differ from one architecture to the other. Perhaps not surprisingly, we also observe that additive angular margin loss works better with lower margins. This is consistent with the margin's role, serving as an upper bound for the distance between an embedding and its centroid, while the margin in contrastive loss serves as a lower bound for the distance between two negatives.

6 Conclusion

In this work we have addressed the problem of misogyny categorization from a metric learning perspective, comparing the performance of sev-

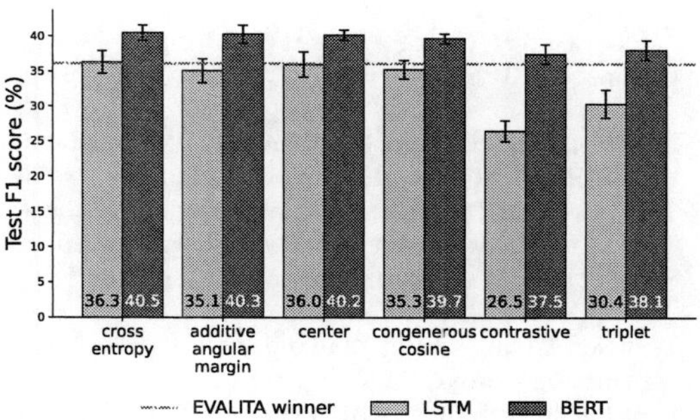

Figure 2: F1 scores on Test for each architecture and loss function. Scores are calculated as the mean of 10 runs and standard deviation is shown as error bars. The baseline of the Evalita 2018 winner (Ahluwalia et al., 2018) is shown for reference.

eral loss functions. We hypothesized that reducing intra-class variability in this way would be beneficial. However, we have shown that none of the considered losses can outperform the regular cross entropy on the task. Our results suggest that metric learning approaches might not be suited to closed-set sentence classification tasks.

Finally, our fine-tuned BERT sets new state-of-the-art performance, with a macro F1 score of 40.5.

Acknowledgements

This work has been partially funded by the LIHLITH project (ANR-17-CHR2-0001-03), and supported by ERA-Net CHIST-ERA, and the "Agence Nationale pour la Recherche" (ANR, France). It has also been made possible thanks to the Saclay-IA computing platform.

Finally, we would like to thank the reviewers for their useful comments.

References

Resham Ahluwalia, Himani Soni, Edward Callow, Anderson Nascimento, and Martine De Cock. 2018. Detecting Hate Speech Against Women in English Tweets. In Tommaso Caselli, Nicole Novielli, Viviana Patti, and Paolo Rosso, editors, *EVALITA Evaluation of NLP and Speech Tools for Italian*, pages 194–199. Accademia University Press.

Steven Bird, Ewan Klein, and Edward Loper. 2009. *Natural Language Processing with Python*. O'Reilly Media.

Herve Bredin. 2017. TristouNet: Triplet loss for speaker turn embedding. In *2017 IEEE International Conference on Acoustics, Speech and Signal*

Processing (ICASSP), pages 5430–5434, New Orleans, LA. IEEE.

Tommaso Caselli, Nicole Novielli, Viviana Patti, and Paolo Rosso. 2018. Tweetaneuse@ AMI EVALITA2018: Character-based Models for the Automatic Misogyny Identification Task. In *Proceedings of the Final Workshop*, volume 12, page 13.

Joon Son Chung, Arsha Nagrani, and Andrew Zisserman. 2018. VoxCeleb2: Deep Speaker Recognition. In *Interspeech*, pages 1086–1090. ISCA.

Jiankang Deng, Jia Guo, Niannan Xue, and Stefanos Zafeiriou. 2019. ArcFace: Additive Angular Margin Loss for Deep Face Recognition. In *The IEEE Conference on Computer Vision and Pattern Recognition (CVPR)*.

Jacob Devlin, Ming-Wei Chang, Kenton Lee, and Kristina Toutanova. 2019. BERT: Pre-training of Deep Bidirectional Transformers for Language Understanding. In *Proceedings of the 2019 Conference of the North American Chapter of the Association for Computational Linguistics: Human Language Technologies, Volume 1 (Long and Short Papers)*, pages 4171–4186, Minneapolis, Minnesota. Association for Computational Linguistics.

Elisabetta Fersini, Debora Nozza, and Paolo Rosso. 2018a. Overview of the Evalita 2018 Task on Automatic Misogyny Identification (AMI). In Tommaso Caselli, Nicole Novielli, Viviana Patti, and Paolo Rosso, editors, *EVALITA Evaluation of NLP and Speech Tools for Italian*, pages 59–66. Accademia University Press.

Elisabetta Fersini, Paolo Rosso, and Maria Anzovino. 2018b. Overview of the Task on Automatic Misogyny Identification at IberEval 2018. In *IberEval@ SEPLN*, pages 214–228.

G. Gelly and J.L. Gauvain. 2017. Spoken Language Identification Using LSTM-Based Angular Proximity. In *Interspeech*, pages 2566–2570. ISCA.

R. Hadsell, S. Chopra, and Y. LeCun. 2006. Dimensionality Reduction by Learning an Invariant Mapping. In *The IEEE Conference on Computer Vision and Pattern Recognition (CVPR)*, volume 2, pages 1735–1742, New York, NY, USA. IEEE.

Sepp Hochreiter and Jürgen Schmidhuber. 1997. Long Short-Term Memory. *Neural Computation*, 9(8):1735–1780.

Yu Liu, Hongyang Li, and Xiaogang Wang. 2017. Rethinking Feature Discrimination and Polymerization for Large-scale Recognition. *ArXiv*, abs/1710.00870.

Tomas Mikolov, Kai Chen, Greg S. Corrado, and Jeffrey Dean. 2013. Efficient Estimation of Word Representations in Vector Space. *ArXiv*, abs/1301.3781.

Nils Reimers and Iryna Gurevych. 2019. Sentence-BERT: Sentence Embeddings using Siamese BERT-Networks. In *Proceedings of the 2019 Conference on Empirical Methods in Natural Language Processing and the 9th International Joint Conference on Natural Language Processing (EMNLP-IJCNLP)*, pages 3982–3992, Hong Kong, China. Association for Computational Linguistics.

Florian Schroff, Dmitry Kalenichenko, and James Philbin. 2015. FaceNet: A Unified Embedding for Face Recognition and Clustering. *The IEEE Conference on Computer Vision and Pattern Recognition (CVPR)*, pages 815–823.

Yash Srivastava, Vaishnav Murali, and Shiv Ram Dubey. 2019. A Performance Comparison of Loss Functions for Deep Face Recognition. *ArXiv*, abs/1901.05903.

Hao Wang, Yitong Wang, Zheng Zhou, Xing Ji, Dihong Gong, Jingchao Zhou, Zhifeng Li, and Wei Liu. 2018. CosFace: Large Margin Cosine Loss for Deep Face Recognition. In *The IEEE Conference on Computer Vision and Pattern Recognition (CVPR)*.

Yandong Wen, Kaipeng Zhang, Zhifeng Li, and Yu Qiao. 2016. A Discriminative Feature Learning Approach for Deep Face Recognition. In *Computer Vision – ECCV 2016*, volume 9911, pages 499–515, Cham. Springer International Publishing.

Thomas Wolf, Lysandre Debut, Victor Sanh, Julien Chaumond, Clement Delangue, Anthony Moi, Pierric Cistac, Tim Rault, R'emi Louf, Morgan Funtowicz, and Jamie Brew. 2019. HuggingFace's Transformers: State-of-the-art Natural Language Processing. *ArXiv*, abs/1910.03771.

Sarthak Yadav and Atul Rai. 2018. Learning Discriminative Features for Speaker Identification and Verification. In *Interspeech*, pages 2237–2241.

On the Choice of Auxiliary Languages for Improved Sequence Tagging

Lukas Lange[1,2,3]   **Heike Adel**[1]   **Jannik Strötgen**[1]

[1] Bosch Center for Artificial Intelligence, Renningen, Germany
[2] Spoken Language Systems (LSV), Saarland University, Saarbrücken, Germany
[3] Saarbrücken Graduate School of Computer Science, Saarbrücken, Germany
{Lukas.Lange,Heike.Adel,Jannik.Stroetgen}@de.bosch.com

Abstract

Recent work showed that embeddings from related languages can improve the performance of sequence tagging, even for monolingual models. In this analysis paper, we investigate whether the best auxiliary language can be predicted based on language distances and show that the most related language is not always the best auxiliary language. Further, we show that attention-based meta-embeddings can effectively combine pre-trained embeddings from different languages for sequence tagging and set new state-of-the-art results for part-of-speech tagging in five languages.

1 Introduction

State-of-the-art methods for sequence tagging tasks, such as named entity recognition (NER) and part-of-speech (POS) tagging, exploit embeddings as input representation. Recent work suggested to include embeddings trained on related languages as auxiliary embeddings to improve model performance: Catalan and Portuguese embeddings, for instance, help NER models on Spanish-English code-switching data (Winata et al., 2019a). In this paper, we analyze whether auxiliary embeddings should be chosen from related languages, or if embeddings from more distant languages could also help.

For this, we revisit current language distance measures (Gamallo et al., 2017) and adapt them to the embeddings and training data used in our experiments. We investigate the question, whether we can predict the best auxiliary language based on those language distance measures. Our results suggest that no strong correlation exists between language distance and performance and that even less related languages can be a good choice as auxiliary languages.

In our experiments, we explore both available monolingual and multilingual pre-trained byte-pair encoding (Heinzerling and Strube, 2018) and FLAIR embeddings (Akbik et al., 2018). For combining monolingual subword embeddings from different languages, we investigate two different methods: the concatenation of embeddings and the use of attention-based meta-embeddings (Kiela et al., 2018; Winata et al., 2019a).

We perform experiments on CoNLL and universal dependency datasets for NER and POS tagging in five languages and show that meta-embeddings are a promising alternative to the concatenation of additional auxiliary embeddings as they learn to decide on the auxiliary languages in an unsupervised way. Moreover, the inclusion of more languages is often beneficial and meta-embeddings can be effectively used to leverage a larger number of embeddings and achieve new state-of-the-art performance on all five POS tagging tasks. Finally, we propose guidelines to decide which auxiliary languages one should use in which setting.

2 Related Work

Combination of Embeddings. Previous work has seen performance gains by combining, e.g., various types of word embeddings (Tsuboi, 2014) or variants of the same type of embeddings trained on different corpora (Luo et al., 2014). For the combination, alternative solutions have been proposed, such as different input channels (Zhang et al., 2016), concatenation (Yin and Schütze, 2016), averaging of embeddings (Coates and Bollegala, 2018), and attention (Kiela et al., 2018). In this paper, we compare the inclusion of auxiliary languages via concatenation to the dynamic combination with attention.

Auxiliary Languages. Winata et al. (2019a) proposed to include embeddings from closely-related languages to improve NER performance

Proceedings of the 5th Workshop on Representation Learning for NLP (RepL4NLP-2020), pages 95–102
July 9, 2020. ©2020 Association for Computational Linguistics

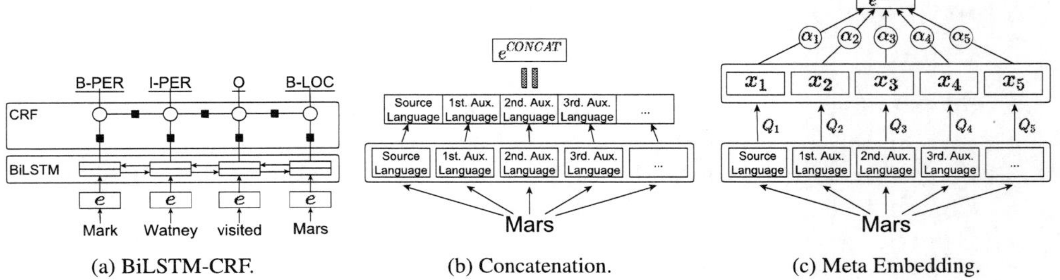

(a) BiLSTM-CRF.   (b) Concatenation.   (c) Meta Embedding.

Figure 1: Overview of our model architecture (left). The embedding combination e can be either computed using the concatenation e^{CONCAT} (middle) or the meta embedding method e^{ATT} (right).

in code-switching settings, i.e., it was shown that Catalan and Portuguese embeddings help for Spanish-English NER. In a later work, it was shown that also more distant languages can be beneficial (Winata et al., 2019b), but only tests in the special setting of code-switching NER were performed and no connection between the relatedness of languages and the performance increase was analyzed. In contrast, our work shows that the inclusion of auxiliary languages increases performance in monolingual settings as well and we analyze whether language distance measures can be used to select the best auxiliary language in advance.

Language Distance Measures. Gamallo et al. (2017) proposed to measure distances between languages by using the perplexity of language models trained on one language and applied to another language. Campos et al. (2019) used a similar method to retrace changes in multilingual diachronic corpora over time. Another popular measure of similarity is based on vocabulary overlap, assuming that similar languages share a large portion of their vocabulary (Brown et al., 2008).

3 Sequence Tagging Model

Following Lample et al. (2016), we use a bidirectional long short-term memory network (BiLSTM) (Hochreiter and Schmidhuber, 1997) followed by a conditional random field (CRF) classifier (Lafferty et al., 2001) (see Figure 1a).

3.1 Embeddings

Each input word is represented with a pretrained word vector. We experiment with byte-pair encoding (BPEmb) (Heinzerling and Strube, 2018) and FLAIR embeddings (Akbik et al., 2018), as

for both of them pretrained embeddings are publicly available for all the languages we consider.[1]

3.2 Combination of Embeddings

As we experiment with multiple word embeddings, we compare two combination methods: a simple **concatenation** e^{CONCAT} and attention-based **meta-embeddings** e^{ATT} as shown in Figure 1b and 1c, respectively, and described next.

In both cases, the input are n embeddings $e_i, 1 \leq i \leq n$ that should be combined. In our experiments, we use embeddings from n different languages.

For concatenation, we simply stack the individual embeddings into a single vector: $e^{CONCAT} = [e_1, e_2, .., e_n]$.

In the case of meta-embeddings, we follow Kiela et al. (2018) and compute the combination as a weighted sum of embeddings. For this, all n embeddings e_i need to be mapped to the same size first. In contrast to previous work, we use a nonlinear mapping as this yielded better performance in our experiments. Thus, we compute $x_i = tanh(Q_i \cdot e_i + b_i)$ with weight matrix Q_i, bias b_i and $x_i \in \mathbb{R}^E$ being the i-th embedding e_i mapped to the size E of the largest embedding. The attention weight α_i for each embedding x_i is then computed with a fully-connected hidden layer of size H with parameters $W \in \mathbb{R}^{H \times E}$ and $V \in \mathbb{R}^{1 \times H}$, followed by a softmax layer.

$$\alpha_i = \frac{\exp(V \cdot \tanh(W x_i))}{\sum_{l=1}^{n} \exp(V \cdot \tanh(W x_l))}$$

The parameters of the meta-embedding layer $(Q_1, ..., Q_n, b_1, ..., b_n, W, V)$ are randomly initialized and learnt during training.

---

[1] https://github.com/flairNLP/flair
https://nlp.h-its.org/bpemb/

NER	De	En	Es	Fi	Nl
Monolingual	79.78 ± .49	86.78 ± .15	78.99 ± .91	78.00 ± .87	78.91 ± .42
Multilingual	75.37 ± .87	86.52 ± .34	78.33 ± .47	77.41 ± .86	77.49 ± .45
Mono + Multi	81.13 ± .46	**88.01 ± .27**	80.32 ± .50	81.44 ± .36	81.15 ± .43
Mono + DE	-	87.46 ± .19	79.79 ± .74	80.31 ± .21	81.31 ± .15
Mono + EN	80.92 ± .29	-	80.48 ± .56	81.22 ± .26	80.84 ± .30
Mono + ES	80.29 ± .20	87.37 ± .30	-	80.80 ± .83	80.62 ± .39
Mono + FI	81.10 ± .36	87.94 ± .17	79.91 ± .82	-	80.65 ± .48
Mono + NL	81.25 ± .14	87.38 ± .22	80.93 ± .25	80.67 ± .49	-
Mono + All	81.52 ± .33	87.70 ± .06	80.63 ± .34	82.07 ± .33 [†]	81.73 ± .26 [†]
Meta-Embeddings	**81.75 ± .50** [†]	87.87 ± .23	80.84 ± .52	**83.12 ± .12** [†]	**82.13 ± .50** [†]

POS	De	En	Es	Fi	Nl
Monolingual	93.02 ± .11	94.17 ± .09	96.23 ± .04	92.84 ± .13	94.01 ± .21
Multilingual	92.19 ± .20	94.10 ± .06	96.01 ± .07	91.95 ± .11	93.35 ± .22
Mono + Multi	93.40 ± .08	95.11 ± .07	**96.54 ± .03**	94.70 ± .12	94.94 ± .13
Mono + DE	-	95.11 ± .09	96.43 ± .13	94.43 ± .18	94.70 ± .09
Mono + EN	93.26 ± .11	-	96.52 ± .06	94.45 ± .14	94.80 ± .12
Mono + ES	93.31 ± .13	95.03 ± .09	-	94.48 ± .14	94.79 ± .17
Mono + FI	93.41 ± .12	94.97 ± .04	96.34 ± .08	-	94.92 ± .13
Mono + NL	93.52 ± .10	94.99 ± .08	96.41 ± .07	94.42 ± .08	-
Mono + All	**93.60 ± .14** [†]	**95.40 ± .04** [†]	96.46 ± .09	**95.61 ± .08** [†]	95.31 ± .08
Meta-Embeddings	93.51 ± .08	95.36 ± .10 [†]	96.48 ± .06	**95.61 ± .11** [†]	**95.34 ± .14** [†]

Table 1: Results of NER (F_1, above) and POS (Accuracy, below) experiments with BPE embeddings. [†] marks models that are statistically significant to the best Mono + X model. box highlights the closest auxiliary language according to language distance measure d_{MV}, and box the best auxiliary language according to performance.

		De	En	Es	Fi	Nl
NER	Straková et al. (2019)	**85.1**	**93.3**	**88.8**	-	**92.7**
	Meta-Emb. (BPEmb)	81.8	87.9	80.8	83.1	82.1
	Meta-Emb. (FLAIR)	83.9	90.7	86.2	**85.1**	86.6
POS	Yasunaga et al. (2018)	94.4	95.8	96.8	95.4	93.1
	Meta-Emb. (BPEmb)	93.5	95.4	96.5	95.6	95.3
	Meta-Emb. (FLAIR)	**94.8**	**96.5**	**97.2**	**97.8**	**96.8**

Table 2: Comparison with state of the art.

Finally, the embeddings x_i are weighted using the attention weights α_i resulting in the word representation $e^{ATT} = \sum_i \alpha_i \cdot x_i$

4 Experiments and Results

We perform NER and POS experiments on five languages: German (De), English (En), Spanish (Es), Finnish (Fi), and Dutch (Nl). Note that we assume at least a character overlap to use auxiliary embeddings from another language. Thus, languages with a different character set, e.g., Asian languages, cannot be used, in this setting. Future work could investigate the inclusion of languages with different character sets, e.g., by using bilingual dictionaries or machine translation.

For NER, we use the CoNLL 2002/03 datasets (Tjong Kim Sang, 2002; Tjong Kim Sang and De Meulder, 2003) and the FiNER corpus (Ruokolainen et al., 2019). For POS tagging, we experiment with the universal dependencies treebanks.[2] For each language, we report results for the following methods:

Monolingual (Mono). Only embeddings from the source language were taken for the experiments. This is the baseline setting. We also compare our results to **multilingual embeddings (Multi)** which have been successfully used in monolingual settings as well (Heinzerling and Strube, 2019). To ensure comparability, we use the multilingual versions of BPEmb and FLAIR, which were trained simultaneously on 275 and 300 languages, respectively.

Mono + X. A second set of embeddings from a different language X is concatenated with the original monolingual embeddings. While for this typically embeddings from a related language are chosen, we report results for all language combinations and investigate in particular whether relatedness is necessary for improvement.

---

[2]We predict the UPOS tag from the following UD v2.0 treebanks: de_gsd, en_ewt, es_gsd, fi_tdt, nl_alpino.

Mono + All & Meta-Embeddings. We also experiment with the combination of all embeddings from all languages from our experiments. In this setting, we use all six embeddings (five monolingual embeddings and the multilingual embeddings) and combine them either using concatenation (Mono + All) or meta-embeddings.

We have chosen these settings that are mainly based on monolingual embeddings, as the current state-of-the-art for named entity recognition is based on monolingual FLAIR embeddings (Akbik et al., 2019). In addition, multilingual embeddings, such as multilingual BERT (Devlin et al., 2019) tend to perform worse than their monolingual counterparts[3] in monolingual experiments. For completeness, we include experiments with multilingual embeddings as mentioned before.

4.1 Results

Following Reimers and Gurevych (2017), we report all experimental results as the mean of five runs and their standard deviation in Table 1 for experiments with byte-pair encoding embeddings. The results with FLAIR embeddings can be found in the appendix. We performed statistical significance testing to check if the concatenation (Mono + All) and meta-embeddings models are better than the best Mono + X model. We used paired permutation testing with 2^{20} permutations and a significance level of 0.05 and performed the Fischer correction following Dror et al. (2017).[4]

For meta-embeddings, we found statistically significant differences in 12 out of 20 settings (6 with BPEmb, 6 with FLAIR) against the best monolingual + X model, while we found statistically significant differences for Mono + All in only 7 out of 20 cases. This suggests that meta-embeddings are superior to monolingual settings with one auxiliary language as well as to the concatenation of all embeddings. Further, we found that the combination of monolingual and multilingual byte-pair encoding embeddings is always superior to either monolingual or multilingual embeddings alone for both tasks. Even though the multilingual embeddings have seen many languages during pre-training, they can still benefit from the high performance of monolingual embeddings and vice versa. As the meta-embeddings

---

[3]https://github.com/google-research/bert/blob/master/multilingual.md

[4]We take the model with median performance on the development set for significance testing.

Rank	d_{MV}				
	De	En	Es	Fi	Nl
1	Nl	Nl	En	En	De*
2	En	Fi	Nl	De	En*
3	Fi	De	Fi	Nl	Fi
4	Es	Es	Es	Es	Es

Table 3: Language ranking according to the majority voting distance d_{MV}. * highlights equal ranks.

assign attention weights for each embedding, we can inspect the importance the models give to the different embeddings. An analysis for an example sentence can be found in Section D in the appendix. Table 2 provides the results of BPEmb and FLAIR meta-embeddings in comparison to state of the art, showing that we set the new state of the art for POS tagging.

4.2 Analysis of Language Distances

To evaluate how useful language distances are for predicting the best auxiliary language, we compare rankings based on language distances and the observed performance rankings based on Table 1. For this, we take the language distance from Gamallo et al. (2017), which is based on language modeling perplexity PP of unigram language models LM applied to texts of foreign languages CH. Lower language model perplexities on a foreign dataset indicate higher language relatedness.

$$d_P(L1, L2) = \text{PP}(\text{CH}_{L2}, \text{LM}_{L1})$$

We also test language similarities based on vocabulary overlap with $W(L1|L2)$ being the number of words of $L1$ which are shared with $L2$ and $N(L1)$ the number of words of $L1$ shared with other languages.

$$d_V(L1, L2) = \frac{W(L1|L2) + W(L2|L1)}{2 \cdot \min(N(L1), N(L2))}$$

For our experiments, we further adapt d_P to use the perplexity of the FLAIR forward language models on the test data provided by Gamallo et al. (2017) and call it d_P^*. Similarly, we adapt d_V^* to compute the overlap of words in our training data. Note that both variants, d_P^* and d_V^*, are based on properties from either our model or training data and are, therefore, specific to our setting. Finally, we create a ranking d_{MV} which combines the rankings from d_P, d_P^*, d_V, d_V^* with majority voting. The ranking of d_{MV} is provided in Table 3, the rankings of the individual distance measures are given in the appendix.

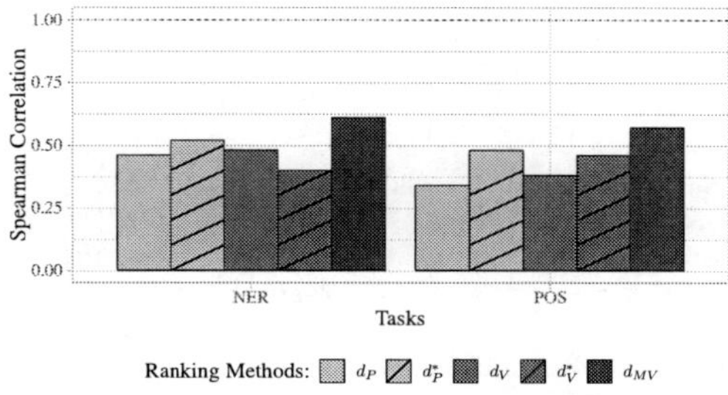

Figure 2: Spearman's rank correlation between language distance and model performance rankings for NER and POS tasks for different language distances.

To analyze the correlation between language distance measures and the performance of our model, we compute the Spearman's rank correlation coefficient between the real rankings based on performance and predicted rankings from our language distances. The results are shown in Figure 2. We conclude that predicting the auxiliary language ranking is a hard task and see that the most related language is not always the best auxiliary language in practice (cf., Table 1). This holds in particular for POS tagging, where the performance differences of models are quite small.

In general, d_P^* shows a higher correlation with model performance than d_P and d_V, indicating that not only word overlap plays a role but also context information. The majority voting d_{MV} achieves the highest correlation and often predicts the best auxiliary language for NER models using byte-pair encoding. However, the actual ranking of all languages does not match the performance ranking, which results in a relatively low correlation with only a little above 0.5.

4.3 Practical Guide

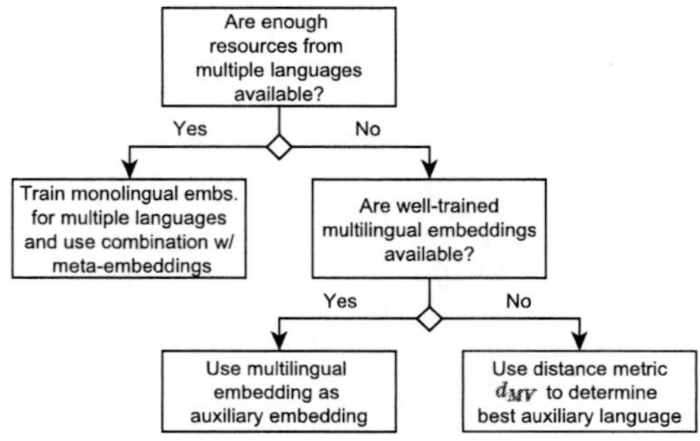

Figure 3: Proposal for auxiliary embedding selection.

Finally, we propose a small guide in Figure 3 to decide which auxiliary languages one can use to improve performance over monolingual embeddings. Depending on the available amount of data, it is recommended to train multiple monolingual embeddings and combine them using meta-embeddings, which was observed to be the best method in our experiments. If not enough data is available to train monolingual embeddings, the best solution would be the inclusion of multilingual embeddings, assuming the existence of high-quality embeddings, such as multilingual byte-pair encoding. If none of the above applies, language distance measures, in particular the combination of multiple distances, can help to identify the most promising auxiliary embeddings. Despite not always predicting the best model, the predicted auxiliary language often led to improvements over the monolingual baseline in our experiments.

5 Conclusion

In this paper, we investigated the benefits of auxiliary languages for sequence tagging. We showed that it is hard to predict the best auxiliary language based on language distances. We further showed that meta-embeddings can leverage multiple embeddings effectively for those tasks and set the new state of the art on part-of-speech tagging across different languages. Finally, we proposed a guide on how to decide which method of including auxiliary languages one should use.

Acknowledgments

We would like to thank Dietrich Klakow, Marius Mosbach, Michael A. Hedderich, the members of the BCAI NLP&KRR research group and the anonymous reviewers for their helpful comments and suggestions.

References

Alan Akbik, Tanja Bergmann, and Roland Vollgraf. 2019. Pooled contextualized embeddings for named entity recognition. In *Proceedings of the 2019 Conference of the North American Chapter of the Association for Computational Linguistics: Human Language Technologies, Volume 1 (Long and Short Papers)*, pages 724–728, Minneapolis, Minnesota. Association for Computational Linguistics.

Alan Akbik, Duncan Blythe, and Roland Vollgraf. 2018. Contextual string embeddings for sequence labeling. In *Proceedings of the 27th International*

Conference on Computational Linguistics, pages 1638–1649, Santa Fe, New Mexico, USA. Association for Computational Linguistics.

Cecil H Brown, Eric W Holman, Søren Wichmann, and Viveka Velupillai. 2008. Automated classification of the world s languages: a description of the method and preliminary results. *STUF-Language Typology and Universals Sprachtypologie und Universalienforschung*, 61(4):285–308.

Jos Ramom Pichel Campos, Pablo Gamallo Otero, and Iaki Alegria Loinaz. 2019. Measuring diachronic language distance using perplexity: Application to english, portuguese, and spanish. *Natural Language Engineering*, page 122.

Joshua Coates and Danushka Bollegala. 2018. Frustratingly easy meta-embedding – computing meta-embeddings by averaging source word embeddings. In *Proceedings of the 2018 Conference of the North American Chapter of the Association for Computational Linguistics: Human Language Technologies, Volume 2 (Short Papers)*, pages 194–198, New Orleans, Louisiana. Association for Computational Linguistics.

Jacob Devlin, Ming-Wei Chang, Kenton Lee, and Kristina Toutanova. 2019. BERT: Pre-training of deep bidirectional transformers for language understanding. In *Proceedings of the 2019 Conference of the North American Chapter of the Association for Computational Linguistics: Human Language Technologies, Volume 1 (Long and Short Papers)*, pages 4171–4186, Minneapolis, Minnesota. Association for Computational Linguistics.

Rotem Dror, Gili Baumer, Marina Bogomolov, and Roi Reichart. 2017. Replicability analysis for natural language processing: Testing significance with multiple datasets. *Transactions of the Association for Computational Linguistics*, 5:471–486.

Pablo Gamallo, José Ramom Pichel, and Iñaki Alegria. 2017. From language identification to language distance. *Physica A: Statistical Mechanics and its Applications*, 484:152–162.

Benjamin Heinzerling and Michael Strube. 2018. BPEmb: Tokenization-free pre-trained subword embeddings in 275 languages. In *Proceedings of the Eleventh International Conference on Language Resources and Evaluation (LREC 2018)*, Miyazaki, Japan. European Language Resources Association (ELRA).

Benjamin Heinzerling and Michael Strube. 2019. Sequence tagging with contextual and non-contextual subword representations: A multilingual evaluation. In *Proceedings of the 57th Annual Meeting of the Association for Computational Linguistics*, pages 273–291, Florence, Italy. Association for Computational Linguistics.

Sepp Hochreiter and Jürgen Schmidhuber. 1997. Long short-term memory. *Neural Computing*, 9(8):1735–1780.

Douwe Kiela, Changhan Wang, and Kyunghyun Cho. 2018. Dynamic meta-embeddings for improved sentence representations. In *Proceedings of the 2018 Conference on Empirical Methods in Natural Language Processing*, pages 1466–1477, Brussels, Belgium. Association for Computational Linguistics.

John D. Lafferty, Andrew McCallum, and Fernando C. N. Pereira. 2001. Conditional random fields: Probabilistic models for segmenting and labeling sequence data. In *Proceedings of the Eighteenth International Conference on Machine Learning*, ICML '01, pages 282–289, San Francisco, CA, USA. Morgan Kaufmann Publishers Inc.

Guillaume Lample, Miguel Ballesteros, Sandeep Subramanian, Kazuya Kawakami, and Chris Dyer. 2016. Neural architectures for named entity recognition. In *Proceedings of the 2016 Conference of the North American Chapter of the Association for Computational Linguistics: Human Language Technologies*, pages 260–270, San Diego, California. Association for Computational Linguistics.

Yong Luo, Jian Tang, Jun Yan, Chao Xu, and Zheng Chen. 2014. Pre-trained multi-view word embedding using two-side neural network. In *Proceedings of the Twenty-Eighth AAAI Conference on Artificial Intelligence*, AAAI'14, pages 1982–1988. AAAI Press.

Nils Reimers and Iryna Gurevych. 2017. Reporting score distributions makes a difference: Performance study of LSTM-networks for sequence tagging. In *Proceedings of the 2017 Conference on Empirical Methods in Natural Language Processing*, pages 338–348, Copenhagen, Denmark. Association for Computational Linguistics.

Teemu Ruokolainen, Pekka Kauppinen, Miikka Silfverberg, and Krister Lindén. 2019. A finnish news corpus for named entity recognition. *Language Resources and Evaluation*, pages 1–26.

Jana Straková, Milan Straka, and Jan Hajič. 2019. Neural Architectures for Nested NER through Linearization. In *Proceedings of the 57th Annual Meeting of the Association for Computational Linguistics*, pages 5326–5331, Florence, Italy. Association for Computational Linguistics.

Erik F. Tjong Kim Sang. 2002. Introduction to the CoNLL-2002 shared task: Language-independent named entity recognition. In *COLING-02: The 6th Conference on Natural Language Learning 2002 (CoNLL-2002)*.

Erik F. Tjong Kim Sang and Fien De Meulder. 2003. Introduction to the CoNLL-2003 shared task: Language-independent named entity recognition. In

Proceedings of the Seventh Conference on Natural Language Learning at HLT-NAACL 2003, pages 142–147.

Yuta Tsuboi. 2014. Neural networks leverage corpus-wide information for part-of-speech tagging. In *Proceedings of the 2014 Conference on Empirical Methods in Natural Language Processing (EMNLP)*, pages 938–950, Doha, Qatar. Association for Computational Linguistics.

Genta Indra Winata, Zhaojiang Lin, and Pascale Fung. 2019a. Learning multilingual meta-embeddings for code-switching named entity recognition. In *Proceedings of the 4th Workshop on Representation Learning for NLP (RepL4NLP-2019)*, pages 181–186, Florence, Italy. Association for Computational Linguistics.

Genta Indra Winata, Zhaojiang Lin, Jamin Shin, Zihan Liu, and Pascale Fung. 2019b. Hierarchical meta-embeddings for code-switching named entity recognition. In *Proceedings of the 2019 Conference on Empirical Methods in Natural Language Processing and the 9th International Joint Conference on Natural Language Processing (EMNLP-IJCNLP)*, pages 3541–3547, Hong Kong, China. Association for Computational Linguistics.

Michihiro Yasunaga, Jungo Kasai, and Dragomir Radev. 2018. Robust multilingual part-of-speech tagging via adversarial training. In *Proceedings of the 2018 Conference of the North American Chapter of the Association for Computational Linguistics: Human Language Technologies, Volume 1 (Long Papers)*, pages 976–986, New Orleans, Louisiana. Association for Computational Linguistics.

Wenpeng Yin and Hinrich Schütze. 2016. Learning word meta-embeddings. In *Proceedings of the 54th Annual Meeting of the Association for Computational Linguistics (Volume 1: Long Papers)*, pages 1351–1360, Berlin, Germany. Association for Computational Linguistics.

Ye Zhang, Stephen Roller, and Byron C. Wallace. 2016. MGNC-CNN: A simple approach to exploiting multiple word embeddings for sentence classification. In *Proceedings of the 2016 Conference of the North American Chapter of the Association for Computational Linguistics: Human Language Technologies*, pages 1522–1527, San Diego, California. Association for Computational Linguistics.

A Hyperparameters and Training

We use the Byte-Pair-Encoding embeddings (Heinzerling and Strube, 2018) with 300 dimensions and a vocabulary size of 200k tokens for all languages. For FLAIR, we use the embeddings provided by the FLAIR framework (Akbik et al., 2018) with 2048 dimensions for each language model resulting in a total embedding size of 4096 dimensions. The bidirectional LSTM has a hidden size of 256 units. For training, we use stochastic gradient descent with a learning rate of 0.1 and a batch size of 64 sentences. The learning rate is halved after 3 consecutive epochs without improvement on the development set. We apply dropout with probability 0.1 after the input layer.

B Language Distances

We report the language rankings of the single metrics d_P, d_P^*, d_V and d_V^* in Table 4.

C Results on NER and POS tagging with FLAIR embeddings

We performed the same experiments as in Section 4.1 with FLAIR embeddings as well and report the results in Table 5 for NER and for POS tagging.

In difference to the BPE experiments reported in the paper, we do not include multilingual embeddings in the Mono + All and meta-embedding versions of FLAIR. The reason is prior experiments in which multilingual embeddings led to reduced performance. This is also reflected in the poor performance of the multilingual FLAIR embeddings alone. It seems that the multilingual BPE embeddings are more effective in downstream tasks than the multilingual FLAIR embeddings.

D Analysis of Attention Weights

As the meta-embeddings assign attention weights for each embedding, we can inspect the importance the models give to the different embeddings. Figure 4 shows the assigned weights for an English sentence. In general, the model assigns most weight to the English embeddings. However, we observe an increased weight for German and the multilingual embedding for the German word *Bayerische*. Even though *Vereinsbank* is also a German word, the model focuses more on English for this word, probably because the subword *bank* has the same meaning in English.

E Study: Increased Number of Parameters vs. Auxiliary Language

To investigate whether the performance increase comes from the increased number of parameters rather than the inclusion of more embeddings, we also investigated including the same embedding type twice (Mono + Mono). However, we found

Rank	de				en				es				fi				nl			
	d_P	d_P^*	d_V	d_V^*	d_P	d_P^*	d_V	d_V^*	d_P	d_P^*	d_V	d_V^*	d_P	d_P^*	d_V	d_V^*	d_P	d_P^*	d_V	d_V^*
1	nl	nl	en	nl	nl	nl	de	fi	en	nl	en	en	de	nl	en	en	de	de	en	en
2	en	en	nl	en	es	fi	nl	nl	nl	en	de	nl	nl	de	de	nl	en	en	de	de
3	fi	fi	es*	fi	de	de	fi	es	fi	de	fi	fi	en	en	es*	de	fi	fi	es*	es
4	es	es	fi*	es	fi	es	es	de	de	fi	nl	de	es	es	nl*	es	es	es	fi*	fi

Table 4: Language distances. Languages marked with * are ranked the same.

NER	De	En	Es	Fi	Nl
Straková et al. (2019)	85.10	93.28	88.81	-	92.69
Monolingual	82.66 ± .11	89.98 ± .11	85.08 ± .68	83.38 ± .31	85.68 ± .27
Multilingual	66.21 ± .79	82.87 ± .24	77.87 ± .93	73.95 ± .74	77.44 ± .52
Mono + Mono	82.45 ± .45	89.95 ± 0.21	85.26 ± .06	83.37 ± .48	85.67 ± .06
Mono + Multi	82.95 ± .21	90.04 ± .11	84.70 ± .50	83.46 ± .37	86.04 ± .28
Mono + DE	-	90.24 ± .19	85.16 ± .23	84.23 ± .22	85.82 ± .22
Mono + EN	83.27 ± .36	-	85.53 ± .20	84.10 ± .26	86.73 ± .09
Mono + ES	82.85 ± .34	90.14 ± .13	-	83.88 ± .31	86.16 ± .09
Mono + FI	83.10 ± .45	90.14 ± .09	85.06 ± .64	-	86.14 ± .31
Mono + NL	82.79 ± .24	90.18 ± .15	85.77 ± .27	83.65 ± .31	-
Mono + All	83.43 ± .29	90.29 ± .18	85.48 ± .78	84.32 ± .32	86.43 ± .33
Meta-Embeddings	83.90 ± .14 [†]	90.70 ± .29 [†]	86.18 ± .35	85.09 ± .30 [†]	86.58 ± .58

POS	De	En	Es	Fi	Nl
Yasunaga et al. (2018)	94.35	95.82	96.84	95.40	93.09
Monolingual	94.72 ± .07	96.28 ± .05	97.08 ± .03	97.52 ± .03	96.48 ± .11
Multilingual	92.82 ± .20	93.69 ± .07	96.06 ± .13	92.98 ± .10	94.85 ± .11
Mono + Mono	94.74 ± .15	96.24 ± .02	97.04 ± .08	97.55 ± .05	96.45 ± .13
Mono + Multi	94.72 ± .13	96.29 ± .04	97.04 ± .05	97.52 ± .05	96.77 ± .02
Mono + DE	-	96.41 ± .07	97.11 ± .08	97.64 ± .04	96.62 ± .06
Mono + EN	94.71 ± .04	-	97.13 ± .12	97.52 ± .06	96.49 ± .09
Mono + ES	94.67 ± .06	96.36 ± .03	-	97.48 ± .03	96.61 ± .13
Mono + FI	94.65 ± .05	96.38 ± .03	97.14 ± .05	-	96.68 ± .05
Mono + NL	94.64 ± .03	96.31 ± .07	97.06 ± .04	97.51 ± .04	-
Mono + All	94.64 ± .10	96.48 ± .05	97.11 ± .04	97.52 ± .06	96.54 ± .20
Meta-Embeddings	94.78 ± .09	96.49 ± .03 [†]	97.18 ± .07	97.82 ± .03 [†]	96.83 ± .13 [†]

Table 5: Results of NER (F_1, above) and POS (Accuracy, below) experiments with FLAIR embeddings. [†] marks models that are statistically significant to the best Mono + X model. box highlights the closest auxiliary language according to language distance measure d_{MV}, and box the best auxiliary language according to performance.

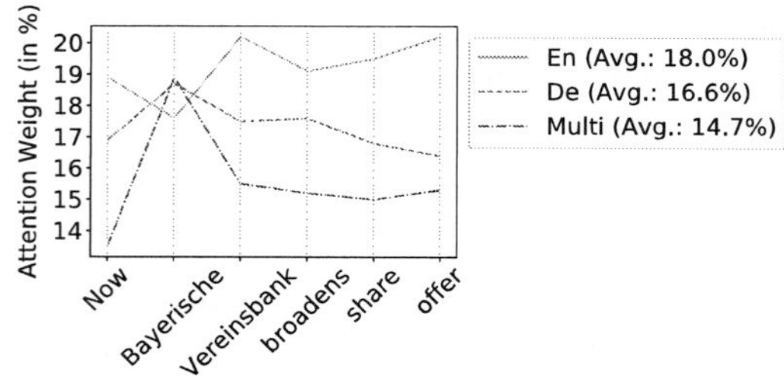

Figure 4: Learned attention weights of the meta-embeddings model with byte-pair encoding embeddings for English NER.

that this does not help: The performance is comparable to the monolingual baseline. Thus, the performance increase for Mono + X really comes from additional information provided by the embeddings of the auxiliary language.

Adversarial Alignment of Multilingual Models
for Extracting Temporal Expressions from Text

Lukas Lange[1,2,3]   **Anastasiia Iurshina**[1]   **Heike Adel**[1]   **Jannik Strötgen**[1]

[1] Bosch Center for Artificial Intelligence, Renningen, Germany
[2] Spoken Language Systems (LSV), Saarland University, Saarbrücken, Germany
[3] Saarbrücken Graduate School of Computer Science, Saarbrücken, Germany
`{Lukas.Lange,Heike.Adel,Jannik.Stroetgen}@de.bosch.com`

Abstract

Although temporal tagging is still dominated by rule-based systems, there have been recent attempts at neural temporal taggers. However, all of them focus on monolingual settings. In this paper, we explore multilingual methods for the extraction of temporal expressions from text and investigate adversarial training for aligning embedding spaces to one common space. With this, we create a single multilingual model that can also be transferred to unseen languages and set the new state of the art in those cross-lingual transfer experiments.

1 Introduction

The extraction of temporal expressions from text is an important processing step for many applications, such as topic detection and questions answering (Strötgen and Gertz, 2016). However, there is a lack of multilingual models for this task. While recent temporal taggers, such as the work by Laparra et al. (2018) focus on English, only little work was dedicated to multilingual temporal tagging so far.

Strötgen and Gertz (2015) proposed to automatically generate language resources for the rule-based temporal tagger HeidelTime, but all of these models are language specific and can only process texts from a fixed language. In this paper, we propose to overcome this limitation by training a single model on multiple languages to extract temporal expressions from text. We experiment with recurrent neural networks using FastText embeddings (Bojanowski et al., 2017) and the multilingual version of BERT (Devlin et al., 2019). In order to process multilingual texts, we investigate an unsupervised alignment technique based on adversarial training, making it applicable to zero- or low-resource scenarios and compare it to standard dictionary-based alternatives (Mikolov et al., 2013).

We demonstrate that it is possible to achieve competitive performance with a single multilingual model trained jointly on English, Spanish and Portuguese. Further, we demonstrate that this multilingual model can be transferred to new languages, for which the model has not seen any labeled sentences during training by applying it to unseen French, Catalan, Basque, and German data. Our model shows superior performance compared to HeidelTime (Strötgen and Gertz, 2015) and sets new state-of-the-art results in the cross-lingual extraction of temporal expressions.

2 Related Work

Temporal Tagging. The current state of the art for temporal tagging are rule-based systems, such as HeidelTime (Strötgen and Gertz, 2013) or SUTime (Chang and Manning, 2012). In particular, HeidelTime uses a different set of rules depending on the language and domain. Strötgen and Gertz (2015) automatically generated HeidelTime rules for more than 200 languages in order to support many languages. However, the quality of these rules does not match the high quality of manually created rules and the models are still language specific. Aside from rule-based systems, Lee et al. (2014) proposed to learn context-dependent semantic parsers for extracting temporal expressions from text. Laparra et al. (2018) made a first step towards neural models by using recurrent neural networks. However, they only performed experiments on English corpora using monolingual models. In contrast, we propose a truly multilingual model.

Multilingual Embeddings. Recently, it became popular to train embedding models on resources from many languages jointly (Lample and Conneau, 2019; Conneau et al., 2019). For example, multilingual BERT (Devlin et al., 2019) was trained on Wikipedia articles from more than 100 languages. Although performance improvements show the possibility to use multilingual BERT in

Proceedings of the 5th Workshop on Representation Learning for NLP (RepL4NLP-2020), pages 103–109
July 9, 2020. ©2020 Association for Computational Linguistics

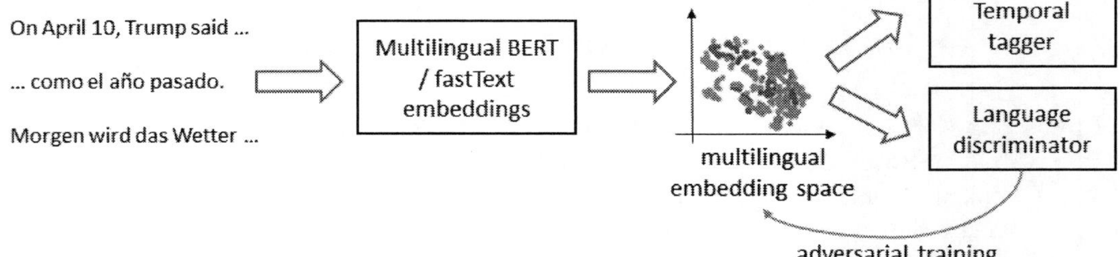

Figure 1: Overview of our multilingual system with adversarial training for improving the embedding space.

monolingual (Hakala and Pyysalo, 2019), multilingual (Tsai et al., 2019) and cross-lingual settings (Wu and Dredze, 2019), it has been questioned whether multilingual BERT is truly multilingual (Pires et al., 2019; Singh et al., 2019; Libovický et al., 2019). Therefore, we will investigate the benefits of aligning its embeddings in our experiments.

Aligning Embedding Spaces. A common method to create multilingual embedding spaces is the alignment of monolingual embeddings (Mikolov et al., 2013; Joulin et al., 2018). Smith et al. (2017) proposed to align embedding spaces by creating orthogonal transformation matrices based on bilingual dictionaries, which we use as baseline alignment method.

It was shown that BERT can also benefit from alignment, i.a. in cross-lingual (Schuster et al., 2019; Liu et al., 2019) or multilingual settings (Cao et al., 2020). In contrast to prior work, we experiment with aligning BERT using adversarial training, which is related to using adversarial training for domain adaptation (Ganin et al., 2016), coping with bias or confounding variables (Li et al., 2018; Raff and Sylvester, 2018; Zhang et al., 2018; Barrett et al., 2019; McHardy et al., 2019) or transferring models from a source to a target language (Zhang et al., 2017; Keung et al., 2019; Wang et al., 2019). Similar to Chen and Cardie (2018), we use a multinomial discriminator in our setting.

3 Methods

We model the task of extracting temporal expressions as a sequence tagging problem and explore the performance of state-of-the-art recurrent neural networks with FastText and BERT embeddings, respectively. In particular, we train multilingual models that process all languages in the same model. To create and improve the multilingual embedding

spaces, we propose an unsupervised alignment approach based on adversarial training and compare it to two baseline approaches. Figure 1 provides an overview of the system. The different components are described in detail in the following.

3.1 Temporal Expression Extraction Model

Following previous work, e.g., Lample et al. (2016), we train a bidirectional long-short term memory network (BiLSTM) (Hochreiter and Schmidhuber, 1997) with a conditional random field (CRF) (Lafferty et al., 2001) output layer. As input, we experiment with two embedding methods: (i) pre-trained FastText (Bojanowski et al., 2017) word embeddings from multiple languages,[1] and (ii) multilingual BERT (Devlin et al., 2019) embeddings.[2] For BERT, we use the averaged output of the last four layers as input to the BiLSTM and fine-tune the whole model during the training of temporal information extraction. We also experimented with a BERT setup similar to Devlin et al. (2019) where the embeddings are directly mapped to the label space and the softmax function is used to compute the label probabilities instead of a CRF. However, we found superior performance for the BiLSTM-CRF models.

3.2 Alignment of Embeddings

We propose an unsupervised approach based on adversarial training to align multilingual embeddings in a common space (Section 3.2.2) and compare it with two approaches from related work based on linear transformation matrices (Section 3.2.1).

---

[1] https://fasttext.cc/docs/en/crawl-vectors.html

[2] https://github.com/google-research/bert/blob/master/multilingual.md

3.2.1 Baseline Alignment

Embedding spaces are typically aligned using a linear transformation based on bilingual dictionaries. We follow the work from Smith et al. (2017), and align embedding spaces based on orthogonal transformation matrices. These matrices can either be constructed in an unsupervised way by using words that appear in the vocabularies from both languages, i.e., equal words that can be identified using string matching, or in a supervised way based on real-world dictionaries (Mikolov et al., 2013; Joulin et al., 2018). For the latter method, we build dictionaries based on translations from wiktionary.[3] For both methods, we reduce the vocabularies to the most frequent 5k words per language and treat English as the pivot language.

3.2.2 Adversarial Alignment

We propose to use gradient reversal training to align embeddings from different (sub)spaces in an unsupervised way. Note that neither dictionaries nor other language resources are needed for this approach, making it applicable to zero- or low-resource scenarios. In particular, we extend the extraction model C with a discriminator D. Both model parts are trained alternately in a multi-task fashion. The *feature extractor* F is shared among them and consists of the embedding layer E, followed by a non-linear mapping: $F(x) = \tanh(W^{\top}E(x))$ with x being the current word, $W \in \mathbb{R}^{S \times S}$ and S being the embedding dimensionality.

The *discriminator* D is a multinomial non-linear classifier consisting of one hidden layer with ReLU activation (Hahnloser et al., 2000): $D(x) = \text{softmax}(T^{\top}\text{ReLU}(V^{\top}F(x)))$ with $V \in \mathbb{R}^{S \times H}$, $T \in \mathbb{R}^{H \times O}$, H being a hyperparameter and O the number of different languages.

In total, we distinguish three sets of parameters: θ_C: the parameters of the downstream classification model (i.e., the temporal tagger), θ_D: the parameters of the discriminator, and θ_F: the parameters of the feature extractor. The loss functions of the temporal tagger L_C and of the discriminator L_D are cross-entropy loss functions. While θ_C and θ_D are updated using standard gradient descent, gradient reversal training updates θ_F as follows:

$$\theta_F = \theta_F - \eta\left(\frac{\partial L_C}{\partial \theta_F} - \lambda\frac{\partial L_D}{\partial \theta_F}\right) \qquad (1)$$

---

[3] https://github.com/open-dsl-dict/wiktionary-dict

Dataset	Train	Dev	Test
English (EN)	3,461/*1,456*	420/*164*	354/*202*
Spanish (ES)	1,705/*972*	189/*122*	332/*199*
Portuguese (PT)	3,501/*948*	389/*100*	481/*172*
French (FR)	-	-	708/*424*
German (DE)	-	-	2,666/*500*
Catalan (CA)	-	-	1,944/*1389*
Basque (EU)	-	-	163/*123*

Table 1: Number of sentences / *temporal expressions* per corpus. The lower part is only used for evaluation.

with η being the learning rate and λ a hyperparameter to control the discriminator influence. Thus, θ_F is updated in the opposite direction of the gradients from the discriminator loss, making the discriminator an adversary. With this, the discriminator is optimized for predicting the correct origin language of a given sentence, but at the same time the feature extractor gets updated with gradient reversal, such that the language detection becomes harder and the discriminator cannot easily distinguish the word representations from different languages.

4 Experiments and Results

4.1 Evaluation Metrics and Datasets

For evaluation, we use the TempEval3 evaluation script and report strict and relaxed extraction F_1 score for complete and partial overlap to gold standard annotations, respectively. We also report the type F_1 score for the classification into the four temporal types: Date, Time, Duration, and Set.

Our multilingual models are trained using the Portuguese TimeBank (Costa and Branco, 2012) and TempEval3 (UzZaman et al., 2013) for Spanish and English (TimeBank subset). To demonstrate that our model is able to generalize to unseen languages, we perform tests using the French (Bittar et al., 2011), Catalan (Saurı and Badia, 2012) and Basque (Altuna et al., 2016) TimeBanks and the Zeit subset of the German KRAUTS corpus (Strötgen et al., 2018). Corpus statistics are shown in Table 1.

4.2 Hyperparameters and Model Training

We use the AdamW optimizer (Loshchilov and Hutter, 2019) with a learning rate of 1e−5 for the BiLSTM-CRF model part and 1e−6 for BERT. The model is trained for a maximum of 50 epochs using early stopping on the development set. The BiLSTM has a hidden size of 128 units per direction. The labels are encoded in the IOB2 format. For

Task	Metric	HeidelTime	FastText				BERT	
			unaligned	aligned w/o Dict.	aligned w/ Dict	aligned w/ AT	unaligned	aligned w/ AT
EN	strict	**81.78**	68.36	69.10	70.80	75.63 [†]	73.09	74.80 [†]
	relaxed	**90.71**	79.14	79.03	81.21	82.03 [†]	84.34	86.61 [†]
	type	**83.27**	72.13	72.18	73.32	72.85 [†]	75.50	79.53 [†]
ES	strict	**85.87**	75.67	76.53	77.44	79.64 [†]	79.11	79.55
	relaxed	**90.13**	82.43	82.45	82.47	84.46 [†]	84.12	85.71
	type	**87.47**	78.07	78.46	78.24	80.88 [†]	80.22	80.11
PT	strict	71.59	70.36	70.20	70.48	72.41	74.52	**75.47**
	relaxed	81.18	76.77	75.86	76.29	78.15	80.75	**81.51**
	type	**76.75**	72.29	71.50	72.26	73.84	75.47	76.23

Table 2: Results for multilingual models trained on English, Spanish and Portuguese data jointly. [†]highlights aligned models with statistical significant differences to the unaligned model (paired permutation test, p=0.05).

regularization, we apply dropout with a rate of 10% after the input embeddings. The discriminator for adversarial training has a hidden size H of 100 units and is trained after every 10th batch of the sequence tagger with λ set to 0.001.

4.3 Results

The results for the multilingual experiments are shown in Table 2. We trained three models with different random seeds and report the performance of the model with median performance on the combined development set of all languages. Current state of the art for English (Lee et al., 2014) achieves 83.1/91.4/85.4 for strict/relaxed/type F_1. However, this is a monolingual model that can only be applied to English.

The effects of aligning FastText embeddings are clearly visible in Table 2. The supervised alignment using a dictionary is always superior compared to the unsupervised alignment without a dictionary or the unaligned embeddings. Our proposed adversarial alignment (w/ AT) leads to the best results across languages. The performance of BERT is close to the best FastText model.[4] Aligning BERT with adversarial training also increases performance. The improvements are smaller compared to FastText but still statistically significant for English.

Table 3 provides transfer results of the models with BERT embeddings to languages without labeled training data.[5] In particular, the model using the Wikipedia data for training the discriminator is effective in generalizing to languages without train-

Task	Metric	HeidelTime -Auto	BERT	
			unalign.	aligned w/ AT
FR	strict	52.35	60.12	**62.58**
	relaxed	72.02	74.23	**75.46**
	type	**68.70**	61.96	62.07
DE	strict	38.87	63.34	**66.53**
	relaxed	52.11	76.51	**77.82**
	type	50.15	66.95	**69.04**
CA	strict	28.11	63.24	**64.21**
	relaxed	62.81	74.95	**77.00**
	type	60.84	65.66	**67.85**
EU	strict	22.54	43.96	**47.87**
	relaxed	26.76	61.54	**63.83**
	type	23.94	57.14	**58.51**

Table 3: Results for the unsupervised cross-lingual setting. We compare to HeidelTime with automatically generated resources, which resembles a similar setting.

ing resources for temporal expression extraction, as these languages are also aligned during model training. It outperforms the state-of-the-art Heidel-Time models by a large margin. The impressive performance of the multilingual BERT in the cross-lingual setting can be explained by the fact that the model has seen many sentences in our target languages during the pre-training phase, which can now be effectively leveraged in this new setting.

4.4 Analysis

The embedding spaces of BERT before and after aligning are shown in Figure 2. The left sub-figure presents the original BERT embeddings without any fine-tuning. In this visualization, clear clusters for each language exist. After fine-tuning on multilingual temporal expression extraction and adversarial alignment (right sub-figure) the clusters for each language mostly disappear.

---

[4]Additional experiments with the multilingual XLM model (Lample and Conneau, 2019) trained on 100 languages led to similar results as the multilingual BERT model.

[5]The results of the FastText models were considerably lower for cross-lingual transfer.

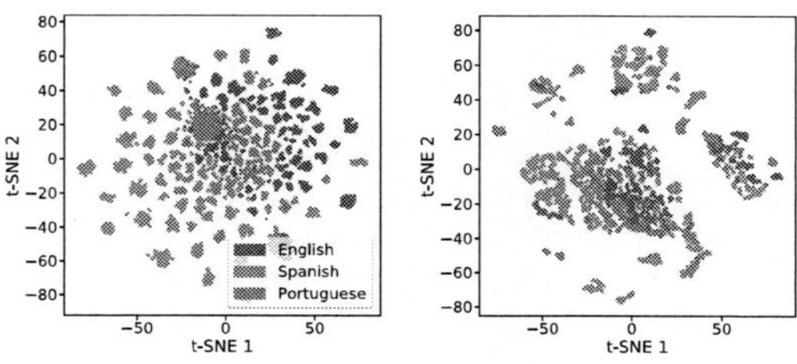

(a) without training.   (b) after joint temporal extraction and adversarial training.

Figure 2: t-SNE plots of the last BERT layer without any training (left) and after training (right).

5 Conclusion

In this paper, we investigated how a multilingual neural model with FastText or BERT embeddings can be used to extract temporal expressions from text. We investigated adversarial training for creating multilingual embedding spaces. The model can effectively be transferred to unseen languages in a cross-lingual setting and outperforms a state-of-the-art model by a large margin.

Acknowledgments

We would like to thank the members of the BCAI NLP&KRR research group and the anonymous reviewers for their helpful comments.

References

Begoña Altuna, María Jesús Aranzabe, and Arantza Díaz de Ilarraza. 2016. Adapting timeml to basque: Event annotation. In *International Conference on Intelligent Text Processing and Computational Linguistics*.

Maria Barrett, Yova Kementchedjhieva, Yanai Elazar, Desmond Elliott, and Anders Søgaard. 2019. Adversarial removal of demographic attributes revisited. In *Proceedings of the 2019 Conference on Empirical Methods in Natural Language Processing and the 9th International Joint Conference on Natural Language Processing (EMNLP-IJCNLP)*.

André Bittar, Pascal Amsili, Pascal Denis, and Laurence Danlos. 2011. French TimeBank: An ISO-TimeML annotated reference corpus. In *Proceedings of the 49th Annual Meeting of the Association for Computational Linguistics: Human Language Technologies*.

Piotr Bojanowski, Edouard Grave, Armand Joulin, and Tomas Mikolov. 2017. Enriching word vectors with subword information. *Transactions of the Association for Computational Linguistics*, 5.

Steven Cao, Nikita Kitaev, and Dan Klein. 2020. Multilingual alignment of contextual word representations. In *International Conference on Learning Representations*.

Angel X. Chang and Christopher Manning. 2012. SUTime: A library for recognizing and normalizing time expressions. In *Proceedings of the Eighth International Conference on Language Resources and Evaluation (LREC'12)*.

Xilun Chen and Claire Cardie. 2018. Multinomial adversarial networks for multi-domain text classification. In *Proceedings of the 2018 Conference of the North American Chapter of the Association for Computational Linguistics: Human Language Technologies, Volume 1 (Long Papers)*.

Alexis Conneau, Kartikay Khandelwal, Naman Goyal, Vishrav Chaudhary, Guillaume Wenzek, Francisco Guzmán, Edouard Grave, Myle Ott, Luke Zettlemoyer, and Veselin Stoyanov. 2019. Unsupervised cross-lingual representation learning at scale. *arXiv preprint arXiv:1911.02116*.

Francisco Costa and António Branco. 2012. TimeBankPT: A TimeML annotated corpus of Portuguese. In *Proceedings of the Eighth International Conference on Language Resources and Evaluation (LREC'12)*.

Jacob Devlin, Ming-Wei Chang, Kenton Lee, and Kristina Toutanova. 2019. BERT: Pre-training of deep bidirectional transformers for language understanding. In *Proceedings of the 2019 Conference of the North American Chapter of the Association for Computational Linguistics: Human Language Technologies, Volume 1 (Long and Short Papers)*.

Yaroslav Ganin, Evgeniya Ustinova, Hana Ajakan, Pascal Germain, Hugo Larochelle, François Laviolette, Mario Marchand, and Victor Lempitsky. 2016. Domain-adversarial training of neural networks. *J. Mach. Learn. Res.*, 17(1).

Richard HR Hahnloser, Rahul Sarpeshkar, Misha A Mahowald, Rodney J Douglas, and H Sebastian Seung. 2000. Digital selection and analogue amplification coexist in a cortex-inspired silicon circuit. *Nature*, 405(6789).

Kai Hakala and Sampo Pyysalo. 2019. Biomedical named entity recognition with multilingual BERT. In *Proceedings of The 5th Workshop on BioNLP Open Shared Tasks*.

Sepp Hochreiter and Jürgen Schmidhuber. 1997. Long short-term memory. *Neural Computing*, 9(8).

Armand Joulin, Piotr Bojanowski, Tomas Mikolov, Hervé Jégou, and Edouard Grave. 2018. Loss in translation: Learning bilingual word mapping with a retrieval criterion. In *Proceedings of the 2018 Conference on Empirical Methods in Natural Language Processing*.

Phillip Keung, yichao lu, and Vikas Bhardwaj. 2019. Adversarial learning with contextual embeddings for zero-resource cross-lingual classification and NER. In *Proceedings of the 2019 Conference on Empirical Methods in Natural Language Processing and the 9th International Joint Conference on Natural Language Processing (EMNLP-IJCNLP)*.

John D. Lafferty, Andrew McCallum, and Fernando C. N. Pereira. 2001. Conditional random fields: Probabilistic models for segmenting and labeling sequence data. In *Proceedings of the Eighteenth International Conference on Machine Learning*, ICML '01.

Guillaume Lample, Miguel Ballesteros, Sandeep Subramanian, Kazuya Kawakami, and Chris Dyer. 2016. Neural architectures for named entity recognition. In *Proceedings of the 2016 Conference of the North American Chapter of the Association for Computational Linguistics: Human Language Technologies*.

Guillaume Lample and Alexis Conneau. 2019. Cross-lingual language model pretraining. *Advances in Neural Information Processing Systems (NeurIPS)*.

Egoitz Laparra, Dongfang Xu, and Steven Bethard. 2018. From characters to time intervals: New paradigms for evaluation and neural parsing of time normalizations. *Transactions of the Association for Computational Linguistics*, 6.

Kenton Lee, Yoav Artzi, Jesse Dodge, and Luke Zettlemoyer. 2014. Context-dependent semantic parsing for time expressions. In *Proceedings of the 52nd Annual Meeting of the Association for Computational Linguistics (Volume 1: Long Papers)*.

Yitong Li, Timothy Baldwin, and Trevor Cohn. 2018. Towards robust and privacy-preserving text representations. In *Proceedings of the 56th Annual Meeting of the Association for Computational Linguistics (Volume 2: Short Papers)*.

Jindřich Libovický, Rudolf Rosa, and Alexander Fraser. 2019. How language-neutral is multilingual bert? *arXiv preprint arXiv:1911.03310*.

Qianchu Liu, Diana McCarthy, Ivan Vulić, and Anna Korhonen. 2019. Investigating cross-lingual alignment methods for contextualized embeddings with token-level evaluation. In *Proceedings of the 23rd Conference on Computational Natural Language Learning (CoNLL)*.

Ilya Loshchilov and Frank Hutter. 2019. Decoupled weight decay regularization. In *International Conference on Learning Representations*.

Robert McHardy, Heike Adel, and Roman Klinger. 2019. Adversarial training for satire detection: Controlling for confounding variables. In *Proceedings of the 2019 Conference of the North American Chapter of the Association for Computational Linguistics: Human Language Technologies, Volume 1 (Long and Short Papers)*.

Tomas Mikolov, Quoc V. Le, and Ilya Sutskever. 2013. Exploiting similarities among languages for machine translation. *arXiv preprint arXiv:1309.4168*.

Telmo Pires, Eva Schlinger, and Dan Garrette. 2019. How multilingual is multilingual BERT? In *Proceedings of the 57th Annual Meeting of the Association for Computational Linguistics*.

E. Raff and J. Sylvester. 2018. Gradient reversal against discrimination: A fair neural network learning approach. In *2018 IEEE 5th International Conference on Data Science and Advanced Analytics (DSAA)*.

Roser Saurı and Toni Badia. 2012. Catalan timebank 1.0 corpus documentation. Technical report.

Tal Schuster, Ori Ram, Regina Barzilay, and Amir Globerson. 2019. Cross-lingual alignment of contextual word embeddings, with applications to zero-shot dependency parsing. In *Proceedings of the 2019 Conference of the North American Chapter of the Association for Computational Linguistics: Human Language Technologies, Volume 1 (Long and Short Papers)*.

Jasdeep Singh, Bryan McCann, Richard Socher, and Caiming Xiong. 2019. BERT is not an interlingua and the bias of tokenization. In *Proceedings of the 2nd Workshop on Deep Learning Approaches for Low-Resource NLP (DeepLo 2019)*.

Samuel L. Smith, David H. P. Turban, Steven Hamblin, and Nils Y. Hammerla. 2017. Offline bilingual word vectors, orthogonal transformations and the inverted softmax. In *5th International Conference on Learning Representations, ICLR 2017, Toulon, France, April 24-26, 2017, Conference Track Proceedings*.

Jannik Strötgen and Michael Gertz. 2013. Multilingual and cross-domain temporal tagging. *Language Resources and Evaluation*, 47(2).

Jannik Strötgen and Michael Gertz. 2015. A baseline temporal tagger for all languages. In *Proceedings of the 2015 Conference on Empirical Methods in Natural Language Processing*.

Jannik Strötgen and Michael Gertz. 2016. Domain-sensitive temporal tagging. *Synthesis Lectures on Human Language Technologies*, 9(3).

Jannik Strötgen, Anne-Lyse Minard, Lukas Lange, Manuela Speranza, and Bernardo Magnini. 2018. KRAUTS: A German temporally annotated news corpus. In *Proceedings of the Eleventh International Conference on Language Resources and Evaluation (LREC 2018)*.

Henry Tsai, Jason Riesa, Melvin Johnson, Naveen Arivazhagan, Xin Li, and Amelia Archer. 2019. Small and practical BERT models for sequence labeling. In *Proceedings of the 2019 Conference on Empirical Methods in Natural Language Processing and the 9th International Joint Conference on Natural Language Processing (EMNLP-IJCNLP)*.

Naushad UzZaman, Hector Llorens, Leon Derczynski, James Allen, Marc Verhagen, and James Pustejovsky. 2013. SemEval-2013 task 1: TempEval-3: Evaluating time expressions, events, and temporal relations. In *Second Joint Conference on Lexical and Computational Semantics (*SEM), Volume 2: Proceedings of the Seventh International Workshop on Semantic Evaluation (SemEval 2013)*.

Haozhou Wang, James Henderson, and Paola Merlo. 2019. Weakly-supervised concept-based adversarial learning for cross-lingual word embeddings. In *Proceedings of the 2019 Conference on Empirical Methods in Natural Language Processing and the 9th International Joint Conference on Natural Language Processing (EMNLP-IJCNLP)*.

Shijie Wu and Mark Dredze. 2019. Beto, bentz, becas: The surprising cross-lingual effectiveness of BERT. In *Proceedings of the 2019 Conference on Empirical Methods in Natural Language Processing and the 9th International Joint Conference on Natural Language Processing (EMNLP-IJCNLP)*.

Brian Hu Zhang, Blake Lemoine, and Margaret Mitchell. 2018. Mitigating unwanted biases with adversarial learning. In *Proceedings of the 2018 AAAI/ACM Conference on AI, Ethics, and Society*, AIES '18.

Meng Zhang, Yang Liu, Huanbo Luan, and Maosong Sun. 2017. Adversarial training for unsupervised bilingual lexicon induction. In *Proceedings of the 55th Annual Meeting of the Association for Computational Linguistics (Volume 1: Long Papers)*.

Contextual and Non-Contextual Word Embeddings:
an in-depth Linguistic Investigation

Alessio Miaschi*◦, Felice Dell'Orletta◦
*Department of Computer Science, University of Pisa
◦ItaliaNLP Lab, Istituto di Linguistica Computazionale "Antonio Zampolli", Pisa
`alessio.miaschi@phd.unipi.it, felice.dellorletta@ilc.cnr.it`

Abstract

In this paper we present a comparison between the linguistic knowledge encoded in the internal representations of a contextual Language Model (BERT) and a contextual-independent one (Word2vec). We use a wide set of probing tasks, each of which corresponds to a distinct sentence-level feature extracted from different levels of linguistic annotation. We show that, although BERT is capable of understanding the full context of each word in an input sequence, the implicit knowledge encoded in its aggregated sentence representations is still comparable to that of a contextual-independent model. We also find that BERT is able to encode sentence-level properties even within single-word embeddings, obtaining comparable or even superior results than those obtained with sentence representations.

1 Introduction

Distributional word representations (Mikolov et al., 2013) trained on large-scale corpora have rapidly become one of the most prominent component in modern NLP systems. In this context, the recent development of context-dependent embeddings (Peters et al., 2018; Devlin et al., 2019) has shown that such representations are able to achieve state-of-the-art performance in many complex NLP tasks.

However, the introduction of such models made the interpretation of the syntactic and semantic properties learned by their inner representations more complex. Recent studies have begun to study these models in order to understand whether they encode linguistic phenomena even without being explicitly designed to learn such properties (Marvin and Linzen, 2018; Goldberg, 2019; Warstadt et al., 2019). Much of this work focused on the definition of *probing models* trained to predict simple linguistic properties from unsupervised representations. In particular, those work provided evidences that

contextualized Neural Language Models (NLMs) are able to capture a wide range of linguistic phenomena (Adi et al., 2016; Perone et al., 2018; Tenney et al., 2019b) and even to organize this information in a hierarchical manner (Belinkov et al., 2017; Lin et al., 2019; Jawahar et al., 2019). Despite this, less study focused on the analysis and the comparison of contextual and non-contextual NLMs according to their ability to encode implicit linguistic properties in their representations.

In this paper we perform a large number of probing experiments to analyze and compare the implicit knowledge stored by a contextual and a non-contextual model within their inner representations. In particular, we define two research questions, aimed at understanding: (i) which is the best method for combining BERT and Word2vec word representations into sentence embeddings and how they differently encode properties related to the linguistic structure of a sentence; (ii) whether such sentence-level knowledge is preserved within BERT single-word representations.

To answer our questions, we rely on a large suite of probing tasks, each of which codifies a particular propriety of a sentence, from very shallow features (such as sentence length and average number of characters per token) to more complex aspects of morphosyntactic and syntactic structure (such as the depth of the whole syntactic tree), thus making them as suitable to assess the implicit knowledge encoded by a NLM at a deep level of granularity.

The remainder of the paper is organized as follows. First we present related work (Sec. 2), then, after briefly presenting our approach (Sec. 3), we describe in more details the data (Sec. 3.1), our set of probing features (Sec. 3.2) and the models used for the experiments (Sec. 3.3). Experiments and results are described in Sec. 4 and 5. To conclude, in Sec. 6 we summarize the main findings of the study.

Proceedings of the 5th Workshop on Representation Learning for NLP (RepL4NLP-2020), pages 110–119
July 9, 2020. ©2020 Association for Computational Linguistics

Contributions In this paper: (i) we perform an in-depth study aimed at understanding the linguistic knowledge encoded in a contextual (BERT) and a contextual-independent (Word2vec) Neural Language Model; (ii) we evaluate the best method for obtaining sentence-level representations from BERT and Word2vec according to a wide spectrum of probing tasks; (iii) we compare the results obtained by BERT and Word2vec according to the different combining methods; (iv) we study whether BERT is able to encode sentence-level properties within its single word representations.

2 Related Work

In the last few years, several methods have been devised to open the black box and understand the linguistic information encoded in NLMs (Belinkov and Glass, 2019). They range from techniques to examine the activations of individual neurons (Karpathy et al., 2015; Li et al., 2016; Kádár et al., 2017) to more domain specific approaches, such as interpreting attention mechanisms (Raganato and Tiedemann, 2018; Kovaleva et al., 2019; Vig and Belinkov, 2019) or designing specific *probing tasks* that a model can solve only if it captures a precise linguistic phenomenon using the *contextual* word/sentence embeddings of a pre-trained model as training features (Conneau et al., 2018; Zhang and Bowman, 2018; Hewitt and Liang, 2019). These latter studies demonstrated that NLMs are able to encode a wide range of linguistic information in a hierarchical manner (Belinkov et al., 2017; Blevins et al., 2018; Tenney et al., 2019b) and even to support the extraction of dependency parse trees (Hewitt and Manning, 2019). Jawahar et al. (2019) investigated the representations learned at different layers of BERT, showing that lower layer representations are usually better for capturing surface features, while embeddings from higher layers are better for syntactic and semantic properties. Using a suite of probing tasks, Tenney et al. (2019a) found that the linguistic knowledge encoded by BERT through its 12/24 layers follows the traditional NLP pipeline: POS tagging, parsing, NER, semantic roles and then coreference. Liu et al. (2019), instead, quantified differences in the transferability of individual layers between different models, showing that higher layers of RNNs (ELMo) are more task-specific (less general), while transformer layers (BERT) do not exhibit this increase in task-specificity.

Closer to our study, Adi et al. (2016) proposed a method for analyzing and comparing different sentence representations and different dimensions, exploring the effect of the dimensionality on the resulting representations. In particular, they showed that sentence representations based on averaged Word2vec embeddings are particularly effective and encode a wide amount of information regarding sentence length, while LSTM auto-encoders are very effective at capturing word order and word content. Similarly, but focused on the resolution of specific downstream tasks, Shen et al. (2018) compared a Single Word Embedding-based model (SWEM-based) with existing recurrent and convolutional networks using a suite of 17 NLP datasets, demonstrating that simple pooling operations over SWEM-based representations exhibit comparable or even superior performance in the majority of cases considered. On the contrary, Joshi et al. (2019) showed that, in the context of three different classification problems in health informatics, context-based representations are a better choice than word-based representations to create vectors. Focusing instead on the geometry of the representation space, Ethayarajh (2019) first showed that the contextualized word representations of ELMo, BERT and GPT-2 produce more context specific representations in the upper layers and then proposed a method for creating a new type of static embedding that outperforms GloVe and FastText on many benchmarks, by simply taking the first principal component of contextualized representations in lower layers of BERT.

Differently from those latter work, our aim is to investigate the implicit linguistic knowledge encoded in pre-trained contextual and contextual-independent models both at sentence and word levels.

3 Our Approach

We studied how layer-wise internal representations of BERT encode a wide spectrum of linguistic properties and how such implicit knowledge differs from that learned by a context-independent model such as Word2vec. Following the probing task approach as defined in Conneau et al. (2018), we proposed a suite of 68 probing tasks, each of which corresponds to a distinct linguistic feature capturing raw-text, lexical, morpho-syntactic and syntactic characteristics of a sentence. More specifically, we defined two sets of experiments. The

Level of Annotation	Linguistic Feature	Label
Raw Text	Sentence Length	sent_length
	Word Length	char_per_tok
	Type/Token Ratio for words and lemmas	ttr_form, ttr_lemma
POS tagging	Distibution of UD and language–specific POS	upos_dist_*, xpos_dist_*
	Lexical density	lexical_density
	Inflectional morphology of lexical verbs and auxiliaries (Mood, Number, Person, Tense and VerbForm)	verbs_*, aux_*
Dependency Parsing	Depth of the whole syntactic tree	parse_depth
	Average length of dependency links and of the longest link	avg_links_len, max_links_len
	Average length of prepositional chains and distribution by depth	avg_prepositional_chain_len, prep_dist_*
	Clause length (n. tokens/verbal heads)	avg_token_per_clause
	Order of subject and object	subj_pre, obj_post
	Verb arity and distribution of verbs by arity	avg_verb_edges, verbal_arity_*
	Distribution of verbal heads and verbal roots	verbal_head_dist, verbal_root_perc
	Distribution of dependency relations	dep_dist_*
	Distribution of subordinate and principal clauses	principal_proposition_dist, subordinate_proposition_dist
	Average length of subordination chains and distribution by depth	avg_subordinate_chain_len, subordinate_dist_1
	Relative order of subordinate clauses	subordinate_post

Table 1: Linguistic Features used in the probing tasks.

first consists in evaluating which is the best method for generating sentence-level embeddings using BERT and Word2vec single-word representations. In particular, we defined a simple probing model that takes as input layer-wise BERT and Word2vec combined representations for each sentence of a gold standard Universal Dependencies (UD) (Nivre et al., 2016) English dataset and predicts the actual value of a given probing feature. Moreover, we compared the results to understand which model performs better according to different levels of linguistic sophistication.

In the second set of experiments, we measured how many sentence-level properties are encoded in single-word representations. To do so, we performed our set of probing tasks using the embeddings extracted from both BERT and Word2vec individual tokens. In particular, we considered the word representations corresponding to the first, last and two internal tokens for each sentence of the UD dataset.

3.1 Data

In order to perform the probing experiments on gold annotated sentences, we relied on the Universal Dependencies (UD) English dataset. The dataset includes three UD English treebanks: UD_English-ParTUT, a conversion of a multilin-gual parallel treebank consisting of a variety of text genres, including talks, legal texts and Wikipedia articles (Sanguinetti and Bosco, 2015); the Universal Dependencies version annotation from the GUM corpus (Zeldes, 2017); the English Web Treebank (EWT), a gold standard universal dependencies corpus for English (Silveira et al., 2014). Overall, the final dataset consists of 23,943 sentences.

3.2 Probing Features

As previously mentioned, our method is in line with the probing tasks approach defined in Conneau et al. (2018), which aims to capture linguistic information from the representations learned by a NLM. Specifically, in our work, each probing task correspond to predict the value of a specific linguistic feature automatically extracted from the POS tagged and dependency parsed sentences in the English UD dataset. The set of features is based on the ones described in Brunato et al. (2020) and it includes characteristics acquired from raw, morphosyntactic and syntactic levels of annotation. As described in Brunato et al. (2020), this set of features has been shown to have a highly predictive role when leveraged by traditional learning models on a variety of classification problems, covering different aspects of stylometric and complexity analysis.

As shown in Table 1, these features capture several linguistic phenomena ranging from the average length of words and sentence, to morpho–syntactic information both at the level of POS distribution and about the inflectional properties of verbs. More complex aspects of sentence structure are derived from syntactic annotation and model global and local properties of parsed tree structure, with a focus on subtrees of verbal heads, the order of subjects and objects with respect to the verb, the distribution of UD syntactic relations and features referring to the use of subordination.

3.3 Models

We relied on a pre-trained English version of BERT (BERT-base uncased, 12 layers) for the extraction of the contextual word embeddings. To obtain the representations for our sentence-level tasks we experimented the activation of the first input token ($[CLS]$)[1] and four different combining methods: *Max-pooling*, *Min-pooling*, *Mean* and *Sum*. Each of this four combining methods returns a single $\vec{s}$ vector, such that each s_n is obtained by combining the nth components $w_{1n}, w_{2n}, ..., w_{mn}$ of the embedding of each word in the input sentence.

In order to conduct a comparison of context-based and word-based representations when solving our set of probing tasks, we performed all the probing experiments using also the embeddings extracted from a pre-trained version of Word2vec. In particular, we trained the model on the English Wikipedia dataset (dump of March 2020), resulting in 300-dimensional vectors. In the same manner as BERT's contextual representations, we experimented four combining methods: *Max-pooling*, *Min-pooling*, *Mean* and *Sum*.

We used a linear Support Vector Regression model (LinearSVR) as probing model.

4 Evaluating Sentence Representations

The first set of experiments consists in evaluating which is the best method for combining word-level embeddings into sentence representations in order to understand what kind of implicit linguistic properties are encoded within both contextual and non-contextual representations using different combining methods. To do so, we firstly extracted from each sentence in the UD dataset the corresponding word embeddings using the output of the internal representations of Word2vec and BERT layers

---

[1]As suggested in Jawahar et al. (2019), the *[CLS]* token somehow summarizes the information encoded in the input sequence.

Categories	BERT	Word2vec	Baseline
Raw text	**0.65**	0.51	0.37
Morphosyntax	0.49	**0.57**	0.28
Syntax	0.55	**0.56**	0.44
All features	0.53	**0.56**	0.38

Table 2: BERT (average between layers) and Word2vec ρ scores computed by averaging *Max-*, *Min-*, *Mean* and *Sum* scores according to the three linguistic levels of annotations and considering all the probing features (*All features*). Baseline scores are also reported.

Categories	Sum	Min	Max	Mean
Raw text	**0.56**	0.51	0.51	0.46
Morphosyntax	0.59	0.52	0.54	**0.61**
Syntax	**0.61**	0.55	0.55	0.54
All features	**0.60**	0.54	0.55	0.57

Table 3: Word2vec probing scores obtained with the four sentence combining methods.

(from input layer *-12* to output layer *-1*). Secondly, we computed the sentence-representations according to the different combining strategies defined in 3.3. We then performed our set of 68 probing tasks using the LinearSVR model for each sentence representation. Since the majority of our probing features is correlated to sentence length, we compared probing results with the ones obtained with a baseline computed by measuring the ρ coefficient between the length of the UD sentences and each of the 68 probing features.

Evaluation was performed with a 5-cross fold validation and using Spearman correlation score (ρ) between predicted and gold labels as evaluation metric.

Table 2 report average ρ scores aggregating all probing results (*All features*) and according to raw text (*Raw text*), morphosyntactic (*Morphosyntax*) and syntactic (*Syntax*) levels of annotations. Scores are computed by averaging *Max-*, *Min-pooling*, *Mean* and *Sum results*. As a general remark, we notice that the scores obtained by Word2vec and BERT's internal representations outperforms the ones obtained with the correlation baseline, thus showing that both models are capable of implicitly encoding a wide spectrum of linguistic phenomena. Interestingly, we can notice that Word2vec sentence representations outperform BERT ones when considering all the probing features in average.

We report in Table 3 and Figure 1 the probing scores obtained by the two models. For what concerns Word2vec representations, we notice that the *Sum* method prove to be the best one for encoding raw text and syntactic features, while mo-

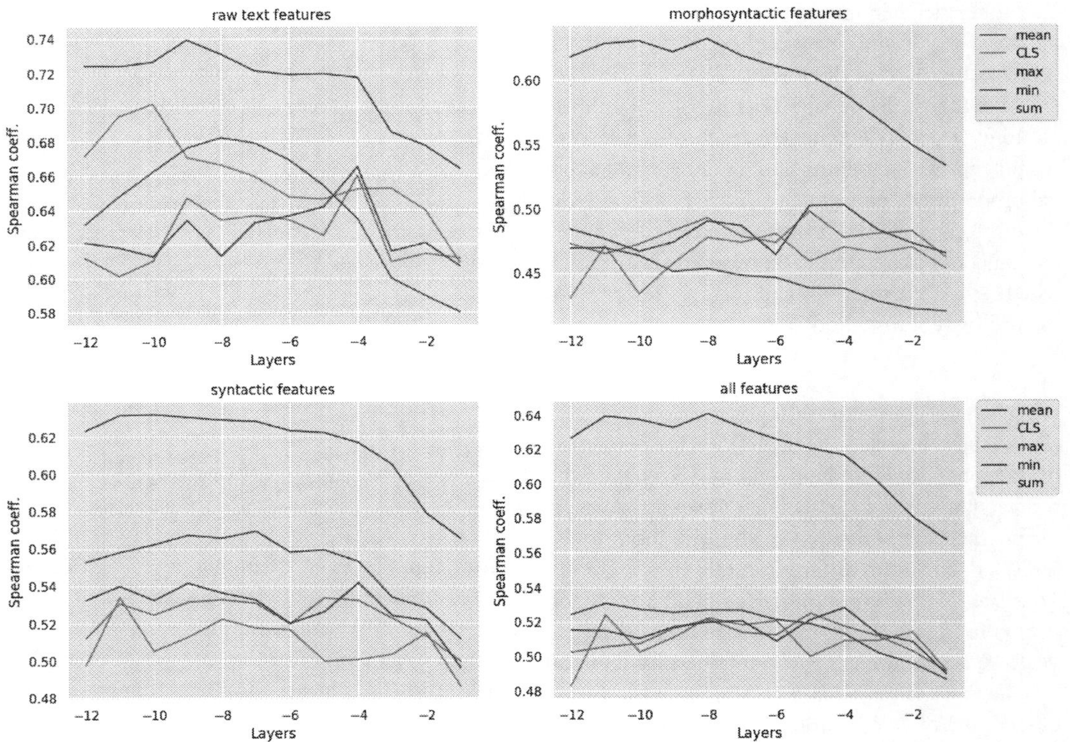

Figure 1: Layerwise ρ scores for the three categories of raw-text, morphosyntactic and syntactic features. Layerwise average results are also reported. Each line in the four plots corresponds to a different aggregating strategy.

rophosyntactic properties are better represented averaging all the word embeddings (*Mean*). In general, best results are obtained with probing tasks related to morphosyntactic and syntactic features, like the distribution of POS (e.g. *upos_dist_PRON*, *upos_dist_VERB*) or the maximum depth of the syntactic tree (*parse_depth*). If we look instead at the average ρ scores obtained with BERT layerwise representations (Figure 1), we observe that, differently from Word2vec, best results are the ones related to raw-text features, such as sentence length or Type/Token Ratio. The *Mean* method prove to be the best one for almost all the probing tasks, achieving highest scores in the first five layers. The only exceptions mainly concern some of the linguistic features related to syntactic properties, e.g. the average length of dependency links (*avg_links_len*) or the maximum depth of the syntactic tree (*parse_depth*), for which best scores across layers are obtained with the *Sum* strategy. The *Max-* and *Min-pooling* methods, instead, show a similar trend for almost all the probing features. Interestingly, the representations corresponding to the

Layers	Mean	Max-pooling	Min-pooling	Sum
-12	.052	-.058	-.038	-.091
-11	.065	-.055	-.038	-.084
-10	.063	-.053	-.043	-.088
-9	.058	-.044	-.036	-.089
-8	.066	-.039	-.034	-.088
-7	.058	-.046	-.033	-.088
-6	.051	-.048	-.045	-.094
-5	.046	-.035	-.032	-.096
-4	.042	-.043	-.025	-.102
-3	.026	-.049	-.041	-.113
-2	.006	-.057	-.045	-.119
-1	-.007	-.069	-.063	-.128

Table 4: Average ρ differences between BERT and Word2vec probing results according to the four embedding-aggregation strategies.

[CLS] token, although considered as a summarization of the entire input sequence, achieve results comparable to those obtained with *Max-* and *Min-pooling* methods. Moreover, it can be noticed that, unlike *Max-* and *Min-pooling*, the representations computed with *Mean* and *Sum* methods tend to lose their average precision in encoding our set of linguistic properties across the 12 layers.

Features

Feature	-12	-11	-10	-9	-8	-7	-6	-5	-4	-3	-2	-1
sent_length	35	34	33	33	33	31	33	33	34	34	34	33
max_links_len	32	31	31	30	33	33	31	31	32	32	33	32
parse_depth	24	23	23	24	25	25	25	26	25	26	25	25
avg_links_len	29	29	29	29	29	30	31	29	32	31	31	29
verbal_heads_dist	20	24	18	20	21	20	20	19	24	23	23	22
avg_subord_chain_len	17	17	17	16	17	17	16	15	15	15	14	10
avg_token_per_clause	9.3	12	13	15	15	16	15	14	14	12	10	9.2
subord_prop_dist	15	16	16	15	16	16	15	15	14	14	13	10
avg_verb_edges	9.1	0.23	8.5	8.3	9	8.9	9	7.9	0.012	10	8.3	9.4
subord_post	12	13	12	12	12	13	12	12	9.8	11	10	7.3
subj_pre	3.7	4.6	4.4	4.4	5.7	5.9	6.4	5.8	5.9	5.7	7.1	1.2
avg_prep_chain_len	-0.83	-0.95	-0.79	-0.77	-1.4	-1.8	-2.4	-2.9	-3.4	-4.1	-4.5	-5.2
verbal_root_perc	-2.1	-1.4	0.85	3.3	3.8	5.6	5.8	6.6	6.9	3.7	2.6	2.3
subord_dist_1	14	14	14	14	14	14	14	14	13	13	13	11
obj_post	0.79	1.9	1.8	1.8	3.5	4.2	4.1	3	2.8	3.1	2.8	-2.1
prep_dist_1	-0.71	-0.77	-1.8	-0.74	-1.3	-1.6	-2.1	-2.4	-2.9	-3	-3.3	-4.1
dep_dist_conj	18	19	16	20	15	7.4	6.3	10	14	15	13	11
dep_dist_case	4.4	6.6	8	-12	-18	5.6	4.8	3.5	2.3	-1.7	-4.9	-9.8
upos_dist_ADP	3.5	4.6	5.4	5.7	5.1	3.4	1.7	-0.085	-2.1	-6.7	-11	-15
dep_dist_nmod	-2.3	-2.3	-1.8	-2.2	-2.6	-3.2	-4	-4.7	-5.4	-6.7	-11	-8
dep_dist_mark	4.5	5.2	5.9	6.2	6.7	6.2	5.9	5	4	2.2	0.95	-2.1
upos_dist_CCONJ	17	17	17	16	14	3.4	-4	-5.6	8.9	4.9	-0.14	1.1
dep_dist_cc	17	17	17	17	12	-3.4	-3	-5.3	-3.3	6	0.28	2
dep_dist_obl	-6.4	-5.8	-5.5	-5.7	-5.7	-6.6	-6.7	-7.6	-8.4	-9.8	-25	-18
dep_dist_det	16	17	-5.9	-8.4	-1.9	2.9	8	13	12	8.5	5.1	5.2
upos_dist_DET	15	15	9.6	-8.9	15	15	14	12	10	6.3	2.8	3.3
aux_form_dist_Fin	-7.4	-6.9	-7.2	-9	-8.4	-9.1	-9.3	-10	-11	-11	-10	-14
aux_mood_dist_Ind	-9.4	-7.8	-7.6	-9.4	-8.3	-9.2	-9.1	-11	-11	-11	-11	-15
verbal_arity_4	13	13	13	13	13	13	13	12	12	12	11	8.5
dep_dist_advcl	9.5	10	10	11	11	11	11	11	10	8.7	7.4	4.9
upos_dist_SCONJ	7	7.9	8.4	8.1	8.5	8.7	8.6	7.7	7.3	5.7	4.8	2.4
dep_dist_amod	-5.6	-0.4	3.4	8.2	8.7	5.9	5.6	0.33	-2.1	-12	-23	-18
xpos_dist_	51	52	53	54	54	51	48	50	48	39	32	33
verbal_arity_3	6.9	7.3	6.9	6.9	7.2	7.3	7.2	6.8	6.3	6.6	6.5	3.9

Feature	-12	-11	-10	-9	-8	-7	-6	-5	-4	-3	-2	-1
upos_dist_PART	-0.3	1.9	4.2	4.8	3.9	2.2	1.1	-0.33	-2.8	-5	-6.8	-15
xpos_dist_TO	-7.8	-6.8	-5.9	-5.5	-6.7	-8.3	-9.5	-10	-12	-14	-15	-17
xpos_dist_VBN	-5.6	-6	-4.1	-6.6	-4.8	-5	-6.2	-7.3	-8.4	-8.6	-8.9	-12
aux_tense_dist_Pres	-8.9	-7.7	-8.2	-10	-7.8	-9	-8.9	-7.8	-6.6	-5.2	-5.2	-9.7
xpos_dist_NNS	-11	-12	-8	-4	-4.6	-3.7	-5.3	-5	-6.3	-8.7	-10	-14
dep_dist_obj	-5.9	-1.9	5.6	9.8	8.9	4.4	0.11	5.9	2.9	-1.2	-6.1	-14
dep_dist_nmod:poss	-0.64	7.8	8.3	4	1.7	0.53	-3.1	-5.4	-7.4	-10	-13	-15
dep_dist_aux	-3.5	-1.5	-3.1	-1.8	-1.7	-2.6	-4.4	-4.4	-5.3	-9	-9.1	-12
dep_dist_advmod	8.6	1.9	1	-0.025	-2.7	-1.2	-4	-3.6	-7.7	-8.9	-16	-18
upos_dist_ADV	0.16	3.6	1.9	0.61	-0.29	-5.5	-6.1	-11	-16	-20	-26	-15
dep_dist_compound	-2.8	-0.38	2.2	5.5	5.3	5	4.4	4.1	3.8	3.2	3.1	1.4
upos_dist_ADJ	-17	-12	-12	-11	-11	-11	-12	-20	-24	-27	-33	-16
aux_Sing+3	-14	-12	-13	-16	-15	-16	-16	-17	-18	-20	-19	-21
xpos_dist_.	14	20	26	32	32	31	29	30	26	21	16	6.7
ttr_lemma	48	50	52	53	52	51	51	51	49	47	45	44
upos_dist_VERB	-17	-12	-7.3	-7.8	-8.3	-10	-9.6	-9.7	-17	-21	-27	-38
upos_dist_AUX	-9.5	-7.3	-6.4	-7.4	-7.3	-8.5	-11	-12	-14	-3.6	-4.6	-6.3
xpos_dist_VBD	2.4	3.3	2.6	-0.93	3.5	3.7	3.6	5	5.6	4.2	3.4	3.5
verbal_arity_2	-2.3	-1.1	-1.3	-1.1	0.076	0.042	-0.092	-0.39	-0.99	-2.4	-2.7	-4.8
xpos_dist_RB	5	6.8	4.2	3.9	3.2	0.51	-1.2	-3.9	-9.7	-11	-14	-21
upos_dist_PRON	6.7	2.2	-0.32	0.52	-1.6	-1.8	-1.5	-2.8	-5.7	0.7	-0.17	-0.35
xpos_dist_VB	-14	-13	-11	-7.8	-7	-6.7	-5.2	-6.3	-6.2	-9.2	-12	-13
dep_dist_nsubj	-3.1	-2.1	-2.3	-2.2	0.4	0.58	1.5	5.3	11	9	8.7	8.4
ttr_form	49	50	52	53	52	51	51	51	49	47	46	44
xpos_dist_VBZ	0.27	0.83	-6.2	-8.6	-8.8	-9.6	-11	2	0.12	-10	-1.9	-0.96
dep_dist_cop	-8.1	-4.8	-3	-2.7	-3.8	-5.1	-7.6	-9.5	-12	-16	-16	-16
lexical_density	3.3	4	4.1	3.8	3.3	3	2.1	1.1	0.57	-2	-3	-4.9
upos_dist_NUM	18	20	20	13	13	12	15	14	8.4	8.9	4.7	2.6
xpos_dist_VBP	4.8	-3.9	-3.9	-4.1	-3.9	-5.4	-5.7	-6	-4.7	-7.5	-6.8	-7.9
dep_dist_punct	51	53	54	54	52	52	51	52	51	45	37	31
xpos_dist_NN	-20	-17	-16	-15	-14	-14	-14	-16	-19	-22	-25	-26
upos_dist_PROPN	-9	-6.7	-4.7	-3.4	-2.3	-2.2	-1.1	-1.6	-3.1	-5	-5.3	-7.1
principal_prop_dist	-2.4	4.4	14	13	14	15	17	13	9.5	8.7	-0.19	-1.7
char_per_tok	-28	-30	-32	-28	-30	-32	-32	-32	-31	-39	-39	-41

Figure 2: Differences between BERT and Word2vec scores (multiplied by 100) for all the 68 probing features (ranked by correlation with sentence length), obtained with the *Mean* aggregation strategy. BERT scores are reported for all the 12 layers. Positive (*red*) and negative (*blue*) cells correspond to scores for which BERT outperforms Word2vec and vice versa.

In order to investigate more in depth how the linguistic knowledge encoded by BERT across its layers differs from that learned by Word2vec, we report in Table 4 average ρ differences between the two models according to the four combining strategies. As a general remark, we can notice that, regardless of the aggregation strategy taken into account, BERT and Word2vec sentence representations achieve quite similar results on average. Hence, although BERT is capable of understanding the full context of each word in an input sequence, the amount of linguistic knowledge implicitly encoded in its aggregated sentence representations is still comparable to that which can be achieved with a non-contextual language model.

In Figure 2 we report instead the differences between BERT and Word2vec scores for all the 68 probing features (ordered by correlation with sentence length). For the comparison, we used the representations obtained with the *Mean* combining method. As a first remark, we notice that there is a clear distinction in terms of ρ scores between features better predicted by BERT and Word2vec. In fact, features most related to syntactic properties (left heatmap) are those for which BERT results are generally higher with respect to those obtained with Word2vec. This result demonstrates that BERT, unlike a non-contextual language model as Word2vec, is able to encode information within its representa-tions that involves the entire input sequence, thus making more simple to solve probing tasks that refer to syntatic characteristics.

Focusing instead on the right heatmap, we observe that Word2vec non-contextual representations are still capable of encoding a wide spectrum of linguistic properties with higher ρ values compared to BERT ones, especially if we consider scores closer to BERT's output layers (from *-4* to *-1*). This is particularly evident for morphosyntactic features related to the distribution of POS categories (*xpos_dist_**, *upos_dist_**), most likely because non-contextual representations tend to encode properties related to single tokens rather than syntactic relations between them.

5 Evaluating Word Representations

Once we have probed the linguistic knowledge encoded by BERT and Word2vec using different strategies for computing sentence embeddings, we investigated how much information about the structure of a sentence is encoded within single-word contextual representations. For doing so, we performed our sentence-level probing tasks using a single BERT word embedding for each sentence in the UD dataset. We tested four different words, corresponding to the first, the last and two internal tokens for each sentence in the UD dataset. In

Feature	tok-1 (-8)	tok-2 (-8)	tok-3 (-8)	tok-4 (-8)	mean (-8)	tok-1 (-1)	tok-2 (-1)	tok-3 (-1)	tok-4 (-1)	mean (-1)
sent_length	0.93	0.93	0.93	0.96	0.94	0.86	0.87	0.88	0.89	0.94
max_links_len	0.77	0.78	0.78	0.81	0.86	0.72	0.74	0.74	0.74	0.85
parse_depth	0.79	0.79	0.79	0.82	0.87	0.74	0.75	0.75	0.76	0.87
avg_links_len	0.66	0.66	0.66	0.72	0.74	0.6	0.62	0.61	0.63	0.74
verbal_heads_dist	0.79	0.78	0.78	0.83	0.86	0.74	0.72	0.73	0.76	0.87
avg_subord_chain_len	0.68	0.67	0.67	0.72	0.74	0.64	0.62	0.62	0.64	0.68
avg_token_per_clause	0.55	0.54	0.55	0.62	0.73	0.51	0.48	0.5	0.55	0.67
subord_prop_dist	0.64	0.6	0.6	0.67	0.69	0.6	0.56	0.57	0.6	0.63
avg_verb_edges	0.52	0.5	0.49	0.56	0.64	0.5	0.48	0.47	0.51	0.65
subord_post	0.62	0.55	0.54	0.64	0.62	0.57	0.51	0.52	0.52	0.57
subj_pre	0.53	0.45	0.44	0.53	0.62	0.53	0.46	0.44	0.52	0.58
avg_prep_chain_len	0.58	0.6	0.6	0.64	0.62	0.53	0.55	0.55	0.55	0.58
verbal_root_perc	0.52	0.44	0.42	0.51	0.61	0.53	0.45	0.45	0.5	0.59
subord_dist_1	0.36	0.33	0.34	0.36	0.52	0.35	0.32	0.32	0.33	0.49
obj_post	0.56	0.54	0.53	0.62	0.57	0.54	0.5	0.5	0.53	0.52
prep_dist_1	0.45	0.46	0.46	0.5	0.52	0.41	0.42	0.43	0.43	0.5
dep_dist_conj	0.63	0.65	0.65	0.74	0.73	0.54	0.58	0.59	0.64	0.7
dep_dist_case	0.61	0.63	0.63	0.7	0.6	0.55	0.55	0.55	0.56	0.68
upos_dist_ADP	0.58	0.6	0.61	0.69	0.86	0.52	0.52	0.52	0.53	0.65
dep_dist_nmod	0.53	0.55	0.55	0.6	0.61	0.49	0.51	0.51	0.51	0.55
dep_dist_mark	0.6	0.57	0.57	0.66	0.67	0.55	0.53	0.52	0.56	0.58
upos_dist_CCONJ	0.63	0.61	0.61	0.76	0.8	0.54	0.54	0.54	0.62	0.67
dep_dist_cc	0.63	0.61	0.61	0.76	0.77	0.54	0.54	0.55	0.63	0.67
dep_dist_obl	0.44	0.44	0.44	0.52	0.53	0.39	0.38	0.38	0.4	0.41
dep_dist_det	0.62	0.61	0.61	0.76	0.7	0.55	0.53	0.54	0.55	0.77
upos_dist_DET	0.62	0.6	0.6	0.75	0.88	0.54	0.53	0.53	0.55	0.76
aux_form_dist_Fin	0.54	0.46	0.43	0.57	0.55	0.5	0.44	0.42	0.5	0.49
aux_mood_dist_Ind	0.61	0.51	0.49	0.68	0.56	0.57	0.49	0.49	0.57	0.5
verbal_arity_4	0.31	0.27	0.28	0.33	0.45	0.29	0.26	0.28	0.3	0.4
dep_dist_advcl	0.47	0.42	0.42	0.52	0.53	0.43	0.38	0.4	0.43	0.46
upos_dist_SCONJ	0.51	0.43	0.43	0.56	0.53	0.47	0.4	0.4	0.46	0.47
dep_dist_amod	0.49	0.51	0.51	0.58	0.62	0.46	0.47	0.46	0.48	0.35
xpos_dist_,	0.58	0.51	0.5	0.72	0.67	0.54	0.48	0.49	0.64	0.46
verbal_arity_3	0.25	0.22	0.19	0.26	0.41	0.22	0.24	0.24	0.23	0.36

Feature	tok-1 (-8)	tok-2 (-8)	tok-3 (-8)	tok-4 (-8)	mean (-8)	tok-1 (-1)	tok-2 (-1)	tok-3 (-1)	tok-4 (-1)	mean (-1)
upos_dist_PART	0.47	0.47	0.47	0.57	0.63	0.44	0.44	0.45	0.48	0.44
xpos_dist_TO	0.39	0.39	0.38	0.48	0.53	0.36	0.36	0.36	0.4	0.43
xpos_dist_VBN	0.37	0.32	0.32	0.46	0.47	0.37	0.34	0.32	0.38	0.4
aux_tense_dist_Pres	0.61	0.51	0.49	0.68	0.52	0.61	0.55	0.53	0.62	0.5
xpos_dist_NNS	0.48	0.5	0.5	0.59	0.56	0.48	0.5	0.5	0.54	0.47
dep_dist_obj	0.57	0.56	0.54	0.64	0.67	0.55	0.52	0.51	0.54	0.44
dep_dist_nmod:poss	0.42	0.38	0.38	0.57	0.59	0.38	0.38	0.38	0.42	0.42
dep_dist_aux	0.6	0.52	0.5	0.67	0.64	0.58	0.52	0.52	0.6	0.54
dep_dist_advmod	0.55	0.48	0.49	0.62	0.59	0.52	0.48	0.48	0.53	0.44
upos_dist_ADV	0.51	0.43	0.44	0.6	0.6	0.47	0.43	0.43	0.48	0.45
dep_dist_compound	0.5	0.49	0.49	0.57	0.52	0.5	0.49	0.49	0.53	0.48
upos_dist_ADJ	0.5	0.52	0.51	0.58	0.52	0.48	0.49	0.49	0.51	0.48
aux_Sing+3	0.57	0.46	0.43	0.64	0.49	0.51	0.43	0.41	0.5	0.43
xpos_dist_.	0.73	0.69	0.69	0.85	0.73	0.71	0.69	0.69	0.81	0.48
ttr_lemma	0.64	0.59	0.59	0.75	0.77	0.54	0.54	0.53	0.62	0.69
upos_dist_VERB	0.67	0.65	0.64	0.74	0.7	0.62	0.59	0.6	0.63	0.4
upos_dist_AUX	0.68	0.61	0.58	0.75	0.71	0.62	0.56	0.55	0.63	0.72
xpos_dist_VBD	0.65	0.57	0.57	0.68	0.64	0.68	0.63	0.62	0.68	0.64
verbal_arity_2	0.23	0.22	0.22	0.33	0.36	0.29	0.2	0.22	0.26	0.31
xpos_dist_RB	0.54	0.47	0.48	0.6	0.62	0.53	0.49	0.49	0.54	0.58
upos_dist_PRON	0.8	0.74	0.73	0.84	0.79	0.78	0.73	0.73	0.77	0.81
xpos_dist_VB	0.65	0.59	0.58	0.7	0.64	0.63	0.61	0.61	0.65	0.58
dep_dist_nsubj	0.74	0.69	0.68	0.78	0.72	0.72	0.67	0.67	0.72	0.8
ttr_form	0.63	0.58	0.57	0.75	0.76	0.53	0.52	0.53	0.62	0.68
xpos_dist_VBZ	0.57	0.45	0.43	0.62	0.52	0.57	0.48	0.47	0.57	0.6
dep_dist_cop	0.52	0.47	0.44	0.59	0.56	0.48	0.41	0.4	0.47	0.44
lexical_density	0.62	0.58	0.57	0.7	0.81	0.58	0.54	0.54	0.61	0.72
upos_dist_NUM	0.48	0.44	0.43	0.58	0.56	0.46	0.44	0.44	0.53	0.45
xpos_dist_VBP	0.59	0.45	0.45	0.62	0.51	0.58	0.5	0.5	0.57	0.47
dep_dist_punct	0.63	0.54	0.55	0.81	0.82	0.58	0.53	0.53	0.69	0.6
xpos_dist_NN	0.47	0.47	0.48	0.58	0.47	0.48	0.47	0.48	0.52	0.35
upos_dist_PROPN	0.67	0.63	0.63	0.71	0.69	0.67	0.64	0.63	0.68	0.64
principal_prop_dist	0.57	0.49	0.48	0.62	0.57	0.55	0.46	0.46	0.56	0.42
char_per_tok	0.28	0.26	0.26	0.29	0.46	0.26	0.24	0.24	0.23	0.35

Figure 3: Probing scores obtained by BERT word (*tok_**) and sentence (*mean*) representations extracted from layers *-1* and *-8*. Sentence embeddings are computed using the *Mean* method.

Embeddings	Raw	Morphoyntax	Syntax	All
BERT-1 (-8)	0.62	0.57	0.55	0.57
BERT-2 (-8)	0.59	0.53	0.53	0.53
BERT-3 (-8)	0.59	0.52	0.52	0.53
BERT-4 (-8)	0.65	**0.66**	**0.62**	**0.64**
BERT-1 (-1)	0.55	0.55	0.51	0.53
BERT-2 (-1)	0.54	0.51	0.49	0.50
BERT-3 (-1)	0.54	0.51	0.49	0.50
BERT-4 (-1)	0.59	0.57	0.53	0.55
[CLS] (-8)	**0.66**	0.47	0.52	0.51
[CLS] (-1)	0.61	0.45	0.49	0.48
Word2vec-1	0.26	0.26	0.22	0.24
Word2vec-2	0.17	0.21	0.18	0.19
Word2vec-3	0.17	0.19	0.17	0.18
Word2vec-4	0.13	0.15	0.12	0.13

Table 5: Average ρ scores obtained by BERT and Word2vec according to word representations corresponding to the first, the last and two internal tokens of each input sentence. Results are computed according to the three linguistic levels of annotation and considering all the probing features (*All*). Average scores obtained with the *[CLS]* token are also reported.

particular, we extracted the embeddings from the output layer (*-1*) and from the layer that achieved best results in the previous experiments (*-8*). We used probing scores obtained with Word2vec embeddings for the same tokens as baseline. In Table 5 we report average ρ scores obtained by BERT (*BERT-**) and Word2vec (*Word2vec-**) according to word-level representations extracted from the four tokens mentioned above. Results were computed aggregating all probing results (*All*) and according

to raw text (*Raw*), morphosyntactic (*Morphosyntax*) and syntatic (*Syntax*) levels of annotation. For comparison, we also report average scores obtained with the *[CLS]* token.

As a first remark, we can clearly notice that even with a single-word embedding BERT is able to encode a wide spectrum of sentence-level linguistic properties. This result allows us to highlight the main potential of contextual representations, i.e. the capability of capturing linguistic phenomena that refer to the entire input sequence within single-word representations. An interesting observation is that, except for the raw text features, for which the best scores are achieved using *[CLS]*, higher performance are obtained with the embeddings corresponding to *BERT-4*, i.e. the last token of each sentence. This result seems to indicate that *[CLS]*, although being used for classification predictions, does not necessarily correspond to the most linguistically informative token within each input sequence.

Comparing the results with those achieved using Word2vec word embeddings, we notice that BERT scores greatly outperform Word2vec for all the probing tasks. This is a straightforward result and can be easily explained by the fact that the lack of contextual knowledge does not allow single-word representations to encode information that are related to the structure of the whole sentence.

Since the latter results demonstrated that BERT is capable of encoding many sentence-level properties within its single word representations, as a last analysis, we decided to compare these results with the ones obtained using sentence embeddings. In particular, Figure 3 reports probing scores obtained by BERT single word (*tok_**) and *Mean* sentence representations (*sent*) extracted from the output layer (*-1*) and from the layer that achieved best results in average (*-8*).

As already mentioned, for many of these probing tasks, word embeddings performance is comparable to that obtained with the aggregated sentence representations. Nevertheless, there are several cases in which the difference between performance is particularly significant. Interestingly, we can notice that aggregated sentence representations are generally better for predicting properties belonging to the left heatmap, i.e. to the group of features more related to syntactic properties. This is particularly noticeable for the average number of tokens per clause (*avg_token_per_clause*) or the distribution of subordinate chains by length (*sub-ord_dist*), for which we observe an improvement from word-level to sentence-level representations of more than .10 ρ points. On the contrary, probing features belonging to the right heatmap, therefore more close to raw text and morphosyntactic properties, are generally better predicted using single word embeddings, especially when considering the inner representations corresponding to the last token in each sentence (*tok_4*). The property most affected by the difference in scores between word- and sentence-level embeddings is the the distribution of periods (*xpos_dist_*).

Focusing instead on differences in performance between the two considered layers, we can notice that regardless of the method used to predict each feature, the representations learned by BERT tend to lose their precision in encoding our set of linguistic properties, most likely because the model is storing task-specific information (Masked Language Modeling task) at the expense of its ability to encode general knowledge about the language.

6 Conclusion

In this paper we studied the linguistic knowledge implicitly encoded in the internal representations of a contextual Language Model (BERT) and a contextual-independent one (Word2vec). Using a suite of 68 probing tasks and testing different methods for combining word embeddings into sentence representations, we showed that BERT and Word2vec encode a wide set of sentence-level linguistic properties in a similar manner. Nevertheless, we found that for Word2vec the best method for obtaining sentence representations is the *Sum*, while BERT is more effective when averaging all the single-word representations (*Mean* method). Moreover, we showed that BERT is able in storing features that are mainly related to raw text and syntactic properties, while Word2vec is good at predicting morphosyntactic characteristics.

Finally, we showed that BERT is able to encode sentence-level linguistic phenomena even within single-word embeddings, exhibiting comparable or even superior performance than those obtained with aggregated sentence representations. Moreover, we found that, at least for morphosyntactic and syntactic characteristics, the most informative word representation is the one that correspond to the last token of each input sequence and not, as might be expected, to the *[CLS]* special token.

References

Yossi Adi, Einat Kermany, Yonatan Belinkov, Ofer Lavi, and Yoav Goldberg. 2016. Fine-grained analysis of sentence embeddings using auxiliary prediction tasks. *arXiv preprint arXiv:1608.04207*.

Yonatan Belinkov and James Glass. 2019. Analysis methods in neural language processing: A survey. *Transactions of the Association for Computational Linguistics*, 7:49–72.

Yonatan Belinkov, Lluís Màrquez, Hassan Sajjad, Nadir Durrani, Fahim Dalvi, and James Glass. 2017. Evaluating layers of representation in neural machine translation on part-of-speech and semantic tagging tasks. In *Proceedings of the Eighth International Joint Conference on Natural Language Processing (Volume 1: Long Papers)*, pages 1–10.

Terra Blevins, Omer Levy, and Luke Zettlemoyer. 2018. Deep rnns encode soft hierarchical syntax. In *Proceedings of the 56th Annual Meeting of the Association for Computational Linguistics (Volume 2: Short Papers)*, pages 14–19.

Dominique Brunato, Andrea Cimino, Felice Dell'Orletta, Giulia Venturi, and Simonetta Montemagni. 2020. Profiling-ud: a tool for linguistic profiling of texts. In *Proceedings of The 12th Language Resources and Evaluation Conference*, pages 7147–7153, Marseille, France. European Language Resources Association.

Alexis Conneau, Germán Kruszewski, Guillaume Lample, Loïc Barrault, and Marco Baroni. 2018. What you can cram into a single $&!#* vector: Probing sentence embeddings for linguistic properties. In *Proceedings of the 56th Annual Meeting of the Association for Computational Linguistics (Volume 1: Long Papers)*, pages 2126–2136.

Jacob Devlin, Ming-Wei Chang, Kenton Lee, and Kristina Toutanova. 2019. Bert: Pre-training of deep bidirectional transformers for language understanding. In *Proceedings of the 2019 Conference of the North American Chapter of the Association for Computational Linguistics: Human Language Technologies, Volume 1 (Long and Short Papers)*, pages 4171–4186.

Kawin Ethayarajh. 2019. How contextual are contextualized word representations? comparing the geometry of BERT, ELMo, and GPT-2 embeddings. In *Proceedings of the 2019 Conference on Empirical Methods in Natural Language Processing and the 9th International Joint Conference on Natural Language Processing (EMNLP-IJCNLP)*, pages 55–65, Hong Kong, China. Association for Computational Linguistics.

Yoav Goldberg. 2019. Assessing bert's syntactic abilities. *arXiv preprint arXiv:1901.05287*.

John Hewitt and Percy Liang. 2019. Designing and interpreting probes with control tasks. In *Proceedings of the 2019 Conference on Empirical Methods in Natural Language Processing and the 9th International Joint Conference on Natural Language Processing (EMNLP-IJCNLP)*, pages 2733–2743.

John Hewitt and Christopher D Manning. 2019. A structural probe for finding syntax in word representations. In *Proceedings of the 2019 Conference of the North American Chapter of the Association for Computational Linguistics: Human Language Technologies, Volume 1 (Long and Short Papers)*, pages 4129–4138.

Ganesh Jawahar, Benoît Sagot, Djamé Seddah, Samuel Unicomb, Gerardo Iñiguez, Márton Karsai, Yannick Léo, Márton Karsai, Carlos Sarraute, Éric Fleury, et al. 2019. What does bert learn about the structure of language? In *57th Annual Meeting of the Association for Computational Linguistics (ACL), Florence, Italy*.

Aditya Joshi, Sarvnaz Karimi, Ross Sparks, Cecile Paris, and C Raina MacIntyre. 2019. A comparison of word-based and context-based representations for classification problems in health informatics. In *Proceedings of the 18th BioNLP Workshop and Shared Task*, pages 135–141, Florence, Italy. Association for Computational Linguistics.

Akos Kádár, Grzegorz Chrupała, and Afra Alishahi. 2017. Representation of linguistic form and function in recurrent neural networks. *Computational Linguistics*, 43(4):761–780.

Andrej Karpathy, Justin Johnson, and Li Fei-Fei. 2015. Visualizing and understanding recurrent networks. *arXiv preprint arXiv:1506.02078*.

Olga Kovaleva, Alexey Romanov, Anna Rogers, and Anna Rumshisky. 2019. Revealing the dark secrets of BERT. In *Proceedings of the 2019 Conference on Empirical Methods in Natural Language Processing and the 9th International Joint Conference on Natural Language Processing (EMNLP-IJCNLP)*, pages 4365–4374, Hong Kong, China. Association for Computational Linguistics.

Jiwei Li, Xinlei Chen, Eduard Hovy, and Dan Jurafsky. 2016. Visualizing and understanding neural models in nlp. In *Proceedings of the 2016 Conference of the North American Chapter of the Association for Computational Linguistics: Human Language Technologies*, pages 681–691.

Yongjie Lin, Yi Chern Tan, and Robert Frank. 2019. Open sesame: Getting inside BERT's linguistic knowledge. In *Proceedings of the 2019 ACL Workshop BlackboxNLP: Analyzing and Interpreting Neural Networks for NLP*, pages 241–253, Florence, Italy. Association for Computational Linguistics.

Nelson F Liu, Matt Gardner, Yonatan Belinkov, Matthew E Peters, and Noah A Smith. 2019. Linguistic knowledge and transferability of contextual representations. In *Proceedings of the 2019 Conference of the North American Chapter of the Association for Computational Linguistics: Human Language Technologies, Volume 1 (Long and Short Papers)*, pages 1073–1094.

Rebecca Marvin and Tal Linzen. 2018. Targeted syntactic evaluation of language models. In *Proceedings of the 2018 Conference on Empirical Methods in Natural Language Processing*, pages 1192–1202.

Tomas Mikolov, Ilya Sutskever, Kai Chen, Greg S Corrado, and Jeff Dean. 2013. Distributed representations of words and phrases and their compositionality. In *Advances in neural information processing systems*, pages 3111–3119.

Joakim Nivre, Marie-Catherine De Marneffe, Filip Ginter, Yoav Goldberg, Jan Hajic, Christopher D Manning, Ryan McDonald, Slav Petrov, Sampo Pyysalo, Natalia Silveira, et al. 2016. Universal dependencies v1: A multilingual treebank collection. In *Proceedings of the Tenth International Conference on Language Resources and Evaluation (LREC'16)*, pages 1659–1666.

Christian S Perone, Roberto Silveira, and Thomas S Paula. 2018. Evaluation of sentence embeddings in downstream and linguistic probing tasks. *arXiv preprint arXiv:1806.06259*.

Matthew Peters, Mark Neumann, Mohit Iyyer, Matt Gardner, Christopher Clark, Kenton Lee, and Luke Zettlemoyer. 2018. Deep contextualized word representations. In *Proceedings of the 2018 Conference of the North American Chapter of the Association for Computational Linguistics: Human Language Technologies, Volume 1 (Long Papers)*, pages 2227–2237.

Alessandro Raganato and Jörg Tiedemann. 2018. An analysis of encoder representations in transformer-based machine translation. In *Proceedings of the 2018 EMNLP Workshop BlackboxNLP: Analyzing and Interpreting Neural Networks for NLP*. Association for Computational Linguistics.

Manuela Sanguinetti and Cristina Bosco. 2015. Parttut: The turin university parallel treebank. In *Harmonization and Development of Resources and Tools for Italian Natural Language Processing within the PARLI Project*, pages 51–69. Springer.

Dinghan Shen, Guoyin Wang, Wenlin Wang, Martin Renqiang Min, Qinliang Su, Yizhe Zhang, Chunyuan Li, Ricardo Henao, and Lawrence Carin. 2018. Baseline needs more love: On simple word-embedding-based models and associated pooling mechanisms. In *Proceedings of the 56th Annual Meeting of the Association for Computational Linguistics (Volume 1: Long Papers)*, pages 440–450, Melbourne, Australia. Association for Computational Linguistics.

Natalia Silveira, Timothy Dozat, Marie-Catherine De Marneffe, Samuel R Bowman, Miriam Connor, John Bauer, and Christopher D Manning. 2014. A gold standard dependency corpus for english. In *LREC*, pages 2897–2904.

Ian Tenney, Dipanjan Das, and Ellie Pavlick. 2019a. BERT rediscovers the classical NLP pipeline. In *Proceedings of the 57th Annual Meeting of the Association for Computational Linguistics*, pages 4593–4601, Florence, Italy. Association for Computational Linguistics.

Ian Tenney, Patrick Xia, Berlin Chen, Alex Wang, Adam Poliak, R Thomas McCoy, Najoung Kim, Benjamin Van Durme, Samuel R Bowman, Dipanjan Das, et al. 2019b. What do you learn from context? probing for sentence structure in contextualized word representations. *arXiv preprint arXiv:1905.06316*.

Jesse Vig and Yonatan Belinkov. 2019. Analyzing the structure of attention in a transformer language model. In *Proceedings of the 2019 ACL Workshop BlackboxNLP: Analyzing and Interpreting Neural Networks for NLP*, pages 63–76, Florence, Italy. Association for Computational Linguistics.

Alex Warstadt, Yu Cao, Ioana Grosu, Wei Peng, Hagen Blix, Yining Nie, Anna Alsop, Shikha Bordia, Haokun Liu, Alicia Parrish, et al. 2019. Investigating bert's knowledge of language: Five analysis methods with npis. In *Proceedings of the 2019 Conference on Empirical Methods in Natural Language Processing and the 9th International Joint Conference on Natural Language Processing (EMNLP-IJCNLP)*, pages 2870–2880.

Amir Zeldes. 2017. The GUM corpus: Creating multilayer resources in the classroom. *Language Resources and Evaluation*, 51(3):581–612.

Kelly Zhang and Samuel Bowman. 2018. Language modeling teaches you more than translation does: Lessons learned through auxiliary syntactic task analysis. In *Proceedings of the 2018 EMNLP Workshop BlackboxNLP: Analyzing and Interpreting Neural Networks for NLP*, pages 359–361.

Are All Languages Created Equal in Multilingual BERT?

Shijie Wu and **Mark Dredze**
Department of Computer Science
Johns Hopkins University
shijie.wu@jhu.edu, mdredze@cs.jhu.edu

Abstract

Multilingual BERT (mBERT) (Devlin, 2018) trained on 104 languages has shown surprisingly good cross-lingual performance on several NLP tasks, even without explicit cross-lingual signals (Wu and Dredze, 2019; Pires et al., 2019). However, these evaluations have focused on cross-lingual transfer with high-resource languages, covering only a third of the languages covered by mBERT. We explore how mBERT performs on a much wider set of languages, focusing on the quality of representation for low-resource languages, measured by within-language performance. We consider three tasks: Named Entity Recognition (99 languages), Part-of-speech Tagging, and Dependency Parsing (54 languages each). mBERT does better than or comparable to baselines on high resource languages but does much worse for low resource languages. Furthermore, monolingual BERT models for these languages do even worse. Paired with similar languages, the performance gap between monolingual BERT and mBERT can be narrowed. We find that better models for low resource languages require more efficient pretraining techniques or more data.

1 Introduction

Pretrained contextual representation models trained with language modeling (Peters et al., 2018; Yang et al., 2019) or the cloze task objectives (Devlin et al., 2019; Liu et al., 2019) have quickly set a new standard for NLP tasks. These models have also been trained in multilingual settings. As the authors of BERT say "[...] (they) do not plan to release more single-language models", they instead train a single BERT model with Wikipedia to serve 104 languages, without any explicit cross-lingual links, yielding a multilingual BERT (mBERT) (Devlin, 2018). Surprisingly, mBERT learn high-quality cross-lingual representation and show strong zero-shot cross-lingual transfer performance (Wu and Dredze, 2019; Pires et al., 2019). However, evaluations have focused on high resource languages, with cross-lingual transfer using English as a source language or within language performance. As Wu and Dredze (2019) evaluated mBERT on 39 languages, this leaves the majority of mBERT's 104 languages, most of which are low resource languages, untested.

Does mBERT learn equally high-quality representation for its 104 languages? If not, which languages are hurt by its massively multilingual style pretraining? While it has been observed that for high resource languages like English, mBERT performs worse than monolingual BERT on English with the same capacity (Devlin, 2018). It is unclear that for low resource languages (in terms of monolingual corpus size), how does mBERT compare to a monolingual BERT? And, does multilingual joint training help mBERT learn better representation for low resource languages?

We evaluate the representation quality of mBERT on 99 languages for NER, and 54 for part-of-speech tagging and dependency parsing. In this paper, we show mBERT does not have equally high-quality representation for all of the 104 languages, with the bottom 30% languages performing much worse than a non-BERT model on NER. Additionally, by training various monolingual BERT for low-resource languages with the same data size, we show the low representation quality of low-resource languages is not the result of the hyper-parameters of BERT or sharing the model with a large number of languages, as monolingual BERT performs worse than mBERT. On the contrary, by pairing low-resource languages with linguistically-related languages, we show low-resource languages benefit from multilingual joint training, as bilingual BERT outperforms monolingual BERT while still lacking behind mBERT,

Proceedings of the 5th Workshop on Representation Learning for NLP (RepL4NLP-2020), pages 120–130
July 9, 2020. ©2020 Association for Computational Linguistics

Our findings suggest, with small monolingual corpus, BERT does not learn high-quality representation for low resource languages. To learn better representation for low resource languages, we suggest either collect more data to make low resource language high resource (Conneau et al., 2019), or consider more data-efficient pretraining techniques like Clark et al. (2020). We leave exploring more data-efficient pretraining techniques as future work.

2 Related Work

Multilingual Contextual Representations Deep contextualized representation models such as ELMo (Peters et al., 2018) and BERT (Devlin et al., 2019) have set a new standard for NLP systems. Their application to multilingual settings, pretraining one model on text from multiple languages with a single vocabulary, has driven forward work in cross-language learning and transfer (Wu and Dredze, 2019; Pires et al., 2019; Mulcaire et al., 2019). BERT-based pretraining also benefits language generation tasks like machine translation (Conneau and Lample, 2019). BERT can be further improve with explicit cross-language signals including: bitext (Conneau and Lample, 2019; Huang et al., 2019) and word translation pairs from a dictionary (Wu et al., 2019) or induced from a bitext (Ji et al., 2019).

Several factors need to be considered in understanding mBERT. First, the 104 most common Wikipedia languages vary considerably in size (Table 1). Therefore, mBERT training attempted to equalize languages by up-sampling words from low resource languages and down-sampling words from high resource languages. Previous work has found that shared strings across languages provide sufficient signal for inducing cross-lingual word representations (Lample et al., 2018; Artetxe et al., 2017). While Wu and Dredze (2019) finds the number of shared subwords across languages correlates with cross-lingual performance, multilingual BERT can still learn cross-lingual representation without any vocabulary overlap across languages (Wu et al., 2019; K et al., 2020). Additionally, Wu et al. (2019) find bilingual BERT can still achieve decent cross-lingual transfer by sharing only the transformer layer across languages. Artetxe et al. (2019) shows learning the embedding layer alone while using a fixed transformer encoder from English monolingual BERT can also produce decent cross-lingual transfer performance. Second, while each language may be similarly represented in the training data, subwords are not evenly distributed among the languages. Many languages share common characters and cognates, biasing subword learning to some languages over others. Both of these factors may influence how well mBERT learns representations for low resource languages.

Finally, Baevski et al. (2019) show that in general larger pretraining data for English leads to better downstream performance, yet increasing the size of pretraining data exponentially only increases downstream performance linearly. For a low resource language with limited pretraining data, it is unclear whether contextual representations outperform previous methods.

Representations for Low Resource Languages Embeddings with subword information, a non-contextual representation, like fastText (Bojanowski et al., 2017) and BPEmb (Heinzerling and Strube, 2018) are more data-efficient compared to contextual representation like ELMo and BERT when a limited amount of text is available. For low resource languages, there are usually limits on **monolingual corpora** and **task specific supervision**. When task-specific supervision is limited, e.g. sequence labeling in low resource languages, mBERT performs better than fastText while underperforming a single BPEmb trained on all languages (Heinzerling and Strube, 2019). Contrary to this work, we focus on mBERT from the perspective of representation learning for each language in terms of monolingual corpora resources and analyze how to improve BERT for low resource languages. We also consider parsing in addition to sequence labeling tasks.

Concurrently, Conneau et al. (2019) train a multilingual masked language model (Devlin et al., 2019) on 2.5TB of CommonCrawl filtered data covering 100 languages and show it outperforms a Wikipedia-based model on low resource languages (Urdu and Swahili) for XNLI (Conneau et al., 2018). Using CommonCrawl greatly increases monolingual resource especially for low resource languages, and makes low resource languages in terms of Wikipedia size high resource. For example, Mongolian has 6 million and 248 million tokens in Wikipedia and CommonCrawl, respectively. Indeed, a 40-fold data increase of Mongolian (mn) increases its WikiSize, a measure of monolingual corpus size introduced in §3.1, from 5 to roughly 10, as shown in Tab. 1, making it relatively high resource with respect to mBERT.

3 Experimental Setup

We begin by defining high and low resource languages in mBERT, a description of the models and downstream tasks we use for evaluation, followed by a description of the masked language model pretraining.

3.1 High/Low Resource Languages

Since mBERT was trained on articles from Wikipedia, a language is considered a high or low resource for mBERT based on the size of Wikipedia in that language. Size can be measured in many ways (articles, tokens, characters); we use the size of the raw dump archive file;[1] for convenience we use $\log_2$ of the size in MB (**WikiSize**). English is the highest resource language (15.5GB) and Yoruba the lowest (10MB).[2] Tab. 1 shows languages and their relative resources.

3.2 Downstream Tasks

mBERT supports 104 languages, and we seek to evaluate the learned representations for as many of these as possible. We consider three NLP tasks for which annotated task data exists in a large number of languages: named entity recognition (NER), universal part-of-speech (POS) tagging and universal dependency parsing. For each task, we train a task-specific model using within-language supervised data on top of the mBERT representation with fine-tuning.

For NER we use data created by Pan et al. (2017) automatically built from Wikipedia, which covers 99 of the 104 languages supported by mBERT. We evaluate NER with entity-level F1. This data is in-domain as mBERT is pretrained on Wikipedia. For POS tagging and dependency parsing, we use Universal Dependencies (UD) v2.3 (Nivre et al., 2018), which covers 54 languages (101 treebanks) supported by mBERT. We evaluate POS with accuracy (ACC) and Parsing with label attachment score (LAS) and unlabeled attachment score (UAS). For POS, we consider UPOS within the treebank. For parsing, we only consider universal dependency labels. The domain is treebank-specific so we use all treebanks of a language for completeness.

Task Models For sequence labeling tasks (NER and POS), we add a linear function with a softmax on top of mBERT. For NER, at test time, we adopt a simple post-processing heuristic as a structured decoder to obtain valid named entity spans. Specifically, we rewrite stand-alone prediction of `I-X` to `B-X` and inconsistent prediction of `B-X I-Y` to `B-Y I-Y`, following the final entity. For dependency parsing, we replace the LSTM in the graph-based parser of Dozat and Manning (2017) with mBERT. For the parser, we use the original hyperparameters. Note we do not use universal part-of-speech tags as input for dependency parsing. We fine-tune all parameters of mBERT for a specific task. We use a maximum sequence length of 128 for sequence labeling tasks. For sentences longer than 128, we use a sliding window with 64 previous tokens as context. For dependency parsing, we use sequence length 128 due to memory constraints and drop sentences with more than 128 subwords. We also adopt the same treatment for the baseline (Che et al., 2018) to obtain comparable results. Since mBERT operates on the subword-level, we select the first subword of each word for the task-specific layer with masking.

Task Optimization We train all models with Adam (Kingma and Ba, 2014). We warm up the learning rate linearly in the first 10% steps then decrease linearly to 0. We select the hyperparameters based on dev set performance by grid search, as recommended by Devlin et al. (2019). The search includes a learning rate (2e-5, 3e-5, and 5e-5), batch size (16 and 32). As task-specific supervision size differs by language or treebank, we fine-tune the model for 10k gradient steps and evaluate the model every 200 steps. We select the best model and hyperparameters for a language or treebank by the corresponding dev set.

Task Baselines We compare our mBERT models with previously published methods: Pan et al. (2017) for NER; For POS and dependency parsing the best performing system ranked by LAS in the 2018 universal parsing shared task (Che et al., 2018)[3], which use ELMo as well as word embeddings. Additionally, Che et al. (2018) is trained on POS and dependency parsing jointly while we trained mBERT to perform each task separately. As a result, the dependency parsing with mBERT

---

[1] The size of English (en) is the size of this file: `https://dumps.wikimedia.org/enwiki/latest/enwiki-latest-pages-articles.xml.bz2`

[2] The ordering does not necessarily match the number of speakers for a language.

[3] The shared task uses UD v2.2 while we use v2.3. However, treebanks contain minor changes from version to version.

WikiSize	Languages	# Languages	Size Range (GB)
3	io, pms, scn, **yo**	4	[0.006, 0.011]
4	cv, lmo, mg, min, su, vo	6	[0.011, 0.022]
5	an, bar, br, ce, fy, ga, gu, is, jv, ky, lb, **mn**, my, nds, ne, pa, pnb, sw, tg	19	[0.022, 0.044]
6	**af**, ba, cy, kn, la, mr, oc, sco, sq, tl, tt, uz	12	[0.044, 0.088]
7	az, bn, bs, eu, hi, ka, kk, lt, **lv**, mk, ml, nn, ta, te, ur	15	[0.088, 0.177]
8	ast, be, bg, da, el, et, gl, hr, hy, ms, sh, sk, sl, th, war	15	[0.177, 0.354]
9	fa, fi, he, id, ko, no, ro, sr, tr, vi	10	[0.354, 0.707]
10	ar, ca, cs, hu, nl, sv, uk	7	[0.707, 1.414]
11	ceb, it, ja, pl, pt, zh	6	[1.414, 2.828]
12	de, es, fr, ru	4	[2.828, 5.657]
14	en	1	[11.314, 22.627]

Table 1: List of 99 languages we consider in mBERT and its pretraining corpus size. Languages in **bold** are the languages we consider in §5.

does not have access to POS tags. By comparing mBERT to these baselines, we control for task and language-specific supervised training set size.

3.3 Masked Language Model Pretraining

We include several experiments in which we pretrain BERT from scratch. We use the PyTorch (Paszke et al., 2019) implementation by Conneau and Lample (2019).[4] All sentences in the corpus are concatenated. For each language, we sample a batch of N sequence and each sequence contains M tokens, ignoring sentence boundaries. When considering two languages, we sample each language uniformly. We then randomly select 15% of the input tokens for masking, proportionally to the exponentiated token count of power -0.5, favoring rare tokens. We replace selected masked token with <MASK> 80% of the time, the original token 10% of the time, and uniform random token within the vocabulary 10% of the time. The model is trained to recover the original token (Devlin et al., 2019). We drop the next sentence prediction task as Liu et al. (2019) find it does not improve downstream performance.

Data Processing We extract text from a Wikipedia dump with Gensim (Řehůřek and Sojka, 2010). We learn vocabulary for the corpus using SentencePiece (Kudo and Richardson, 2018) with the unigram language model (Kudo, 2018). When considering two languages, we concatenate the corpora for the two languages while sampling the same number of sentences from both corpora when learning vocabulary. We learn a vocabulary

of size V, excluding special tokens. Finally, we tokenized the corpora using the learned SentencePiece model and did not apply any further preprocessing.

BERT Models Following mBERT, We use 12 Transformer layers (Vaswani et al., 2017) with 12 heads, embedding dimensions of 768, hidden dimension of the feed-forward layer of 3072, dropout of 0.1 and GELU activation (Hendrycks and Gimpel, 2016). We tied the output softmax layer and input embeddings (Press and Wolf, 2017). We consider both a 12 layer model (**base**) and a smaller 6 layer model (**small**).

BERT Optimization We train BERT with Adam and an inverse square root learning rate scheduler with warmup (Vaswani et al., 2017). We warm up linearly for 10k steps and the learning rate is 0.0001. We use batch size $N = 88$ and mixed-precision training. We trained the model for roughly 115k steps and save a checkpoint every 23k steps, which correspond to 10 epochs. We select the best out of five checkpoints with a task-specific dev set. We train each model on a single NVIDIA RTX Titan with 24GB of memory for roughly 20 hours.

4 Are All Languages Created Equal in mBERT?

Fig. 1 shows the performance of mBERT and the baseline averaged across all languages by Wikipedia size (see Tab. 1 for groupings). For WikiSize over 6, mBERT is comparable or better than baselines in all three tasks, with the exception of NER. For NER in very high resource languages (WikiSize over 11, i.e. top 10%) mBERT performs worse than baseline, suggesting high resource languages could benefit from monolingual pretraining.

---

[4]`https://github.com/facebookresearch/XLM`

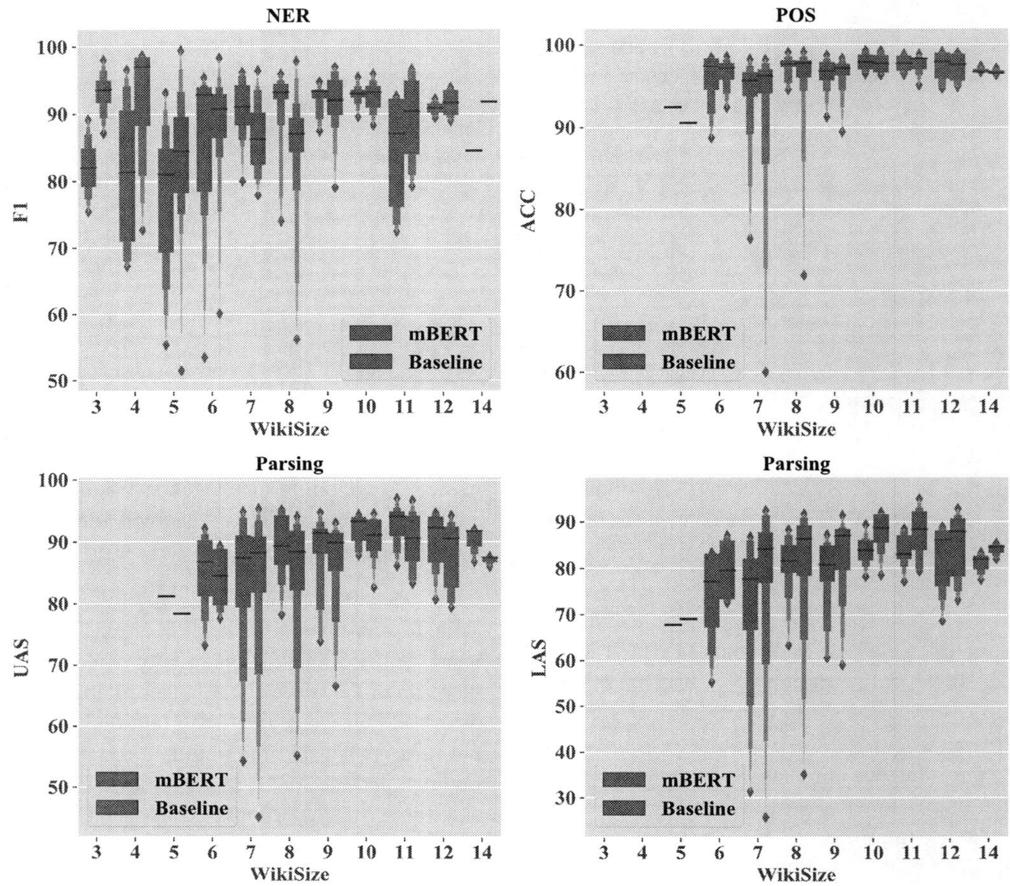

Figure 1: mBERT vs baseline grouped by WikiSize. mBERT performance drops much more than baseline models on languages lower than WikiSize 6 – the bottom 30% languages supported by mBERT – especially in NER, which covers nearly all mBERT supported languages.

Note mBERT has strong UAS on parsing but weak LAS compared to the baseline; Wu and Dredze (2019) finds adding POS to mBERT improve LAS significantly. We expect multitask learning on POS and parsing could further improve LAS. While POS and Parsing only cover half (54) of the languages, NER covers 99 of 104 languages, extending the curve to the lowest resource languages. mBERT performance drops significantly for languages with WikiSize less than 6 (bottom 30% languages). For the smallest size, mBERT goes from being competitive with state-of-the-art to being *over 10 points behind*. Readers may find this surprising since while these are very low resource languages, mBERT training up-weighted these languages to counter this effect.

Fig. 2 shows the performance of mBERT (only)

for NER over languages with *different resources*, where we show how much task-specific supervised training data was available for each language. For languages with only 100 labeled sentences, the performance of mBERT drops significantly as these languages also had less pretraining data. While we may expect that pretraining representations with mBERT would be most beneficial for languages with only 100 labels, as Howard and Ruder (2018) show pretraining improve data-efficiency for English on text classification, our results show that on low resource languages this strategy performs much worse than a model trained directly on the available task data. Clearly, mBERT provides variable quality representations depending on the language. While we confirm the finding of others that mBERT is excellent for high resource languages, it

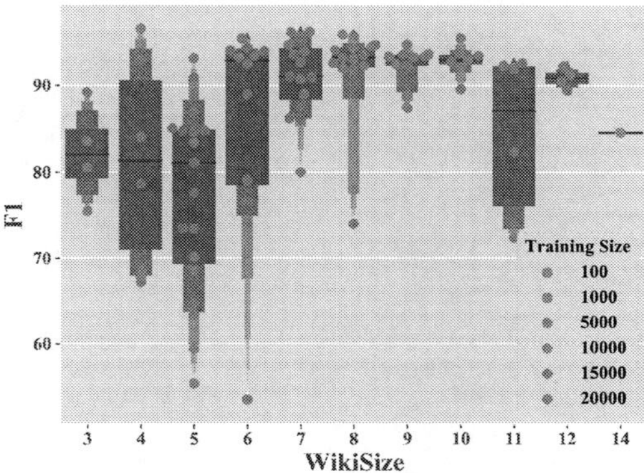

Figure 2: NER with mBERT on 99 languages, ordered by size of pretraining corpus (WikiSize). Task-specific supervised training size differs by language. Performance drops dramatically with less pretraining and supervised training data.

	Coefficient	p-value	CI
Univariate			
Training Size	0.035	<0.001	[0.029, 0.041]
Training Vocab	0.021	<0.001	[0.017, 0.025]
WikiSize	0.015	<0.001	[0.007, 0.023]
Multivariate			
Training Size	0.029	<0.001	[0.023, 0.035]
WikiSize	-0.014	<0.001	[-0.022, -0.006]

Table 2: Statistical analysis on what factors predict downstream performance. We fit two types of linear models, which consider either single factor or multiple factors.

is much worse for low resource languages. Our results suggest caution for those expecting a reliable model for *all* 104 mBERT languages.

5 Why Are All Languages Not Created Equal in mBERT?

5.1 Statistical Analysis

We present a statistical analysis to understand why mBERT does so poorly on some languages. We consider three factors that might affect the downstream task performance: pretraining Wikipedia size (WikiSize), task-specific supervision size, and vocabulary size in task-specific data. Note we take $\log_2$ of training size and training vocab following WikiSize. We consider NER because it covers nearly all languages of mBERT.

We fit a linear model to predict task performance (F1) using a single factor. Tab. 2 shows that each factor has a statistically significant positive correlation. One unit increase of training size leads to the biggest performance increase, then training vocabulary followed by WikiSize, all in log scale. Intuitively, training size and training vocab correlate with each other. We confirm this with a log-likelihood ratio test; adding training vocabulary to a linear model with training size yields a statistically insignificant improvement. As a result, when considering multiple factors, we consider training size and WikiSize. Interestingly, Tab. 2 shows training size still has a positive but slightly smaller slope, but the slope of WikiSize change sign, which suggests WikiSize might correlate with training size. We confirm this by fitting a linear model with training size as x and WikiSize as y and the slope is over 0.5 with $p < 0.001$. This finding is unsurprising as the NER dataset is built from Wikipedia so larger Wikipedia size means larger training size.

In conclusion, the larger the task-specific supervised dataset, the better the downstream performance on NER. Unsurprisingly, while pretraining improve data-efficiency (Howard and Ruder, 2018), it still cannot solve a task with limited supervision. Training vocabulary and Wikipedia size correlate with training size, and increasing either one factor leads to better performance. A similar conclusion could be found when we try to predict the performance ratio of mBERT and the baseline instead. Statistical analysis shows a correlation between resource and mBERT performance but can not give a causal answer on why low resource languages within mBERT perform poorly.

5.2 mBERT vs monolingual BERT

We have established that mBERT does not perform well in low-resource languages. Is this because we are relying on a multilingual model that favors high-resource over low-resource languages? To answer this question we train mono-lingual BERT models on several low resource languages with different hyperparameters. Since pretraining a BERT model from scratch is computationally intensive, we select four low resource languages: Latvian (lv), Afrikaans (af), Mongolian (mn), and Yoruba (yo). These four languages (bold font in Tab. 3) reflect varying amounts of monolingual training data.

It turns out that these low resource languages are reasonably covered by mBERT's vocabulary: 25% to 50% of the subword types within the mBERT 115K vocabulary appear in these lan-

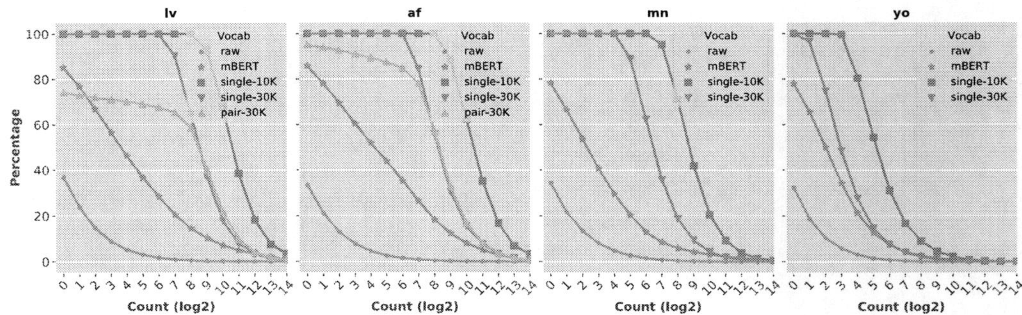

Figure 3: Percentage of vocabulary containing word count larger than a threshold. "Raw" is the vocabulary segmented by space. Single-30K and Single-10K are 30K/10K vocabularies learned from single languages. Pair-30K is 30K vocabulary learned from the selected language and a closely related language, described in §5.3.

	lv	af	mn	yo
Genus	Baltic	Germanic	Mongolic	Defoid
Family	Indo-Eur	Indo-Eur	Altaic	Niger-Congo
WikiSize	7	6	5	3
# Sentences (M)	2.9	2.3	0.8	0.1
# Tokens (M)	21.8	28.8	6.4	0.9
mBERT vocab (K)	56.6	59.0	42.3	29.3
mBERT vocab (%)	49.2	51.3	36.8	25.5

Table 3: Statistic of four low resource languages.

guages' Wikipedia. However, the mBERT vocabulary is by no means optimal for these languages. Fig. 3 shows that a large amount of the mBERT vocabulary that appears in these languages is low frequency while the language-specific Sentence-Piece vocabulary has a much higher frequency. In other words, the vocabulary of mBERT is not distributed uniformly.

To train the monolingual BERTs properly for low resource languages, we consider four different sets of hyperparameters. In **base**, we follow English monolingual BERT on learning vocabulary size $V = 30K$, 12 layers of transformer (base). To ensure we have a reasonable batch size for training using our GPU, we set the training sequence length to $M = 256$. Since a smaller model can prevent overfitting smaller datasets, we consider 6 transformer layers (**small**). We do not change the batch size as a larger batch is observed to improve performance (Liu et al., 2019). As low resource languages have small corpora, 30K vocabulary items might not be optimal. We consider **smaller vocabulary** with $V = 10K$. Finally, since in fine-tuning we only use a maximum sequence length of 128, in **smaller sequence length**, we match the fine-tuning phrase with $M = 128$. As a benefit of half the self-attention range, we can increase the batch

size over 2.5 times to $N = 220$.

Tab. 4 shows the performance of monolingual BERT in four settings. The model with smaller sequence length performs best for monolingual BERT and outperforms the base model in 5 out of 8 tasks and languages combination. The model with smaller vocabulary has mixed performance in the low resource languages (mn, yo) but falls short for (relatively) higher resource languages (lv, af). Finally, the smaller model underperforms the base model in 5 out of 8 cases. In conclusion, the best way to pretrain BERT with a limited amount of computation for low resource languages is to use a smaller sequence length to allow a larger batch size. Future work could look into a smaller self-attention span with a restricted transformer (Vaswani et al., 2017) to improve training efficiency.

Despite these insights, no monolingual BERT outperforms mBERT (except Latvian POS). For higher resource languages (lv, af) we hypothesize that training longer with larger batch size could further improve the downstream performance as the cloze task dev perplexity was still improving. Fig. 4 supports this hypothesis showing downstream dev performance of lv and af improves as pretraining continues. Yet for lower resource languages (mn, yo), the cloze task dev perplexity is stuck and we began to overfit the training set. At the same time, Fig. 4 shows the downstream performance of mn fluctuates. It suggests the cloze task dev perplexity correlates with downstream performance when dev perplexity is not decreasing.

The fact that monolingual BERT underperforms mBERT on four low resource languages suggests that mBERT style multilingual training benefits low resource languages by transferring from other

Model Size	Vocabulary	Max Length	lv			af			mn	yo
			NER	POS	Parsing (LAS/UAS)	NER	POS	Parsing (LAS/UAS)	NER	NER
Baseline										
	Baseline		92.10	**96.19**	**84.47**/88.28	**94.00**	97.50	**85.69**/88.67	**76.40**	**94.00**
	mBERT		**93.88**	95.69	77.78/**88.69**	93.36	**98.26**	83.18/**89.69**	64.71	80.54
Monolingual BERT (§5.2)										
base	30k	256	93.02	<u>95.76</u>	<u>74.18</u>/<u>85.35</u>	90.90	97.76	80.08/86.92	56.20	72.57
small	-	-	92.75	95.41	71.67/83.34	90.67	<u>98.02</u>	80.60/87.40	<u>58.92</u>	70.80
-	10k	-	92.68	95.65	73.94/85.20	89.55	97.66	79.91/86.93	41.70	<u>80.18</u>
-	-	128	<u>93.38</u>	95.57	73.21/84.53	<u>91.84</u>	97.87	<u>80.83</u>/<u>87.59</u>	55.91	73.45
Bilingual BERT (§5.3)			lv + lt			af + nl				
base	30k	256	93.22	96.03	74.42/85.60	91.85	97.98	81.73/88.55	n/a	n/a

Table 4: Monolingual BERT on four languages with different hyperparameters. <u>Underscore</u> denotes best within monolingual BERT and **bold** denotes best among all models. Monolingual BERT underperforms mBERT in most cases. "-" denotes same as base case.

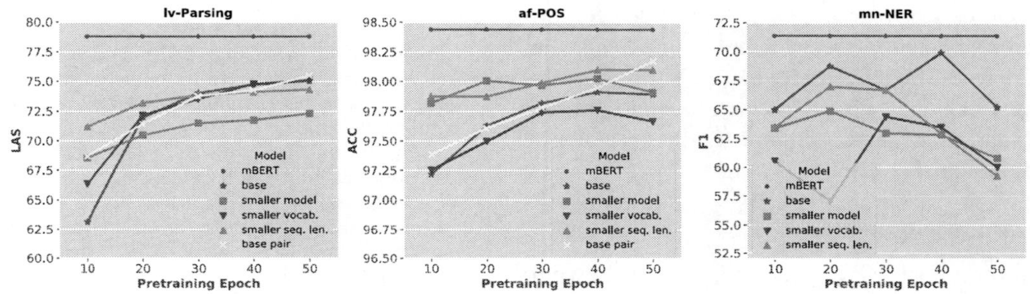

Figure 4: Dev performance with different pretraining epochs on three languages and tasks. Dev performance on higher resources languages (lv, af) improves as training continues, while lower resource languages (mn) fluctuate.

languages; monolingual training produces worse representations due to small corpus size. Additionally, the poor performance of mBERT on low resource languages does not emerge from balancing between languages. Instead, it appears that we do not have sufficient data, or the model is not sufficiently data-efficient.

5.3 mBERT vs Bilingual BERT

Finally, we consider a middle ground between monolingual training and massively multilingual training. We train a BERT model on a low resource language (lv and af) paired with a related higher resource language. We pair Lithuanian (lt) with Latvian and Dutch (nl) with Afrikaans.[5] Lithuanian has a similar size to Latvian while Dutch is over 10 times bigger. Lithuanian belong to the same Genus as Latvian while Afrikaans is a daughter language of Dutch. The **base pair** model has the same hyperparameters as the base model.

Tab. 4 shows that pairing low resource languages with closely related languages improves downstream performance. The Afrikaans-Dutch BERT improves more compared to Latvian-Lithuanian, possibly because Dutch is much larger than Afrikaans, as compared to Latvian and Lithuanian. These experiments suggest that pairing linguistically related languages can benefit representation learning and adding extra languages can further improve the performance as demonstrated by mBERT. It echos the finding of Conneau and Lample (2019) where multilingual training improves uni-directional language model perplexity for low resource languages. Concurrent work shows similar findings as the performance of low resource languages (Urdu and Swahili) improves on XNLI when more languages are trained jointly then decrease with an increasing number of languages (Conneau et al., 2019). However, they do not consider the effect of language similarity.

---

[5]We did not consider mn and yo since neither has a closely related language in mBERT.

6 Discussion

While mBERT covers 104 languages, the 30% languages with least pretraining resources perform worse than using no pretrained language model at all. Therefore, we caution against using mBERT alone for low resource languages. Furthermore, training a monolingual model on low resource languages does no better. Training on pairs of closely related low resource languages helps but still lags behind mBERT. On the other end of the spectrum, the highest resource languages (top 10%) are hurt by massively multilingual joint training. While mBERT has access to numerous languages, the resulting model is worse than a monolingual model when sufficient training data exists.

Developing pretrained language models for low-resource languages remains an open challenge. Future work should consider more efficient pretraining techniques, how to obtain more data for low resource languages, and how to best make use of multilingual corpora.

Acknowledgments

This research is supported in part by ODNI, IARPA, via the BETTER Program contract #2019-19051600005. The views and conclusions contained herein are those of the authors and should not be interpreted as necessarily representing the official policies, either expressed or implied, of ODNI, IARPA, or the U.S. Government. The U.S. Government is authorized to reproduce and distribute reprints for governmental purposes notwithstanding any copyright annotation therein.

References

Mikel Artetxe, Gorka Labaka, and Eneko Agirre. 2017. Learning bilingual word embeddings with (almost) no bilingual data. In *Proceedings of the 55th Annual Meeting of the Association for Computational Linguistics (Volume 1: Long Papers)*, pages 451–462, Vancouver, Canada. Association for Computational Linguistics.

Mikel Artetxe, Sebastian Ruder, and Dani Yogatama. 2019. On the cross-lingual transferability of monolingual representations. *arXiv preprint arXiv:1910.11856*.

Alexei Baevski, Sergey Edunov, Yinhan Liu, Luke Zettlemoyer, and Michael Auli. 2019. Cloze-driven pretraining of self-attention networks. In *Proceedings of the 2019 Conference on Empirical Methods in Natural Language Processing and the 9th International Joint Conference on Natural Language Processing (EMNLP-IJCNLP)*, pages 5359–5368, Hong Kong, China. Association for Computational Linguistics.

Piotr Bojanowski, Edouard Grave, Armand Joulin, and Tomas Mikolov. 2017. Enriching word vectors with subword information. *Transactions of the Association for Computational Linguistics*, 5:135–146.

Wanxiang Che, Yijia Liu, Yuxuan Wang, Bo Zheng, and Ting Liu. 2018. Towards better UD parsing: Deep contextualized word embeddings, ensemble, and treebank concatenation. In *Proceedings of the CoNLL 2018 Shared Task: Multilingual Parsing from Raw Text to Universal Dependencies*, pages 55–64, Brussels, Belgium. Association for Computational Linguistics.

Kevin Clark, Minh-Thang Luong, Quoc V. Le, and Christopher D. Manning. 2020. Electra: Pretraining text encoders as discriminators rather than generators. In *International Conference on Learning Representations*.

Alexis Conneau, Kartikay Khandelwal, Naman Goyal, Vishrav Chaudhary, Guillaume Wenzek, Francisco Guzmán, Edouard Grave, Myle Ott, Luke Zettlemoyer, and Veselin Stoyanov. 2019. Unsupervised cross-lingual representation learning at scale. *arXiv preprint arXiv:1911.02116*.

Alexis Conneau and Guillaume Lample. 2019. Cross-lingual language model pretraining. In *Advances in Neural Information Processing Systems*, pages 7057–7067.

Alexis Conneau, Ruty Rinott, Guillaume Lample, Adina Williams, Samuel Bowman, Holger Schwenk, and Veselin Stoyanov. 2018. XNLI: Evaluating cross-lingual sentence representations. In *Proceedings of the 2018 Conference on Empirical Methods in Natural Language Processing*, pages 2475–2485, Brussels, Belgium. Association for Computational Linguistics.

Jacob Devlin. 2018. Multilingual bert readme document.

Jacob Devlin, Ming-Wei Chang, Kenton Lee, and Kristina Toutanova. 2019. BERT: Pre-training of deep bidirectional transformers for language understanding. In *Proceedings of the 2019 Conference of the North American Chapter of the Association for Computational Linguistics: Human Language Technologies, Volume 1 (Long and Short Papers)*, pages 4171–4186, Minneapolis, Minnesota. Association for Computational Linguistics.

Timothy Dozat and Christopher D Manning. 2017. Deep biaffine attention for neural dependency parsing. In *International Conference on Learning Representations*.

Benjamin Heinzerling and Michael Strube. 2018. BPEmb: Tokenization-free pre-trained subword embeddings in 275 languages. In *Proceedings of the Eleventh International Conference on Language Resources and Evaluation (LREC 2018)*, Miyazaki, Japan. European Language Resources Association (ELRA).

Benjamin Heinzerling and Michael Strube. 2019. Sequence tagging with contextual and non-contextual subword representations: A multilingual evaluation. In *Proceedings of the 57th Annual Meeting of the Association for Computational Linguistics*, pages 273–291, Florence, Italy. Association for Computational Linguistics.

Dan Hendrycks and Kevin Gimpel. 2016. Bridging nonlinearities and stochastic regularizers with gaussian error linear units.

Jeremy Howard and Sebastian Ruder. 2018. Universal language model fine-tuning for text classification. In *Proceedings of the 56th Annual Meeting of the Association for Computational Linguistics (Volume 1: Long Papers)*, pages 328–339, Melbourne, Australia. Association for Computational Linguistics.

Haoyang Huang, Yaobo Liang, Nan Duan, Ming Gong, Linjun Shou, Daxin Jiang, and Ming Zhou. 2019. Unicoder: A universal language encoder by pretraining with multiple cross-lingual tasks. In *Proceedings of the 2019 Conference on Empirical Methods in Natural Language Processing and the 9th International Joint Conference on Natural Language Processing (EMNLP-IJCNLP)*, pages 2485–2494, Hong Kong, China. Association for Computational Linguistics.

Baijun Ji, Zhirui Zhang, Xiangyu Duan, Min Zhang, Boxing Chen, and Weihua Luo. 2019. Cross-lingual pre-training based transfer for zero-shot neural machine translation. *arXiv preprint arXiv:1912.01214*.

Karthikeyan K, Zihan Wang, Stephen Mayhew, and Dan Roth. 2020. Cross-lingual ability of multilingual bert: An empirical study. In *International Conference on Learning Representations*.

Diederik P Kingma and Jimmy Ba. 2014. Adam: A method for stochastic optimization. *arXiv preprint arXiv:1412.6980*.

Taku Kudo. 2018. Subword regularization: Improving neural network translation models with multiple subword candidates. In *Proceedings of the 56th Annual Meeting of the Association for Computational Linguistics (Volume 1: Long Papers)*, pages 66–75, Melbourne, Australia. Association for Computational Linguistics.

Taku Kudo and John Richardson. 2018. SentencePiece: A simple and language independent subword tokenizer and detokenizer for neural text processing. In *Proceedings of the 2018 Conference on Empirical Methods in Natural Language Processing: System Demonstrations*, pages 66–71, Brussels, Belgium. Association for Computational Linguistics.

Guillaume Lample, Alexis Conneau, Marc'Aurelio Ranzato, Ludovic Denoyer, and Herv Jgou. 2018. Word translation without parallel data. In *International Conference on Learning Representations*.

Yinhan Liu, Myle Ott, Naman Goyal, Jingfei Du, Mandar Joshi, Danqi Chen, Omer Levy, Mike Lewis, Luke Zettlemoyer, and Veselin Stoyanov. 2019. Roberta: A robustly optimized bert pretraining approach. *arXiv preprint arXiv:1907.11692*.

Phoebe Mulcaire, Jungo Kasai, and Noah A. Smith. 2019. Polyglot contextual representations improve crosslingual transfer. In *Proceedings of the 2019 Conference of the North American Chapter of the Association for Computational Linguistics: Human Language Technologies, Volume 1 (Long and Short Papers)*, pages 3912–3918, Minneapolis, Minnesota. Association for Computational Linguistics.

Joakim Nivre, Manying Zhang, and Hanzhi Zhu. 2018. Universal dependencies 2.3. LINDAT/CLARIN digital library at the Institute of Formal and Applied Linguistics (ÚFAL), Faculty of Mathematics and Physics, Charles University.

Xiaoman Pan, Boliang Zhang, Jonathan May, Joel Nothman, Kevin Knight, and Heng Ji. 2017. Cross-lingual name tagging and linking for 282 languages. In *Proceedings of the 55th Annual Meeting of the Association for Computational Linguistics (Volume 1: Long Papers)*, pages 1946–1958, Vancouver, Canada. Association for Computational Linguistics.

Adam Paszke, Sam Gross, Francisco Massa, Adam Lerer, James Bradbury, Gregory Chanan, Trevor Killeen, Zeming Lin, Natalia Gimelshein, Luca Antiga, et al. 2019. Pytorch: An imperative style, high-performance deep learning library. In *Advances in Neural Information Processing Systems*, pages 8024–8035.

Matthew Peters, Mark Neumann, Mohit Iyyer, Matt Gardner, Christopher Clark, Kenton Lee, and Luke Zettlemoyer. 2018. Deep contextualized word representations. In *Proceedings of the 2018 Conference of the North American Chapter of the Association for Computational Linguistics: Human Language Technologies, Volume 1 (Long Papers)*, pages 2227–2237, New Orleans, Louisiana. Association for Computational Linguistics.

Telmo Pires, Eva Schlinger, and Dan Garrette. 2019. How multilingual is multilingual BERT? In *Proceedings of the 57th Annual Meeting of the Association for Computational Linguistics*, pages 4996–5001, Florence, Italy. Association for Computational Linguistics.

Ofir Press and Lior Wolf. 2017. Using the output embedding to improve language models. In *Proceedings of the 15th Conference of the European Chapter of the Association for Computational Linguistics:*

Volume 2, Short Papers, pages 157–163, Valencia, Spain. Association for Computational Linguistics.

Radim Řehůřek and Petr Sojka. 2010. Software Framework for Topic Modelling with Large Corpora. In *Proceedings of the LREC 2010 Workshop on New Challenges for NLP Frameworks*, pages 45–50, Valletta, Malta. ELRA. `http://is.muni.cz/publication/884893/en`.

Ashish Vaswani, Noam Shazeer, Niki Parmar, Jakob Uszkoreit, Llion Jones, Aidan N Gomez, Łukasz Kaiser, and Illia Polosukhin. 2017. Attention is all you need. In *Advances in Neural Information Processing Systems*, pages 5998–6008.

Shijie Wu, Alexis Conneau, Haoran Li, Luke Zettlemoyer, and Veselin Stoyanov. 2019. Emerging cross-lingual structure in pretrained language models. *arXiv preprint arXiv:1911.01464*.

Shijie Wu and Mark Dredze. 2019. Beto, bentz, becas: The surprising cross-lingual effectiveness of BERT. In *Proceedings of the 2019 Conference on Empirical Methods in Natural Language Processing and the 9th International Joint Conference on Natural Language Processing (EMNLP-IJCNLP)*, pages 833–844, Hong Kong, China. Association for Computational Linguistics.

Zhilin Yang, Zihang Dai, Yiming Yang, Jaime Carbonell, Russ R Salakhutdinov, and Quoc V Le. 2019. Xlnet: Generalized autoregressive pretraining for language understanding. In *Advances in neural information processing systems*, pages 5754–5764.

Staying True to Your Word: (How) Can Attention Become Explanation?

Martin Tutek and **Jan Šnajder**
Text Analysis and Knowledge Engineering Lab
Faculty of Electrical Engineering and Computing, University of Zagreb
Unska 3, 10000 Zagreb, Croatia
`{martin.tutek,jan.snajder}@fer.hr`

Abstract

The attention mechanism has quickly become ubiquitous in NLP. In addition to improving performance of models, attention has been widely used as a glimpse into the inner workings of NLP models. The latter aspect has in the recent years become a common topic of discussion, most notably in work of Jain and Wallace, 2019; Wiegreffe and Pinter, 2019. With the shortcomings of using attention weights as a tool of transparency revealed, the attention mechanism has been stuck in a limbo without concrete proof when and whether it can be used as an explanation. In this paper, we provide an explanation as to why attention has seen rightful critique when used with recurrent networks in sequence classification tasks. We propose a remedy to these issues in the form of a word level objective and our findings give credibility for attention to provide faithful interpretations of recurrent models.

1 Introduction

Not long since its introduction, the attention mechanism (Bahdanau et al., 2014) has become a staple of many NLP models. Apart from enhancing prediction performance of models and starting the trend of fully attentional networks (Vaswani et al., 2017), attention weights have been widely used as a method for interpreting decisions of neural models.

Recently, the validity of interpreting the decision making process of a model through its attention weights came under question. Jain and Wallace (2019) introduced a set of experiments on English language sequence classification tasks which demonstrated that attention weights do not correlate with feature importance measures, and that attention weights generated by a trained model can be substituted and modified without detriment to model performance. While it is natural to assume that multiple plausible explanations for a model's decision can coexist, the authors show the existence of attention distributions that assign most of their mass to words seemingly irrelevant to the task, while still not affecting neither the decision nor the confidence of the model. In the follow-up work, Wiegreffe and Pinter (2019) find that, while such *adversarial* attention distributions do exist, they are seldom converged to in the training process, even when one introduces a training signal with the sole purpose of guiding the model to such distributions.

In this paper, we aim to tackle the difficult question of the relationship between attention and explanation from a different angle – is there any modification we can make to the existing models so that attention could be reliably used as a tool of model transparency? For the sake of consistency, we follow previous work (Jain and Wallace, 2019; Wiegreffe and Pinter, 2019) and limit our scope to single-sequence binary classification tasks, where we consider models from the *RNN + self-attention* family. Concretely, we analyse single-layer bidirectional LSTM-s (Hochreiter and Schmidhuber, 1997) equipped with the additive (Bahdanau et al., 2014) and dot-product (Vaswani et al., 2017) self-attention mechanisms.

Inspired by the recent results (Voita et al., 2019), which show that optimizing the masked language modelling (MLM) (Devlin et al., 2019) objective results in high mutual information between the input and output layers of models, we ask ourselves whether such a trait is beneficial for interpretability. The task of sequence classification in no way incentivizes a model to retain information from the input, and the model is likely to filter out information irrelevant to the task.[1] We believe this lack

---

[1] The LSTM cell even has an inductive bias towards forgetting information, as we cannot expect the cell gates to always be saturated on the positive side.

Proceedings of the 5th Workshop on Representation Learning for NLP (RepL4NLP-2020), pages 131–142
July 9, 2020. ©2020 Association for Computational Linguistics

of enforced information retention causes a discrepancy between the input and hidden vectors, which results in reduced model interpretability. To enforce information retention, we propose a number of techniques to keep the hidden representations closer to their input representations, improving the faithfulness of interpreting models through inspecting their attention weights.

The contributions of this paper are as follows: we (1) investigate whether the lack of a word-level objective causes attention not to be a faithful interpretation, (2) propose various regularization methods in order to improve interpretability through inspecting attention weights, and (3) quantitatively and qualitatively evaluate whether and how these methods help model interpretability.

The rest of the paper is organized as follows. Firstly (§2), we position ourselves within current work and discuss the use of attention as interpretation in NLP,. We then (§3) present our experimental setup, introduce various regularization methods, and briefly describe the experiments we use to evaluate our regularized models. In §4, we offer a quantitative evaluation of the effect of regularizes on the trained models across a number of datasets. We then (§5) qualitatively and quantitatively inspect the effect of regularization on a trained model, identifying what we believe to be the cause of negative results reported in previous work. Finally (§6), we summarize our findings and propose possible lines of future work.

2   Attention and Interpretability in NLP

Preliminaries: Let the input sequence of word embeddings be denoted as $\{w_t\}_{t=1}^{T}$, where T is the length of the sequence. The sequence of hidden states produced by the encoder is then $\{h_t\}_{t=1}^{T}$, where each $h_t = \text{rnn}(x_t, h_{(t-1)})$. The RNN used is a bidirectional LSTM. When discussing a hidden state h_t, we refer only to x_t as its *input* for convenience. The attention mechanism produces a probability distribution over the hidden states, the elements of which we denote $\{\alpha_t\}_{t=1}^{T}$, and refer to as *attention weights*.

2.1   Attention as Interpretation

When interpreting models through the attention mechanism, we assume that the attention weight on the t-th word, α_t, is a *faithful* measure of importance of the input word x_t for the classifier decision. This assumption allows us to *interpret* the decision

of the classifier by retrieving the highest attention weights assigned by the model, and then identifying the input words in these timesteps. Thus, in the terminology of Doshi-Velez and Kim (2017), our *cognitive chunk* (a basic unit of explanation) is a single word. However, we are using a BiLSTM as an encoder, and every hidden state is contextualized by virtue of observing the entire input sequence, so the attention weights actually pertain to the input word in context. A faithful measure of importance should by definition accurately represent the true reasoning behind the final decision of the model.[2] So, if attention weights are a faithful measure of importance of word inputs, they will assign large weights to words relevant for the classifier decision.

To define faithfulness more clearly, we can assume the existence of an oracle method which can partition each input sequence of words[3] into *decision-relevant* and *decision-irrelevant* words, where relevance is defined by the judgment of a human reading the text with respect to a task. By this definition, a faithful attention distribution would consistently attribute all or at least most of its probability mass to the decision-relevant words, making it a *plausible* explanation for humans. In contrast, a *counterfactual* attention distribution (Jain and Wallace, 2019) attributes most (or a significant amount) of its probability mass to task-irrelevant words. Obviously, infinitely many plausible and counterfactual explanations exist for a given input instance – merely by redistributing the original attention mass within the same set of words we can obtain infinitely many *alternative* interpretations that are still either plausible or counterfactual.

Jain and Wallace (2019) and Vashishth et al. (2019) demonstrate that, if we permute or substitute the weights of a learned attention distribution, our model can still retain high (and in some cases, unchanged) classification performance and prediction confidence. Even more worryingly, some of the modified attention distributions assign high attention weights to task-irrelevant words while not affecting the instance classification. The existence of such counterfactual attention distributions raises doubts whether inspecting attention weights can be used as a faithful interpretation of the model's decision making process at all.

---

[2]For an excellent discussion on interpretation faithfulness, see Alon Jacovi's post on `https://tinyurl.com/y92rskfr`
[3]The instance-level definition is important here, as the same word can bear different meanings in different contexts.

Wiegreffe and Pinter (2019) provide two counter-arguments – (1) *Existence does not entail exclusivity*, suggesting that, just because our model has converged to an attention distribution (a *base* attention distribution), that distribution is not necessarily unique, and alternative attention distributions can still be faithful; (2) while models which produce counterfactual distributions do exist and can be found by post-hoc modifications, these distributions are difficult to converge to naturally through the optimization process of a neural network. This is demonstrated by the authors in experiments where they specifically optimize for a distribution significantly different from the base one.

In contrast, Rudin (2019) states that even if a small fraction of explanations produced by the model is counterfactual, one cannot trust other explanations produced by the same model. Lipton (2016) is more forgiving, and allows that models can still be trusted if they make mistakes, provided humans would also make mistakes on the same instances. The work of Pruthi et al. (2019) emphasizes the threat of interpreting models through attention weights, as they show a regularization term can be introduced to guide the attention weights away from focusing on subsets of words while retaining model accuracy, implying that models which exploit bias in data can be trained to hide the true reasoning behind their decisions.

Among other work, Serrano and Smith (2019) apply an array of tests to analyse whether attention weights correlate with impact on model prediction, concluding again that attention is not a fail-safe (faithful) indicator of importance. The experiments of Vashishth et al. (2019) show that for single-sequence classification, learned attention distributions can be replaced without affecting performance – indicating that attention might not be all we need, after all.

3 Experimental Setup

The **base** model used in (Jain and Wallace, 2019; Wiegreffe and Pinter, 2019) is a single-layer bidirectional LSTM augmented with either a dot-product or an additive attention mechanism, the output of which is then fed into a linear classifier (decoder). We use the same base model as a baseline throughout our experiments.

3.1 Regularizing Models

As mentioned before, we suspect that the lack of a word-level objective weakens the relationship between h_t and x_t, and, consequently, the faithfulness of interpreting attention weights α_t as an explanation of the decision making process of the model diminishes. We will now present a number of methods constructed with the goal of improving information retention between the inputs and hidden states.

Our self-attention augmented LSTM encoder with inputs x_t is defined as:

$$
\begin{aligned}
e_t &= \text{emb}(x_t) & \alpha_t &= \text{attn}(h_t) \\
h_t &= \text{rnn}(e_t) & s &= \sum \alpha_i h_i
\end{aligned}
\tag{1}
$$

where attn is either the dot-product or additive attention mechanism. The sequence representation s is then fed into a linear decoder.

The simplest way to retain information from input is to include it explicitly in the hidden representations. This can be done by concatenating the embeddings to the hidden representation:

$$
h_t^{cat} = [\text{rnn}(e_t); e_t]
\tag{2}
$$

where $[\cdot; \cdot]$ is the concatenation operator. Another method is to incorporate a residual connection:

$$
h_t^{res} = e_t + \text{rnn}(e_t)
\tag{3}
$$

We use these two methods as our regularized baselines (**concat**, **residual**), along with the unreguralized **base** model.

Our next proposed method is to add a regularization term constraining the L2 norm of the difference between a word embedding and its corresponding hidden representation. As we suspect that the base model discards a lot of word information it deems task-irrelevant, we wish to penalize it for doing so where this information filtering is not crucial.

$$
\mathcal{L}_{tying} = \frac{\delta}{T} \sum_i^T \|h_t - e_t\|_2^2
\tag{4}
$$

where δ is the regularization scale hyperparameter, and we minimize the average across all tokens in the batch. We consider values $[1, 10, 20, 30]$ for δ and perform ablation for these values. Further on, we only report results of the model with the best-performing results due to space limitations. We further refer to this method as **tying**.

The last model we propose is inspired by results in (Voita et al., 2019), where we introduce the masked language modelling objective (Devlin et al., 2019), in which input tokens from a sequence are masked at random.[4] The task of the model is then to correctly predict the masked tokens based on contextual cues from the unmasked tokens in the sequence.

In addition to the standard model in (1), the **MLM** model also performs the following:

$$\hat{x}_t = \text{mask}(x_t)$$
$$\hat{e}_t = \text{emb}(\hat{x}_t) \qquad (5)$$
$$\hat{h}_t = \text{rnn}(\hat{e}_t)$$

The hidden states $\hat{h}_t$ for the corresponding masked tokens are then fed into a linear decoder which predicts the masked word. The encoder and embedding matrix are shared between the MLM and classification tasks.

The MLM linear decoder also introduces no new parameters as we tie the weights (Inan et al., 2016) of the MLM decoder and the input embedding matrix and keep them frozen during training. Both of these choices are motivated by the fact that the model might converge to a solution which does not require retention of information from inputs. In order to apply weight tying, we have to ensure that the dimension of the BiLSTM hidden state equal to the input embedding, and therefore we increase the LSTM hidden state size to 150, compared to 128 in (Jain and Wallace, 2019; Wiegreffe and Pinter, 2019). We also use the new hidden state size for all experiments with the base model.

The MLM setup introduces two hyperparameters: p_{mlm}, denoting the probability of masking a token in a sequence, and η, denoting the weight of the MLM loss. We keep p_{mlm} fixed at 0.15 throughout the experiments, as in (Devlin et al., 2019), and adjust η with respect to the average sequence length in various datasets so that the MLM loss would not dominate the optimization process.[5]

3.2 Post-hoc Modification of Attention Distributions

As suggested by Jain and Wallace (2019), robustness of classifier confidence with respect to atten-

tion weight modifications is not a desirable property of interpretable models. Ideally, if a model produces the same decision for an alternative set of attention weights, we would like to be sure that the alternative explanation is faithful. This is not the case in practice as Jain and Wallace (2019) and Vashishth et al. (2019) show that a trained network is surprisingly robust to changes to the attention weights and produces nearly unchanged classification scores even for adversarial distributions. So, while attention is an integral part of training the network, the weights it produces do not greatly affect the classifier decision once trained.

While we agree with the observation of Wiegreffe and Pinter (2019) that robustness of model decisions with respect to attention weights is not necessarily bad as the model is unlikely to naturally converge to such a solution, we believe that fragility of model decisions is an argument **in favor** of interpretability as it indicates that the number of explanations plausible to the model has been reduced, and we perform experiments with that in mind.

3.3 Training an Adversary

In the experiment introduced by Jain and Wallace (2019), for a trained model we attempt to find an adversarial attention distribution which maximizes the Jensen-Shannon divergence (JSD) from the base distribution produced by the trained model, while at the same time minimizing the total variation distance (TVD) from the confidence of the predictions of the base model. The authors demonstrate that it is possible to find an attention distribution that obtains a high JSD while still producing the same prediction confidence consistently across multiple tasks.

As these adversarial distributions were found in an artificial setting, Wiegreffe and Pinter (2019) explore a more realistic scenario and construct an optimization task where, given a fixed (original) model, they train an adversary to minimize TVD from per-instance prediction confidences, while maximizing JSD between per-instance attention distributions of the original model and the adversary. The optimization objective for our adversarial model a given a base model b is defined as follows:

$$\mathcal{L} = \text{TVD}(\hat{y}_a, \hat{y}_b) - \lambda\text{JSD}(\alpha_a, \alpha_b) \qquad (6)$$

This training setup introduces another hyperparameter λ, which weighs the JSD component of the

---

[4]To be precise, either masked, replaced by a random word, or left unchanged. We direct the reader to (Devlin et al., 2019) for a detailed explanation of the MLM task.

[5]As due to keeping p_{mlm} fixed, the longer the sequence is, the more masked predictions we are expected to make.

optimization objective. TVD and JSD are defined as follows:

$$\text{TVD}(\hat{y}_a, \hat{y}_b) = \frac{1}{2} \sum_{i=1}^{|\mathcal{Y}|} |y_{ai} - y_{bi}| \tag{7}$$

$$\text{JSD}(\alpha_a, \alpha_b) = \frac{1}{2}(\text{KL}[\alpha_a||\bar{\alpha}] + \text{KL}[\alpha_b||\bar{\alpha}]) \tag{8}$$

where $\bar{\alpha} = \frac{\alpha_a + \alpha_b}{2}$.

Initially, we were enthusiastic about this setup and conducted the same experiments with our model variants, but drawing any conclusions from the analysis proved to be hard. Firstly, by optimizing for TVD from a trained model instead of on the raw labels, we bias our new model to make the exact same mistakes as the trained model. We believe this severely limits the search space of the adversarial model, as repeating the same mistakes will also bias the model towards exploiting similar patterns in data and, consequently, a similar attention distribution. Secondly, without knowing what the plausible explanations are for the dataset, it is impossible to determine whether a high JSD is a symptom of the model finding an alternative or adversarial explanation. Thus, we do not attempt to draw many conclusions from this experiment, but we reproduce it for completeness with previous work.

3.4 Mutual Information

To quantitatively evaluate whether the regularization has strengthened the relationship between the hidden states and input representations of our model, we look into a recent method of Voita et al. (2019) inspired by the "Information Bottleneck" (IB) theory (Tishby, 1999), where the authors measure an estimate of mutual information (MI). Originally applied to transformers (Devlin et al., 2018), this method is straightforward to adapt to the bidirectional LSTM.

Similarly to our point of view, the IB theory states that neural networks, in general, aim to extract a compressed representation of input in which information relevant for the output is retained while irrelevant is discarded. Mutual information is used as a method of measuring how much information is lost between the input and hidden representation of a certain network. Voita et al. (2019) show transformer networks discard progressively more information in deeper layers. This phenomenon is different for the case of MLM in transformers, where MI is higher in the uppermost layers, likely due to the task of reconstructing corresponding input tokens.

The strength of the relationship between e_t and h_t can be quantified by estimating MI. As MI is intractable to compute in the continuous form, we first discretize the vector representations and estimate MI in the discrete form. Following Voita et al. (2019) and Sajjadi et al. (2018), we perform this discretization by clustering the embedding and hidden representations to a large number of clusters and using the obtained cluster labels in place of the continuous vectors to estimate MI.

Concretely, we select a subset of 1000 words from the vocabulary and gather at most 1M representations of these tokens at input and hidden level. We then cluster the obtained representations into $k = 1000$ clusters with mini-batch $k-$means with batch size of 100. We obtain the vocabulary sample in two ways: as the top 1k most frequent words (**MF**), as in (Voita et al., 2019), but also as a random sample (**RS**) of from the scaled unigram distribution.[6]

3.5 Datasets

We experiment on the following English language datasets for binary classification tasks, which were either originally built for this task or were adapted for it by Jain and Wallace (2019):

(1) *The Stanford Sentiment Treebank (SST)* (Socher et al., 2013), a collection of sentences tagged with sentiment on a discrete scale from 1 to 5, where 1 is the most negative and 5 the most positive. We omit the neutral class (3) and conflate scores 1 and 2 as well as 4 and 5 into negative and positive class, respectively;

(2) *IMDB Large Movie Reviews Corpus* (IMDB) (Maas et al., 2011), a binary sentiment classification dataset of movie reviews;

(3) *AG News Corpus*, a categorized set of news articles from various sources. We limit ourselves to binary classification between articles labelled as *world* (0) and *business* (1);

(4) *20 Newsgroups* similarly, we consider the task of discriminating between *baseball* (0) and *hockey* (1) in this dataset of newsgroup correspondences labelled with 20 categories;

(5,6) *MIMIC ICD9* (Johnson et al., 2016), a dataset of patient discharge summaries from a database of electronic health records. Here, we

---

[6]The sample is drawn from the unigram distribution raised to the power of $\frac{3}{4}$.

analyse two classification tasks on different subsets of the data: whether a summary is labelled with the ICD9 code for *diabetes* (1) or *not* (0) (henceforth *Diabetes*) and whether a summary corresponds to a patient with *acute* (0) or *chronic* anemie (henceforth *Anemia*);

For consistency, we use the train/test/dev splits produced by Jain and Wallace (2019).[7]

4 Results

4.1 Attention is Fragile

We report the average F1-scores of five runs for the **base** model and the following regularization variants: **concat**, **tying**, and **MLM**. We omit results on **residual** due to space, but they are consistently comparable to **concat** due to their similar nature. For each model variant we report results of experiments with the dot-product ($\cdot$) and additive (+) attention mechanism. Due to space constraints, we omit the full results and refer the reader to Appendix for more details.

We report the performance of each model in scenarios where we use trained attention (**Tr.**), a random permutation of the trained attention (**Pm.**) or substitute the attention distribution with the uniform (**Un.**). For the uniform and permutation settings, we report the drop in F1-score when compared to trained attention performance.

We omit the results on the Diabetes dataset, as every modification of attention weights on this dataset results with an F1-score of 0, due to a very small number of tokens being a high-precision indicator of the positive class, as noted by Jain and Wallace (2019). As shown in Table 1, regularization setups increase fragility of model performance with respect to modifications of the attention distribution, while retaining similar classification scores to the base model. These results indicate that we have successfully reduced the space of possible alternative explanations for the model by tying the input and hidden representations closer together. By doing this, we show that lateral information leakage (between hidden states) is reduced when proper regularization is applied, and that, as a consequence, alternative explanations are also plausible. Having shown this, we still need to determine whether a high attention weight on a hidden state is a faithful measure of importance of a corresponding input.

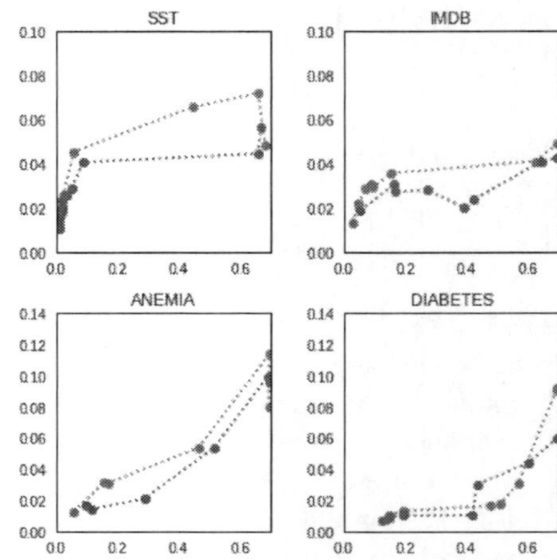

Figure 1: Averaged per-instance test set JSD (x-axis) and TVD (y-axis)

4.2 Mutual Information is Higher

In Table 3 we report mutual information scores across datasets for the most frequent words (MF) and a random sample drawn from the scaled unigram distribution of the vocabulary (RS).

The increase in mutual information scores between inputs x_t and hidden states h_t implies that more information from the inputs is retained during encoding. While retention of input information is not a desirable trait of a model performing pure sequence classification, as the only goal the model optimizes is producing the correct class label with high confidence, it is beneficial for interpretability. If we wish to interpret classifier decisions through inspecting attention weights on hidden states, we have to ensure that a hidden state preserves a significant degree of information from the input. A significant increase in mutual information suggests that the base model was filtering or overwriting a large amount of information from the input, making attention inspection less credible. It is not possible to report mutual information for the **concat** setup as the dimensionality of the hidden vector is larger than the input embedding, so we report the results for **Residual**. The results for the Residual setup can be considered close to the best realistically obtainable MI score as the model explicitly includes the input embedding in the hidden state.

4.3 Adversarial Attention Distributions are Harder to Find

In Fig. 1 we report results where for a fixed oracle model we train an adversary with the objective

---

[7] https://github.com/successar/AttentionExplanation

	α	Base			Concat			Tying			MLM		
		↑ Tr.	↓ Un.	↓ Pm.	↑ Tr.	↓ Un.	↓ Pm.	↑ Tr.	↓ Un.	↓ Pm.	↑ Tr.	↓ Un.	↓ Pm.
SST	+	**84.2**	−2.8	−5.0	83.7	−1.9	−4.7	83.5	**−7.0**	**−18.0**	82.8	−5.9	−15.6
	·	**84.3**	−2.6	−6.5	84.1	−3.4	−7.4	83.5	**−9.9**	**−20.0**	82.7	−3.0	−5.4
AG	+	**95.9**	−2.3	−3.9	**95.9**	−1.5	−2.6	95.0	**−3.3**	**−14.6**	95.2	−1.5	−6.6
	·	95.9	−2.3	−3.8	**96.1**	−1.9	−3.0	95.4	**−3.0**	**−12.2**	95.4	−2.0	−5.3
NG	+	90.9	−9.8	−14.1	91.3	−25.0	−28.2	91.4	−39.7	−43.2	**91.5**	**−76.3**	**−66.0**
	·	**91.1**	−35.2	−36.8	91.0	−40.4	−37.1	90.9	−37.0	−42.8	89.1	**−79.6**	**−72.8**
IM	+	**88.3**	−10.0	−13.4	**88.3**	−10.2	−14.0	87.1	**−56.2**	**−43.3**	87.5	−22.8	−26.5
	·	**88.2**	−18.6	−22.9	87.9	−17.2	−20.8	87.2	**−57.7**	**−45.3**	87.8	−15.3	−18.5
ANM	+	92.4	−21.6	−22.4	**92.8**	−19.3	−22.2	91.3	−31.4	−27.6	89.7	**−35.0**	**−37.7**
	·	**92.7**	−10.2	−14.4	92.4	−15.2	−17.2	91.0	**−91.0**	**−59.7**	90.7	−37.8	−33.9

Table 1: % F1-scores for trained models (higher is better) and drops in performance (Δ F1) when applying regularization (lower is better). Scores reported are averages over five runs.

	$\sim$	Base	Resid	Tying	MLM
SST	MF	2.324	**5.062**	4.870	3.662
	RS	2.435	**4.289**	4.216	3.808
AG	MF	1.940	**5.467**	4.075	3.845
	RS	2.078	**4.518**	4.177	3.980
NG	MF	1.566	**4.345**	3.985	3.677
	RS	1.828	**3.843**	3.784	3.458
IM	MF	2.455	4.998	**5.186**	3.728
	RS	2.682	**4.366**	4.434	3.885
ANM	MF	3.711	**5.253**	4.239	4.016
	RS	3.780	**4.477**	3.950	3.921

Table 2: Mutual information scores between the input and hidden representations. Higher is better. Due to space limitations, results are only reported on additive attention.

of minimizing the TVD between the predictions of the model and, at the same time, maximizing JSD between per-instance averaged attention distributions. Due to space limitations, we only report results for the MLM regularised model, while the others fare comparably. The red dotted line indicates the imitation setup of the base model, and the green dotted line indicates imitation setup for the MLM model. Consistently, except for an outlier point in the Diabetes dataset, the imitation setup of the MLM model produces larger drops of TVD in order to increase the JSD between attention distributions, corroborating the claim that attention distribution of the MLM model is more fragile.

5 Understanding the Effect of Model Regularization

To visually demonstrate the undesired effect of attention mechanisms when trained in the **base** setting, as well as to illustrate the effect of regularizations we applied, we first analyse how we obtain the classifier prediction. The output of the classifier is an affine transformation of the attention output:

$$p_{logit} = W_d(\sum_{i=1}^{T} \alpha_i h_i) + b_d$$

$$= \sum_{i=1}^{T} \alpha_i (W_d h_i + b_d) \qquad (9)$$

$$= \sum_{i=1}^{T} \alpha_i \hat{p}_t$$

We can reformulate this as a convex attention-weighted sum of logits ($\hat{p}_t$) obtained by running each individual hidden state through the decoder. Once we scale the logits for individual timesteps, we obtain the prediction probability as if the whole attention mass was on that hidden representation. For attention weights to be a faithful measure of interpretability, this probability should be high only on tokens which are decision-relevant.

In Fig. 2, we plot these token-level probabilities for a single example to demonstrate that in the **base** model, this is not the case. We can see that for the base model, the probabilities for most tokens have nearly the **same** probability as the final prediction, while the regularization keeps the representations for neutral words grounded closer to the decision boundary. As a direct result of this, the model predictions are much more fragile to change of attention weights, as only a small number of hidden states are far enough from the decision boundary to produce an equally confident classification.

We now quantitatively formulate and measure this criterion – **if** the accuracy of a regularized classifier isn't hurt by the regularization, when optimizing for interpretability we should prefer models that have a lower per-token average prediction probability (given that the prediction for that instance is correct).

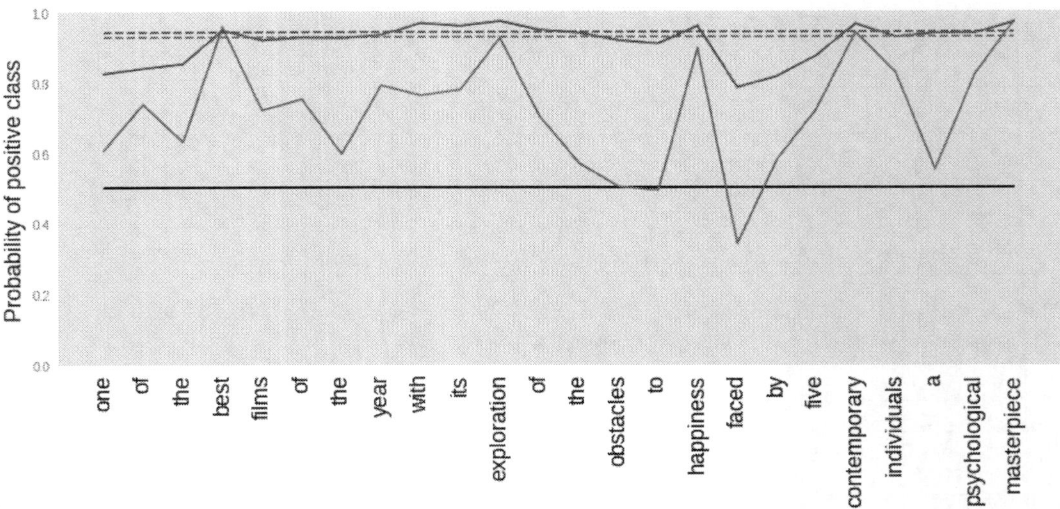

Figure 2: Per-token prediction probability for an example from the SST dataset for the base model (red) and a regularized (tying) model (green). The dotted lines indicate the classification probability of the model. More instances and examples of other regularization techniques can be found in the Appendix.

		Base	Resid	Tying	MLM
SST	+	0.712	0.685	**0.586**	0.630
	•	0.693	0.701	**0.600**	0.664
AG	+	0.887	0.822	**0.615**	0.695
	•	0.862	0.876	**0.646**	0.698
NG	+	0.811	0.551	0.577	**0.514**
	•	0.687	0.755	0.516	**0.482**
IM	+	0.625	0.609	**0.533**	0.562
	•	0.590	0.608	**0.539**	0.553
AN	+	0.568	0.547	0.531	**0.515**
	•	0.542	0.534	0.515	**0.519**

Table 3: Average per-token prediction probability across models and tasks. From the perspective of interpretability, lower is better, given the classifier performance is not significantly affected.

6 Conclusion

We have identified the lack of a word-level objective as the likely cause of attention weights not being a faithful tool of interpretability in the case of sequence classification with attention mechanism augmented recurrent networks. We experimentally establish that we can add regularization methods to sequence classification which strengthen the relationship between the input and hidden states while not being a detriment to classification performance. If one wishes to interpret classifier decisions through inspecting attention weights, we strongly suggest inclusion of a technique such as weight tying or adding masked language modelling as an auxiliary. Adding such methods causes the model to become more susceptible to attacks modifying the attention weights of a trained model, and increases faithfulness of explanations produced by attention weights.

While we believe our work is a step forward towards using attention weights as a faithful explanation, by no means do we claim that the modification is sufficient. As was our primary concern, the risk with using attention weights as a tool of interpretability is that a single bad explanation could have consequences in decision-making scenarios, and while our methods improve the faithfulness of such interpretability, it is by no means foolproof. We have only scratched the surface of faithful interpretability, and most of the datasets in our and previous work do not have human annotated rationales. In order to fully understand the cases in which attention provides a reliable explanation, we believe that datasets with annotated rationales or decision-relevant tokens should be used. This analysis should also be extended to more complex models which better capture the nuances of language. We believe that the experiments we presented demonstrate the shortcomings of interpreting model decisions through inspecting attention weights, however we acknowledge that this branch of research sorely lacks evaluation methods that include humans in the loop.

References

Dzmitry Bahdanau, Kyunghyun Cho, and Yoshua Bengio. 2014. Neural machine translation by jointly learning to align and translate. *arXiv preprint arXiv:1409.0473*.

Jacob Devlin, Ming-Wei Chang, Kenton Lee, and Kristina Toutanova. 2018. Bert: Pre-training of deep bidirectional transformers for language understanding. *arXiv preprint arXiv:1810.04805*.

Jacob Devlin, Ming-Wei Chang, Kenton Lee, and Kristina Toutanova. 2019. Bert: Pre-training of deep bidirectional transformers for language understanding. In *Proceedings of the 2019 Conference of the North American Chapter of the Association for Computational Linguistics: Human Language Technologies, Volume 1 (Long and Short Papers)*, pages 4171–4186.

Finale Doshi-Velez and Been Kim. 2017. Towards a rigorous science of interpretable machine learning. *arXiv preprint arXiv:1702.08608*.

Sepp Hochreiter and Jürgen Schmidhuber. 1997. Long short-term memory. *Neural computation*, 9(8):1735–1780.

Hakan Inan, Khashayar Khosravi, and Richard Socher. 2016. Tying word vectors and word classifiers: A loss framework for language modeling. *arXiv preprint arXiv:1611.01462*.

Sarthak Jain and Byron C. Wallace. 2019. Attention is not Explanation. In *Proceedings of the 2019 Conference of the North American Chapter of the Association for Computational Linguistics: Human Language Technologies, Volume 1 (Long and Short Papers)*, pages 3543–3556, Minneapolis, Minnesota. Association for Computational Linguistics.

Alistair EW Johnson, Tom J Pollard, Lu Shen, H Lehman Li-wei, Mengling Feng, Mohammad Ghassemi, Benjamin Moody, Peter Szolovits, Leo Anthony Celi, and Roger G Mark. 2016. Mimic-iii, a freely accessible critical care database. *Scientific data*, 3:160035.

Zachary C Lipton. 2016. The mythos of model interpretability. *arXiv preprint arXiv:1606.03490*.

Andrew L. Maas, Raymond E. Daly, Peter T. Pham, Dan Huang, Andrew Y. Ng, and Christopher Potts. 2011. Learning word vectors for sentiment analysis. In *Proceedings of the 49th Annual Meeting of the Association for Computational Linguistics: Human Language Technologies*, pages 142–150, Portland, Oregon, USA. Association for Computational Linguistics.

Danish Pruthi, Mansi Gupta, Bhuwan Dhingra, Graham Neubig, and Zachary C Lipton. 2019. Learning to deceive with attention-based explanations. *arXiv preprint arXiv:1909.07913*.

Cynthia Rudin. 2019. Stop explaining black box machine learning models for high stakes decisions and use interpretable models instead. *Nature Machine Intelligence*, 1(5):206–215.

Mehdi SM Sajjadi, Olivier Bachem, Mario Lucic, Olivier Bousquet, and Sylvain Gelly. 2018. Assessing generative models via precision and recall. In *Advances in Neural Information Processing Systems*, pages 5228–5237.

Sofia Serrano and Noah A. Smith. 2019. Is attention interpretable? In *Proceedings of the 57th Annual Meeting of the Association for Computational Linguistics*, pages 2931–2951, Florence, Italy. Association for Computational Linguistics.

Richard Socher, Alex Perelygin, Jean Wu, Jason Chuang, Christopher D Manning, Andrew Ng, and Christopher Potts. 2013. Recursive deep models for semantic compositionality over a sentiment treebank. In *Proceedings of the 2013 conference on empirical methods in natural language processing*, pages 1631–1642.

N Tishby. 1999. The information bottleneck method. In *Proc. 37th Annual Allerton Conference on Communications, Control and Computing, 1999*, pages 368–377.

Shikhar Vashishth, Shyam Upadhyay, Gaurav Singh Tomar, and Manaal Faruqui. 2019. Attention interpretability across NLP tasks. *arXiv preprint arXiv:1909.11218*.

Ashish Vaswani, Noam Shazeer, Niki Parmar, Jakob Uszkoreit, Llion Jones, Aidan N Gomez, Łukasz Kaiser, and Illia Polosukhin. 2017. Attention is all you need. In *Advances in neural information processing systems*, pages 5998–6008.

Elena Voita, Rico Sennrich, and Ivan Titov. 2019. The bottom-up evolution of representations in the transformer: A study with machine translation and language modeling objectives. In *Proceedings of the 2019 Conference on Empirical Methods in Natural Language Processing and the 9th International Joint Conference on Natural Language Processing (EMNLP-IJCNLP)*, pages 4387–4397.

Sarah Wiegreffe and Yuval Pinter. 2019. Attention is not not explanation. In *Proceedings of the 2019 Conference on Empirical Methods in Natural Language Processing and the 9th International Joint Conference on Natural Language Processing (EMNLP-IJCNLP)*, pages 11–20, Hong Kong, China. Association for Computational Linguistics.

General parameters	
Embedding dim	300
RNN hidden dim	150
Learning rate	$1e{-}3$
Grad. clipping	5
Batch size	32
Weight decay	$1e{-}5$
Regularization parameters	
Masking prob.	0.15
Masking weight η	$\{0.1, 0.3, 1, 3, 5\}$
Tying weight δ	$\{10, 20, 30\}$

Table 4: Model hyperparameters

A Model Hyperparameters

Since we analyse a number of models and regularization techniques, we naturally also have a large number of hyperparameters. We do not tune any of them except for regularization-specific ones and we inherit others them from previous work (Jain and Wallace, 2019; Wiegreffe and Pinter, 2019). A notable change is the dimension of the hidden state, which we increase from 128 to 150 due to the nature of the MLM regularization. We, however, repeat the experiments for the base model with this increased dimensionality.

We report our parameters in Table 4. While we have considered other values in a brief search for η and δ, but we have only ablated over the mentioned ones as they have proven to be (locally) optimal.

Dataset	Avg. len.	Vocabulary
SST	17	17310
AG News	31	15286
20NG	164	15590
IMDB	234	41919
Diabetes	1700	23778
Anemia	1927	20290

Table 5: Statistics of datasets used in experiments

We also report the statistics of datasets used in experiments in Table 5. The average instance length had a significant impact on the experiments as datasets with longer instances were naturally more fragile to attention distribution modifications.

B Experiments on Multilayer LSTMs

All of the experiments performed in the paper used single-layer LSTMs. Even though the considered binary classification tasks could be considered some of the simplest NLP problems, one still wonders what would the effect be if a more complex encoder was used. To this end, we perform a preliminary set of experiments where we use the best hyperparameters used for training of the single-layer networks and increase the number of layers of the LSTM network.

The results in Table 6, while far from conclusive, show that (1) among all tasks, the base model consistently becomes **more robust** to attention perturbation the more layers we add. Inconsistently, we further observe a (2) **diminishing return** of regularization techniques among tasks as the number of layers increases. In some cases, the 3-layer results do not follow this trend (but, curiously, the regularization seems to have a stronger effect). We believe that these results should be taken with a grain of salt prior to a careful ablation study, but still might interest the reader.

C Importance of Initialisation in Dot-Product Attention

Initially, the experiments we conducted worked well for additive attention but not for scaled dot-product attention. While the various regularization techniques produced significant changes in F1-scores when the additive attention distribution was modified post-hoc, this was not the case for dot-product attention and the F1-scores remained constant no matter the modification. This was caused by the fact that the attention distribution of the model consistently converged to a uniform one.

After exhaustive experimenting, the only change that fixed this behavior was changing the default initialization scheme for the query parameter. The dot-product self-attention mechanism for a **single instance** (for illustrative purposes) is generally defined as follows:

$$\text{Attention}(q, K, V) = \text{softmax}\left(\frac{qK^T}{\sqrt{d_k}}\right)V \quad (10)$$

where q is the query vector, while K and V are stacked representations for each timestep. In practice, when using self-attention for single-sequence classification, the query is a model parameter,[8] while the keys and values are functions of RNN hidden states. In our case concretely (following Jain and Wallace (2019); Wiegreffe and Pinter (2019)),

---

[8]This independence of the query vector from the instance is not intuitive in our perspective (it seems natural to us that different information is relevant for different instances), but in practice we find that both approaches work equally well.

	#L	Base			Concat			Tying			MLM		
		↑Tr.	↓Un.	↓Pm.	↑Tr.	↓Un.	↓Pm.	↑Tr.	↓Un.	↓Pm.	↑Tr.	↓Un.	↓Pm.
SST	1	**84.2**	−2.8	−5.0	83.7	−1.9	−4.7	83.5	**−7.0**	**−18.0**	82.8	−5.9	−15.6
	2	84.2	−1.0	−1.2	**84.5**	−0.8	−4.6	84.1	−3.7	**−14.5**	84.4	**−3.8**	−5.9
	3	84.2	−0.7	−0.7	83.3	−1.3	−1.3	**84.6**	−2.7	−13.9	82.3	**−7.3**	**−18.0**
AG	1	**95.9**	−2.3	−3.9	**95.9**	−1.5	−2.6	95.0	**−3.3**	−14.6	95.2	−1.5	−6.6
	2	95.7	−0.3	−0.3	**95.9**	−1.4	−2.0	95.5	**−3.7**	−14.8	95.6	−1.6	−3.8
	3	**95.9**	−0.0	−0.1	95.7	−1.0	−1.6	95.4	−2.0	−12.8	95.8	**−13.2**	**−62.5**
NG	1	90.9	−9.8	−14.1	91.3	−25.0	−28.2	91.4	−39.7	−43.2	**91.5**	**−76.3**	**−66.0**
	2	93.7	−0.9	−5.6	**94.0**	−6.3	−11.9	92.8	−17.5	−25.5	89.8	−31.6	**−35.0**
	3	**92.0**	0.0	0.0	91.5	−30.2	−35.7	89.0	**−30.3**	**−39.3**	88.5	−17.9	−17.4
IM	1	**88.3**	−10.0	−13.4	**88.3**	−10.2	−14.0	87.1	**−56.2**	**−43.3**	87.5	−22.8	−26.5
	2	88.4	−3.1	−3.8	**88.9**	−7.2	−9.1	87.6	**−51.2**	**−41.1**	87.4	−14.5	−21.7
	3	88.5	−1.2	−1.4	**88.8**	−5.7	−7.8	87.9	−7.6	−21.3	87.1	**−87.1**	**−84.5**

Table 6: % F1-scores for trained models (higher is better) and drops in performance (Δ F1) for LSTM models with multiple layers. The number of layers is indicated in the second column.

the keys and values are the hidden states themselves.

With this in mind, Eq. 10 can be written as follows:

$$\text{Attention}(H) = \text{softmax}(\frac{L_q(H)}{\sqrt{d_k}})H \qquad (11)$$

where L_q is the trainable query parameter. In our `Pytorch` implementation, L_q is a `Linear` layer, which is initialised from the Kaiming uniform[9] distribution with the scale parameter $\sqrt{5}$. With this initialisation, the dot-product attention distribution in our experiments has always converged to a uniform one. When we changed the initialisation to instead sample from a standard normal distribution, the dot-product attention converges to a sensible distribution. We suspect this problem occurs because the small initial weights of the linear transform scale down the difference norm between the attention probabilities too much to be distinguished from the uniform distribution.

D Additional Visualisations of Regularization Effects

To expand on Fig. 2, we now plot per-token prediction probabilities for multiple models. We sometimes omit the model classification probabilities not to clutter the plots too much. We select diverse examples (Figs. 3–7) from the first three batches of the SST validation split.

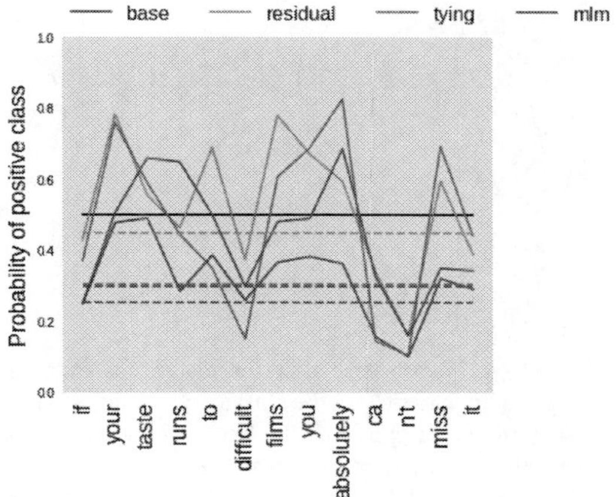

Figure 3: A negative example: perhaps the analysed single-layer LSTM is unable to understand even the simple nuances of language. Here the instance is classified as negative across all models only due to presence of the word "difficult". Note that these models obtain a near 0.9 F1-score on this dataset.

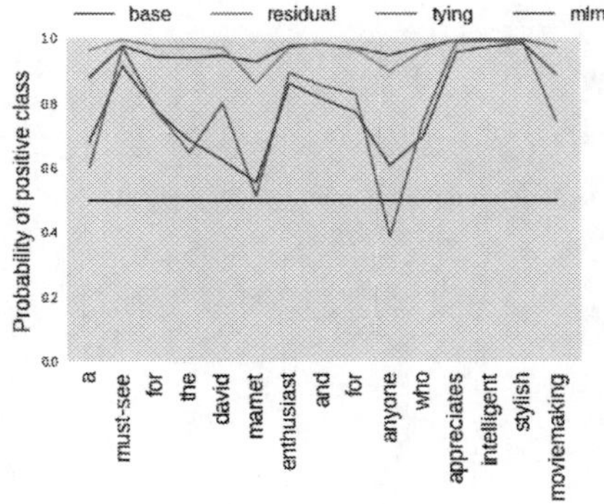

Figure 4: A clear-cut instance

[9]`https://github.com/pytorch/pytorch/blob/master/torch/nn/modules/linear.py#L79`

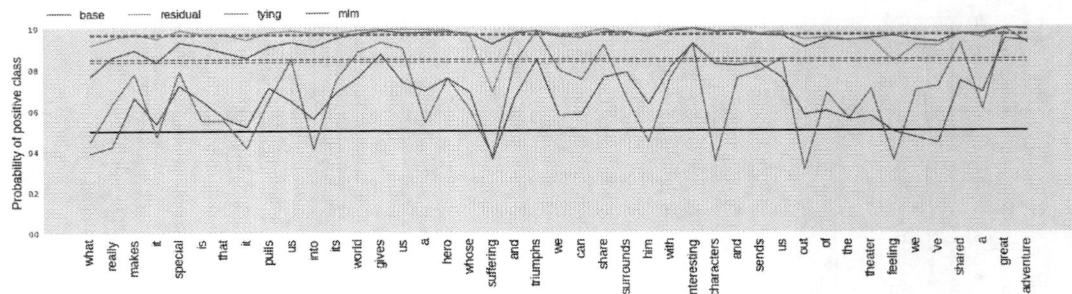

Figure 5: A long example which further demonstrates lateral information leakage

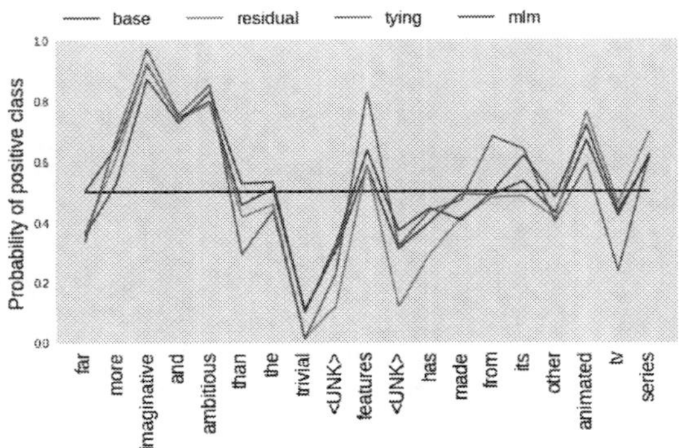

Figure 6: We observe that for instances where the model is not clear about the classification, the per-word probabilities are pretty similar between regularizations. We believe that lateral information leakage happens only when the model is confident in its prediction. Base model prediction confidence is indicated in this example (it overlaps with the 0.5 line).

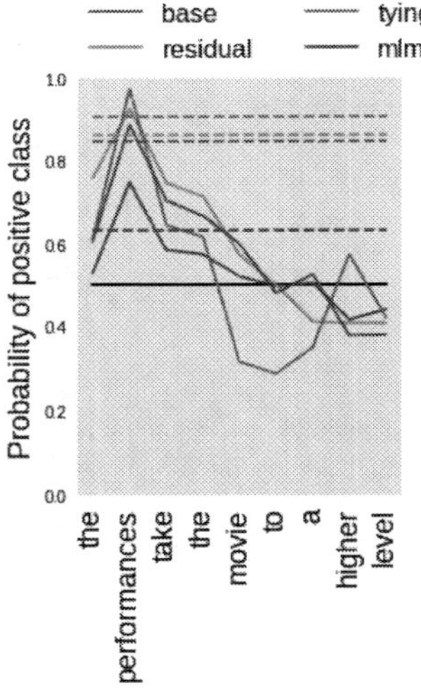

Figure 7: A rare example where the regularised models are more confident in the correct prediction than the base model

Compressing BERT: Studying the Effects of Weight Pruning on Transfer Learning

Mitchell A. Gordon & Kevin Duh & Nicholas Andrews
Johns Hopkins University
`mitchg@jhu.edu, kevinduh@cs.jhu.edu, noa@jhu.edu`

Abstract

Pre-trained feature extractors, such as BERT for natural language processing and VGG for computer vision, have become effective methods for improving deep learning models without requiring more labeled data. While effective, these feature extractors may be prohibitively large for some deployment scenarios. We explore weight pruning for BERT and ask: how does compression during pre-training affect transfer learning? We find that pruning affects transfer learning in three broad regimes. Low levels of pruning (30-40%) do not affect pre-training loss or transfer to downstream tasks at all. Medium levels of pruning increase the pre-training loss and prevent useful pre-training information from being transferred to downstream tasks. High levels of pruning additionally prevent models from fitting downstream datasets, leading to further degradation. Finally, we observe that fine-tuning BERT on a specific task does not improve its prunability. We conclude that BERT can be pruned once during pre-training rather than separately for each task without affecting performance.

1 Introduction

Pre-trained feature extractors, such as BERT (Devlin et al., 2018) for natural language processing and VGG (Simonyan and Zisserman, 2014) for computer vision, have become effective methods for improving the performance of deep learning models. In the last year, models similar to BERT have become state-of-the-art in many NLP tasks, including natural language inference (NLI), named entity recognition (NER), sentiment analysis, etc. These models follow a pre-training paradigm: they are trained on a large amount of unlabeled text via a task that resembles language modeling (Yang et al., 2019; Chan et al., 2019) and are then fine-tuned on a smaller amount of "downstream" data, which is labeled for a specific task. Pre-trained models usually achieve higher accuracy than any model trained on downstream data alone.

The pre-training paradigm, while effective, still has some problems. While some claim that language model pre-training is a "universal language learning task" (Radford et al., 2019), there is no theoretical justification for this, only empirical evidence. Second, due to the size of the pre-training dataset, BERT models tend to be slow and require impractically large amounts of GPU memory. BERT-Large can only be used with access to a Google TPU, and BERT-Base requires some optimization tricks such as gradient checkpointing or gradient accumulation to be trained effectively on consumer hardware (Sohoni et al., 2019). Training BERT-Base from scratch costs $\sim$\$7k and emits $\sim$1438 pounds of CO_2 (Strubell et al., 2019).

Model compression (Bucila et al., 2006), which attempts to shrink a model without losing accuracy, is a viable approach to decreasing GPU usage. It might also be used to trade accuracy for memory in some low-resource cases, such as deploying to smartphones for real-time prediction. The main questions this paper attempts to answer are: **Does compressing BERT impede it's ability to transfer to new tasks?** And **does fine-tuning make BERT more or less compressible?**

To explore these questions, we compressed English BERT using magnitude weight pruning (Han et al., 2015) and observed the results on transfer learning to the General Language Understanding Evaluation (GLUE) benchmark (Wang et al., 2019), a diverse set of natural language understanding tasks including sentiment analysis, NLI, and textual similarity evaluation. We chose magnitude weight pruning, which compresses models by removing weights close to 0, because it is one of the most fine-grained and effective compression methods and because there are many interesting ways to

Proceedings of the 5th Workshop on Representation Learning for NLP (RepL4NLP-2020), pages 143–155
July 9, 2020. ©2020 Association for Computational Linguistics

view pruning, which we explore in the next section.

Our findings are as follows: Low levels of pruning (30-40%) do not increase pre-training loss or affect transfer to downstream tasks at all. Medium levels of pruning increase the pre-training loss and prevent useful pre-training information from being transferred to downstream tasks. This information is not equally useful to each task; tasks degrade linearly with pre-train loss, but at different rates. High levels of pruning, depending on the size of the downstream dataset, may additionally degrade performance by preventing models from fitting downstream datasets. Finally, we observe that fine-tuning BERT on a specific task does not improve its prunability or change the order of pruning by a meaningful amount.

To our knowledge, prior work had not shown whether BERT could be compressed in a task-generic way, keeping the benefits of pre-training while avoiding costly experimentation associated with compressing and re-training BERT multiple times. Nor had it shown whether BERT could be over-pruned for a memory / accuracy trade-off for deployment to low-resource devices. In this work, we conclude that *BERT can be pruned prior to distribution without affecting it's universality*, and that *BERT may be over-pruned during pre-training for a reasonable accuracy trade-off for certain tasks.*

2 Pruning: Compression, Regularization, Architecture Search

Neural network pruning involves examining a trained network and removing parts deemed to be unnecessary by some heuristic saliency criterion. One might remove weights, neurons, layers, channels, attention heads, etc. depending on which heuristic is used. Below, we describe three different lenses through which we might interpret pruning.

Compression Pruning a neural network decreases the number of parameters required to specify the model, which decreases the disk space required to store it. This allows large models to be deployed on edge computing devices like smartphones. Pruning can also increase inference speed if whole neurons or convolutional channels are pruned, which reduces GPU usage.[1]

Regularization Pruning a neural network also regularizes it. We might consider pruning to be

a form of permanent dropout (Molchanov et al., 2017) or a heuristic-based L0 regularizer (Louizos et al., 2018). Through this lens, pruning decreases the complexity of the network and therefore narrows the range of possible functions it can express.[2] The main difference between L0 or L1 regularization and weight pruning is that the former induce sparsity via a penalty on the loss function, which is learned during gradient descent via stochastic relaxation. It's not clear which approach is more principled or preferred. (Gale et al., 2019)

Sparse Architecture Search Finally, we can view neural network pruning as a type of sparse architecture search. Liu et al. (2019b) and Frankle and Carbin (2019) show that they can train carefully re-initialized pruned architectures to similar performance levels as dense networks. Under this lens, stochastic gradient descent (SGD) induces network sparsity, and pruning simply makes that sparsity explicit. These sparse architectures, along with the appropriate initializations, are sometimes referred to as "lottery tickets."[3]

2.1 Magnitude Weight Pruning

In this work, we focus on weight magnitude pruning because it is one of the most fine-grained and effective pruning methods. It also has a compelling saliency criterion (Han et al., 2015): if a weight is close to zero, then its input is effectively ignored, which means the weight can be pruned.

Magnitude weight pruning itself is a simple procedure: 1. Pick a target percentage of weights to be pruned, say 50%. 2. Calculate a threshold such that 50% of weight magnitudes are under that threshold. 3. Remove those weights. 4. Continue training the network to recover any lost accuracy. 5. Optionally, return to step 1 and increase the percentage of weights pruned. This procedure is conveniently implemented in a Tensorflow (Abadi et al., 2016) package[4], which we use (Zhu and Gupta, 2017).

Calculating a threshold and pruning can be done for all network parameters holistically (global pruning) or for each weight matrix individually (matrix-

---

[1]If weights are pruned, however, the weight matrices become sparse. Sparse matrix multiplication is difficult to optimize on current GPU architectures (Han et al., 2016), although progress is being made.

[2]Interestingly, recent work used compression not to induce simplicity but to measure it (Arora et al., 2018).

[3]Sparse networks are difficult to train from scratch (Evci et al., 2019). However, Dettmers and Zettlemoyer (2019) and Mostafa and Wang (2019) present methods to do this by allowing SGD to search over the space of possible subnetworks. Our findings suggest that these methods might be used to train sparse BERT from scratch.

[4]`https://www.tensorflow.org/versions/r1.15/api_docs/python/tf/contrib/model_pruning`

local pruning). Both methods will prune to the same sparsity, but in global pruning the sparsity might be unevenly distributed across weight matrices. We use matrix-local pruning because it is more popular in the community.[5] For information on other pruning techniques, we recommend Gale et al. (2019) and Liu et al. (2019b).

3 Experimental Setup

BERT is a large Transformer encoder; for background, we refer readers to Vaswani et al. (2017) or one of these excellent tutorials (Alammar, 2018; Klein et al., 2017).

3.1 Implementing BERT Pruning

BERT-Base consists of 12 encoder layers, each of which contains 6 prunable matrices: 4 for the multi-headed self-attention and 2 for the layer's output feed-forward network.

Recall that self-attention first projects layer inputs into key, query, and value embeddings via linear projections. While there is a separate key, query, and value projection matrix for each attention head, implementations typically "stack" matrices from each attention head, resulting in only 3 parameter matrices: one for key projections, one for value projections, and one for query projections. We prune each of these matrices separately, calculating a threshold for each. We also prune the linear output projection, which combines outputs from each attention head into a single embedding.[6]

We prune word embeddings in the same way we prune feed-foward networks and self-attention parameters.[7] The justification is similar: if a word embedding value is close to zero, we can assume it's zero and store the rest in a sparse matrix. This is useful because token / subword embeddings tend to account for a large portion of a natural language model's memory. In BERT-Base specifically,

the embeddings account for $\sim 21\%$ of the model's memory.

Our experimental code for pruning BERT, based on the public BERT repository, is available here.[8]

3.2 Pruning During Pre-Training

We perform weight magnitude pruning on a pre-trained BERT-Base model.[9] We select sparsities from 0% to 90% in increments of 10% and gradually prune BERT to this sparsity over the first 10k steps of training. We continue pre-training on English Wikipedia and BookCorpus for another 90k steps to regain any lost accuracy.[10] The resulting pre-training losses are shown in Table 1.

We then fine-tune these pruned models on tasks from the General Language Understanding Evaluation (GLUE) benchmark, which is a standard set of 9 tasks that include sentiment analysis, natural language inference, etc. We avoid WNLI, which is known to be problematic.[11] We also avoid tasks with less than 5k training examples because the results tend to be noisy (RTE, MRPC, STS-B). We fine-tune a separate model on each of the remaining 5 GLUE tasks for 3 epochs and try 4 learning rates: $[2, 3, 4, 5] \times 10^{-5}$. The best evaluation accuracies are averaged and plotted in Figure 1. Individual task results are in Table 1.

BERT can be used as a static feature-extractor or as a pre-trained model which is fine-tuned end-to-end. In all experiments, we fine-tune weights in all layers of BERT on downstream tasks.

3.3 Disentangling Complexity Restriction and Information Deletion

Pruning involves two steps: it deletes the information stored in a weight by setting it to 0 and then regularizes the model by preventing that weight from changing during further training.

To disentangle these two effects (model complexity restriction and information deletion), we repeat the experiments from Section 3.2 with an identical pre-training setup, but instead of pruning we simply set the weights to 0 and allow them to vary during downstream training. This deletes the pre-training information associated with the weight but does not prevent the model from fitting downstream datasets by keeping the weight at zero during downstream training. We also fine-tune on downstream tasks

---

[5]The weights in almost every matrix in BERT-Base are approximately normally distributed with mean 0 and variance between 0.03 and 0.05 (Table A). This similarity may imply that global pruning would perform similarly to matrix-local pruning.

[6]We could have calculated a single threshold for the entire self-attention layer or for each attention head separately. Similar to global pruning vs. matrix-local pruning, it's not clear which one should be preferred.

[7]Interestingly, pruning word embeddings is slightly more interpretable that pruning other matrices. See Figure ?? for a heatmap of embedding magnitudes, which shows that shorter subwords tend to be pruned more than longer subwords and that certain dimensions are almost never pruned in any subword.

[8]https://github.com/mitchellgordon95/bert-prune
[9]https://github.com/google-research/bert
[10]Evaluation curves leveled out at 20k steps.
[11]https://gluebenchmark.com/faq

until training loss becomes comparable to models with no pruning. We trained most models for 13 epochs rather than 3. Models with 70-90% information deletion required 15 epochs to fit the training data. The results are also included in Figure 1 and Table 1.

3.4 Pruning After Downstream Fine-tuning

We might expect that BERT would be more compressible after downstream fine-tuning. Intuitively, the information needed for downstream tasks is a subset of the information learned during pre-training; some tasks require more semantic information than syntactic, and vice-versa. We should be able to discard the "extra" information and only keep what we need for, say, parsing (Li and Eisner, 2019).

For magnitude weight pruning specifically, we might expect downstream training to change the distribution of weights in the parameter matrices. This, in turn, changes the sort-order of the absolute values of those weights, which changes the order that we prune them in. This new pruning order, hypothetically, would be less degrading to our specific downstream task.

To test this, we fine-tuned pre-trained BERT-Base on downstream data for 3 epochs. We then pruned at various sparsity levels and continued training for 5 more epochs (7 for 80/90% sparsity), at which point the training losses became comparable to those of models pruned during pre-training. We repeat this for learning rates in $[2, 3, 4, 5] \times 10^{-5}$ and show the results with the best development accuracy in Figure 1 / Table 1. We also measure the difference in which weights are selected for pruning during pre-training vs. downstream fine-tuning and plot the results in Figure 3.

4 Pruning Regimes

4.1 30-40% of Weights Are Discardable

Figure 1 shows that the first 30-40% of weights pruned by magnitude weight pruning do not impact pre-training loss or inference on any downstream task. These weights can be pruned either before or after fine-tuning. This makes sense from the perspective of pruning as sparse architecture search: when we initialize BERT-Base, we initialize many possible subnetworks. SGD selects the best one for pre-training and pushes the rest of the weights to 0. We can then prune those weights without affecting

the output of the network.[12]

4.2 Medium Pruning Levels Prevent Information Transfer

Past 40% pruning, performance starts to degrade. Pre-training loss increases as we prune weights necessary for fitting the pre-training data (Table 1). Feature activations of the hidden layers start to diverge from models with low levels of pruning (Figure 2).[13] Downstream accuracy also begins to degrade at this point.

Why does pruning at these levels hurt downstream performance? On one hand, pruning deletes pre-training information by setting weights to 0, preventing the transfer of the useful inductive biases learned during pre-training. On the other hand, pruning regularizes the model by keeping certain weights at zero, which might prevent fitting downstream datasets.

Figure 1 and Table 1 show information deletion is the main cause of performance degradation between 40 - 60% sparsity, since pruning and information deletion degrade models by the same amount. Information deletion would not be a problem if pre-training and downstream datasets contained similar information. However, pre-training is effective precisely because the pre-training dataset is much larger than the labeled downstream dataset, which allows learning of more robust representations.

We see that the main obstacle to compressing pre-trained models is maintaining the inductive bias of the model learned during pre-training. Encoding this bias requires many more weights than fitting downstream datasets, and it cannot be recovered due to a fundamental information gap between pre-training and downstream datasets.[14] This leads us to believe that *the amount a model can be pruned*

---

[12] We know, however, that increasing the size of BERT to BERT-Large improves performance. This view does not fully explain why even an obviously under-parameterized model should become sparse. This may be caused by dropout, or it may be a general property of our training regime (SGD). Perhaps an extension of Tian et al. (2019) to under-parameterized models would provide some insight.

[13] We believe this observation may point towards a more principled stopping criterion for pruning. Currently, the only way to know how much to prune is by trial and (dev-set) error. Predictors of performance degradation while pruning might help us decide which level of sparsity is appropriate for a given trained network without trying many at once.

[14] We might consider finding a lottery ticket for BERT, which we would expect to fit the GLUE training data just as well as pre-trained BERT (Morcos et al., 2019; Yu et al., 2019). However, we predict that the lottery-ticket will not reach similar generalization levels unless the lottery ticket encodes enough information to close the information gap.

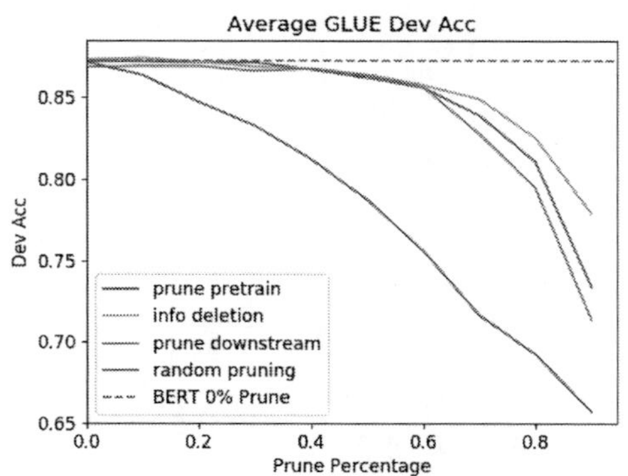
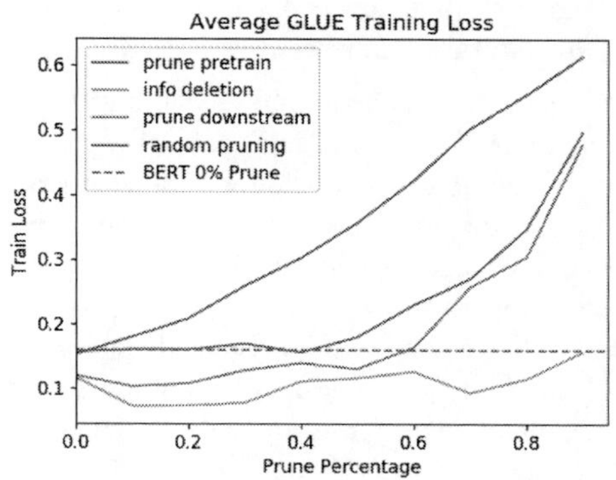

Figure 1: (Blue) The best GLUE dev accuracy and training losses for models pruned during pre-training, averaged over 5 tasks. Also shown are models with information deletion during pre-training (orange), models pruned after downstream fine-tuning (green), and models pruned randomly during pre-training instead of by lowest magnitude (red). 30-40% of weights can be pruned using magnitude weight pruning without decreasing dowsntream accuracy. Notice that information deletion fits the training data better than un-pruned models at all sparsity levels but does not fully recover evaluation accuracy. Also, models pruned after downstream fine-tuning have the same or worse development accuracy, despite achieving lower training losses. Note: none of the pruned models are overfitting because un-pruned models have the lowest training loss and the highest development accuracy. While the results for individual tasks are in Table 1, each task does not vary much from the average trend, with an exception discussed in Section 4.3.

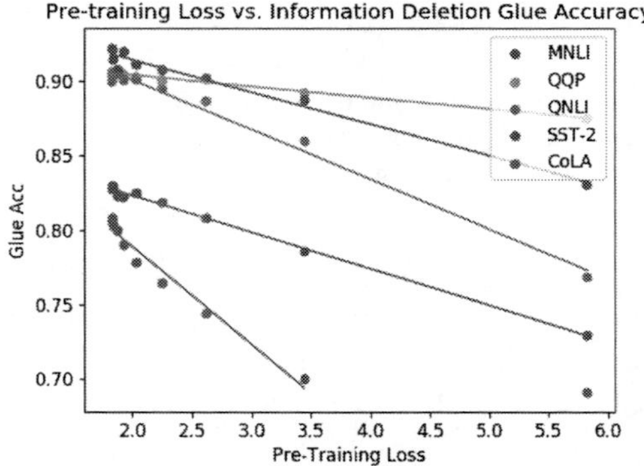
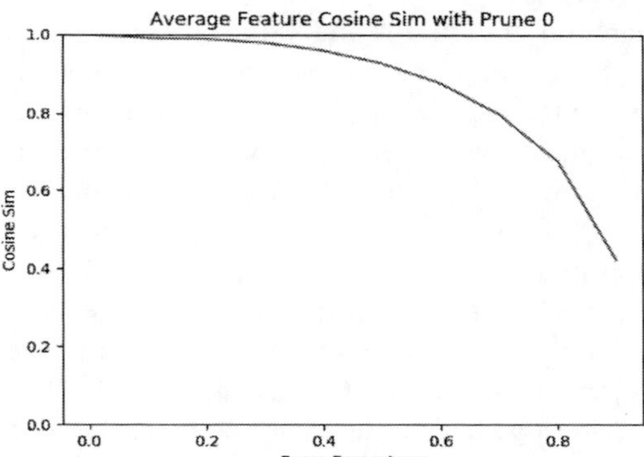

Figure 2: (Left) Pre-training loss predicts information deletion GLUE accuracy linearly as sparsity increases. We believe the slope of each line tells us how much a bit of BERT is worth to each task. (CoLA at 90% is excluded from the line of best fit.) (Right) The cosine similarities of features extracted for a subset of the pre-training development data before and after pruning. Features are extracted from activations of all 12 layers of BERT and compared layer-wise to a model that has not been pruned. As performance degrades, cosine similarities of features decreases.

is limited by the largest dataset the model has been trained on: in this case, the pre-training dataset. [15]

4.3 High Pruning Levels Also Prevent Fitting Downstream Datasets

At 70% sparsity and above, models with information deletion recover some accuracy w.r.t. pruned models, so complexity restriction is a secondary cause of performance degradation. However, these models do not recover all evaluation accuracy, despite matching un-pruned model's training loss.

Table 1 shows that on the MNLI and QQP tasks, which have the largest amount of training data, information deletion performs much better than pruning. In contrast, models do not recover as well on SST-2 and CoLA, which have less data. We believe this is because the larger datasets require larger models to fit, so complexity restriction becomes an issue earlier.

We might be concerned that poorly performing models are over-fitting, since they have lower training losses than unpruned models. But the best performing information-deleted models have the lowest training error of all, so overfitting seems unlikely.[16]

4.4 How Much Is A Bit Of BERT Worth?

We've seen that over-pruning BERT deletes information useful for downstream tasks. Is this information equally useful to all tasks? We might consider the pre-training loss as a proxy for how much pre-training information we've deleted in total. Similarly, the performance of information-deletion models is a proxy for how much of that information was useful for each task. Figure 2 shows that *the pre-training loss linearly predicts the effects of information deletion on downstream accuracy.*

For every bit of information we delete from BERT, it appears only a fraction is useful for CoLA, and an even smaller fraction useful for QQP.[17] This relationship should be taken into account when considering the memory / accuracy trade-off of over-pruning. Pruning an extra 30% of BERT's weights

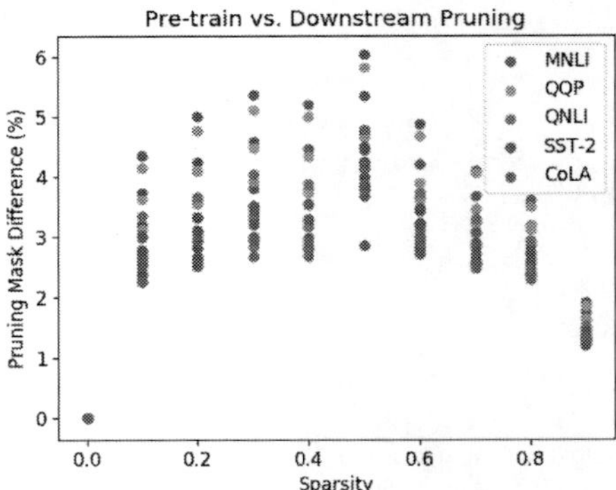

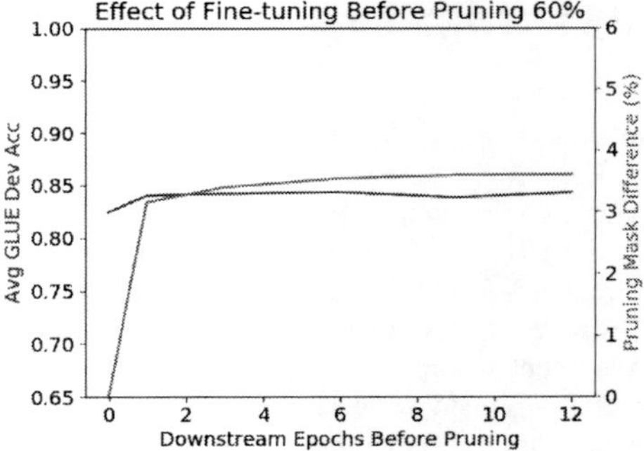

Figure 3: (Top) The measured difference in pruning masks between models pruned during pre-training and models pruned during downstream fine-tuning. As predicted, the differences are less than 6%, since fine-tuning only changes the magnitude sorting order of weights locally, not globally. (Bottom) The average GLUE development accuracy and pruning mask difference for models trained on downstream datasets before pruning 60% at learning rate 5e-5. After pruning, models are trained for an additional 2 epochs to regain accuracy. We see that training between 3 and 12 epochs before pruning does not change which weights are pruned or improve performance.

is worth only one accuracy point on QQP but 10 points on CoLA. It's unclear, however, whether this is because the pre-training task is less relevant to QQP or whether QQP simply has a bigger dataset with more information content.[18]

5 Downstream Fine-tuning Does Not Improve Prunability

Since pre-training information deletion plays a central role in performance degradation while over-pruning, we might expect that downstream fine-

---

[15] We would have more confidence in this supposition if we had experiments where the pre-training data is much smaller than the downstream data. It would also be useful to have a more information-theoretic analysis of how data complexity influences model compressibility. This is may be an interesting direction for future work.

[16] We are reminded of the double-descent risk curve proposed by Belkin et al. (2018).

[17] We can't quantify this now, but perhaps compression will help quantify the "universality" of the LM task.

[18] Hendrycks et al. (2019) suggest that pruning these weights might have a hidden cost: decreasing model robustness.

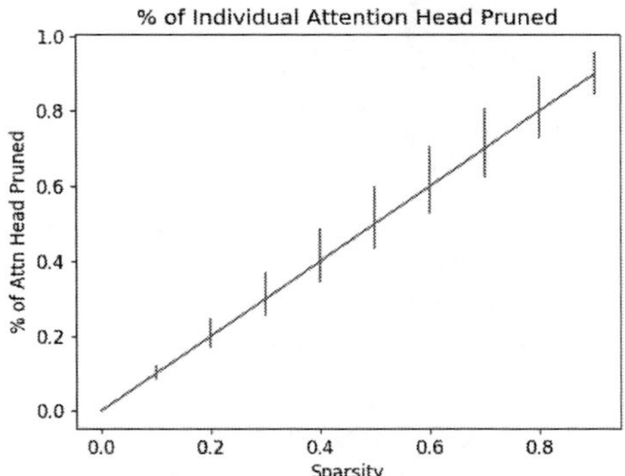
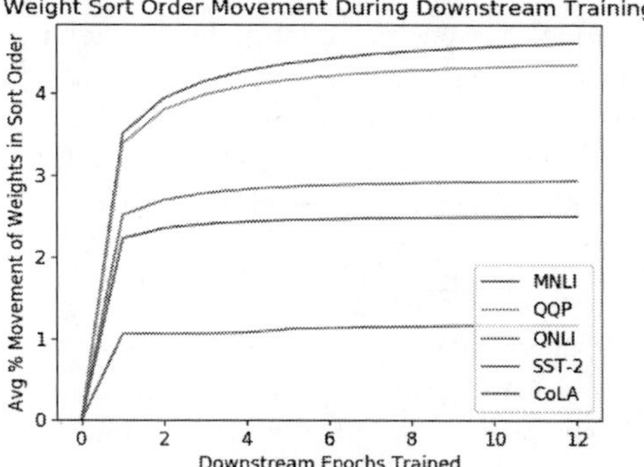

Figure 4: (Left) The average, min, and max percentage of individual attention heads pruned at each sparsity level. We see at 60% sparsity, each attention head individually is pruned strictly between 55% and 65%. (Right) We compute the magnitude sorting order of each weight before and after downstream fine-tuning. If a weight's original position is 59 / 100 before fine-tuning and 63 / 100 after fine-tuning, then that weight moved 4% in the sorting order. After even an epoch of downstream fine-tuning, weights quickly stabilize in a new sorting order which is not far from the original sorting order. Variances level out similarly.

tuning would improve prunability by making important weights more salient (increasing their magnitude). However, Figure 1 shows that models pruned after downstream fine-tuning do not surpass the development accuracies of models pruned during pre-training, despite achieving similar training losses. Figure 3 shows fine-tuning changes which weights are pruned by less than 6%.

Why doesn't fine-tuning change which weights are pruned much? Table 2 shows that the magnitude sorting order of weights is mostly preserved; weights move on average 0-4% away from their starting positions in the sort order. We also see that high magnitude weights are more stable than lower ones (Figure 6).

Our experiments suggest that training on downstream data before pruning is too blunt an instrument to improve prunability. Even so, we might consider simply training on the downstream tasks for much longer, which would increase the difference in weights pruned. However, Figure 4 shows that even after an epoch of downstream fine-tuning, weights quickly re-stabilize in a new sorting order, meaning longer downstream training will have only a marginal effect on which weights are pruned. Indeed, Figure 3 shows that the weights selected for 60% pruning quickly stabilize and evaluation accuracy does not improve with more training before pruning.

6 Related Work

Compressing BERT for Specific Tasks Section 5 showed that downstream fine-tuning does not increase prunability. However, several alternative compression approaches have been proposed to discard non-task-specific information. Li and Eisner (2019) used an information bottleneck to discard non-syntactic information. Tang et al. (2019) used BERT as a knowledge distillation teacher to compress relevant information into smaller Bi-LSTMs, while Kuncoro et al. (2019) took a similar distillation approach. While fine-tuning does not increase prunability, task-specific knowledge might be extracted from BERT with other methods.

Attention Head Pruning previously showed redundancy in transformer models by pruning entire attention heads. Michel et al. (2019) showed that after fine-tuning on MNLI, up to 40% of attention heads can be pruned from BERT without affecting test accuracy. They show redundancy in BERT after fine-tuning on a single downstream task; in contrast, our work emphasizes the interplay between compression and transfer learning to many tasks, pruning both before and after fine-tuning. Also, magnitude weight pruning allows us to additionally prune the feed-foward networks and sub-word embeddings in BERT (not just self-attention), which account for ~72% of BERT's total memory usage.

We suspect that attention head pruning and weight pruning remove different redundancies from

BERT. Figure 4 shows that weight pruning does not prune any specific attention head much more than the pruning rate for the whole model. It is not clear, however, whether weight pruning and recovery training makes attention heads less prunable by distributing functionality to unused heads.

7 Conclusion And Future Work

We've shown that encoding BERT's inductive bias requires many more weights than are required to fit downstream data. Future work on compressing pre-trained models should focus on maintaining that inductive bias and quantifying its relevance to various tasks during accuracy/memory trade-offs.

For magnitude weight pruning, we've shown that 30-40% of the weights do not encode any useful inductive bias and can be discarded without affecting BERT's universality. The relevance of the rest of the weights vary from task to task, and fine-tuning on downstream tasks does not change the nature of this trade-off by changing which weights are pruned. In future work, we will investigate the factors that influence language modeling's relevance to downstream tasks and how to improve compression in a task-general way.

It's reasonable to believe that these conclusions will generalize to other pre-trained language models such as Kermit (Chan et al., 2019), XLNet (Yang et al., 2019), GPT-2 (Radford et al., 2019), RoBERTa (Liu et al., 2019a) or ELMO (Peters et al., 2018). All of these learn some variant of language modeling, and most use Transformer architectures. While it remains to be shown in future work, viewing pruning as architecture search implies these models will be prunable due to the training dynamics inherent to neural networks.

References

Martín Abadi, Ashish Agarwal, Paul Barham, Eugene Brevdo, Zhifeng Chen, Craig Citro, Gregory S. Corrado, Andy Davis, Jeffrey Dean, Matthieu Devin, Sanjay Ghemawat, Ian J. Goodfellow, Andrew Harp, Geoffrey Irving, Michael Isard, Yangqing Jia, Rafal Józefowicz, Lukasz Kaiser, Manjunath Kudlur, Josh Levenberg, Dan Mané, Rajat Monga, Sherry Moore, Derek Gordon Murray, Chris Olah, Mike Schuster, Jonathon Shlens, Benoit Steiner, Ilya Sutskever, Kunal Talwar, Paul A. Tucker, Vincent Vanhoucke, Vijay Vasudevan, Fernanda B. Viégas, Oriol Vinyals, Pete Warden, Martin Wattenberg, Martin Wicke, Yuan Yu, and Xiaoqiang Zheng. 2016. Tensorflow: Large-scale machine learning on heterogeneous distributed systems. *CoRR*, abs/1603.04467.

Jay Alammar. 2018. The illustrated transformer.

Sanjeev Arora, Rong Ge, Behnam Neyshabur, and Yi Zhang. 2018. Stronger generalization bounds for deep nets via a compression approach. *CoRR*, abs/1802.05296.

Mikhail Belkin, Daniel Hsu, Siyuan Ma, and Soumik Mand al. 2018. Reconciling modern machine learning practice and the bias-variance trade-off. *arXiv e-prints*, page arXiv:1812.11118.

Cristian Bucila, Rich Caruana, and Alexandru Niculescu-Mizil. 2006. Model compression. In *Proceedings of the Twelfth ACM SIGKDD International Conference on Knowledge Discovery and Data Mining, Philadelphia, PA, USA, August 20-23, 2006*, pages 535–541.

William Chan, Nikita Kitaev, Kelvin Guu, Mitchell Stern, and Jakob Uszkoreit. 2019. KERMIT: generative insertion-based modeling for sequences. *CoRR*, abs/1906.01604.

Tim Dettmers and Luke S. Zettlemoyer. 2019. Sparse networks from scratch: Faster training without losing performance. *ArXiv*, abs/1907.04840.

Jacob Devlin, Ming-Wei Chang, Kenton Lee, and Kristina Toutanova. 2018. Bert: Pre-training of deep bidirectional transformers for language understanding. *CoRR*, abs/1810.04805.

Utku Evci, Fabian Pedregosa, Aidan N. Gomez, and Erich Elsen. 2019. The difficulty of training sparse neural networks. *CoRR*, abs/1906.10732.

Jonathan Frankle and Michael Carbin. 2019. The lottery ticket hypothesis: Finding sparse, trainable neural networks. In *International Conference on Learning Representations*.

Trevor Gale, Erich Elsen, and Sara Hooker. 2019. The state of sparsity in deep neural networks. *CoRR*, abs/1902.09574.

Song Han, Xingyu Liu, Huizi Mao, Jing Pu, Ardavan Pedram, Mark A. Horowitz, and William J. Dally. 2016. Eie: Efficient inference engine on compressed deep neural network. In *Proceedings of the 43rd International Symposium on Computer Architecture*, ISCA '16, pages 243–254, Piscataway, NJ, USA. IEEE Press.

Song Han, Jeff Pool, John Tran, and William Dally. 2015. Learning both weights and connections for efficient neural network. In C. Cortes, N. D. Lawrence, D. D. Lee, M. Sugiyama, and R. Garnett, editors, *Advances in Neural Information Processing Systems 28*, pages 1135–1143. Curran Associates, Inc.

Dan Hendrycks, Kimin Lee, and Mantas Mazeika. 2019. Using pre-training can improve model robustness and uncertainty. In *ICML*, pages 2712–2721.

Guillaume Klein, Yoon Kim, Yuntian Deng, Jean Senellart, and Alexander M. Rush. 2017. Opennmt: Open-source toolkit for neural machine translation. In *Proc. ACL*.

Adhiguna Kuncoro, Chris Dyer, Laura Rimell, Stephen Clark, and Phil Blunsom. 2019. Scalable syntax-aware language models using knowledge distillation. *CoRR*, abs/1906.06438.

Xiang Lisa Li and Jason Eisner. 2019. Specializing word embeddings (for parsing) by information bottleneck. In *Proceedings of the 2019 Conference on Empirical Methods in Natural Language Processing and 9th International Joint Conference on Natural Language Processing*, Hong Kong.

Yinhan Liu, Myle Ott, Naman Goyal, Jingfei Du, Mandar Joshi, Danqi Chen, Omer Levy, Mike Lewis, Luke Zettlemoyer, and Veselin Stoyanov. 2019a. Roberta: A robustly optimized BERT pretraining approach. *CoRR*, abs/1907.11692.

Zhuang Liu, Mingjie Sun, Tinghui Zhou, Gao Huang, and Trevor Darrell. 2019b. Rethinking the value of network pruning. In *International Conference on Learning Representations*.

Christos Louizos, Max Welling, and Diederik P. Kingma. 2018. Learning sparse neural networks through l-0 regularization. In *International Conference on Learning Representations*.

Paul Michel, Omer Levy, and Graham Neubig. 2019. Are sixteen heads really better than one? *ArXiv*, abs/1905.10650.

Dmitry Molchanov, Arsenii Ashukha, and Dmitry Vetrov. 2017. Variational dropout sparsifies deep neural networks. In *Proceedings of the 34th International Conference on Machine Learning - Volume 70*, ICML'17, pages 2498–2507. JMLR.org.

Ari S. Morcos, Haonan Yu, Michela Paganini, and Yuand ong Tian. 2019. One ticket to win them all: generalizing lottery ticket initializations across datasets and optimizers. *arXiv e-prints*, page arXiv:1906.02773.

Hesham Mostafa and Xin Wang. 2019. Parameter efficient training of deep convolutional neural networks by dynamic sparse reparameterization.

Matthew E. Peters, Mark Neumann, Mohit Iyyer, Matt Gardner, Christopher Clark, Kenton Lee, and Luke Zettlemoyer. 2018. Deep contextualized word representations. *CoRR*, abs/1802.05365.

Alec Radford, Jeff Wu, Rewon Child, David Luan, Dario Amodei, and Ilya Sutskever. 2019. Language models are unsupervised multitask learners.

Karen Simonyan and Andrew Zisserman. 2014. Very Deep Convolutional Networks for Large-Scale Image Recognition. *arXiv e-prints*, page arXiv:1409.1556.

Nimit Sharad Sohoni, Christopher Richard Aberger, Megan Leszczynski, Jian Zhang, and Christopher Ré. 2019. Low-memory neural network training: A technical report. *CoRR*, abs/1904.10631.

Emma Strubell, Ananya Ganesh, and Andrew McCallum. 2019. Energy and policy considerations for deep learning in NLP. *CoRR*, abs/1906.02243.

Raphael Tang, Yao Lu, Linqing Liu, Lili Mou, Olga Vechtomova, and Jimmy Lin. 2019. Distilling task-specific knowledge from BERT into simple neural networks. *CoRR*, abs/1903.12136.

Yuandong Tian, Tina Jiang, Qucheng Gong, and Ari S. Morcos. 2019. Luck matters: Understanding training dynamics of deep relu networks. *CoRR*, abs/1905.13405.

Ashish Vaswani, Noam Shazeer, Niki Parmar, Jakob Uszkoreit, Llion Jones, Aidan N. Gomez, Lukasz Kaiser, and Illia Polosukhin. 2017. Attention is all you need. *CoRR*, abs/1706.03762.

Alex Wang, Amanpreet Singh, Julian Michael, Felix Hill, Omer Levy, and Samuel R. Bowman. 2019. GLUE: A multi-task benchmark and analysis platform for natural language understanding. In *International Conference on Learning Representations*.

Zhilin Yang, Zihang Dai, Yiming Yang, Jaime G. Carbonell, Ruslan Salakhutdinov, and Quoc V. Le. 2019. Xlnet: Generalized autoregressive pretraining for language understanding. *CoRR*, abs/1906.08237.

Haonan Yu, Sergey Edunov, Yuandong Tian, and Ari S. Morcos. 2019. Playing the lottery with rewards and multiple languages: lottery tickets in RL and NLP. *arXiv e-prints*, page arXiv:1906.02768.

Michael Zhu and Suyog Gupta. 2017. To prune, or not to prune: exploring the efficacy of pruning for model compression. *arXiv e-prints*, page arXiv:1710.01878.

A Appendix

Pruned	Pre-train Loss	MNLI 392k	QQP 363k	QNLI 108k	SST-2 67k	CoLA 8.5k	AVG
0	1.82	83.1|0.25	90.5|0.10	91.1|0.12	92.1|0.06	79.1|0.26	87.2|15.7
10	1.82	83.3|0.21	90.4|0.10	91.0|0.12	91.6|0.07	79.4|0.30	87.2|16.0
20	1.83	83.3|0.24	90.5|0.11	91.1|0.11	91.6|0.05	79.1|0.30	87.1|16.0
30	1.86	83.3|0.23	90.2|0.12	90.7|0.12	91.9|0.06	79.5|0.31	87.1|16.9
40	1.93	83.0|0.25	90.1|0.12	90.4|0.12	91.5|0.06	78.4|0.23	86.7|15.6
50	2.03	82.6|0.27	89.8|0.13	90.2|0.13	90.9|0.07	77.4|0.30	86.2|18.0
60	2.25	81.8|0.32	89.4|0.16	89.3|0.16	91.4|0.07	75.9|0.44	85.6|23.0
70	2.62	79.5|0.40	88.6|0.18	88.4|0.21	90.1|0.10	72.7|0.47	83.9|27.1
80	3.44	75.9|0.49	86.9|0.24	85.3|0.29	88.1|0.12	69.1|0.61	81.1|34.8
90	5.83	64.8|0.76	81.1|0.36	71.7|0.52	80.3|0.25	69.1|0.61	73.4|49.8
				Information Deletion			
0	1.82	83.0|0.20	90.6|0.06	90.0|0.10	92.1|0.03	80.6|0.18	87.3|11.6
10	1.82	82.8|0.01	90.5|0.05	90.5|0.09	92.2|0.05	80.8|0.16	87.4|07.2
20	1.83	82.9|0.01	90.5|0.05	90.5|0.09	91.5|0.05	80.3|0.16	87.2|07.3
30	1.86	82.3|0.01	90.6|0.04	90.5|0.10	90.8|0.05	80.0|0.18	86.9|07.7
40	1.93	82.2|0.19	90.5|0.05	90.1|0.10	92.0|0.05	79.0|0.17	86.7|11.1
50	2.03	82.5|0.19	90.3|0.05	90.2|0.10	91.2|0.05	77.9|0.19	86.4|11.6
60	2.25	81.9|0.20	90.1|0.05	89.5|0.10	90.8|0.05	76.4|0.23	85.7|12.6
70	2.62	80.8|0.01	90.2|0.01	88.7|0.10	90.3|0.06	74.4|0.28	84.9|09.3
80	3.44	78.6|0.01	89.3|0.02	86.0|0.02	88.8|0.07	70.0|0.45	82.5|11.5
90	5.83	72.9|0.01	87.5|0.02	76.8|0.06	83.0|0.09	69.1|0.61	77.9|15.7
			Pruned after Downstream Fine-tuning				
0	-	82.6|0.15	90.6|0.06	90.1|0.10	92.1|0.04	78.7|0.25	86.8|12.0
10	-	82.9|0.19	90.6|0.06	90.3|0.10	91.6|0.05	79.0|0.11	86.9|10.3
20	-	82.7|0.15	90.6|0.07	90.2|0.07	92.0|0.04	79.0|0.22	86.9|10.7
30	-	82.7|0.23	90.4|0.07	89.7|0.07	91.6|0.04	78.5|0.23	86.6|12.8
40	-	82.7|0.25	90.5|0.11	89.9|0.12	91.7|0.05	78.8|0.17	86.7|13.9
50	-	82.6|0.19	90.3|0.08	89.7|0.11	90.8|0.06	78.0|0.22	86.3|13.0
60	-	81.8|0.22	90.2|0.10	89.3|0.12	90.6|0.06	76.1|0.31	85.6|16.4
70	-	80.5|0.30	89.4|0.14	86.2|0.19	88.2|0.07	69.5|0.58	82.7|25.8
80	-	73.7|0.53	87.8|0.12	80.4|0.21	86.4|0.07	69.1|0.59	79.5|30.5
90	-	58.7|0.86	82.5|0.26	65.2|0.52	81.5|0.16	69.1|0.61	71.4|47.9
				Random Pruning			
0	1.82	83.3|0.26	90.5|0.10	90.6|0.15	92.4|0.07	78.7|0.18	87.1|15.3
10	2.09	82.0|0.27	90.1|0.12	90.3|0.13	92.3|0.05	77.0|0.32	86.3|18.0
20	2.46	80.6|0.32	89.8|0.12	88.5|0.14	91.1|0.07	73.5|0.39	84.7|20.8
30	2.98	79.1|0.36	89.2|0.14	86.9|0.23	89.3|0.10	71.8|0.47	83.3|25.9
40	3.76	75.4|0.45	88.2|0.16	84.5|0.23	88.6|0.09	69.3|0.57	81.2|30.3
50	4.73	71.6|0.60	86.6|0.20	81.5|0.28	85.0|0.10	69.1|0.61	78.8|35.8
60	5.63	70.4|0.60	85.2|0.24	71.7|0.45	81.5|0.21	69.1|0.61	75.6|42.3
70	6.22	64.1|0.76	81.4|0.34	63.0|0.62	80.6|0.20	69.1|0.61	71.6|50.3
80	6.87	58.8|0.84	76.6|0.46	61.1|0.64	80.6|0.23	69.1|0.61	69.3|55.6
90	7.37	49.8|0.98	74.3|0.51	60.2|0.65	75.1|0.33	69.1|0.61	65.7|61.4

Table 1: Pre-training development losses and GLUE task development accuracies for various levels of pruning. Each development accuracy is accompanied on its right by the achieved training loss, evaluated on the entire training set. Averages are summarized in Figure 1. Pre-training losses are omitted for models pruned after downstream fine-tuning because it is not clear how to measure their performance on the pre-training task in a fair way.

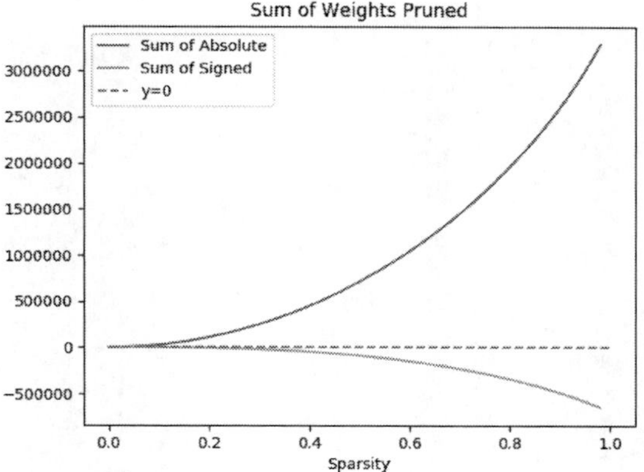

Figure 5: The sum of weights pruned at each sparsity level for one shot pruning of BERT. Given the motivation for our saliency criterion, it seems strange that such a large magnitude of weights can be pruned without decreasing accuracy.

LR	MNLI	QQP	QNL	SST-2	CoLA
2e-5	1.91 ± 1.81	1.82 ± 1.72	1.27 ± 1.22	1.06 ± 1.03	0.79 ± 0.77
3e-5	2.68 ± 2.51	2.56 ± 2.40	1.79 ± 1.69	1.54 ± 1.47	1.06 ± 1.03
4e-5	3.41 ± 3.18	3.30 ± 3.10	2.31 ± 2.19	1.99 ± 1.89	1.11 ± 1.09
5e-5	4.12 ± 3.83	4.02 ± 3.74	2.77 ± 2.62	2.38 ± 2.29	1.47 ± 1.43

Table 2: We compute the magnitude sorting order of each weight before and after downstream fine-tuning. If a weight's original position is 59 / 100 before fine-tuning and 63 / 100 after fine-tuning, then that weight moved 4% in the sorting order. We then list the average movement of weights in each model, along with the standard deviation. Sorting order changes mostly locally across tasks: a weight moves, on average, 0-4% away from its starting position. As expected, larger datasets and larger learning rates have more movement (per epoch). We also see that higher magnitude weights are more stable than lower weights, see Figure 6.

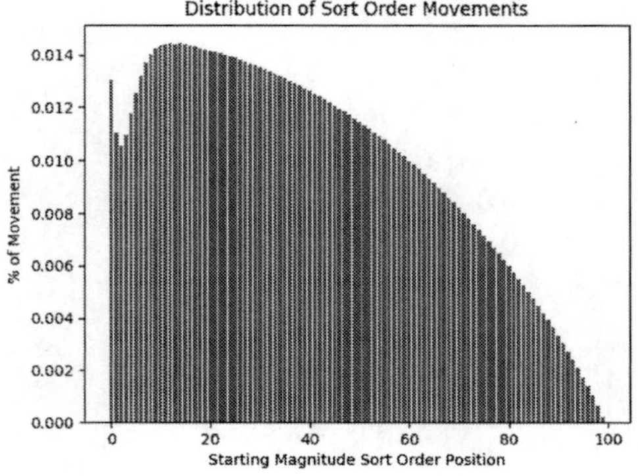

Figure 6: We show how weight sort order movements are distributed during fine-tuning, given a weight's starting magnitude. We see that higher magnitude weights are more stable than lower magnitude weights and do not move as much in the sort order. This plot is nearly identical for every model and learning rate, so we only show it once.

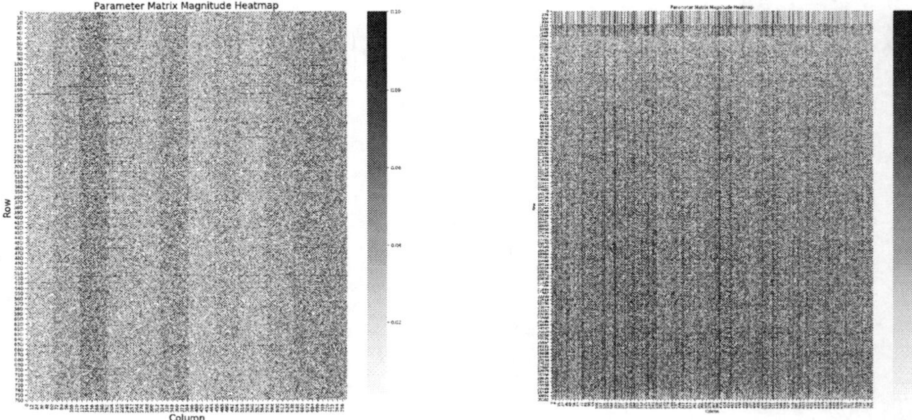

Figure 7: A heatmap of the weight magnitudes of the 12 horizontally stacked self-attention key projection matrices for layer 1. A banding pattern can be seen: the highest values of the matrix tend to cluster in certain attention heads. This pattern appears in most of the self-attention parameter matrices, but it does not cause pruning to prune one head more than another. However, it may prove to be a useful heuristic for attention head pruning, which would not require making many passes over the training data. (Right) A heatmap of the weight magnitudes of BERT's subword embeddings. Interestingly, pruning BERT embeddings are more interpretable; we can see shorter subwords (top rows) have smaller magnitude values and thus will be pruned earlier than other subword embeddings.

Weight Matrix	Weight Mean	Weight STD
embeddings word embeddings	-0.0282	0.042
layer 0 attention output FC	-0.0000	0.029
layer 0 self attn key	0.0000	0.043
layer 0 self attn query	0.0000	0.043
layer 0 self attn value	-0.0000	0.029
layer 0 intermediate FC	-0.0000	0.037
layer 0 output FC	-0.0012	0.036
layer 1 attention output FC	0.0001	0.028
layer 1 self attn key	0.0000	0.043
layer 1 self attn query	-0.0003	0.043
layer 1 self attn value	-0.0000	0.029
layer 1 intermediate FC	0.0001	0.039
layer 1 output FC	-0.0014	0.038
layer 10 attention output FC	-0.0000	0.033
layer 10 self attn key	-0.0000	0.046
layer 10 self attn query	0.0002	0.046
layer 10 self attn value	-0.0000	0.036
layer 10 intermediate FC	0.0000	0.039
layer 10 output FC	-0.0011	0.038
layer 11 attention output FC	-0.0000	0.037
layer 11 self attn key	0.0002	0.044
layer 11 self attn query	-0.0001	0.045
layer 11 self attn value	-0.0000	0.039
layer 11 intermediate FC	0.0004	0.039
layer 11 output FC	-0.0008	0.036

layer 2 attention output FC	0.0000	0.027
layer 2 self attn key	0.0000	0.047
layer 2 self attn query	0.0000	0.048
layer 2 self attn value	-0.0000	0.028
layer 2 intermediate FC	0.0001	0.040
layer 2 output FC	-0.0015	0.038
layer 3 attention output FC	0.0001	0.029
layer 3 self attn key	0.0000	0.043
layer 3 self attn query	0.0003	0.043
layer 3 self attn value	-0.0001	0.031
layer 3 intermediate FC	-0.0001	0.040
layer 3 output FC	-0.0014	0.039
layer 4 attention output FC	0.0000	0.033
layer 4 self attn key	0.0000	0.042
layer 4 self attn query	-0.0001	0.042
layer 4 self attn value	0.0001	0.035
layer 4 intermediate FC	0.0001	0.041
layer 4 output FC	-0.0014	0.040
layer 5 attention output FC	-0.0000	0.033
layer 5 self attn key	-0.0001	0.043
layer 5 self attn query	-0.0000	0.043
layer 5 self attn value	-0.0000	0.035
layer 5 intermediate FC	0.0000	0.041
layer 5 output FC	-0.0014	0.039
layer 6 attention output FC	0.0001	0.032
layer 6 self attn key	-0.0000	0.043
layer 6 self attn query	0.0001	0.043
layer 6 self attn value	0.0000	0.034
layer 6 intermediate FC	-0.0000	0.041
layer 6 output FC	-0.0014	0.039
layer 7 attention output FC	0.0000	0.032
layer 7 self attn key	-0.0000	0.044
layer 7 self attn query	-0.0000	0.044
layer 7 self attn value	0.0001	0.033
layer 7 intermediate FC	0.0003	0.039
layer 7 output FC	-0.0013	0.038
layer 8 attention output FC	0.0000	0.034
layer 8 self attn key	-0.0000	0.044
layer 8 self attn query	0.0001	0.044
layer 8 self attn value	0.0000	0.035
layer 8 intermediate FC	0.0004	0.039
layer 8 output FC	-0.0013	0.037
layer 9 attention output FC	0.0001	0.033
layer 9 self attn key	0.0000	0.046
layer 9 self attn query	-0.0001	0.046
layer 9 self attn value	0.0000	0.035
layer 9 intermediate FC	0.0005	0.040
layer 9 output FC	-0.0012	0.039
pooler FC	0.0000	0.029

Table 3: The values of BERT's weights are normally distributed in each weight matrix. The means and variances are listed for each.

On Dimensional Linguistic Properties of the Word Embedding Space

Vikas Raunak[*]
Carnegie Mellon University
vraunak@cs.cmu.edu

Vaibhav Kumar[*]
Carnegie Mellon University
vaibhav2@cs.cmu.edu

Vivek Gupta
University of Utah
vgupta@cs.utah.edu

Florian Metze
Carnegie Mellon University
fmetze@cs.cmu.edu

Abstract

Word embeddings have become a staple of several natural language processing tasks, yet much remains to be understood about their properties. In this work, we analyze word embeddings in terms of their principal components and arrive at a number of novel and counterintuitive observations. In particular, we characterize the utility of variance explained by the principal components as a proxy for downstream performance. Furthermore, through syntactic probing of the principal embedding space, we show that the syntactic information captured by a principal component does not correlate with the amount of variance it explains. Consequently, we investigate the limitations of variance based embedding post-processing, used in a few algorithms such as (Mu and Viswanath, 2018; Raunak et al., 2019) and demonstrate that such post-processing is counter-productive in sentence classification and machine translation tasks. Finally, we offer a few precautionary guidelines on applying variance based embedding post-processing and explain why non-isotropic geometry might be integral to word embedding performance.

1 Introduction

Word embeddings have revolutionized natural language processing by representing words as dense real-valued vectors in a low dimensional space. Pre-trained word embeddings such as Glove (Pennington et al., 2014), word2vec (Mikolov et al., 2013) and fastText (Bojanowski et al., 2017), trained on large corpora are readily available for use in a variety of tasks. Subsequently, there has been emphasis on post-processing the embeddings to improve their performance on downstream tasks (Mu and Viswanath, 2018) or to induce linguistic properties (Mrkšic et al.; Faruqui et al., 2015).

---

[*]equal contribution

In particular, the Principal Component Analysis (PCA) based post-processing algorithm proposed by (Mu and Viswanath, 2018) has led to significant gains in word and sentence similarity tasks, and has also proved useful in dimensionality reduction (Raunak et al., 2019). Similarly, understanding the geometry of word embeddings is another area of active research (Mimno and Thompson, 2017). In contrast to previous work such as (Yin and Shen, 2018), which focuses on optimal dimensionality selection for word embeddings, we explore the dimensional properties of existing pre-trained word embeddings through their principal components. Specifically, our contributions are as follows:

1. We analyze the word embeddings in terms of their principal components and demonstrate that their performance on both word similarity and sentence classification tasks saturates well before the full dimensionality.

2. We demonstrate that the amount of variance captured by the principal components is a poor representative for the downstream performance of the embeddings constructed using the very same principal components.

3. We investigate the reasons behind the aforementioned result through syntactic information based dimensional linguistic probing tasks (Conneau et al., 2018) and demonstrate that the syntactic information captured by a principal component is independent of the amount of variance it explains.

4. We point out the limitations of variance based post-processing used in a few algorithms (Mu and Viswanath, 2018; Raunak et al., 2019) and demonstrate that it leads to a decrease in performance in sentence classification and machine translation tasks, restricting its efficacy mainly to semantic similarity tasks.

Proceedings of the 5th Workshop on Representation Learning for NLP (RepL4NLP-2020), pages 156–165
July 9, 2020. ©2020 Association for Computational Linguistics

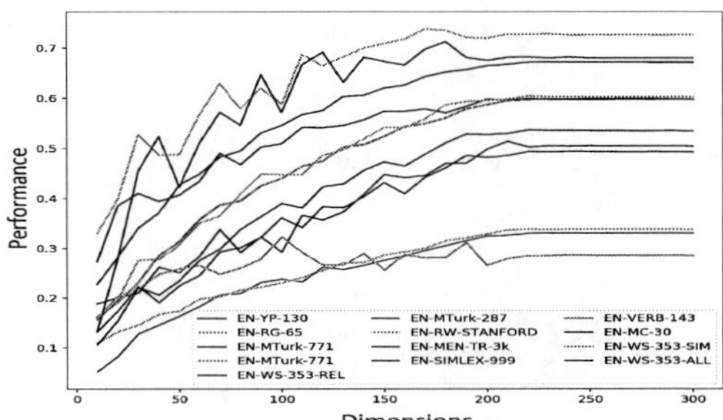

Figure 1: **Rho** x 100 on Word Similarity Tasks

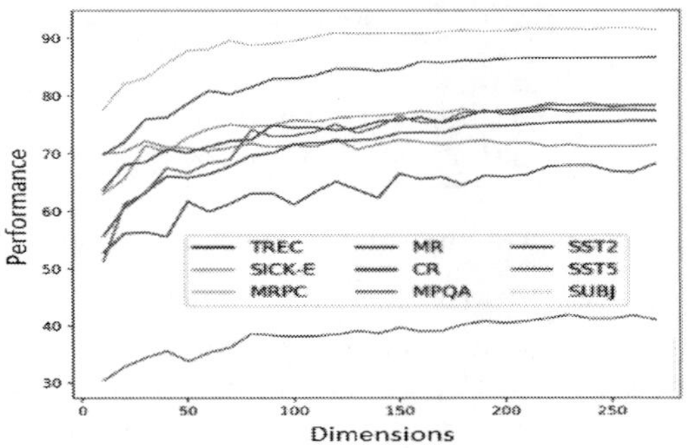

Figure 2: Accuracy on Sentence Classification Tasks

In Section 1, we provide an introduction to the problem statement. In Section 2, we discuss the dimensional properties of word embeddings. In Section 3, we conduct a variance based analysis by evaluating the word embeddings on several downstream tasks. In Section 4, we move on to dimensional linguistic probing tasks followed by Section 5, where we discuss variance based post-processing algorithms, and finally conclude in Section 7. To foster reproducibility, we have released the source code along with paper [1].

2 Dimensional Properties of the Word Embedding Space

Principal components provide a natural basis for studying the properties of an embedding space. In this work, we refer to the properties pertaining to the principal components of the embedding space as dimensional properties and the embedding space obtained by projecting the embeddings on the principal components as the principal embedding space. We study the principal embedding space and the dimensional properties in a number of different contexts such as word similarity, sen-

tence classification. We provide a brief introductions to the both evaluation tasks of our experiment in the sub-sections. For details on the benchmarks, please refer to Conneau and Kiela (2018) for sentence classification and Faruqui and Dyer (2014) for word similarity.

For experiments in this section, we use 300 dimensional a) Glove embeddings (trained on Wikipedia 201 + Gigaword 5 [2]), b) fastText embeddings (trained on Wikipedia, UBMC webbase corpus and statmt.org news dataset [3]) and c) Word2vec embeddings (trained on the Google-News dataset [4]. We use Glove embeddings for the word similarity tasks. For the sentence classification tasks, we show results for fasttext and word2vec as well, in addition to Glove embeddings. For the sentence classification tasks we use Logistic Regression as the classifier, since it is the simplest classification model and we are only interested in evaluating performance variation due the changes in representations. Thus, the convex objective used in the classifier avoids any optimizer instability, making our entire evaluation pipeline deterministic and exactly reproducible.

2.1 Word Similarity Tasks

The word similarity benchmarks (Faruqui and Dyer, 2014) have word pairs (WP) that have been assigned similarity rating by humans. While evaluating word embeddings, the similarity between the words is calculated by the cosine similarity of their vector representations. Then, Spearman's rank correlation co-efficient (*Rho*) between the ranks produced using the cosine similarities and the given human rankings is used for the performance evaluation. Hence, for better word similarity, the evaluation metric (*Rho*) will be higher.

Figure 1 shows the performance (*Rho* x 100) of word embeddings (Glove) on 13 word similarity benchmarks w.r.t varying word embedding dimensions. The similarities are computed by projecting the embeddings in the principal component space. Each new evaluation cumulatively adds 10 more principal components to the earlier embeddings, i.e. the units on the X-axis vary in the increments of 10. Thus, we obtain 30 measurements for each dataset, ranging from word embeddings constructed using the first 10 principal components to orignal 300 principal components. From Figure

Table 1: Test accuracy of embeddings composed of **Top-100 (T)**, **Middle-100 (M)** and **Bottom-100 (B) principal components** on sentence classification datasets. The highlighted cells correspond to one of the three cases - *M outperforms T* (orange), *B outperforms T* (red) and *B outperforms M* (yellow)

Split	MR	CR	SUBJ	MPQA	SST2	SST5	TREC	SICK-E	MRPC
Random-Embeddings	61.65	71.6	78.9	73.79	60.57	31.09	70.0	77.07	69.91
Glove-Full	75.7	77.48	91.76	86.66	78.03	41.0	68.0	78.49	70.61
Glove-T	70.74	73.67	90.1	81.58	72.49	37.24	61.8	75.71	71.94
Glove-M	**72.98**	**75.04**	87.76	**84.07**	**75.34**	**40.5**	57.6	**76.5**	71.42
Glove-B	67.62	73.01	83.68	**81.61**	69.52	36.11	57.0	72.82	70.96
Word2vec-Full	77.65	79.26	90.76	88.3	79.68	42.44	83.0	78.24	72.58
Word2vec-T	74.34	76.29	89.88	85.07	77.16	40.36	70.0	75.46	71.48
Word2vec-M	72.91	73.43	82.39	82.76	72.65	38.69	66.0	70.53	71.36
Word2vec-B	71.42	**74.25**	**82.47**	81.05	**73.48**	38.46	**72.2**	**74.3**	71.01
fastText-Full	67.85	75.39	85.87	79.85	70.57	35.97	68.0	76.66	70.84
fastText-T	69.42	67.76	87.69	84.64	74.35	36.83	74.8	66.04	70.61
fastText-M	68.88	65.3	81.74	81.45	72.1	35.57	65.2	65.01	68.29
fastText-B	66.45	64.21	79.89	79.83	69.96	31.22	**69.4**	63.77	67.94

1, it is evident that the performance saturates consistently at around 200 dimensions for all of the tasks, after which adding new principal components does not lead to much gain in performance.

2.2 Sentence Classification Tasks

The sentence classification tasks (Conneau and Kiela, 2018) include binary classification tasks (MR, CR, SUBJ, MPQA), multiclass classification tasks (SST-FG, TREC), entailment (SICK-E), semantic relatedness (STS-B) and Paraphrase detection (MRPC) tasks. As usual, the evaluation is done by computing the classification accuracy on the test set.

Figure 2 shows the performance (Test accuracy) on 9 standard downstream sentence classification tasks (Conneau and Kiela, 2018) using the same procedure for constructing word embeddings (Glove) as in 2.1. Further, sentence vectors were constructed using an average of the contained word embeddings, which has been demonstrated to be a very strong baseline for downstream tasks (Arora et al., 2017). From Figure 2, we can observe that, similar to the previous word similarity tasks, the performance saturates consistently at around 200 dimensions for all of the tasks, after which incrementing the embeddings with additional principal components does not lead to much gains in performance. We also report results for original ($300D$) and post processed PCA reduced ($200D$) word embeddings for other types (fastText, Glove) in Table 2. In Table 2, we also report results with pretrained $200D$ Glove embedding. [5]

Analysis: To conclude, observations from both word similarity and sentence classification tasks, of saturation in performance around 200, much before the original 300 dimensions implies redundancy among the dimensions (in section 3 we will clarify why it doesn't imply *noise*). Furthermore, this observation is consistent across various embedding types (Glove, fastText and word2vec) for the sentence classification tasks, as demonstrated in Table 2. This also suggests a simple strategy to reduce the embedding size wherein one third of the components could be reliably removed without affecting the performance on word similarity or sentence classification tasks, leading to 33% memory reduction.

3 Variance Based Analysis

In this section, we characterize the redundancy observed in Section 2, in terms of variance of the principal components. Specifically, we measure downstream performance (on the sentence classification tasks of Section 2.2) of word embeddings against the amount of variance captured by the principal components (the variance explained or captured by a principal component is the variance of the embeddings when projected onto that principal component; hereon, we refer to the fraction of variance explained by a principal component simply as variance explained by that component). Similar to the previous sec-

---

[5] word embeddings for $200D$ for other embedding types (fasttext, word2vec) are not publicly available.

Table 2: Performance on sentence classification tasks of various embeddings (300 dimensional) and their post-processed PCA reduced counterparts of 200 dimensions.

Embedding	MR	CR	SUBJ	MPQA	SST2	SST5	TREC	SICK-E	MRPC
Glove	75.7	77.48	91.76	86.66	78.03	41.0	68.0	78.49	70.61
Glove-PCA	74.62	76.95	91.6	85.97	77.16	40.18	66.6	77.02	72.99
Glove-200	74.69	77.91	91.18	86.52	77.98	40.05	66.4	77.47	72.23
Word2vec	77.65	79.26	90.76	88.30	79.68	42.44	83.0	78.24	72.58
Word2vec-PCA	76.53	78.12	90.50	86.74	79.63	41.49	77.6	76.54	72.17
fastText	67.85	75.39	85.87	79.85	70.57	35.9	68.0	76.66	70.84
fastText-PCA	66.83	74.46	85.26	78.91	69.85	36.11	66.0	76.50	68.75

Table 3: The Variance for each of the T, M, B splits of the embeddings.

	Glove	**Word2vec**	**fastText**
T	0.529	0.628	0.745
M	0.371	0.221	0.162
B	0.100	0.151	0.093

tion, we use 300 dimensional Glove embeddings (trained on Wikipedia 201 + Gigaword 5[2]) for experiments in this section, along with publically released fastText (trained on Wikipedia, UBMC webbase corpus and statmt.org news dataset[3] and Word2vec (trained on the GoogleNews dataset[4]) embeddings, both of 300 dimensions.

For each of the embedding types, we first construct word embeddings using only top 100 principal components (T), the middle 100 principal components (M) and the bottom 100 principal components (B). Then, we compute the variance for each split by aggregating the variance of the 100 principal components of each split for all three embedding types. Table 3 highlights how the total variance is divided across the three splits. The T embeddings have the first 100 principal components (PCs), so the highest variance explained, while the B embeddings have the bottom 100 components, thereby the least variance explained. Furthermore, the variance explained by the principal components for the same split also differ significantly across the different embedding types. For example, fastText has more variance explained, when compared to Glove and Word2vec, for the split T, while Glove has the most variance explained, among the three embedding types, for the split M. Lastly, Word2vec explains more variance than Glove and fastText for the split B. The differences are expected since, the three embedding types differ considerably in their training algorithms. While Word2vec uses negative sampling, Glove derives semantic relationships from the word-word co-occurrence matrix and fastText uses subword information. So, to summarize we constructed altogether 9 embedding splits (3 from each of the 3 embedding types), which differ significantly in terms of the variance explained by their constituent components.

We use the 100 dimensional embedding obtain from the several splits (T, M, B) and types (Glove, fastText, Word2vec) as features for downstream sentence classification tasks, as in Section 2.2, except that, now, each of the embedding feature has 100 dimensions. The experiments are designed to test whether the variance explained by a split is closely correlated with the downstream performance metric (classification accuracy) for each of the three embedding types. Table 1 shows the results on 9 sentence classification tasks, for each embedding split, for all the three embedding types. In the table, the highlighted cells represent the cases where classification accuracy of the lower variance split exceeds that of the corresponding higher variance split. Each annotated cell corresponds to one of the three cases - **M outperforms T (orange)**, **B outperforms T (red)** and **B outperforms M (yellow)**. For the comparisons between T and M splits, in 6 out of 27 such comparisons, the M embeddings outperform the T embeddings. Similarly, for comparisons between M and B embeddings, the B embeddings outperform the M embeddings in 7 out of 27 cases and for comparisons between T and B embeddings, in 2 out of 27 cases the B embeddings outperform the T embeddings. Further, in a number of cases (although not highlighted), such as on the MRPC task, the T and M splits differ very little in performance. The same is true for M and B splits on tasks such as MPQA and CR. Such cases are least prominent in fastText, probably due to the extremely large gap in the variance explained between the T, M and T, B splits.

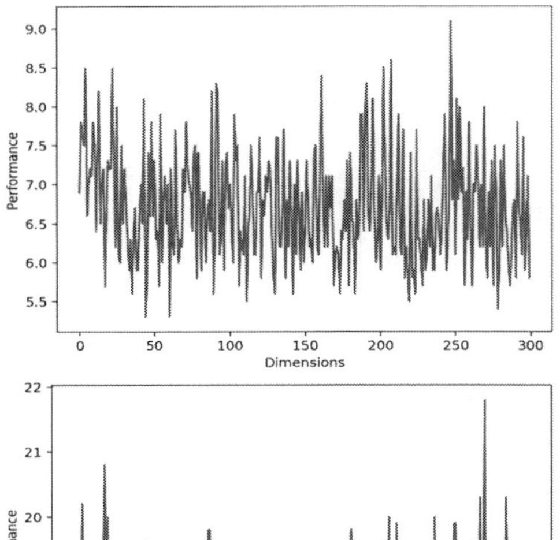

Figure 3: Analysis of individual principal components on the two syntactic information based linguistic probing tasks: TopConst (top) and TreeDepth (bottom). The Y-axis represents the Test accuracy on the two tasks.

Analysis: From Table 1 it is evident that the performance drop between the T, M, B splits is quite low for a number of tasks, which is highly contrary to the expectation, given the large differences in the variance explained (Table 3). Further, there are also many cases where lower variance embeddings (B and M) outperform the emedddings (M and T) with higher variance, for all the three embedding types. These results demonstrate that for word embeddings, *the variance explained by the principal components is not sufficient for explaining their downstream performance. In other words, the variance explained by the principal components is a weak representative of downstream performance.* This is in contrast to the widely used practice of using the variance explained by the principal components as a fundamental tool to assess the quality of the corresponding representations (Jolliffe and Cadima, 2016).

4   Dimensional Linguistic Probing Tasks

A plausible hypothesis to explain the better performance of M and B embeddings (Table 1) in the earlier section is that *'the syntactic informa-*

tion required for downstream sentence classification tasks is distributed independently with respect to the principal components'. To explore the validity of the proposed hypothesis, we leverage two linguistic probing tasks, namely TreeDepth and TopConst (Conneau et al., 2018). These probing tasks are designed to test whether sentence embeddings are sensitive to the syntactic properties of the encoded sentences. The TreeDepth task (a 8-way classification problem) tests whether the model can predict the depth of the hierarchical syntactic structure of the sentence. For doing well on the TreeDepth task, the embeddings have to group sentences by the depth of the longest path from root to any leaf. In the TopConst task (a 20-way classification problem), a sentence must be classified in terms of the sequence of its constituents occurring immediately below the sentence node of its hierarchical structure. Therefore, for good performance on the TopConst task, the embeddings have to capture latent syntactic structures and cluster them by constituent types. The random baselines for the TreeDepth and TopConst tasks are 12.5 and 5.0 respectively, while full 300-dimensional Glove embeddings obtain accuracies of 37 and 68 percent respectively.

To evaluate the syntactic information contained in each of the principal components, we first construct one-dimensional word embeddings by projecting word vectors onto a single principal component. Then we use these word embeddings to construct sentence vectors, as in Section 2.2, which are used as features for the two classification tasks. For good performance, the single component sentence vector has to distinguish between the probing task's output classes. Therefore, the performance on these tasks can be used to isolate the behavior of individual components with respect to the syntactic information captured. The motivation here is that if the syntactically discriminative components would vary considerably, then we can isolate the behavior of the individual components and see their correspondence with the rank of the principal component. Figure 3 depicts the scores (Test classification accuracy) on TopConst and TreeDepth tasks respectively. The average performance of the one-dimensional representations has mean $\pm$ standard deviation of 18.38 ± 0.64 and 6.71 ± 0.72 for the TreeDepth and TopConst tasks respectively.

Analysis: The average performance of the one-dimensional representations on both tasks is much lower than full dimension embeddings but well above the random baseline. However, many individual compoenents far exceed the random baseline as well. As mentioned earlier, we wanted to probe whether such discriminativeness is ranked according to variance. However from Figure 3, it is evident that the performance across the dimensions does not have any particular trend (increasing or decreasing) w.r.t to the rank of the principal components. In fact, the peak performance on both the tasks is achieved by a component in the bottom (B) split of the embeddings. This validates the hypothesis that *the syntactic information captured by a principal component is independent of the amount of variance it explains.*

Table 4: Classification Accuracy for Linguistic Probing Tasks using the **T, M, B** splits of the embeddings. Here also, the highlighted cells correspond to one of the three cases - *M outperforms T (* orange *), B outperforms T (* red *) and B outperforms M (* yellow *)*

Embedding	TopConst	TreeDepth
Glove-T	28.1	28.2
Glove-M	26.0	24.8
Glove-B	**27.1**	**26.9**
Word2vec-T	23.9	42.5
Word2vec-M	**24.3**	**43.5**
Word2vec-B	23.7	**44.6**
fastText-T	31.2	50.7
fastText-M	29.3	**51.0**
fastText-B	**30.6**	**56.8**

To further validate the hypothesis, we repeat the experiment described in Section 3 for each of the embedding types, except on the synctatic probing tasks of TopConst and TreeDepth in Table 4. Similar to Table 1, each annotated cell in Table 4 corresponds to one of the three cases - **M outperforms T (** orange **), B outperforms T (** red **) and B outperforms M (** yellow **)**. For the comparisons between T and M splits, in 3 out of 6 such comparisons, the M embeddings outperform the T embeddings. Similarly, for comparisons between M and B embeddings, the B embeddings outperform the M embeddings in 5 out of 6 cases and for comparisons between T and B embeddings, in 2 out of 6 cases the B embeddings outperform the T embeddings. In other words, table 4 shows that for the TreeDepth task, the B embeddings significantly outperform T and M embeddings for word2vec and fastText, whereas for Glove, it outperforms

the M embeddings. For the TopConst task as well, the B embeddings outperform M embeddings for Glove and fastText, whereas for Word2vec, it outperforms the T embeddings. Thus, the discrepancy in performance on these syntactic probing tasks is even more severe when compared to the sentence classification tasks evaluated in Section 3. The results also validate our hypothesis that *the variance explained by the embeddings is of little predictive strength in predicting its relative performance.*

5 The Post Processing Algorithm (PPA)

In this section, we briefly describe and then evaluate the post-processing algorithm (PPA) by (Mu and Viswanath, 2018), which achieves high scores on Word and Semantic textual similarity tasks (Agirre et al., 2012). The algorithm (PPA) is listed below as Algorithm 1. PPA removes the projections of top principal components from each of the word vectors, making the individual word vectors more discriminative. The algorithm could be regarded as pushing the word embeddings towards a more isotropic space (Arora et al., 2016), by eliminating the common parts (mean vector and top principal components of the embedding space) from the individual word embeddings. However, it is worth revisiting the assumption whether isotropy (or angular isotropy more specifically) of the embedding space is universally beneficial with respect to downstream tasks. In this section, we stress test this assumption on a range of sentence classification and machine translation tasks. Our fundamental intuition is that since these tasks require the embedding space to capture syntactic properties much more significantly than word-similarity tasks, enforcing isotropy could lead to worse performance.

Algorithm 1: Post Processing Algorithm PPA(X, D)

Data: Embedding Matrix X, Threshold Parameter D
Result: Post-Processed Word Embedding Matrix X

```
/* Subtract Mean Embedding */
```
1 $X = X - \overline{X}$;
```
/* Compute PCA Components */
```
2 $u_i = \text{PCA}(X)$, where i = 1, 2, ... d;
```
/* Remove Top-D Components */
```
3 **for** *all v in X* **do**
4      $v = v - \sum_{i=1}^{D}(u_i^T \cdot v)u_i$
5 **end**

Table 5: Performance on sentence classification tasks of various embeddings and their post-processed (PPA) counterparts. The **red** colored cells denote the cases where the original embeddings outperformed their post-processed (PPA) counterparts.

Embedding	MR	CR	SUBJ	MPQA	SST2	SST5	TREC	SICK-E	MRPC
Glove (300 dim)	75.7	77.48	91.76	86.66	78.03	41.0	68.8	78.49	70.61
PPA on Glove	75.57	77.48	91.01	86.67	77.98	40.72	65.8	78.53	71.59
Word2vec (300 dim)	77.65	79.23	90.76	88.30	79.68	42.44	82.6	78.24	72.64
PPA on Word2vec	77.33	79.5	90.59	88.12	79.41	42.71	83.4	78.26	72.58
fastText (300 dim)	74.16	71.63	89.56	87.12	79.24	39.14	79.4	72.34	70.14
PPA on fastText	74.59	71.63	89.4	86.9	79.13	39.64	80.2	72.36	70.09

5.1 Sentence Classification Tasks

We compare the performance of PPA (with a constant D=5 across all the embeddings) on the 9 downstream sentence classification tasks, as in Section 3. The results are presented in Table 5. In our work, we adhere to the linear evaluation protocol and use a simple logistic regression classifier in evaluating word representations (Arora et al., 2019; Gupta et al., 2020), whereas (Mu and Viswanath, 2018) use a neural network as their classifier. The **red** colored cells in Table 5 denote the cases where the original embeddings outperformed their Post Processed (PPA) counterparts. Such cases occurred in 14 out of 27 comparisons in Table 5. The results in Table 5 show that post-processing doesn't always lead to accuracy gains and can be counterproductive in a number of tasks.

Analysis: The results in Table 5 are contrary to the expectation that pushing the word embeddings towards isotropy would lead to better downstream performance. This suggests that within the context of downstream sentence classification tasks, projecting word vectors away from the top components leads to a loss of 'useful' information. To explain this loss of 'useful' information, we could use the analysis from Figure 3. From Figure 3, it is evident that the top dimensions also contain syntactic information, the loss of which adversely impacts downstream classification tasks, which by construction, benefit from both semantic and syntactic information. Also, by just removing the mean (no top component nullification as in PPA), we notice almost zero change in performance for most of the sentence classification tasks in Table 5 (the highest change was for TREC, of -0.4, still quite low when compared to -4.4 for PPA), which demonstrably shows that removing the mean must be ruled out as the possible cause for the drop in classification accuracies.

On the same tasks, we also observe a drop in sentence classification accuracy (2.37, 1.99, 3.94 average drop on word2vec, Glove, fastText respectively) using 150 dimensional embeddings obtained from PPA based dimensionality reduction (Raunak et al., 2019). This shows that the variance based post-processing algorithms such as PPA (Mu and Viswanath, 2018) and PPA-PCA (Raunak et al., 2019), when used in *downstream tasks* have significant limitations, which could be attributed to the loss of syntactic information.

5.2 Machine Translation

Recently, (Qi et al., 2018) have shown that pre-trained embeddings lead to significant gains in performance for the translation of three low resource languages namely, Azerbaijani (AZ), Belarusian (BE) and Galician (GL) into English (EN). Here, we demonstrate the impact of the post processing algorithm on machine translation (MT) tasks. We replicate the experimental settings of (Qi et al., 2018) and use a standard 1 layer encoder-decoder model with attention (Bahdanau et al., 2015) and a beam size of 5. Prior to training, we initialize the encoder with fastText word embeddings (no other embeddings are publically available for these languages) trained on Wikipedia[6]. We then use PPA on the pre-trained embeddings and train again. The results of the experiments are presented in Table 6.

Analysis: From the results, it is evident that removing the top principal component(s) leads to a consistent drop in BLEU scores across the three language pairs. The observations are consistent with the previous section, in that removing top components hurts performance in non-similarity based tasks. This can again be explained using the analysis from earlier section i.e. instead of strengthening the embeddings, removing the top components leads to a loss of 'useful' information

---

[6] https://bit.ly/2WkHQ0Y

for the Machine translation task. Further, similar to the previous section, we can specifically attribute the performance drop to the loss of syntactic information, since the top components are at least as equally important for syntactic information as the other components, thus, nullifying them hurts performance.

Table 6: BLEU scores over three different low-resource language pairs with pretrained emebddings and Top D components removed using PPA. **Green** cells denotes top scores.

	AZ->EN	BE->EN	GL->EN
Pre-Trained	**3.24**	**6.09**	**15.91**
PPA (D = 1)	3.19	6.02	14.81
PPA (D = 2)	3.07	5.50	13.88
PPA (D = 3)	3.04	5.26	13.27
PPA (D = 4)	2.92	4.75	13.24

5.3 Summary and Discussion

To summarize our experiments on variance based post-processing, we conclude the following:

1. We can not rely on principal components for manipulating word embeddings as freely as the current literature suggests. While eliminating the 'common parts' helps improve the discriminativeness between the word embeddings (thereby refining the word similarity scores), pushing the embeddings towards angular isotropy does not lead to performance gain in downstream tasks, e.g. sentence classification and machine translation. Although, we did not assume any generative model for the embeddings in any of the explanations (unlike (Arora et al., 2016), which makes use of the isotropy assumption to explain empirical observations in factorizing the PMI matrix), our work further casts doubt on the isotropy assumption for word embeddings and suggests that non-isotropy may be integral to performance on downstream tasks.

2. Furthermore, worse performance in non-similarity tasks can be attributed to the loss of syntactic information contained in the top components, suggesting that the specific geometry created through the 'common parts' is integral to embeddings capturing syntactic properties. Establishing a link between the syntactic properties of the embedding space and its non-isotropy would be an interesting direction to explore for future work.

6 Related Work

Due to the widespread utility of word embeddings, a number of recent works have explored further improving the embeddings post-hoc, as well as trying to better understand and manipulate the geometry of the embedding space.

Post-Processing Word Embeddings A number of recent works have been proposed to enhance word embedding quality post-hoc (Mrkšic et al.; Faruqui et al., 2014; Mu and Viswanath, 2018). Their applications range from better modeling semantic similarities, improving downstream classification performance to dimensionality reduction of the embeddings (Raunak et al., 2019).

Word Embedding Geometry The linear algebraic structure emergent in word embeddings has received considerable attention (Allen and Hospedales, 2019; Arora et al., 2018), and theoretical links have been established between neural embedding algorithms and factorization based techniques (Levy and Goldberg, 2014). Another prominent line of work has been along the direction of probing tasks (Conneau and Kiela, 2018), which use proxy classification tasks to comparatively measure the presence of certain syntactic/semantic properties in the embedding space.

Our work focuses on the dimensional properties of the embedding space in the principal component basis, and also analyzes a few post-processing algorithms, thus contributing to the existing literature on both the areas of embedding analysis.

7 Conclusion and Future Work

To conclude, besides elucidating redundancy in the word embedding space, we demonstrate that the variance explained by the word embeddings' principal components is not a reliable proxy for the downstream utility of the corresponding representations and that the syntactic information captured by a principal component does not depend on the amount of variance it explains. Further, we show that variance based post-processing algorithms such as PPA is not suitable for tasks which rely more on syntax, such as sentence classification and machine translation. Going further, we wish to explore whether the geometric intuitions developed in our work could be leveraged for contextualized embeddings such as ElMo (Peters et al., 2018), BERT (Devlin et al., 2019), and Roberta (Liu et al., 2019), etc.

References

Eneko Agirre, Mona Diab, Daniel Cer, and Aitor Gonzalez-Agirre. 2012. Semeval-2012 task 6: A pilot on semantic textual similarity. In *Proceedings of the First Joint Conference on Lexical and Computational Semantics-Volume 1: Proceedings of the main conference and the shared task, and Volume 2: Proceedings of the Sixth International Workshop on Semantic Evaluation*, pages 385–393. Association for Computational Linguistics.

Carl Allen and Timothy Hospedales. 2019. Analogies explained: Towards understanding word embeddings. In *International Conference on Machine Learning*, pages 223–231.

Sanjeev Arora, Yuanzhi Li, Yingyu Liang, Tengyu Ma, and Andrej Risteski. 2016. A latent variable model approach to pmi-based word embeddings. *Transactions of the Association for Computational Linguistics*, 4:385–399.

Sanjeev Arora, Yuanzhi Li, Yingyu Liang, Tengyu Ma, and Andrej Risteski. 2018. Linear algebraic structure of word senses, with applications to polysemy. *Transactions of the Association for Computational Linguistics*, 6:483–495.

Sanjeev Arora, Yingyu Liang, and Tengyu Ma. 2017. A simple but tough-to-beat baseline for sentence embeddings. *International Conference of Learning Representation*.

Sanjeev Arora, Yingyu Liang, and Tengyu Ma. 2019. A simple but tough-to-beat baseline for sentence embeddings. In *5th International Conference on Learning Representations, ICLR 2017*.

Dzmitry Bahdanau, Kyunghyun Cho, and Yoshua Bengio. 2015. Neural machine translation by jointly learning to align and translate. In *3rd International Conference on Learning Representations, ICLR 2015*.

Piotr Bojanowski, Edouard Grave, Armand Joulin, and Tomas Mikolov. 2017. Enriching word vectors with subword information. *Transactions of the Association of Computational Linguistics*, 5(1):135–146.

Alexis Conneau and Douwe Kiela. 2018. Senteval: An evaluation toolkit for universal sentence representations. In *Proceedings of the Eleventh International Conference on Language Resources and Evaluation (LREC 2018)*.

Alexis Conneau, German Kruszewski, Guillaume Lample, Loic Barrault, and Marco Baroni. 2018. What you can cram into a single vector: Probing sentence embeddings for linguistic properties. In *Proceedings of the 56th Annual Meeting of the Association for Computational Linguistics (Volume 1: Long Papers)*, pages 2126–2136.

Jacob Devlin, Ming-Wei Chang, Kenton Lee, and Kristina Toutanova. 2019. BERT: Pre-training of deep bidirectional transformers for language understanding. In *Proceedings of the 2019 Conference of the North American Chapter of the Association for Computational Linguistics: Human Language Technologies, Volume 1 (Long and Short Papers)*, pages 4171–4186, Minneapolis, Minnesota. Association for Computational Linguistics.

Manaal Faruqui, Jesse Dodge, Sujay K Jauhar, Chris Dyer, Eduard Hovy, and Noah A Smith. 2014. Retrofitting word vectors to semantic lexicons. *arXiv preprint arXiv:1411.4166*.

Manaal Faruqui, Jesse Dodge, Sujay Kumar Jauhar, Chris Dyer, Eduard Hovy, and Noah A Smith. 2015. Retrofitting word vectors to semantic lexicons. In *Proceedings of the 2015 Conference of the North American Chapter of the Association for Computational Linguistics: Human Language Technologies*, pages 1606–1615.

Manaal Faruqui and Chris Dyer. 2014. Community evaluation and exchange of word vectors at wordvectors. org. In *Proceedings of 52nd Annual Meeting of the Association for Computational Linguistics: System Demonstrations*, pages 19–24.

Vivek Gupta, Ankit Saw, Pegah Nokhiz, Praneeth Netrapalli, Piyush Rai, and Partha Talukdar. 2020. P-sif: Document embeddings using partition averaging. In *Proceedings of the AAAI Conference on Artificial Intelligence*.

Ian T Jolliffe and Jorge Cadima. 2016. Principal component analysis: a review and recent developments. *Philosophical Transactions of the Royal Society A: Mathematical, Physical and Engineering Sciences*, 374(2065):20150202.

Omer Levy and Yoav Goldberg. 2014. Neural word embedding as implicit matrix factorization. In *Advances in neural information processing systems*, pages 2177–2185.

Yinhan Liu, Myle Ott, Naman Goyal, Jingfei Du, Mandar Joshi, Danqi Chen, Omer Levy, Mike Lewis, Luke Zettlemoyer, and Veselin Stoyanov. 2019. Roberta: A robustly optimized bert pretraining approach. *arXiv preprint arXiv:1907.11692*.

Tomas Mikolov, Ilya Sutskever, Kai Chen, Greg S Corrado, and Jeff Dean. 2013. Distributed representations of words and phrases and their compositionality. In *Advances in neural information processing systems*, pages 3111–3119.

David Mimno and Laure Thompson. 2017. The strange geometry of skip-gram with negative sampling. In *Proceedings of the 2017 Conference on Empirical Methods in Natural Language Processing*, pages 2873–2878.

Nikola Mrkšic, Diarmuid OSéaghdha, Blaise Thomson, and pages=142–148 year=2016 Gašić, Milica and Rojas-Barahona, Lina and Su, Pei-Hao and Vandyke, David and Wen, Tsung-Hsien and

Young, Steve, booktitle=Proceedings of NAACL-HLT. Counter-fitting word vectors to linguistic constraints.

Jiaqi Mu and Pramod Viswanath. 2018. All-but-the-top: Simple and effective postprocessing for word representations. In *International Conference on Learning Representations*.

Jeffrey Pennington, Richard Socher, and Christopher Manning. 2014. Glove: Global vectors for word representation. In *Proceedings of the 2014 conference on empirical methods in natural language processing (EMNLP)*, pages 1532–1543.

Matthew Peters, Mark Neumann, Mohit Iyyer, Matt Gardner, Christopher Clark, Kenton Lee, and Luke Zettlemoyer. 2018. Deep contextualized word representations. In *Proceedings of the 2018 Conference of the North American Chapter of the Association for Computational Linguistics: Human Language Technologies, Volume 1 (Long Papers)*, pages 2227–2237.

Ye Qi, Devendra Sachan, Matthieu Felix, Sarguna Padmanabhan, and Graham Neubig. 2018. When and why are pre-trained word embeddings useful for neural machine translation? In *Proceedings of the 2018 Conference of the North American Chapter of the Association for Computational Linguistics: Human Language Technologies, Volume 2 (Short Papers)*, pages 529–535.

Vikas Raunak, Vivek Gupta, and Florian Metze. 2019. Effective dimensionality reduction for word embeddings. In *Proceedings of the 4th Workshop on Representation Learning for NLP (RepL4NLP-2019)*, pages 235–243, Florence, Italy. Association for Computational Linguistics.

Zi Yin and Yuanyuan Shen. 2018. On the dimensionality of word embedding. In S. Bengio, H. Wallach, H. Larochelle, K. Grauman, N. Cesa-Bianchi, and R. Garnett, editors, *Advances in Neural Information Processing Systems 31*, pages 895–906. Curran Associates, Inc.

A Cross-Task Analysis of Text Span Representations

Shubham Toshniwal, Haoyue Shi, Bowen Shi, Lingyu Gao, Karen Livescu, Kevin Gimpel
Toyota Technological Institute at Chicago

{shtoshni, freda, bshi, lygao, klivescu, kgimpel}@ttic.edu

Abstract

Many natural language processing (NLP) tasks involve reasoning with textual spans, including question answering, entity recognition, and coreference resolution. While extensive research has focused on functional architectures for representing words and sentences, there is less work on representing arbitrary spans of text within sentences. In this paper, we conduct a comprehensive empirical evaluation of six span representation methods using eight pretrained language representation models across six tasks, including two tasks that we introduce. We find that, although some simple span representations are fairly reliable across tasks, in general the optimal span representation varies by task, and can also vary within different facets of individual tasks. We also find that the choice of span representation has a bigger impact with a fixed pretrained encoder than with a fine-tuned encoder.

1 Introduction

Fixed-dimensional span representations are often used as a component in recent models for a number of natural language processing (NLP) tasks, such as question answering (Lee et al., 2016; Seo et al., 2019), coreference resolution (Lee et al., 2017), and constituency parsing (Stern et al., 2017; Kitaev and Klein, 2018; Kitaev et al., 2019, *inter alia*). Such models initialized with contextualized word embeddings (Peters et al., 2018; Devlin et al., 2019) have achieved new state-of-the-art results for these tasks (Kitaev et al., 2019; Joshi et al., 2019b).

Since spans can have arbitrary length (i.e., number of tokens), fixed-dimensional span representations involve some form of (parameterized) pooling of the token representations. Existing models typically pick a *span representation* method (dashed boxes in Figure 1) that works well for the task(s) of interest. However, a comprehensive evaluation com-

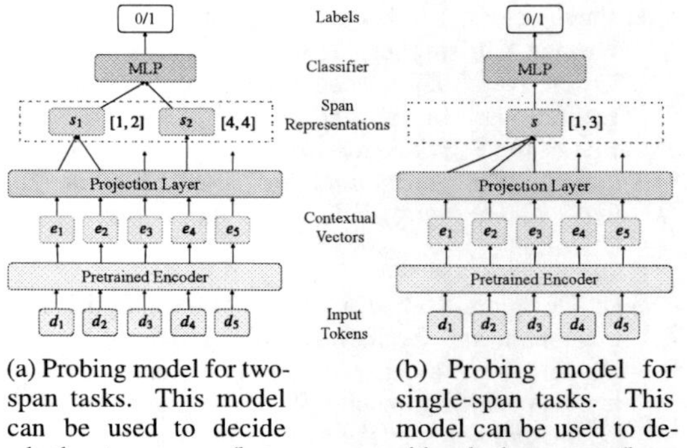

(a) Probing model for two-span tasks. This model can be used to decide whether two spans (here [1, 2] and [4, 4]) are coreferent or not.

(b) Probing model for single-span tasks. This model can be used to decide whether a span (here [1, 3]) refers to a constituent or not.

Figure 1: Probing architectures for span representation methods. The models are very similar to that of Tenney et al. (2019b) but we explicitly separate the span representation part into a projection step followed by a choice among span representation methods.

paring various span representation methods across tasks is still lacking.

In this work, we systematically compare and analyze a wide range of span representations (Section 3.2) by probing the representations via various NLP tasks, including constituent detection, constituent labeling, named entity labeling, semantic role labeling, mention detection, and coreference arc prediction (Section 2).[1] All of the tasks we consider naturally involve span representations. Similar comparisons are done by Tenney et al. (2019b), where they use this probing approach to compare several pretrained contextual embedding models, while keeping the span representation method fixed to self-attentive pooling (Lin et al., 2017; Lee et al., 2017). Here we vary both the choice of contextualized embedding models (among BERT (Devlin et al., 2019), RoBERTa (Liu et al., 2019b), XL-

---

[1]Code available at `https://github.com/shtoshni92/span-rep`

Proceedings of the 5th Workshop on Representation Learning for NLP (RepL4NLP-2020), pages 166–176
July 9, 2020. ©2020 Association for Computational Linguistics

Net (Yang et al., 2019), and SpanBERT (Joshi et al., 2019a)) and the span representation methods. By analyzing the performance of each span representation method for multiple tasks, we aim to uncover the importance of choice of span representation.

We follow the "edge probing" setup of Tenney et al. (2019b) and introduce two new tasks to this setup, namely constituent detection and mention detection, which complement the constituent labeling and coreference arc prediction tasks, respectively, that are part of the original setup. For the full-scale comparison, we follow the original setup and keep the pretrained token representation models fixed, learning only layer weights and additional task-specific parameters on top of the weighted pretrained representations. We also conduct a small-scale study to compare the effect of fine-tuning on different span representations in terms of their relative ordering and for comparison with their non fine-tuned counterparts.

Overall, we find that the behavior of span representations tends to pattern according to whether they are based on information at the span boundaries versus using the entire span content. When pretrained models are frozen, we find that the choice of span representation is more important than the choice of pretrained model. When fine-tuning, the choice of span representation still has an impact on performance though it is much less pronounced than in the frozen case. Although the best-performing method can vary greatly among tasks, we find in general that a span representation that simply takes the max over time is a reliable choice across tasks.

2 Span Probing Tasks

We borrow four probing tasks applied by Tenney et al. (2019b), namely constituent labeling, named entity labeling, semantic role labeling, and coreference arc prediction. We also introduce two new tasks: constituent detection and mention detection. The specific tasks are described below.

Constituent labeling is the task of predicting the non-terminal label (e.g., noun phrase, verb phrase, etc.) for a span corresponding to a constituent.

Constituent detection is the task of determining whether a span of words corresponds to a constituent (i.e., a nonterminal node) in the constituency parse tree of the input sentence. We introduce this task as a complement to the task of constituent labeling, to further evaluate the syntactic ability of the span representation methods.

Named entity labeling (NEL) is the task of predicting the entity type of a given span corresponding to an entity, e.g., whether the span "German" in its sentence context refers to people, an organization, or a language.

Semantic role labeling (SRL) is concerned with predicting the semantic roles of phrases in a sentence. In this probing task the locations of the predicate and its argument are given, and the goal is to classify the argument into its specific semantic roles (ARG0, ARG1, etc.).

Mention detection is the task of predicting whether a span represents a mention of an entity or not. For example, in the sentence *"Mary goes to the market"*, the spans *"Mary"* and *"the market"* refer to mentions while all other spans are not mentions. The task is similar to named entity recognition (Tjong Kim Sang and De Meulder, 2003), but the mentions are not limited to named entities. We introduce this task as it is the first step for coreference resolution (Pradhan et al., 2012), if the candidate mentions are not explicitly given.

Coreference arc prediction is the task of predicting whether a pair of spans refer to the same entity. For example, in the sentence "John is his own enemy", "John" and "his" refer to the same entity.

3 Models

In this section, we first briefly describe the probing model, which is borrowed from Tenney et al. (2019b) with the extension to different span representations (Figure 1), followed by details of the various span representation methods we compare in this work.

3.1 Probing Model

The input to the model is a sentence $\mathbf{d} = \{d_1, \cdots, d_T\}$ where the d_i are tokens (produced by a tokenizer specific to a given choice of encoder). The sentence is first passed through a fixed, pretrained encoder, such as BERT, followed by a learned projection layer to obtain contextualized token embeddings $\{e_1, \cdots, e_T\}$. These embeddings are then fed to span representation modules to get fixed-dimensional contextual span embeddings. Finally, the span embeddings are fed into a two-layer MLP followed by a sigmoid layer to predict the labels. For multiclass probing tasks with $|\mathcal{L}|$ labels, the predictions are made independently with separate MLPs per label resulting in a $[0, 1]^{|\mathcal{L}|}$ vector. Finally, some tasks involve a single span, whereas others (coreference, semantic role labeling) involve two spans; in the latter case, the MLP takes as input the concatenation of the representations corresponding to the two spans.

3.2 Span Representation Methods

Given a span $s = [i, j]$ and its corresponding contextualized embeddings $[e_i, \cdots, e_j]$, where $e_k \in \mathbb{R}^d$, a span representation module outputs a fixed-dimensional span representation s_{ij}. Below we describe the various span representation methods compared in this work.

Average pooling is a simple average of the contextualized embeddings in the span window:

$$s_{ij} = \frac{1}{j - i + 1} \sum_{k=i}^{j} e_k$$

Attention pooling or self-attention pooling is a learned weighted average over the contextualized token embeddings in the span:

$$\alpha_k = v \cdot e_k; \quad a_k = \frac{\exp(\alpha_k)}{\sum_{\ell=i}^{j} \exp(\alpha_\ell)}$$

$$s_{ij} = \sum_{k=i}^{j} a_k \cdot e_k$$

where v is a learned parameter vector. This pooling method is a popular choice for many NLP tasks (Lee et al., 2017; Lin et al., 2017), and is the one used by Tenney et al. (2019b).

Max pooling takes the maximum value over time for each dimension of the contextualized embeddings within the span. Max pooling has been frequently used to obtain fixed-dimensional sentence representations for classification tasks (Collobert et al., 2011; Hashimoto et al., 2017; Conneau et al., 2017).

Endpoint is a simple concatenation of the endpoints of the span: $s_{ij} = [e_i; e_j]$. This is a popular choice for representing answer spans (Lee et al., 2016) in extractive question-answering tasks such as SQuAD (Rajpurkar et al., 2016). Note that in this case $s_{ij} \in \mathbb{R}^{2d}$.

Diff-Sum is a variant of endpoint where we concatenate the sum and difference of the span endpoints: $s_{ij} = [e_j + e_i; e_j - e_i]$. Diff-sum and its close

variants have been used in parsing and SRL (Stern et al., 2017; Ouchi et al., 2018). As in endpoint, $s_{ij} \in \mathbb{R}^{2d}$.

Coherent is a span representation proposed by Seo et al. (2019) for indexing phrases in a query-agnostic manner for question answering. First, the endpoints of the span are split into four parts:

$$e_i = [e_i^1; e_i^2; e_i^3; e_i^4]$$

where $e_i^1, e_i^2 \in \mathbb{R}^a$ and $e_i^3, e_i^4 \in \mathbb{R}^b$, and therefore $2a + 2b = d$. The endpoints are then combined as:

$$s_{ij} = [e_i^1; e_j^2; e_i^3 \cdot e_j^4]$$

where the last term $e_i^3 \cdot e_j^4$ is referred to as the *coherence* term; hence the name "coherent" (assigned by us). In this case, $s_{ij} \in \mathbb{R}^{2a+1}$ where $2a + 1 < d$ since $2a + 2b = d$.[2]

4 Experimental Setup

4.1 Implementation details

All input strings are passed through contextual encoder models to obtain an embedding for each token. With frozen encoders the weighted average of outputs from all layers is used as the token representation e_k (Tenney et al., 2019b), while for fine-tuned encoders the last layer output is used unless otherwise stated. We investigate four pretrained models: BERT (Devlin et al., 2019), RoBERTa (Liu et al., 2019b), SpanBERT (Joshi et al., 2019a), and XLNet (Yang et al., 2019). Each has both "base" and "large" variants, and we experiment with both. Since some of the models, such as XLNet, only have cased versions, we use the cased version for all models. We use the HuggingFace (Wolf et al., 2019) implementation of the four models, which is based on PyTorch (Paszke et al., 2019).

Embeddings are first projected down to 256 dimensions.[3] For each span, a representation method (one of the methods from Section 3.2) is then applied to its sequence of projected vectors to obtain a fixed-length representation for the span. The span representations are concatenated (if there are more than one) and fed into a two-layer MLP followed by a sigmoid output layer. The two-layer MLP is a

---

[2] Seo et al. (2019) used a=480 and b=32 for 1024-dimensional BERT-large embeddings. We use the same proportions for the projected contextualized embeddings.

[3] For SRL we use separate projection matrices for the two spans involved in the task, as the two spans may require different types of information to be extracted. For all of the other tasks, a single projection matrix is used.

Task	Task Type	$|\mathcal{L}|$	#Examples (Train / Val. / Test)
Constituent labeling	Syntactic	30	1.9M / 255K / 191K
Constituent detection	Syntactic	2	3.1M / 426K / 318K
NEL	Semantic	18	128K / 20K / 13K
SRL	Semantic/Syntactic	66	599K / 83K / 62K
Mention detection	Syntactic	2	387K / 49K / 48K
Coreference arc prediction	Semantic	2	208K / 27K / 28K

Table 1: Dataset statistics for the six tasks.

stack of a linear layer, a non-linear layer with tanh activations, layer normalization, dropout (0.3 zeroing probability), and a second linear layer. The hidden dimension of the MLP is 256. Models are trained by minimizing binary cross-entropy loss against the set of true labels. Though some tasks (e.g., SRL) are multi-class classification, we make predictions for each label independently i.e. binary classification, which facilitates analysis on individual labels or label groups. The binary classification setting also allows using the micro-averaged F-score as the evaluation metric across tasks.

In experiments with frozen encoders, we only learn the encoder layer mixing weights, projection parameters, and MLP parameters, keeping the encoder parameters themselves fixed. For optimization we use Adam (Kingma and Ba, 2015) with an initial learning rate of 5×10^{-4} and a batch size of 64.[4] The model is evaluated on the validation set every 1000 steps and the learning rate is reduced by a factor of 2 if no improvement is seen in the previous 5 validation evaluations. Training stops if no improvement is seen for 20 validation evaluations.

In experiments with fine-tuning the encoders, we focus on only a subset of the frozen-encoder configurations for computational reasons. In particular, we only experiment with the "base" versions of BERT, RoBERTa, and SpanBERT.[5] All models are trained using Adam with an initial learning rate of 3×10^{-5} and a batch size of 64. Finally, the token embedding is either a layer-weighted combination or just the last layer.[6]

4.2 Data

Table 1 shows the dataset statistics of the six tasks evaluated in this study. For SRL, NEL, coreference arc prediction and constituent labeling, we use the annotations in the OntoNotes 5.0 corpus (Weischedel et al., 2013) and cast the original annotations into the edge probing format, following the same procedure as Tenney et al. (2019b) for pre-processing.

For the newly proposed constituent detection and mention detection tasks, we create our own datasets using the existing annotations and random negative sampling. For constituent detection, we use the constituent labeling annotations to get actual constituents, and for each constituent we sample a random negative span of the same length. We ensure that all negative spans are different and that we don't sample an actual constituent. We follow a similar procedure to get mention detection annotations from coreference arc prediction annotations. To make the mention detection task harder and more realistic, we sample 5 times more negatives than actual mentions.

5 Results

5.1 Results without Fine-Tuning

The results across tasks and models are shown in Figure 2. Overall we find max pooling to be the most robust and effective choice across tasks. Boundary-based span representations (i.e., ENDPOINT, DIFFSUM, COHERENT) are superior to entire-span methods (i.e., ATTN, MAX, AVG) on tasks which are more shallow/syntactic (e.g., constituent labeling and constituent detection), though max pooling is competitive with the boundary-based methods.

On the other hand, entire-span representations are good at semantic tasks like coreference arc prediction. As SRL has both semantic and syntactic characteristics, COHERENT, MAX, and ATTN show

---

[4]We found non-trivial gains with this choice of higher learning rate compared to 1×10^{-4} used by Tenney et al. (2019b).

[5]We omit XLNet due to its relatively poor performance across tasks in the frozen setting.

[6]Typically the last layer embeddings perform slightly better but a few of those training runs failed and we present the layer-weighted results for those.

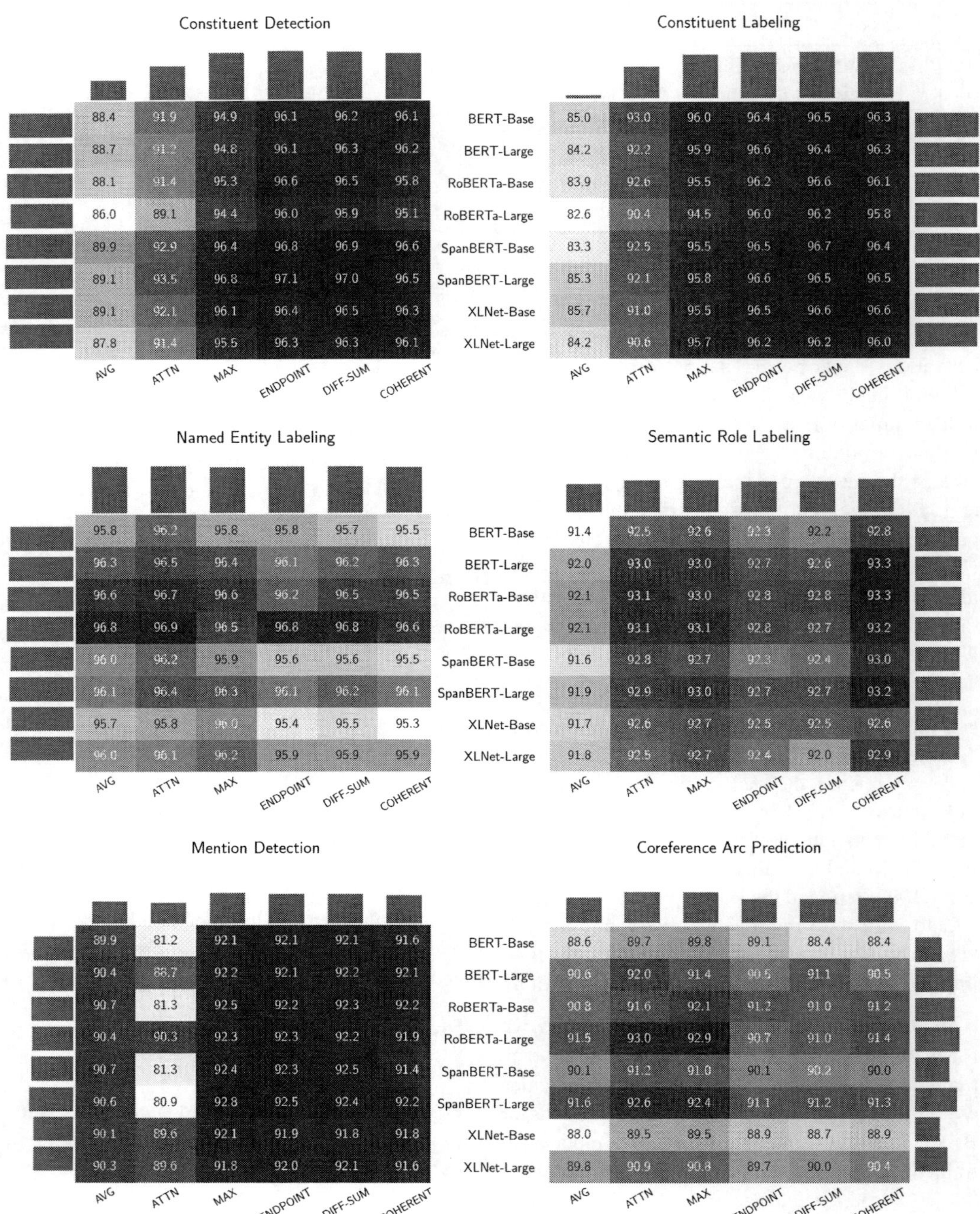

Figure 2: Results with frozen encoders (no fine-tuning) for the 6 different tasks presented as separate heatmap figures. Each heatmap represents the 48 combinations resulting from 6 span representations and 8 pretrained models. The bars at the side of the heatmap represent the max value in the row/column which is right below the bar.

similar performance with the other methods fairly close behind. We do not find large differences between span representation methods for NEL, which mainly contains short spans.

Model-wise, large models are usually better than base models though there exist exceptions (e.g., constituent labeling). RoBERTa shows strong performance across tasks. We also find that SpanBERT

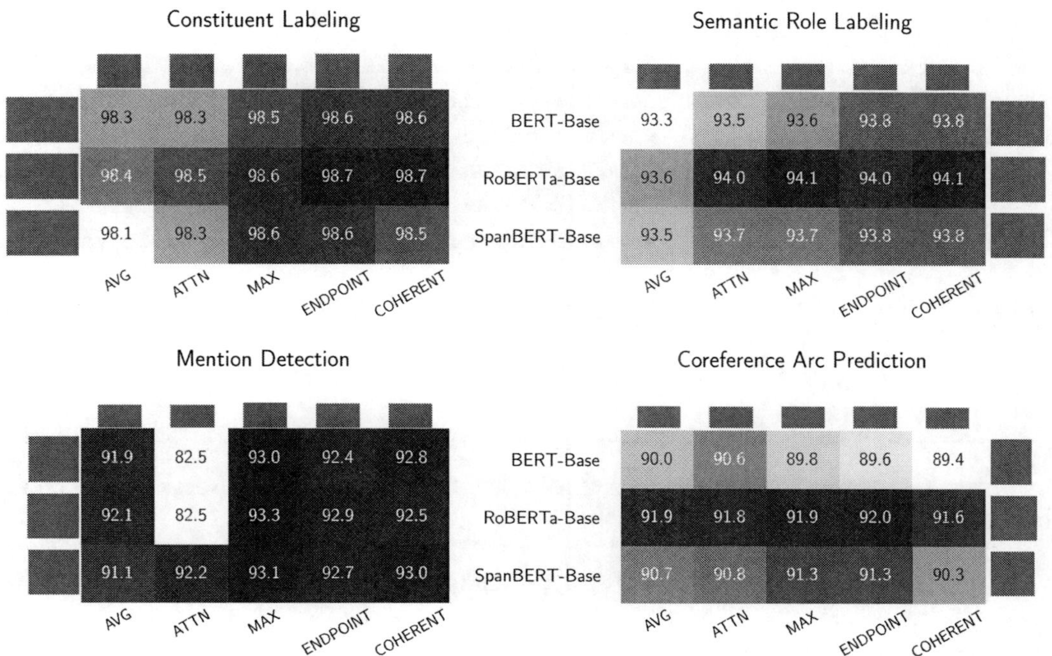

Figure 3: Results with fine-tuned encoders for four tasks, namely constituent labeling, SRL, mention detection, and coreference arc prediction, presented as separate heatmaps.

excels for tasks where boundary-based methods are superior, which may be because it is explicitly trained with an objective of predicting tokens inside a span given the boundary tokens.

Results for each task are summarized below.

Constituent detection/labeling: Boundary-based representations are better than entire-span ones, though MAX is close behind. Surprisingly, in these two tasks, large models are not as good as their base counterparts (Goldberg (2019) found similar exceptions for syntactic tasks).

Semantic role labeling: COHERENT is the best method on this task with MAX and ATTN being very close behind.

Mention detection and coreference arc prediction: ATTN and MAX perform the best for coreference arc prediction since they benefit from access to the entire span and thus to the semantic head of the span (Lee et al., 2017). For mention detection the trends are reversed, except for MAX, with the boundary-based methods doing quite well. This is not surprising since the mention detection task is somewhat close to constituent tasks. Surprisingly, ATTN shows high variance across models and performs worse than even AVG. Since we initialize

the attention parameter vector v to all zeroes, this result means that not learning the attention vector is surprisingly better than learning them.[7] Preliminary investigation of the learned attention weights did not provide any clues.

Mention detection and coreference arc prediction together complete the pipeline for coreference resolution. The preference for different forms of span representations between the two (except for MAX) suggests that different span representations can be considered for different stages of the coreference resolution task. Interestingly, one of the best performing end-to-end coreference models (Lee et al., 2017) uses a concatenation of a boundary-based span representation, ENDPOINT, and ATTN.

Some of our observations may be confounded with training set sizes, which vary from coreference arc prediction on the small end (208K) up to constituent tasks on the largest end (1.9M), with SRL (599K) in the middle of the range.

5.2 Results with Fine-Tuning

State-of-the-art models almost always fine-tune the pretrained encoders. However, the training is quite

---

[7]Stopping the gradient for the attention vector indeed performed similarly to AVG.

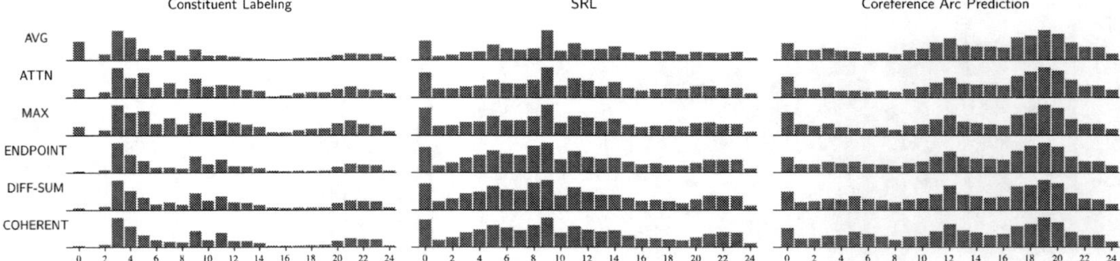

Figure 4: Visualization of layerwise weights learned for all span representation methods for constituent labeling, SRL, and coreference arc prediction for the RoBERTa-large model.

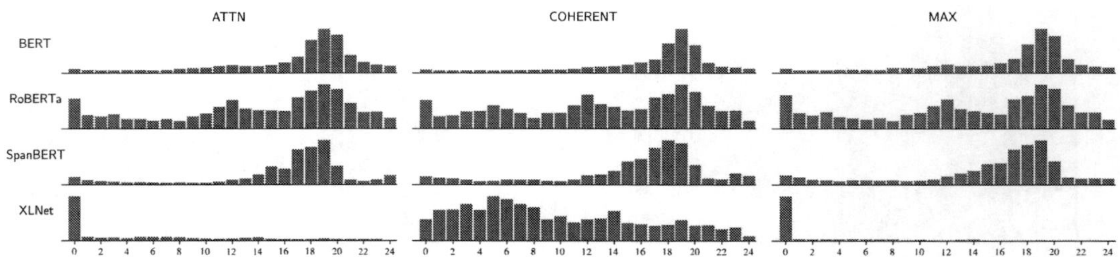

Figure 5: Visualization of layerwise weights learned for the coreference arc prediction task for three span representation methods with {BERT, RoBERTa, SpanBERT, XLNet}-large models. While BERT, SpanBERT, and XLNet have peaked weight distributions, RoBERTa's weights are more spread out. Oddly enough XLNet chooses to place the most weight on the embedding layer for ATTN and MAX (the two best span representations for XLNet-large).

computationally expensive; hence, we perform the span representation comparison for a small set of the total configurations whose results are shown in Figure 3. In general, fine-tuning improves the results for all span representation methods across tasks, with the performance of different span representation methods now more tightly clustered. This is best illustrated by the constituent labeling task where without fine-tuning AVG trails by 10+ F-score with respect to the best span representation but less than 0.5 F-score with fine-tuning.

6 Analysis

In this section we analyze the impact of span representation method with fixed pretrained encoders.

6.1 Layerwise Weight Analysis

Figures 4 and 5 visualize learned layer weights for different task, span representation, and pretrained encoder combinations. Within a model and task, we generally found that the layer weights were fairly consistent across span representation methods. Overall, we find similar trends to prior work in analyzing layer weights for downstream NLP tasks, namely that constituency parsing has higher weight for lower layers and coreference has most weight

on higher layers, with SRL in between (Liu et al., 2019a; Tenney et al., 2019a). For ablation analysis of layer weights, whether to learn them or not, see Appendix A.1.

6.2 Label-Specific Analysis of Span Groups

We seek to determine whether boundary-based span representation methods (COHERENT, DIFFSUM, and ENDPOINT) differ systematically from methods that consider the entire span (ATTN, MAX, and AVG). We pooled predictions from the three methods in each group for RoBERTa-large and calculated the recall for particular labels, for two tasks: SRL and constituent labeling (analysis for NEL appears in Appendix A.2). We found the labels with the largest differences in recall between the two groups, and discuss our findings below.

SRL. Table 2 shows the argument labels with the largest differences in recall (ΔR) between the two groups, limiting our analysis to the 20 most frequent argument labels. Labels with positive ΔR are handled better by boundary-based methods. These tend to be arguments that can be identified based on particular words, often function words, at the boundaries. For example, ARGM-DIS is found

Argument	ΔR	Notes	Examples
C-ARG1 (continuous argument)	10.85	often starts with *to*, similar to `xcomp` in universal dependencies	"were <u>granted</u> the right earlier this year **to ship sugar**", "brought more <u>money</u> into a city **than it took out**", "Food prices are expected **to be unchanged**"
ARGM-DIS (discourse)	3.24	mostly single-word discourse modifiers like *and* or *but*	"**In addition** , the government is <u>figuring</u>", "**But** <u>eluding</u>", "**And** the USIA <u>said</u>", "**of course** , there <u>'s</u> that word"
ARGM-MNR (manner)	2.03	mostly adverbs and prepositional phrases	"...get <u>married</u> **in a tuxedo**", "**relatively** <u>respected</u>", "**Moving rapidly** through school", "...do n't <u>leave</u> home **without the American Express card**"
ARG3 (starting point, benefactive, attribute)	-4.28	multiple functions depending on predicate, and thus a variety of boundary words	"And what I had <u>mentioned</u> **about my mother bugging me** was...", "You should feel comfortable <u>staying</u> **there**", "...he believes that it can bring the market **back** <u>up</u> after a plunge", "Biologists <u>mixed</u> a <u>mold</u> element in the cells of plants with pearl powder **to produce a granulated drug**"
ARGM-DIR (direction)	-5.20	typically a word or short phrase, mostly adverbs, prepositional phrases, particles, and adjectives	"newspapers turning **to color** on their pages", "bond prices rapidly <u>turned</u> **south**", "major brokerage firms <u>rushed</u> **out** ads", "<u>takes</u> the dispute **to the Supreme Court**", "we have to <u>get</u> **out of bed**", "<u>toss</u> the chalk **back and forth**"
ARGM-EXT (extent)	-8.14	often a short phrase like *more, very much, a lot*, etc.; limited semantics, range of surface forms	"you <u>'re</u> critical to yourself **too much**", "of <u>freezing</u> , **at least partially**", "<u>increase</u> **of 32 %**", "life has <u>changed</u> **a lot**", "<u>Thank</u> you **very much**"

Table 2: Analysis of argument labels for semantic role labeling. ΔR = argument recall% with boundary-based span representation methods minus recall% with entire-span methods. In the examples, predicates are underlined and arguments of the given type are shown in boldface.

Label	ΔR	Examples
SBAR	6.1	"that are missing", "who owned the land"
PRN	4.6	", she says ,", ", it turns out ,", "(file photo)", "(hey , it 's possible)"
ADJP	3.3	"liable", "available to anyone", "more generous", "satisfied with where they work", "at least somewhat interesting"
PP	2.7	"in 1966", "within a community"
SBARQ	-6.1	"What can we do ?", "So what should be done .", "and what is money for", "how shall I say"
SQ	-6.5	"Did you see ?", "will I do now", "do you make of", "You still building"
FRAG	-6.5	"Or something .", "well below 1988 activity", "As for Mr. Papandreou ?"
SINV	-15.7	"should the Air Force order the craft", "say Mr. Dinkins 's managers", "notes Huang frankly", "invest they will"

Table 3: Analysis of labels for constituent labeling. ΔR = label recall% with ENDPOINT minus recall% with MAX. We restrict this analysis to labels that appear at least 100 times in our development set.

mostly with single-word modifiers in this dataset (like *and* and *but*). Arguments that are handled better by entire-span methods are more diverse in terms of their boundary words. ARGM-EXT is used for arguments with relatively limited semantics (as shown in the examples) but a variety of surface realizations.

Constituent labeling. Table 3 shows a similar analysis for constituent labeling, though in this case we compare only a single method from each family: ENDPOINT and MAX. We do this because MAX is comparable in performance to the boundary methods while ATTN and AVG are significantly worse. We choose ENDPOINT as our single representative of the boundary methods in order to compare only two methods, though we found the same trends for others in its group.

ENDPOINT has higher recall on several labels, shown in the top part of the table. There is a 6% difference for SBAR, which is a clause introduced by a (possibly empty) subordinating conjunction. About 25% of SBAR constituents begin with *that*, and many others start with some other very common subordinating conjunction, making SBAR easier to find for methods that focus on boundary words. Parentheticals (PRN) frequently begin and end with commas or parentheses. ADJPs typically begin or end with an adjective and PPs nearly always begin with prepositions.

The lower part of Table 3 shows labels where MAX has higher recall than ENDPOINT. The largest difference is in SINV, which is an "inverted" declarative sentence, that is, a sentence in which the subject follows the conjugated verb. These often look like VPs based on boundary words but are more di-

173

verse syntactically; a few short examples are shown in the table. The other labels also show syntactic diversity. FRAG (fragment) has many realizations that vary widely in terms of their syntax. while SBARQ and SQ often start with *wh*-words and end in question marks, they show significant variation.

7   Related Work

Many of the span representations that we consider here were proposed previously for specific tasks, such as the attention-weighted pooling of Lee et al. (2017) for coreference resolution; the endpoint-based representation of Lee et al. (2016) and the "coherent" endpoint-based representation of Seo et al. (2019) for question answering; and combinations of differences and sums of endpoint representations for parsing and semantic role labeling (Stern et al., 2017; Ouchi et al., 2018). These are described in more detail in Section 3.2.

Other recent work has considered pooling approaches such as the difference between endpoint representations (Wang and Chang, 2016; Cross and Huang, 2016) or a concatenation of endpoint and attention-based representations (Li et al., 2016). Other approaches concatenate additional specialized feature vectors, such as the span length or position information (Lee et al., 2017; He et al., 2018; Kuribayashi et al., 2019). Some work has also considered explicitly composing span representations via syntactic parse trees, such as recursive neural networks (Li et al., 2014), and some unsupervised parsing models produce span representations as a byproduct of training (Drozdov et al., 2019; Shi et al., 2019).

At the same time, there has been significant effort devoted to the related problem of learning representations for sentences or even longer texts (Kalchbrenner et al., 2014; Iyyer et al., 2015; Kiros et al., 2015; Wieting et al., 2016; Conneau et al., 2017; Shen et al., 2018, *inter alia*). Much of this work focuses on pooling over word representations, often finding that simple pooling operations like averaging perform surprisingly well (Wieting et al., 2016; Shen et al., 2018). Shen et al. (2018) did a similar empirical study to ours in spirit, comparing a variety of pooling models for sentence representations across tasks.

In this work we are mainly focusing on the models for computing span representations given pretrained token embeddings, but we also include a variety of pretrained contextual embeddings. One in particular, SpanBERT (Joshi et al., 2019a), was designed to enable improved span representations. While recent work has compared across pretrained contextual embeddings for representing spans (Tenney et al., 2019b), to our knowledge there has been no systematic comparison of methods for combining these contextual embeddings into span representations across a variety of tasks.

8   Conclusion

We systematically compared multiple span representation methods, combined with various base embedding models, on various tasks. Our analysis includes two new tasks that we propose to tease apart different aspects of span representations. When using fixed, pretrained encoders, we find that, although max pooling is a fairly reliable representation across tasks, the optimal span representation varies with respect to the syntactic and semantic nature of the task. Finally, fine-tuning reduces the impact of span representation choice on performance, though it involves significant computational expense. Our results are likely to be most useful for those without the computational capabilities to perform fine-tuning of large pretrained encoders, in which case there are significant differences among methods.

References

Ronan Collobert, Jason Weston, Léon Bottou, Michael Karlen, Koray Kavukcuoglu, and Pavel Kuksa. 2011. Natural Language Processing (Almost) from Scratch. *JMLR*, 12:2493–2537.

Alexis Conneau, Douwe Kiela, Holger Schwenk, Loïc Barrault, and Antoine Bordes. 2017. Supervised Learning of Universal Sentence Representations from Natural Language Inference Data. In *EMNLP*.

James Cross and Liang Huang. 2016. Span-Based Constituency Parsing with a Structure-Label System and Provably Optimal Dynamic Oracles. In *EMNLP*.

Jacob Devlin, Ming-Wei Chang, Kenton Lee, and Kristina Toutanova. 2019. BERT: Pre-training of Deep Bidirectional Transformers for Language Understanding. In *NAACL-HLT*.

Andrew Drozdov, Patrick Verga, Mohit Yadav, Mohit Iyyer, and Andrew McCallum. 2019. Unsupervised Latent Tree Induction with Deep Inside-Outside Recursive Auto-Encoders. In *NAACL-HLT*.

Yoav Goldberg. 2019. Assessing BERT's Syntactic Abilities. *arXiv*, abs/1901.05287.

Kazuma Hashimoto, Caiming Xiong, Yoshimasa Tsuruoka, and Richard Socher. 2017. A Joint Many-Task Model: Growing a Neural Network for Multiple NLP Tasks. In *EMNLP*.

Luheng He, Kenton Lee, Omer Levy, and Luke Zettlemoyer. 2018. Jointly Predicting Predicates and Arguments in Neural Semantic Role Labeling. In *ACL*.

Mohit Iyyer, Varun Manjunatha, Jordan Boyd-Graber, and Hal Daumé III. 2015. Deep unordered composition rivals syntactic methods for text classification. In *ACL-IJCNLP*.

Mandar Joshi, Danqi Chen, Yinhan Liu, Daniel S Weld, Luke Zettlemoyer, and Omer Levy. 2019a. Span-BERT: Improving Pre-training by Representing and Predicting Spans. *TACL*.

Mandar Joshi, Omer Levy, Luke Zettlemoyer, and Daniel Weld. 2019b. BERT for Coreference Resolution: Baselines and Analysis. In *EMNLP-IJCNLP*.

Nal Kalchbrenner, Edward Grefenstette, and Phil Blunsom. 2014. A Convolutional Neural Network for Modelling Sentences. In *ACL*.

Diederik P. Kingma and Jimmy Ba. 2015. Adam: A method for stochastic optimization. In *ICLR*.

Ryan Kiros, Yukun Zhu, Russ R Salakhutdinov, Richard Zemel, Raquel Urtasun, Antonio Torralba, and Sanja Fidler. 2015. Skip-thought vectors. In *NeurIPS*.

Nikita Kitaev, Steven Cao, and Dan Klein. 2019. Multilingual Constituency Parsing with Self-Attention and Pre-Training. In *ACL*.

Nikita Kitaev and Dan Klein. 2018. Constituency Parsing with a Self-Attentive Encoder. In *ACL*.

Tatsuki Kuribayashi, Hiroki Ouchi, Naoya Inoue, Paul Reisert, Toshinori Miyoshi, Jun Suzuki, and Kentaro Inui. 2019. An Empirical Study of Span Representations in Argumentation Structure Parsing. In *ACL*.

Kenton Lee, Luheng He, Mike Lewis, and Luke Zettlemoyer. 2017. End-to-end Neural Coreference Resolution. In *EMNLP*.

Kenton Lee, Tom Kwiatkowski, Ankur P. Parikh, and Dipanjan Das. 2016. Learning Recurrent Span Representations for Extractive Question Answering. *CoRR*, abs/1611.01436.

Jiwei Li, Rumeng Li, and Eduard Hovy. 2014. Recursive Deep Models for Discourse Parsing. In *EMNLP*.

Qi Li, Tianshi Li, and Baobao Chang. 2016. Discourse Parsing with Attention-based Hierarchical Neural Networks. In *EMNLP*.

Zhouhan Lin, Minwei Feng, Cicero Nogueira dos Santos, Mo Yu, Bing Xiang, Bowen Zhou, and Yoshua Bengio. 2017. A structured self-attentive sentence embedding. In *ICLR*.

Nelson F. Liu, Matt Gardner, Yonatan Belinkov, Matthew E. Peters, and Noah A. Smith. 2019a. Linguistic Knowledge and Transferability of Contextual Representations. In *NAACL-HLT*.

Yinhan Liu, Myle Ott, Naman Goyal, Jingfei Du, Mandar Joshi, Danqi Chen, Omer Levy, Mike Lewis, Luke Zettlemoyer, and Veselin Stoyanov. 2019b. RoBERTa:A Robustly Optimized BERT Pretraining Approach. *arXiv preprint arXiv:1907.11692*.

Hiroki Ouchi, Hiroyuki Shindo, and Yuji Matsumoto. 2018. A Span Selection Model for Semantic Role Labeling. In *EMNLP*.

Adam Paszke, Sam Gross, Francisco Massa, Adam Lerer, James Bradbury, Gregory Chanan, Trevor Killeen, Zeming Lin, Natalia Gimelshein, Luca Antiga, Alban Desmaison, Andreas Kopf, Edward Yang, Zachary DeVito, Martin Raison, Alykhan Tejani, Sasank Chilamkurthy, Benoit Steiner, Lu Fang, Junjie Bai, and Soumith Chintala. 2019. Pytorch: An Imperative Style, High-Performance Deep Learning Library. In *NeurIPS*.

Matthew E Peters, Mark Neumann, Mohit Iyyer, Matt Gardner, Christopher Clark, Kenton Lee, and Luke Zettlemoyer. 2018. Deep contextualized word representations. In *NAACL-HLT*.

Sameer Pradhan, Alessandro Moschitti, Nianwen Xue, Olga Uryupina, and Yuchen Zhang. 2012. CoNLL-2012 Shared Task: Modeling Multilingual Unrestricted Coreference in OntoNotes. In *EMNLP and CoNLL - Shared Task*.

Pranav Rajpurkar, Jian Zhang, Konstantin Lopyrev, and Percy Liang. 2016. SQuAD: 100,000+ Questions for Machine Comprehension of Text. In *EMNLP*.

Minjoon Seo, Jinhyuk Lee, Tom Kwiatkowski, Ankur Parikh, Ali Farhadi, and Hannaneh Hajishirzi. 2019. Real-Time Open-Domain Question Answering with Dense-Sparse Phrase Index. In *ACL*.

Dinghan Shen, Guoyin Wang, Wenlin Wang, Martin Renqiang Min, Qinliang Su, Yizhe Zhang, Chunyuan Li, Ricardo Henao, and Lawrence Carin. 2018. Baseline Needs More Love: On Simple Word-Embedding-Based Models and Associated Pooling Mechanisms. In *ACL*.

Haoyue Shi, Jiayuan Mao, Kevin Gimpel, and Karen Livescu. 2019. Visually grounded neural syntax acquisition. In *ACL*.

Mitchell Stern, Jacob Andreas, and Dan Klein. 2017. A Minimal Span-Based Neural Constituency Parser. In *ACL*.

Ian Tenney, Dipanjan Das, and Ellie Pavlick. 2019a. BERT Rediscovers the Classical NLP Pipeline. In *ACL*.

Ian Tenney, Patrick Xia, Berlin Chen, Alex Wang, Adam Poliak, R. Thomas McCoy, Najoung Kim, Benjamin Van Durme, Samuel R. Bowman, Dipanjan Das, and Ellie Pavlick. 2019b. What do you learn from context? Probing for sentence structure in contextualized word representations. In *ICLR*.

Erik F. Tjong Kim Sang and Fien De Meulder. 2003. Introduction to the CoNLL-2003 Shared Task: Language-Independent Named Entity Recognition. In *NAACL*.

Wenhui Wang and Baobao Chang. 2016. Graph-based Dependency Parsing with Bidirectional LSTM. In *ACL*.

Ralph Weischedel, Martha Palmer, Mitchell Marcus, Eduard Hovy, Sameer Pradhan, Lance Ramshaw, Nianwen Xue, Ann Taylor, Jeff Kaufman, and Michelle Franchini et al. 2013. OntoNotes release 5.0 LDC2013T19. *Linguistic Data Consortium.*

John Wieting, Mohit Bansal, Kevin Gimpel, and Karen Livescu. 2016. Towards Universal Paraphrastic Sentence Embeddings. In *ICLR*.

Thomas Wolf, Lysandre Debut, Victor Sanh, Julien Chaumond, Clement Delangue, Anthony Moi, Pierric Cistac, Tim Rault, R'emi Louf, Morgan Funtowicz, and Jamie Brew. 2019. HuggingFace's Transformers: State-of-the-art Natural Language Processing. *arXiv, abs/1910.03771.*

Zhilin Yang, Zihang Dai, Yiming Yang, Jaime Carbonell, Ruslan Salakhutdinov, and Quoc V Le. 2019. XLNet: Generalized Autoregressive Pretraining for Language Understanding. In *NeurIPS*.

A Appendix

A.1 Mixing Weights for Layers

Model	AVG	ATT	MAX	EP	DS	COH
BERT-large	90.6	92	91.4	90.5	91.1	90.5
-mix_wt	90.3	91.3	91.5	90.4	90.4	90.3
RoBERTa-large	91.5	93	92.9	90.7	91.0	91.4
-mix_wt	91.0	92.7	92.6	90.9	90.7	90.6
SpanBERT-large	91.6	92.6	92.4	91.1	91.2	91.3
-mix_wt	90.4	91.4	91.5	90.6	90.3	90.2
XLNet-large	89.8	90.9	90.8	89.7	90.0	90.4
-mix_wt	89.4	90.7	90.8	89.5	90.0	90.7

Table 4: Analysis of importance of learning mixing weights for combination of different models and span representations for the coreference arc prediction task.

In the table above we analyze the effect of learning the layerwise mixing weights vs simple averaging over layers in context of the coreference arc prediction task. ATTN-based models suffer the biggest drop with a drop of 0.6% absolute on average. Among pretrained contextual embedding models, SpanBERT-large is hurt the most with a drop of 1% absolute on average. Surprisingly, XLNet drops by only 0.1% on average even though its attention plots looked quite peaky for some of the span representations.

A.2 Label-Specific Analysis of Span Groups for NEL

Label	ΔR	Examples
ORDINAL	1.2	"first", "second", "First", "6th", "ninth"
CARDINAL	0.3	"two", "10", "Dozens", "at least 37"
TIME	-2.3	"seven o'clock", "two hours", "about ten", "eight fifty in the morning"
LAW	-2.9	"Paragraph 14 of Article 19", "the Geneva Convention", "Dru 's Law"
LOC	-3.2	"the Sierra Nevada Mountains", "Asia", "Mai Po Marshes"
WORK_OF_ART	-6.0	"The End of the Day", "Carry On Trading", "News Night Tonight"

Table 5: Analysis of labels for NEL. ΔR = label recall% with boundary-based span representation methods minus recall% with entire-span methods.

NEL. Table 5 shows a similar analysis for entity labeling as done in Section 6.2. The labels with higher recall under the boundary-based methods are limited to ORDINAL and CARDINAL numbers, which tend to be very short and highly regular (nearly all ORDINAL entities are one token and approximately half are *first*). The entire-span methods achieve much higher recall for the WORK_OF_ART label, and also for LOC, LAW, and TIME. These entities tend to be multi-word phrases with a variety of syntactic forms and without consistent boundary words.

It may be surprising that ORDINAL is better detected by the boundary methods, since nearly all ORDINAL entities are a single token, and the entire-span methods reduce to a simple form for single tokens. However, this may show that the entire-span methods are being trained to abstract over the contents of the span, thereby losing some of the surface information. The boundary-based methods, by contrast, devote particular parts of the span representation to the boundary position representations, thereby providing a more direct/explicit connection between those boundary words and the downstream classifier.

Enhancing Transformer with Sememe Knowledge

Yuhui Zhang[1*]   **Chenghao Yang**[2*]   **Zhengping Zhou**[1*]   **Zhiyuan Liu**[3]
[1]Stanford University   [2]Columbia University   [3]Tsinghua University
{yuhuiz, zpzhou}@stanford.edu   chenghao.yang@columbia.edu
liuzy@tsinghua.edu.cn

Abstract

While large-scale pretraining has achieved great success in many NLP tasks, it has not been fully studied whether external linguistic knowledge can improve data-driven models. In this work, we introduce sememe knowledge into Transformer and propose three sememe-enhanced Transformer models. Sememes, by linguistic definition, are the minimum semantic units of language, which can well represent implicit semantic meanings behind words. Our experiments demonstrate that introducing sememe knowledge into Transformer can consistently improve language modeling and downstream tasks. The adversarial test further demonstrates that sememe knowledge can substantially improve model robustness.[1]

1 Introduction

Self-supervised pretraining has significantly improved the performance of Transformer (Vaswani et al., 2017) on a wide range of NLP tasks (Radford et al., 2018; Devlin et al., 2019; Yang et al., 2019). While no explicit linguistic rules and concepts are introduced, models can achieve remarkable performances with extensive training signals provided by large-scale data. Nonetheless, recent works still demonstrate that external syntactic information can improve various NLP tasks, including machine translation (Sennrich and Haddow, 2016; Aharoni and Goldberg, 2017; Bastings et al., 2017) and semantic role labeling (Marcheggiani and Titov, 2017; Strubell et al., 2018).

Can external semantic information benefit the widely-adopted pretraining and fine-tuning framework as well? In response, we explore incorporating sememe knowledge into Transformer (Vaswani et al., 2017). Sememes are the minimum semantic units of meaning for natural language, as some linguists assume that a limited closed set of sememes can be composed to represent the semantic meaning of each word (Bloomfield, 1926). In this work, we adopt a high-quality sememe-based lexical knowledge base, HowNet (Dong and Dong, 2006; Qi et al., 2019), which can provide powerful support for models to understand Chinese word semantics (Gu et al., 2018; Niu et al., 2017). Some examples of sememe annotations can be found in Figure 1.

We propose to combine two simple methods to incorporate sememe knowledge into our framework: 1) based on the linguistic assumption, we add aggregated sememe embeddings to each word embedding to enhance its semantic representation; 2) we use sememe prediction as an auxiliary task to help the model gain deeper understandings of word semantics. We verify the effectiveness of our methods on several Chinese NLP tasks that are closely related to word-level and sentence-level semantics. Following general settings of pretraining and fine-tuning, our experiments show consistent improvements on all the tasks with sememe-enhanced Transformer. We also find that the sememe-enhanced model can achieve the same performance with less fine-tuning data, which is desirable as data annotation processes are always time-consuming and expensive.

We further demonstrate that, by incorporating sememe knowledge using our methods, model robustness can be significantly improved towards adversarial examples, which are generated by replacing nouns, adjectives and adverbs with their synonyms in our experiment. Our case studies further interpret why sememe knowledge can help model defend adversarial attacks.

---

* Indicates equal contribution. Work done at Tsinghua University. Y.Z. and C.Y. designed and evaluated the model architecture and performed the adversarial test. Z.Z. performed the data ablation study and case study. Z.L. supervised the work and is the corresponding author.

[1]Codes are available at https://github.com/yuhui-zh15/SememeTransformer/.

Proceedings of the 5th Workshop on Representation Learning for NLP (RepL4NLP-2020), pages 177–184
July 9, 2020. ©2020 Association for Computational Linguistics

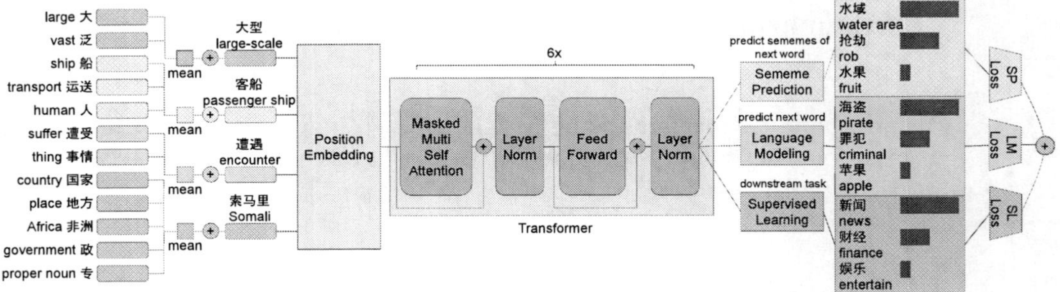

Figure 1: Our proposed model architecture. For each word, we enhance word representation by adding aggregated sememe embeddings. We use multitask learning with three tasks: **sememe prediction** (predicting sememes of next word), **language modeling** (predicting next word) and **supervised learning** (only for downstream tasks).

2 Methodology

In this section, we propose two simple methods to incorporate sememe knowledge into our framework: aggregated sememe embeddings and sememe prediction auxiliary task.

2.1 Transformer

Transformer was originally proposed by Vaswani et al. (2017) as a machine translation architecture. We use a multi-layer Transformer architecture similar to the setup in Radford et al. (2018), which has been verified effectiveness on multiple NLP tasks. At the input layer, a sequence of words $(w_1, w_2, ..., w_T)$ are embedded as $\mathbf{H}^0 = (\mathbf{w}_1, \mathbf{w}_2, ..., \mathbf{w}_T) \in \mathbb{R}^{T \times D}$, where D indicates the hidden size of the model. A positional embedding is then added to inject position information into Transformer. After L residual multi-head self-attention layers with feed-forward connections, we obtain the contextualized sequence embedding $\mathbf{H}^L = (\mathbf{h}_1^L, \mathbf{h}_2^L, ..., \mathbf{h}_T^L) \in \mathbb{R}^{T \times D}$.

2.2 Aggregated Sememe Embeddings

Enhancing word representation is a common approach to introduce linguistic knowledge into neural networks (Sennrich and Haddow, 2016; Niu et al., 2017; Bojanowski et al., 2017). For each word w, **Transformer-SE** considers all of its sememes and enhances word representation by adding its average sememe embeddings to word embedding. Formally, we have:

$$\tilde{\mathbf{w}} = \frac{1}{n_w} \sum_{s \in S(w)} \mathbf{x}_s + \mathbf{w}$$

where $S(w)$ refers to the sememe set associated with word w with the size n_w, $\mathbf{x}_s$ refers to the

embedding of the sememe s, $\mathbf{w}$ refers to the embedding of word w and $\tilde{\mathbf{w}}$ refers to the sememe-enhanced word embedding. Sememe-enhanced representation $\tilde{\mathbf{w}}$ is directly fed into Transformer.

The Transformer-SE model complies with the linguistic assumption that implicit word semantics can be composed of a limited set of sememes. Also, as sememe embeddings are shared among words, latent semantic correlations between words can be well encoded. While our method to incorporate sememe knowledge is rather straightforward, our main purpose is to verify the effectiveness of sememe knowledge. We leave more potential methods to enrich word-level semantics with sememe knowledge such as tree LSTM (Tai et al., 2015) and graph convolutional network (Bastings et al., 2017) in future work.

2.3 Sememe Prediction Auxiliary Task

Sememe prediction task aims to predict sememes for the next word and can be formulated as a multi-label classification task. Inspired by the multitask learning (Caruana, 1997; Collobert et al., 2011), we add the sememe prediction task in addition to the language modeling task for **Transformer-SP**. This task challenges the model's capability to incorporate sememe knowledge, and can be viewed as a complementary task for language modeling, as predicting the sememes of the next word is closely related to understanding semantics and it is often more learnable than directly modeling the probability of the next word. [2]

At each time step, given current contextualized

---

[2]For example, if a sentence starts with "How to cook", it is much easier to predict the next word is a kind of "food" than any specified word. It is worth noting that language modeling has about 20 times larger vocabulary size.

| Task | Language Modeling | Headline Categorization | Sentiment Classification | Semantic Matching | Sememe Prediction |
Metric	PPL	ACC (%)	ACC (%)	ACC (%)	MAP (%)
Transformer	49.01	71.5	52.7	81.2	40.1
Transformer-SE	47.37	72.6	53.7	82.6	52.1
Transformer-SP	49.14	72.3	53.0	81.8	40.3
Transformer-SEP	**46.53**	**72.6**	**54.9**	**83.3**	**52.8**
+ Sememe2Char	48.90	72.3	52.2	81.2	-

Table 1: Experimental results on different tasks. **Transformer**, **Transformer-SE**, **Transformer-SP** and **Transformer-SEP** refers to the vanilla Transformer model (base), Transformer with aggregated sememe embeddings, Transformer with sememe prediction auxiliary task and the hybrid model, respectively. We also compare sememe decomposition to character decomposition for our best model and demonstrate advantages of our methods.

representation $\mathbf{h}^L$ from Transformer, we estimate the probability of sememe s associated with next word w as $p(w,s) = \sigma(\mathbf{w}\mathbf{h}^L + b)$, where $\mathbf{w}$ and b are the weight and bias associated with sememe s, σ is the sigmoid activation function. We then calculate the binary cross-entropy loss of sememe prediction $\mathcal{L}_{SP}$ as:

$$\mathcal{L}_{SP} = -\frac{1}{T}\sum_{t=1}^{T}\frac{1}{n}\sum_{s \in S} g(w_t, s)\log(p(w_t, s))$$
$$+ (1 - g(w_t, s))\log(1 - p(w_t, s))$$

where S refers to the overall sememe set with the size n, $g(w,s)$ is a binary variable indicating whether sememe s is associated with word w. Finally, we formulate the loss as:

$$\mathcal{L}_{PRE} = \mathcal{L}_{LM} + \mathcal{L}_{SP}$$
$$\mathcal{L} = \mathcal{L}_{SL} + \rho\mathcal{L}_{PRE}$$

where $\mathcal{L}_{LM}$ and $\mathcal{L}_{SL}$ are the conventional negative log-likelihood language modeling loss and downstream supervised learning loss. $\mathcal{L}_{PRE}$ is the loss optimized during pretraining, while $\mathcal{L}$ is the loss optimized during supervised training for downstream tasks, ρ serves as a coefficient to control the strength of $\mathcal{L}_{PRE}$ during supervised learning.

2.4 Hybrid Model

Transformer-SE and Transformer-SP are designed based on different ideas. Transformer-SE can well inform sememe knowledge to all self-attention layers, while Transformer-SP utilizes additional training signals through the back-propagation process. To combine the advantages of these models, we propose a hybrid model named **Transformer-SEP**. Transformer-SEP incorporates sememe knowledge into the input layer by adding aggregated sememe embeddings and performs the sememe prediction auxiliary task in the output layer.

3 Experiments

We experiment across a diverse set of five benchmark NLP tasks and demonstrate the effectiveness of introducing sememe knowledge.

3.1 Experimental Setup

We use 6-layer 8-head Transformer with the hidden size of 768 and feedforward size of 2048. We set both word embedding and sememe embedding size as 768. We use batch size of 32 and set dropout rate as 0.2 to alleviate overfitting. The vocabulary size is 39,770 and the total number of sememes is 2,100. We truncate the sequence length to 128 for pretraining and supervised learning. When performing supervised training, we set the coefficient ρ to be 0.5. Embeddings are tied for the input layer and output layer to speed up convergence. We clip gradients less than 2 and use Adam optimizer (Kingma and Ba, 2014) with 0.001 learning rate and 8000 warmup steps. For downstream tasks, we use the best pretrained model from language modeling to initialize.

3.2 Tasks and Datasets

Language Modeling Language modeling on a large corpus provides additional training signals for supervised downstream tasks. We use perplexity (PPL) to measure the performance of the language model. Lower PPL indicates better performance. We pretrain the language model on the People's Daily corpus, which contains $\sim$ 15M words.

Headline Categorization Automatic and accurate news categorization is essential for recommen-

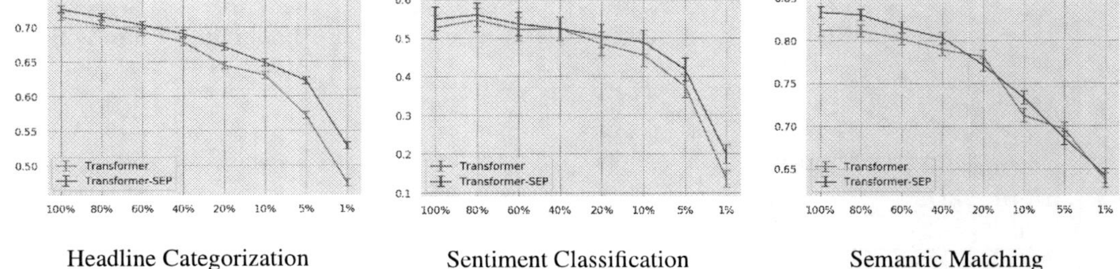

Figure 2: Performance of Transformer and Transformer-SEP with different amounts of training data. More significant improvements can be achieved on tasks that depend more on word-level semantics. X-axis: Percent of supervised training data. Y-axis: Accuracy. The error bars indicate the 95% confidence interval.

dation systems. We use NLPCC 2017 news headline categorization dataset (Qiu et al., 2017), which contains 156,000 news for training and 36,000 news for validation, divided into 18 categories including finance, society, game, etc. We use accuracy (ACC) to measure the performance.

Sentiment Classification   Sentiment classification is a useful task for emoticon recommendation, depression detection, etc. We use NLPCC 2013 Weibo sentiment detection dataset and conduct experiments on sentence-level sentiment classification. The dataset includes 7 different sentiment genres. We remove sentences without any sentiment and resplit the data to 8,225 / 997 / 1,020 for training, validation, test, respectively.

Semantic Matching   Semantic matching is fundamental for question answering, which aims to match the input question to similar questions in an existing database. We use LCQMC (Liu et al., 2018) dataset for this task, which contains 238,766 / 8,802 / 12,500 training, validation, test data, respectively. For each pair of questions, we concatenate them with a special token for classification.

Sememe Prediction   Predicting sememes for given words by its definitions is important for the HowNet extension (Xie et al., 2017). The definitions are extracted from the Contemporary Chinese Dictionary and the sememes of target words are masked for fair comparison. We create a dataset containing 41,081 / 5,135 / 5,136 word-definition pairs for training, validation and test.

3.3   Overall Performance

From Table 1, we observe that simply adding sememe embedding (i.e., Transformer-SE) can lead to significant improvements over all tasks. These

tasks challenge models on the capability of modeling word-level semantics and sentence-level semantics, which demonstrates that sememe knowledge can provide beneficial semantic information for Transformer. The improvement of Transformer-SP is rather less, which may due to the difficulty of predicting new knowledge without previous knowledge. Transformer-SEP achieves further improvements over Transformer-SE. The additional improvement can be interpreted as combining the advantages of these two models.

As characters provide strong semantics for Chinese (Chen et al., 2015), we also compare sememe decomposition with character decomposition (Sememe2Char) for our best model (i.e., with aggregated character embedding and character prediction auxiliary task). From Table 1, we observe clear performance drops over all tasks, which demonstrates that decomposing word into sememes are much more effective.

3.4   Data Ablation Study

We further perform data ablation study and observe overall consistent improvements for downstream tasks over different amounts of training data, indicating that incorporating external sememe knowledge could benefit model robustness when faced with limited training data (Figure 2). It is also worth noting that, when training data is limited, the more a task depends on **word-level semantics** (e.g., headline categorization > sentiment classification > semantic matching[3]), the larger improvement can be achieved by incorporating sememe knowledge. We hypothesize this is due to the increased unseen words in the test set when faced

---

[3]For instance, the word *football* strongly indicates *sport* for headline categorization, while *what's football? ≠ is it a football?* for semantic matching.

Replace	Semantic Matching			Sentiment Classification			Headline Categorization		
	#Count	Base	Ours	#Count	Base	Ours	#Count	Base	Ours
-	0	0.0	0.0	0	0.0	0.0	0	0.0	0.0
Noun.	30,858	18.0	**15.4**(-14%)	2,313	14.1	**11.8**(-16%)	168,516	14.8	**13.4**(-10%)
Adj.	6,498	16.7	**14.8**(-11%)	1,143	20.4	**16.9**(-17%)	54,054	9.4	9.5(+1%)
Adv.	3,306	16.1	**14.1**(-12%)	1,803	14.0	**12.3**(-12%)	65,136	8.5	**8.0**(-6%)
ALL	40,662	17.6	**15.2**(-14%)	5,259	15.4	**13.1**(-15%)	287,706	12.4	**11.4**(-8%)

Table 2: Adversarial test for the base model and our best model (i.e., Transformer v.s. Transformer-SEP). We generate adversarial examples by replacing nouns, adjectives, and adverbs for cases that both models can predict correctly. We report **error rate** (lower the better) categorized by part-of-speech and the number of generated adversarial examples.

with less training data. As semantically similar words would share similar sememes, the sememe-informed model would better understand semantics and outperform the baseline by a large margin.

3.5 Adversarial Test and Case Study

Recent research has demonstrated that neural networks are vulnerable to adversarial examples (Goodfellow et al., 2015; Jia and Liang, 2017; Alzantot et al., 2018). To evaluate the robustness of our models, we generate adversarial examples by replacing similar nouns, adjectives and adverbs for the cases that both Transformer and Transformer-SEP can predict correctly. Intuitively, these words are generally more informative for prediction and models are more likely to overfit such words.

Specifically, we compute the word similarity based on the novel Cilin metric (Tian and Zhao, 2010) and we use THULAC (Sun et al., 2016) for part-of-speech (POS) tagging. For the semantic matching task, we only replace words that occur in both sentences to ensure semantic consistency.

奸商（骗子）如何有工作牌在行李大厅里明目张胆行骗？

How do the profiteers (cheaters) have staff cards and blatantly cheat in the baggage hall?

有罪 guilty 人 human 欺骗 deceive 商业 commerce

有罪 guilty 人 human 骗 cheat

Table 3: Case study for the adversarial test. The **original word** with its sememes is colored in blue, while the **replaced word** with its sememes is colored in red.

We report the adversarial test error rate categorized by POS in Table 2. Sememe-enhanced Transformer-SEP achieves consistent improvement over the vanilla Transformer. An interesting find-ing is that, in headline categorization and semantic matching, the largest performance drops are observed by replacing nouns while intuitively sentiment classification should be more sensitive to adjectives.

We further perform the case study to get a better interpretation of why sememe knowledge can improve model robustness to adversarial attacks. We show an example that Transformer-SEP can predict correctly but get wrong for Transformer in Table 3. As word "cheater" and "profiteer" share the same sememes "guilty" and "human" and similar sememes "deceive" and "cheat", this sememe knowledge can propagate through all self-attention layers, thus it is easy to interpret why sememe knowledge can enhance word representation and defend such word-replacement attack. More examples can be found in the Appendix.

4 Conclusion

In this work, we introduce sememe knowledge into Transformer and verify the effectiveness of external semantic knowledge for data-driven models. We further demonstrate the robustness of our methods via data ablation study and adversarial test. For future work, we would like to explore more ways to leverage semantic knowledge and generate different adversarial examples for evaluation.

Acknowledgments

The authors would like to thank the anonymous reviewers for their many insightful comments. This work is (jointly or partly) funded by the Natural Science Foundation of China (NSFC) and the German Research Foundation (DFG) in Project Crossmodal Learning, NSFC 61621136008 / DFG TRR-169.

References

Roee Aharoni and Yoav Goldberg. 2017. Towards string-to-tree neural machine translation. In *Proceedings of the 55th Annual Meeting of the Association for Computational Linguistics (Volume 2: Short Papers)*, pages 132–140.

Moustafa Alzantot, Yash Sharma Sharma, Ahmed El-gohary, Bo-Jhang Ho, Mani Srivastava, and Kai-Wei Chang. 2018. Generating natural language adversarial examples. In *Proceedings of the 2018 Conference on Empirical Methods in Natural Language Processing*.

Joost Bastings, Ivan Titov, Wilker Aziz, Diego Marcheggiani, and Khalil Sima'an. 2017. Graph convolutional encoders for syntax-aware neural machine translation. In *Proceedings of the 2017 Conference on Empirical Methods in Natural Language Processing*, pages 1957–1967.

Leonard Bloomfield. 1926. A set of postulates for the science of language. *Language*, 2(3).

Piotr Bojanowski, Edouard Grave, Armand Joulin, and Tomas Mikolov. 2017. Enriching word vectors with subword information. *Transactions of the Association for Computational Linguistics*, 5:135–146.

Rich Caruana. 1997. Multitask learning. *Machine learning*, 28(1):41–75.

Xinxiong Chen, Lei Xu, Zhiyuan Liu, Maosong Sun, and Huanbo Luan. 2015. Joint learning of character and word embeddings. In *Twenty-Fourth International Joint Conference on Artificial Intelligence*.

Ronan Collobert, Jason Weston, Léon Bottou, Michael Karlen, Koray Kavukcuoglu, and Pavel Kuksa. 2011. Natural language processing (almost) from scratch. *Journal of Machine Learning Research*, 12:2461–2505.

Jacob Devlin, Ming-Wei Chang, Kenton Lee, and Kristina Toutanova. 2019. Bert: Pre-training of deep bidirectional transformers for language understanding. In *Proceedings of the 2019 Conference of the North American Chapter of the Association for Computational Linguistics: Human Language Technologies, Volume 1 (Long and Short Papers)*, pages 4171–4186.

Zhendong Dong and Qiang Dong. 2006. *Hownet and the computation of meaning (with Cd-rom)*. World Scientific.

Ian Goodfellow, Jonathon Shlens, and Christian Szegedy. 2015. Explaining and harnessing adversarial examples. In *International Conference on Learning Representations*.

Yihong Gu, Jun Yan, Hao Zhu, Zhiyuan Liu, Ruobing Xie, Maosong Sun, Fen Lin, and Leyu Lin. 2018. Language modeling with sparse product of sememe experts. In *Proceedings of the 2018 Conference on Empirical Methods in Natural Language Processing*, pages 4642–4651.

Robin Jia and Percy Liang. 2017. Adversarial examples for evaluating reading comprehension systems. In *Proceedings of the 2017 Conference on Empirical Methods in Natural Language Processing*, pages 2021–2031.

Diederik P Kingma and Jimmy Ba. 2014. Adam: A method for stochastic optimization. *arXiv preprint arXiv:1412.6980*.

Xin Liu, Qingcai Chen, Chong Deng, Huajun Zeng, Jing Chen, Dongfang Li, and Buzhou Tang. 2018. Lcqmc: A large-scale chinese question matching corpus. In *Proceedings of the 27th International Conference on Computational Linguistics*, pages 1952–1962.

Diego Marcheggiani and Ivan Titov. 2017. Encoding sentences with graph convolutional networks for semantic role labeling. In *Proceedings of the 2017 Conference on Empirical Methods in Natural Language Processing*, pages 1506–1515.

Yilin Niu, Ruobing Xie, Zhiyuan Liu, and Maosong Sun. 2017. Improved word representation learning with sememes. In *Proceedings of the 55th Annual Meeting of the Association for Computational Linguistics (Volume 1: Long Papers)*, volume 1, pages 2049–2058.

Fanchao Qi, Chenghao Yang, Zhiyuan Liu, Qiang Dong, Maosong Sun, and Zhendong Dong. 2019. Openhownet: An open sememe-based lexical knowledge base. *arXiv preprint arXiv:1901.09957*.

Xipeng Qiu, Jingjing Gong, and Xuanjing Huang. 2017. Overview of the nlpcc 2017 shared task: Chinese news headline categorization. In *National CCF Conference on Natural Language Processing and Chinese Computing*, pages 948–953. Springer.

Alec Radford, Karthik Narasimhan, Tim Salimans, and Ilya Sutskever. 2018. Improving language understanding by generative pre-training. *URL https://s3-us-west-2. amazonaws. com/openai-assets/research-covers/languageunsupervised/language understanding paper. pdf*.

Rico Sennrich and Barry Haddow. 2016. Linguistic input features improve neural machine translation. In *Proceedings of the First Conference on Machine Translation: Volume 1, Research Papers*, pages 83–91.

Emma Strubell, Patrick Verga, Daniel Andor, David Weiss, and Andrew McCallum. 2018. Linguistically-informed self-attention for semantic role labeling. In *Proceedings of the 2018 Conference on Empirical Methods in Natural Language Processing*, pages 5027–5038.

Maosong Sun, Xinxiong Chen, Kaixu Zhang, Zhipeng Guo, and Zhiyuan Liu. 2016. Thulac: An efficient lexical analyzer for chinese. Technical report, Technical Report. Technical Report.

Kai Sheng Tai, Richard Socher, and Christopher D Manning. 2015. Improved semantic representations from tree-structured long short-term memory networks. In *Proceedings of the 53rd Annual Meeting of the Association for Computational Linguistics and the 7th International Joint Conference on Natural Language Processing (Volume 1: Long Papers)*, pages 1556–1566.

Jiu-le Tian and Wei Zhao. 2010. Words similarity algorithm based on tongyici cilin in semantic web adaptive learning system. *Journal of Jilin University(Information Science Edition)*, 28(6):602–608.

Ashish Vaswani, Noam Shazeer, Niki Parmar, Jakob Uszkoreit, Llion Jones, Aidan N Gomez, Łukasz Kaiser, and Illia Polosukhin. 2017. Attention is all you need. In *Advances in Neural Information Processing Systems*, pages 5998–6008.

Ruobing Xie, Xingchi Yuan, Zhiyuan Liu, and Maosong Sun. 2017. Lexical sememe prediction via word embeddings and matrix factorization. In *IJCAI*, pages 4200–4206.

Zhilin Yang, Zihang Dai, Yiming Yang, Jaime Carbonell, Russ R Salakhutdinov, and Quoc V Le. 2019. Xlnet: Generalized autoregressive pretraining for language understanding. In *Advances in neural information processing systems*, pages 5754–5764.

Task	Input	Ours	Base
Sentiment Classification	奸商 （骗子） 如何有工作牌在行李大厅里明目张胆行骗？ How do the profiteers (cheaters) have staff cards and blatantly cheat in the baggage hall? 有罪 guilty 人 human 欺骗 deceive 商业 commerce 有罪 guilty 人 human 骗 cheat	disgust	surprise
	吓人 （可怕） ，中药比西药更不安全。 Frightful (Fearful), Chinese medicine is less safe than Western medicine. 能 able 促使 urge 害怕 fear 能 able 促使 urge 害怕 fear	fear	disgust
Headline Categorization	转载一个成方 （秘方） ，主治一切骨折，据说一剂见效 We republish a set prescription (secret prescription) , which mainly treats all kinds of fractures, and is said to be effective with only one dose. 医 medical 药物 medicine 准备 prepare 文书 document 命令 order 医 medical 药物 medicine 有效 effective 医治 doctor 全 all 方法 method 疾病 disease	regimen	essay
	他是三征高句丽的强将 （猛将） ，最后死于一群无赖之手 He was a good general (valiant general) that attacked Goguryeo for three times, yet was killed by a group of rogues. 人 human 军 military 官 official 人 human 军 military 官 official 军队 army 勇 brave 争斗 fight	history	story
Semantic Matching	A. 如何选择大哥大 （手机） ？ A. How to choose hand phone (mobile phone)? B. 怎么选择大哥大 （手机） ？ B. What is the way to choose hand phone (cell phone)? 携带 bring 能 able 用具 tool 交流 communicate 样式值 PatternValue 携带 bring 能 able 用具 tool 交流 communicate 样式值 PatternValue	same	different
	A. 初中生 （男生） 暗恋女生会有什么表现？ A. What performance will junior high school students (boy students) have if they secretly love a girl? B. 初中生 （男生） 暗恋女生表现是什么？ B. What is the performance of junior high school students (boy students) if they secretly love a girl? 学习 study 教 teach 场所 InstitutePlace 人 human 教育 education 中等 intermediate 学习 study 教 teach 场所 InstitutePlace 人 human 教育 education 初等 elementary 男 male	same	different

Case Study for adversarial test. The **original words** are shown in parenthesis and colored in blue, while the **replaced words** (similar words calculated by Cilin (Tian and Zhao, 2010)) are colored in red. Both the base model and our model (i.e. Transformer v.s. Transformer-SEP) predict correctly on sentences with the original words, yet only ours succeed in the sentences with the replaced words. We show **sememes for original words** and **sememes for replaced words** in blue and red color boxes respectively. *Best viewed in color.*

Evaluating Compositionality of Sentence Representation Models

Hanoz Bhathena[1], Angelica Willis, Nathan Dass
Stanford University
hanozbhathena@gmail.com, arwillis@stanford.edu,
ndass@stanford.edu

Abstract

We evaluate the compositionality of general-purpose sentence encoders by proposing two metrics to quantify compositional understanding capability of sentence encoders. We introduce a novel metric, Polarity Sensitivity Scoring (PSS), which utilizes sentiment perturbations as a proxy for measuring compositionality. We then compare results from PSS with those obtained via our proposed extension of a metric called Tree Reconstruction Error (TRE) (Andreas, 2019) where compositionality is evaluated by measuring how well a true representation-producing model can be approximated by a model that explicitly combines representations of its primitives.

1 Introduction

Compositionality is the principle inherent in human language whereby the meaning of a complex, compound language expression can be deduced from the meanings of its constituent parts and how they are combined. Compositionality can be thought of as a key ingredient towards making artificial intelligence more like general human intelligence since it enables understanding of highly complex concepts by breaking them down into simpler, more manageable, and modular components. The last couple of years have seen a breathtaking expansion in the research around transfer learning for natural language understanding. BERT (Devlin et al., 2019) has proven to be a highly successful model for learning general, task-agnostic sentence representations that can equal or outperform task-specific ones. Given the strong intuitive connection between compositionality and generalization of representation learning, but the relative difficulty in often quantifying it, our goal is to propose evaluation metrics for compositional understanding of

---

[1] Stanford SCPD student

sentence encoders and evaluate the level of compositional understanding in the current state-of-the-art sentence encoder models.

We propose two new methods to evaluate the compositionality of sentence embedding models. First, we propose a new method called Polarity Sensitivity Scoring (PSS) which measures compositionality via the ability of sentence encoding models to be sensitive to minor perturbations in the input that would flip the sentiment polarity of a sentence. Next, we extend Tree Reconstruction Error (TRE) (Andreas, 2019) to work sentences.

2 Related Work

With the rapid improvement of natural language understanding models in recent years, there has simultaneously been a large increase in research on the nuances and pitfalls of these models, especially in the area of compositionality. Among other methods, measuring performance in classification tasks targeting semantic understanding (Ettinger et al., 2016), lexical composition (Shwartz and Dagan, 2019), synonym substitution (Hupkes et al., 2020), and divergence (Keysers et al., 2020) have all been proposed.

Many researchers have shown evidence that inducing compositionality into deep and shallow models have helped in generalization, data efficiency, and interpretability. Fyshe et al. (2015) evaluates compositionality at the phrase level to make representations more interpretable. Baroni (2020) finds that neural networks are capable of subtle grammar-dependent generalizations, but do not rely on systematic compositional rules. Dessì and Baroni (2019) found that, perhaps counter-intuitively, CNNs were able to significantly outperform LSTMs and GRUs on the more difficult *jump* and *around-right* tasks in the SCAN challenge proposed by Lake and Baroni (2017) and

Proceedings of the 5th Workshop on Representation Learning for NLP (RepL4NLP-2020), pages 185–193
July 9, 2020. ©2020 Association for Computational Linguistics

Loula et al. (2018). However, they still find that CNNs also are not good at learning rule-like compositional generalizations as the mistakes it makes are not systematic and they are evenly spread across different commands.

Stone et al. (2017) explores the compositional properties of deep CNNs for image recognition. Their method quantifies compositionality as the difference in higher layer CNN activations between a network which takes a normal multi-object image as input and masks all activations outside the spatial location of one of the objects and a network which takes as input the same image as above with all other objects except the target object zeroed out. The intuition is that if CNNs are inherently compositional, then the difference in two activations should be zero.

3 Polarity Sensitivity Scoring (PSS)

Our primary contribution is a method we propose is called Polarity Sensitivity Scoring. Here, we posit that a model that has strong compositional understanding can adapt to small changes in the constituent components of a sentence such as sentiment polarity. Generally, the sentiment of a sentence is localized to a small fraction of the words, which can be separated from the overall content of the sentence that is not sentiment bearing. We hypothesize that if a model can accurately detect a sentiment switch when its thematic content remains constant, but only its tonality changes, then it should have a good semantic understanding of the nuances of composition structure. We define the equation for PSS as:

$$PSS = \frac{1}{N} \sum_{n=1}^{N} \mathbb{1}[\hat{y}_s = y_s \wedge \hat{z}_{s'} = z_{s'}]$$

where y_s is the ground truth label for the sentence s and $\hat{y}_s$ is the predicted label produced by a sentiment model trained using the sentence encoding model. Similarly, $z_{s'}$ and $\hat{z}_{s'}$ are the ground truth and predicted labels, respectively, for the sentence s' for which the polarity has been flipped. For PSS, we need sentence pairs which have the same content but differ only in certain sentiment specific attributes. Ideally, we would want human-generated pairs but since that can be cumbersome and expensive we utilize outputs of an off the shelf model for synthetic data generation which generates the sentiment switched sentence. The approach we use was proposed by Li et al. (2018) and the interested reader is encouraged to read the paper to gain a better understanding of the algorithm details. This formula for PSS calculation would be sufficient if the sentiment switching model was perfect, however, this is not the case. To account for this we manually reviewed a subset of examples to come up with a set of rules which removed error-prone switches making our synthetic pairs closer to a gold standard. Details are described in appendix B.

The perturbation-driven nature of PSS might lead one to question whether PSS really captures compositional understanding or is it just a test of the robustness of sentence representations to noise. We believe that, at least with respect to the required compositional understanding to correctly classify sentiment (Socher et al., 2013), it does and might also be more general than that. PSS can actually complement the *consistency score* proposed by Hupkes et al. (2020) which measures substitutivity, one of the five tests for compositionality. While they replace words with their synonyms and expect the same classification, we replace sentiment bearing words and expect the model to accurately reflect this change in sentiment. Since changing a classification label establishes a more direct causal link between change in text and change in label, we believe that our method is better at least for the substitutivity test.

3.1 Experimental Results

We leverage the same dataset used in Li et al. (2018) for our experiments: a sentiment corpus of Yelp Business Reviews. The dataset contains 270K positive examples and 180K negative ones in the train set and an equally balanced 4000-example development set and 1000-example test set. Since our end goal is evaluating compositionality and not developing the most performant sentiment model, we use static hyperparameter configurations (learning rate=2e-5 for BERT and 3e-3 for others) and report test accuracy by combining dev and test sets. For the sentiment switched pairs we directly utilize the 500 reference test pairs released [1]. After the cleaning rules (see appendix) to remove problematic pairs we are left with 353 example pairs for which we have a high degree of confidence that they belong to opposite sentiments. Our PSS metric is therefore calculated on these 353 sentence pairs. If our models predict the correct label for both the

---

[1] https://github.com/rpryzant/delete_retrieve_generate

Encocder Type	Final Layers	Finetune mode	Test Accuracy	PSS	Relative
BERT	Linear	FB	79.2	59.5	75.1
BERT	Linear	FT	81.3	73.7	90.7
ELMo	Linear	FB	75.3	57.2	76.0
ELMo	Linear	FT	75.8	67.9	89.6
ELMo	DNN	FB	77	57.5	74.7
ELMo	DNN	FT	77.2	70	90.7
USE DAN	DNN	FB	75.3	62.3	82.8
USE DAN	DNN	FT	79.6	69.4	87.2
USE DAN	Linear	FB	69.3	49.9	71.9
USE DAN	Linear	FT	78.1	69.1	88.5
USE Transformer	Linear	FB	76.5	65.7	85.9
USE Transformer	Linear	FT	82.3	73.7	89.5
USE Transformer	DNN	FB	78.7	65.7	83.5
USE Transformer	DNN	FT	80.2	69.4	86.5

Table 1: Results from Polarity Sensitivity Scoring (PSS). Linear: Linear projection from sentence embedding to labels. DNN: 2 layer deep neural network. Relative: PSS / Test Accuracy×100. Finetune mode: FT: encoder finetuned, FB: encoder parameters frozen with final layers only trained

positive and negative versions of the sentence, an example gets a score of 1 else 0 and these values are averaged to get the PSS score for a model.

We compare four encoder types: BERT (Devlin et al., 2019), ELMo (Peters et al., 2018), Universal Sentence Encoder (USE) deep averaging network (DAN), and USE Transformer (Cer et al., 2018). For all encoders except BERT, we experiment with different final layer types to isolate impact from the classification layer to the encoding layers: single linear layer (Linear) or 2 layer feedforward deep neural network (DNN) with 500 and 100 units in the first and second layers, respectively. For all encoders, we experiment with the finetuning mode (FT): train the all encoder and classification layers and feature-based mode (FB): freeze the encoder layers and only train the classification layers.

Table 1 shows the results of our polarity sensitivity experiment. Since each encoder has a different sentiment classification performance, we also consider the relative PSS, defined as $(PSS/TestAcc.) \times 100$, which helps us normalize the compositional understanding capability against its task performance.

We observe that BERT FT and USE Transformer FT, both Transformer Vaswani et al. (2017) architectures, are the leading models on absolute PSS and BERT FT and ELMo in DNN FT configuration are joint leaders on relative PSS. The fact that BERT leads in both categories is no surprise given its well known superior performance

on wide-ranging tasks. On absolute PSS alone, ELMo and USE DAN are the least compositional. Given USE DAN's bag of words type architecture this makes sense but is slightly surprising for the ELMo LSTM architecture even though ELMo does better when we normalize by the sentiment classification accuracy. We note that the consistency score of Hupkes et al. (2020) shows quite similar results where the Transformer architecture outperforms both LSTM and CNN architectures substantially. Across the board, models that finetune the sentence encoder decidedly do better in absolute and relative terms than not finetuning which makes sense as encoders should generally be better equipped to pick up compositional generalizations than the classification layers which are the only trainable layers in FB mode. Additionally, comparison of the performance of DNN vs linear classifier types is less conclusive further suggesting that the difference in compositional understanding is most dependent on the sentence encoder versus the classifier chosen.

Since BERT FT is joint best with USE Transformer FT Linear on absolute PSS and they also are both among the top-performing models on test accuracy it validates our key motivation that good compositional understanding contributes towards good downstream performance. However, if we look at when we do not finetune BERT and USE Transformer encoders, we see that even though BERT FB has decent test accuracy, the PSS of BERT FB is 59.5% compared to 65.7% for USE

Transformer FB (linear and DNN). On the surface one would expect that true measurement of raw compositional understanding of a representation must be calculated without encoder fine-tuning however, we must remember that the pre-training mechanism of BERT and USE is quite different. While BERT is completely pre-trained using unsupervised Masked LM and next sentence prediction, USE is also trained using the supervised SNLI dataset (Bowman et al., 2015) which the authors note improves the transfer learning capability of USE. Given that natural language inference is a task that would be very hard to do well without some compositional understanding, it stands to reason that the pre-training phase of USE provides some implicit compositional advantages. This is equally valid for other types of models and so for accurate comparisons across models, we must default to FT mode.

Given that the above results correlate well with our *a priori* expectations based on both theoretical and empirical knowledge about these encoders, we feel confident that absolute and relative PSS can be good estimates of compositional understanding of sentence representation models.

4 Tree Reconstruction Error (TRE)

TRE (Andreas, 2019) measures the vector space distance between a target vector representation produced by an encoding model and a vector representation that is generated from compositions of its primitive units. In the case of sentences, the target representation is produced by a sentence encoding model and the primitives are generally the words in the sentence. The compositions are represented by syntactic parses of the sentences where at every subtree, the representations of the child nodes are composed using some composition function. The primitive representations (word vectors) are trained using RMSProp, fixing the sentence representation and compositional functions, to minimize the cosine distance between the sentence encoding and the output of the compositional function applied to primitives.

We aim to extend TRE [2] from phrases to sentences. Unfortunately, there are not many open source datasets with human-labeled compositionality scores for sentences that we could find. Therefore, using the Stanford Sentiment Treebank (SST) we propose two automated methods to generate ground truth compositionality labels for the SST dataset by using phrase-level sentiment labels in SST.

4.1 Tree Impurity

We start by traversing the constituency parsed tree of each SST sentence and collect the labels of all sub-components and phrases within the parse tree. To compute the Tree Impurity, we take the absolute difference between the root label and the average of all phrase labels within a tree. To understand why this metric is meaningful, let's consider the following example sentence from SST:

"A coda in every sense, The Pinochet Case splits time between a minute-by-minute account of the British court's extradition chess game and the regime's talking-head survivors."

As seen in Figure 3 (appendix), the phrase labels of the two children of the root and all of their children have a label of 2 (neutral). However, at the top, the root level label is 4 (highly positive). This constitutes an example of a sentence with a high degree of compositionality i.e. the overall meaning of a sentence is not just the meaning of the components but also how they are composed.

4.2 Weighted Node Switching (WNS)

Tree Impurity loses crucial information regarding the compositionality within subtrees. Weighted node switching seeks to counteract this by introducing more local compositional information. Here, for every subtree where both children have a sentiment label, we calculate the absolute difference between the sentiment label of the root of the subtree and the average sentiment labels of its children. To introduce global information, we weight this label difference by the height of the root node of the subtree, wherein nodes closer to the tree root are given higher weights than those closer to the leaves. These weighted absolute differences are then averaged to get a measure of the overall compositionality of the entire sentence.

Both methods are generalizable to subtrees whose roots have multiple children and so can be used with constituency and dependency parses. Going forward in our experiments we solely use WNS as our approximation of compositionality scores given that it is more linguistically robust than Tree Impurity.

---

[2] https://github.com/jacobandreas/tre

Encoder Type	SST Correlation
BERT	-0.1997
ELMo	-0.344
USE DAN	-0.485
USE Transformer	-0.168

Table 2: Rank correlations.
* p-value indicated that they are uncorrelated

4.3 Experimental Results

We use SST for compositionality evaluation with TRE. Using TRE, we evaluated the compositionality of sentence representations from BERT (Devlin et al., 2019), ELMo (Peters et al., 2018), Universal Sentence Encoder (USE) deep averaging network (DAN) and USE Transformer (Cer et al., 2018). The lower the value of TRE, the more compositional a given phrase or sentence is. Since we hypothesize that WNS is positively correlated with the degree of compositionality, then the more negatively correlated WNS is with TRE, the more compositional the sentence representation is overall. We evaluate compositionality using the rank correlation between TRE and the WNS compositionality scores.

In Table 2, we notice that the Spearman rank correlations are all negative, indicating that all the sentence representations encode some level of compositionality in their sentence representations. The more negative the correlation, the more compositional the sentence representation. By this metric, USE Transformer seems to be the least compositional while USE DAN seems to be the most compositional.

The under-performance of BERT, at least as measured by compositionality, is quite surprising given the widespread success of BERT on a multitude of downstream tasks and also the PSS metric we proposed and tested above. Given that our results are dependent on machine-generated ground truth compositionality scores, more investigation is crucial.

5 Discussion

Even though our observations from PSS and TRE approaches are not directly correlated, we observe certain consistencies and see that Transformer architectures are different compared to others. While they are more compositional as measured by PSS, they appear to be less compositional according to TRE. We believe this could be because the two methods are quantifying different kinds of compositionality. Pelletier (2011) described two different senses of compositionality; ontological and functional. TRE seems to measure more of the former since it, by nature of its definition, tries to make combination of primitives equal to the whole while PSS measures functional compositionality as it calculates a type of sensitivity which only a model with good compositional understanding can grasp. Furthermore, phrases that are similar in vector space can have opposite sentiment. For example, the *warm* and *cool* could be close in vector space, but could have a high impact on WNS.

In the current state, we believe that PSS is a more mature method to estimate compositionality for sentences especially since our extension of TRE to sentences depends on the efficacy of WNS as a good estimate of sentence compositionality. Furthermore, even if we did not use WNS and had humans tag sentences with scores for compositionality, this would still be quite hard to quantify even for humans given how subjective it can be. Expert labelers would be needed for such labeling tasks. However, looking at a positive sentence and switching its sentiment to negative or vice-versa is a much easier task for a human, so dataset creation and evaluation for PSS is much more practical.

6 Conclusion

We explored two approaches to measure the compositionality of sentence representations. Our primary contribution was proposing polarity switching as a possible measure of compositionality which correlated well with empirical results and our knowledge about inductive biases in sentence encoders. We also extended TRE as proposed in Andreas (2019) beyond bigram phrases to sentence representations. To do this, we needed to come up with a heuristic approximation of a compositional score for a sentence which we did by using weighted node switching.

7 Acknowledgments

This paper originated from our class project for Stanford's CS224U class. We would like to thank our project mentor, Ignacio Cases, for his support and guidance. This work is partly supported by the NSF Graduate Research Fellowship under Grant No. DGE − 1656518.

References

Jacob Andreas. 2019. Measuring compositionality in representation learning. In *International Conference on Learning Representations*.

Marco Baroni. 2020. Linguistic generalization and compositionality in modern artificial neural networks. *Philosophical Transactions of the Royal Society B: Biological Sciences*, 375(1791):20190307.

Samuel R. Bowman, Gabor Angeli, Christopher Potts, and Christopher D. Manning. 2015. A large annotated corpus for learning natural language inference. In *Proceedings of the 2015 Conference on Empirical Methods in Natural Language Processing*, pages 632–642, Lisbon, Portugal. Association for Computational Linguistics.

Daniel Cer, Yinfei Yang, Sheng-yi Kong, Nan Hua, Nicole Limtiaco, Rhomni St. John, Noah Constant, Mario Guajardo-Cespedes, Steve Yuan, Chris Tar, Brian Strope, and Ray Kurzweil. 2018. Universal sentence encoder for English. In *Proceedings of the 2018 Conference on Empirical Methods in Natural Language Processing: System Demonstrations*, pages 169–174, Brussels, Belgium. Association for Computational Linguistics.

Alexis Conneau, Douwe Kiela, Holger Schwenk, Loïc Barrault, and Antoine Bordes. 2017. Supervised learning of universal sentence representations from natural language inference data. *Proceedings of the 2017 Conference on Empirical Methods in Natural Language Processing*.

Roberto Dessì and Marco Baroni. 2019. Cnns found to jump around more skillfully than rnns: Compositional generalization in seq2seq convolutional networks. *arXiv preprint arXiv:1905.08527*.

Jacob Devlin, Ming-Wei Chang, Kenton Lee, and Kristina Toutanova. 2019. BERT: Pre-training of deep bidirectional transformers for language understanding. In *Proceedings of the 2019 Conference of the North American Chapter of the Association for Computational Linguistics: Human Language Technologies, Volume 1 (Long and Short Papers)*, pages 4171–4186, Minneapolis, Minnesota. Association for Computational Linguistics.

Allyson Ettinger, Ahmed Elgohary, and Philip Resnik. 2016. Probing for semantic evidence of composition by means of simple classification tasks. In *Proceedings of the 1st Workshop on Evaluating Vector-Space Representations for NLP*, pages 134–139, Berlin, Germany. Association for Computational Linguistics.

Alona Fyshe, Leila Wehbe, Partha P Talukdar, Brian Murphy, and Tom M Mitchell. 2015. A compositional and interpretable semantic space. In *Proceedings of the 2015 Conference of the North American Chapter of the Association for Computational Linguistics: Human Language Technologies*, pages 32–41.

Dieuwke Hupkes, Verna Dankers, Mathijs Mul, and Elia Bruni. 2020. Compositionality decomposed: How do neural networks generalise? *Journal of Artificial Intelligence Research*, 67:757–795.

Daniel Keysers, Nathanael Schärli, Nathan Scales, Hylke Buisman, Daniel Furrer, Sergii Kashubin, Nikola Momchev, Danila Sinopalnikov, Lukasz Stafiniak, Tibor Tihon, Dmitry Tsarkov, Xiao Wang, Marc van Zee, and Olivier Bousquet. 2020. Measuring compositional generalization: A comprehensive method on realistic data. In *International Conference on Learning Representations*.

Brenden M Lake and Marco Baroni. 2017. Generalization without systematicity: On the compositional skills of sequence-to-sequence recurrent networks. *arXiv preprint arXiv:1711.00350*.

Juncen Li, Robin Jia, He He, and Percy Liang. 2018. Delete, retrieve, generate: a simple approach to sentiment and style transfer. In *Proceedings of the 2018 Conference of the North American Chapter of the Association for Computational Linguistics: Human Language Technologies, Volume 1 (Long Papers)*, pages 1865–1874, New Orleans, Louisiana. Association for Computational Linguistics.

Joao Loula, Marco Baroni, and Brenden M Lake. 2018. Rearranging the familiar: Testing compositional generalization in recurrent networks. *arXiv preprint arXiv:1807.07545*.

Jeff Pelletier. 2011. *Compositionality*. Oxford University Press.

Matthew Peters, Mark Neumann, Mohit Iyyer, Matt Gardner, Christopher Clark, Kenton Lee, and Luke Zettlemoyer. 2018. Deep contextualized word representations. In *Proceedings of the 2018 Conference of the North American Chapter of the Association for Computational Linguistics: Human Language Technologies, Volume 1 (Long Papers)*, pages 2227–2237, New Orleans, Louisiana. Association for Computational Linguistics.

Vered Shwartz and Ido Dagan. 2019. Still a pain in the neck: Evaluating text representations on lexical composition. *Transactions of the Association for Computational Linguistics*, 7:403–419.

Richard Socher, Alex Perelygin, Jean Wu, Jason Chuang, Christopher D Manning, Andrew Ng, and Christopher Potts. 2013. Recursive deep models for semantic compositionality over a sentiment treebank. In *Proceedings of the 2013 conference on empirical methods in natural language processing*, pages 1631–1642.

Austin Stone, Huayan Wang, Michael Stark, Yi Liu, D. Scott Phoenix, and Dileep George. 2017. Teaching compositionality to cnns. *2017 IEEE Conference on Computer Vision and Pattern Recognition (CVPR)*.

Ashish Vaswani, Noam Shazeer, Niki Parmar, Jakob Uszkoreit, Llion Jones, Aidan N Gomez, Łukasz Kaiser, and Illia Polosukhin. 2017. Attention is all you need. In *Advances in neural information processing systems*, pages 5998–6008.

A Encoder Models

For BERT, we use Bert as a service[3] with parameter weights of BERTbase from Google Research[4]. For ELMo, we use AllenNLP[5] for TRE and TensorflowHub [6] for PSS. For Universal Sentence Encoder, we used TensorflowHub[7]

A.1 BERT

This model architecture is a multi-layer bidirectional Transformer (Vaswani et al., 2017). BERT was able to outperform the previous state-of-the-art on the GLUE Benchmark by 7%. The input representation can be an individual sequence or a sequence pair, such as a sentence or question/answer pairs, respectively. The final embeddings are a combination of token embeddings and special classification and segmentation tokens. For our experiments, we take the average of token embeddings to obtain the sentence embeddings. BERT was pre-trained using two novel unsupervised learning tasks: Masked Language Model (LM) and Next Sentence Prediction. BERT is that it is trained in a bidirectional manner, while other language models can only be trained using one direction at a time since being able to see the next word in the classical setting trivializes the task. In Masked LM, a certain percentage of the input tokens are masked at random, and the model is asked to predict the masked words. This allows for the preservation of a learning objective, because the transformer's encoder will not know which words it will need to predict in the future or which words have been replaced by random words, so it is forced to keep a contextual representation of every word in the vocabulary.

A.2 ELMo

ELMo (Embeddings from Language Models) vectors are derived from a bidirectional LSTM that is trained with a coupled language model (LM). We learn a weighted linear combination of the vectors stacked above each input word for each end task. Since ELMo generates three layers of embedding outputs for each word, we leverage the common pooling strategy of averaging across the layers to create a final word-level representation. Sentence-level embeddings are created by simply averaging the final word-level vectors.

A.3 Universal Sentence Encoder

We use two models of the Universal Sentence Encoder: one where the encoder is a deep averaging network (DAN) (Conneau et al., 2017) and one where the encoder is a Transformer (Vaswani et al., 2017). The embeddings are trained on tasks that demand to extract information beyond the word-level. Both models are trained with the aim of dynamically accommodating a wide variety of natural language understanding tasks. The input is variable-length English text and the output is a 512-dimensional vector.

B Synthetic data considerations

The formula for PSS calculation would be sufficient if we were fully confident that our sentiment switching model was always 100% accurate. However, as we know from Li et al. (2018), this is not the case. The polarity switching model at times generates an exact duplicate of its provided input and at other times only removes certain sentiment specific words. For the former case, it is not fair to expect any model to switch polarity, so we remove such examples. Furthermore, we also remove examples where the model only deletes (does not add) sentiment specific keywords as on manual evaluation, the model more often would remove a word/phrase that would not fully preserve the content and only at times removals resulted in negative sentiment switching to positive (e.g. removing "not"). Therefore, we only consider examples where the model adds some words in its generation that were not present in its input. Given that the model adds positive words (for a negative to positive switch), it is much more likely that if a sentiment classifier gets such an example switch wrong (cannot detect negative to positive switch), it is more a function of the sentiment classifier and therefore the sentence encoder and not an error of the data generator.

---

[3]`https://github.com/hanxiao/bert-as-service`

[4]`https://github.com/google-research/bert`

[5]`https://allennlp.org/`

[6]`https://tensorflow.org/hub`

[7]`https://tensorflow.org/hub`

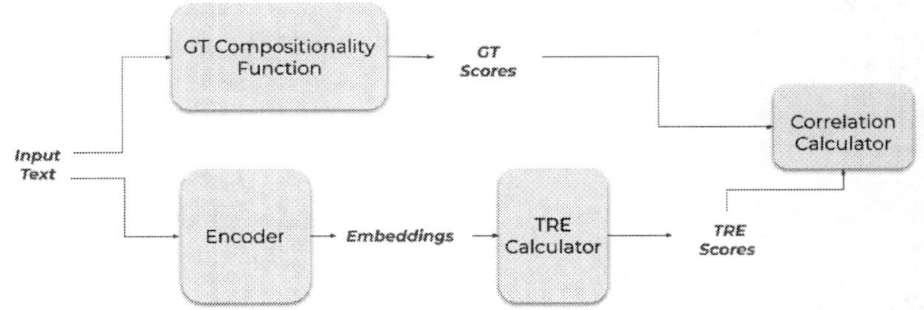

Figure 1: Experimental workflow design: TRE

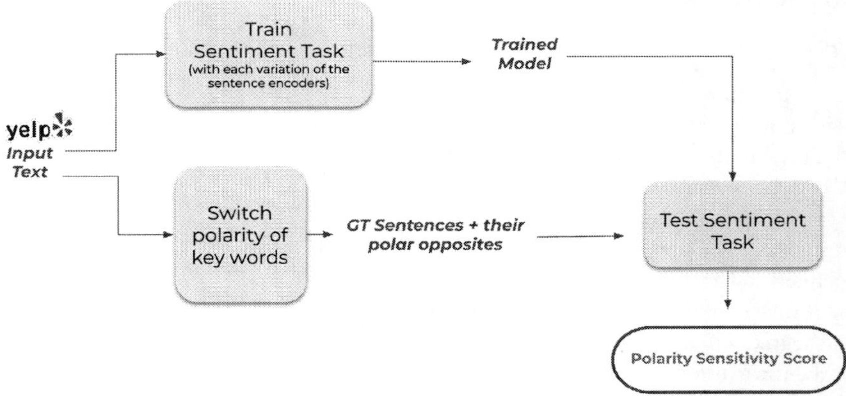

Figure 2: Experimental workflow design: Polarity Sensitivity Scoring

C Effects of the direction of sentiment switch

Given the way PSS is defined, it does not depend on the direction of the sentiment switch. As long as our ground truth sentiment label before and after switching is accurate, PSS does not differentiate between positive to negative or negative to positive switch. As mentioned above, the only source of sensitivity to the polarity switching direction comes from the sentiment switching model. Li et al. (2018) does not highlight any major differences in the direction.

Original Sentence (Negative)	Generated Sentence (Positive)
so , no treatment and no medication to help me deal with my condition . failure	so good , honest treatment and easy to help me deal with my condition .
at this location the service was terrible .	at this location the service was great .
overcooked so badly that it was the consistency of canned tuna fish .	so good that it was the best consistency of tuna fish .

Table 3: Examples of sentences output by the Polarity Switching Model.

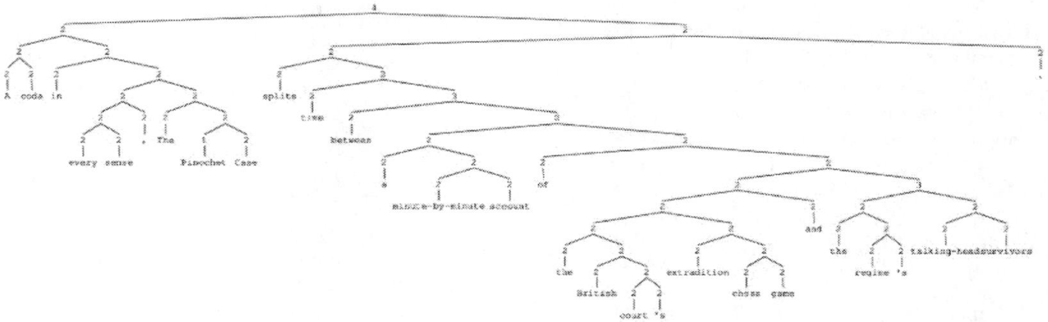

Figure 3: Examples of a sentence sentiment parse tree. The Tree Impurity metric for compositionality gives a somewhat high score of 1.95 while Weighted Node Switching gives it a lower score of 0.37. The higher score TI score is likely due to high numbers of label 1 and 2 nodes, contributing most to the overall average, which is quite different from the root node of 4. WNS, however, considers more local compositionality information which shows that most of the subtrees are not very compositional, that coupled with the overall large quantity of those subtrees, leads to the lower WNS. Additionally, WNS brings in global information via its weighting scheme which more correctly gives higher weights to when local node switches have a sentence level effect.

Sentence	TI	WNS
If Steven Soderbergh 's ' Solaris ' is a failure it is a glorious failure	2.51	1.65
A sober and affecting chronicle of the leveling effect of loss .	0.0	0.23
Cool ?	0.33	2.5
Nothing is black and white .	0.0	0.0

Table 4: Examples of sentences and their ground truth compositionality scores via both proposed metrics: Weighted Node Switching (WNS) and Tree Impurity (TI) methods. Higher scores equate to higher compositionality of the sentence. These examples represent the far ends of the spectrum on on method or the other, as 2.51 is the highest score in TI and 2.5 is the highest score in WNS, and 0.0 is the lowest possible compositionality score for both methods. One of the most telling examples of WNS's superiority over TI can be show in sentence three. Adding a "?" to "Cool" completely changes the tone of the sentence; WNS captures that nuance where TI struggles.

Supertagging with CCG primitives

Aditya Bhargava   **Gerald Penn**
Department of Computer Science
University of Toronto
Toronto, ON, Canada M5S 3G4
{aditya,gpenn}@cs.toronto.edu

Abstract

In CCG and other highly lexicalized grammars, supertagging a sentence's words with their lexical categories is a critical step for efficient parsing. Because of the high degree of lexicalization in these grammars, the lexical categories can be very complex. Existing approaches to supervised CCG supertagging treat the categories as atomic units, even when the categories are not simple; when they encounter words with categories unseen during training, their guesses are accordingly unsophisticated.

In this paper, we make use of the primitives and operators that constitute the lexical categories of categorial grammars. Instead of opaque labels, we treat lexical categories themselves as linear sequences. We present an LSTM-based model that replaces standard word-level classification with prediction of a sequence of primitives, similarly to LSTM decoders. Our model obtains state-of-the-art word accuracy for single-task English CCG supertagging, increases parser coverage and F_1, and is able to produce novel categories. Analysis shows a synergistic effect between this decomposed view and incorporation of prediction history.

1   Introduction

Highly lexicalized grammars, such as lexicalized tree-adjoining grammar (LTAG) and combinatory categorial grammar (CCG), have very large sets of possible lexical categories. Where most phrase-structure and dependency grammars have lexical category sets numbering in the tens for English (Taylor et al., 2003), LTAG and CCG have sets numbering in the hundreds or thousands (Joshi and Srinivas, 1994; Clark, 2002). The large number of possible labels for each word can make the search space for the syntactic tree of the sentence

Category	Count
N	206,312
N/N	152,508
NP_{nb}/N	83,377
(NP\NP)/NP	43,700
((S\NP)\(S\NP))/NP	22,189
conj	20,170
NP	19,749
PP/NP	17,199
(S\NP)\(S\NP)	16,146
((S\NP)\(S\NP))/((S\NP)\(S\NP))	3,820
(((S\NP)\(S\NP))\((S\NP)\(S\NP)))/NP	325

Figure 1: Some sample CCG lexical categories from the CCGbank training set. The first nine are the most frequent non-punctuation categories. The final two are in the top 100 (out of 1285) and illustrate the capacity for syntactic richness and variety in complexity.

intractably large; narrowing the set of viable lexical categories per word is therefore an important step in efficient parsing for such grammars (Clark and Curran, 2007; Lewis et al., 2016). As the tags are much more complex and informative than part-of-speech (POS) tags, tagging the words with these more complex categories is called **supertagging**.

The large number of lexical categories comes from the high degree of complexity that the categories can have. When grammars have small tag sets, the bulk of the work in developing or learning a grammar comes from deciding how to combine the tags and their words. Categorial grammars instead have fewer combination rules, requiring the lexical categories to support much greater syntactic richness; see Figure 1 for some sample categories.

Existing approaches to supervised supertagging operate in the same manner as POS taggers: as a word classifiers, predicting the correct tag from a fixed set. This is relatively straightforward for POS tags: there are relatively few possibilities as the tags are simple–*e.g.*, it is not immediately apparent if or how *VBD* is more complex than *NNP*. By con-

Proceedings of the 5th Workshop on Representation Learning for NLP (RepL4NLP-2020), pages 194–204
July 9, 2020. ©2020 Association for Computational Linguistics

trast, CCG categories have varying complexities and are clearly not atomic units; they are composed from a much smaller vocabulary of primitives.

In this paper, we challenge the usual treatment of CCG supertagging as large-tagset POS tagging, instead treating lexical categories as the complex units that they are. We present a model for CCG supertagging that replaces traditional whole-category prediction with the prediction of their composing primitives. In addition to addressing the incongruity between POS tags and CCG categories, this allows for the generation of new categories that do not occur in the training set, a necessary property for handling the long tail of syntactic phenomena.

We treat supertags as linear sequences, enabling us to employ LSTM decoders to autoregressively predict CCG primitives in sequence. On CCGbank, our model outperforms a bidirectional LSTM classification baseline on word accuracy, parser F_1, and parser coverage, establishing a new state-of-the-art for single-task English CCG supertagging.

Analysis of our model and results shows that our non-atomic view of CCG lexical categories enables more effective incorporation of model prediction history than is the case with atomic category classification. Our model can also generate new categories that it has not seen during training, and even manages to correctly label some words with such out-of-vocabulary (OOV) categories. To the best of our knowledge, our model is the first fully-supervised CCG supertagger that constructs lexical categories from primitive types, and the first to be able to produce OOV categories. Our work presents both a more appropriate view of the problem and establishes a strong baseline for CCG supertagging according to this view.

2 Background and motivation

Supertagging is quite different from POS tagging. CCG lexical categories are composed from a fixed set of more **primitive** units; as a result, CCG supertagging has a much larger set of possible tags than does POS tagging—an open set, in fact. Where the Penn Treebank (PTB) has 48^1 POS tags (Taylor et al., 2003), CCGbank has 1322 lexical categories (Hockenmaier and Steedman, 2007). Selecting from a much larger set is more difficult, of course, and therefore, POS tagging accuracy is substantially higher than for CCG supertagging. Recent POS tagging work has reached up to 98%

accuracy and above, depending on the language and corpus, *without* the use of pre-trained embeddings or other incorporation of external corpora (Plank et al., 2016). English CCG supertagging, meanwhile, has only recently broken past 96%, accuracy and that too with a heavy dependence on pre-trained embeddings, external corpora, and/or multi-task training (Clark et al., 2018).

Given these substantial differences, the complex, structured nature of CCG lexical categories warrants further investigation for supertagging. We see two primary advantages in doing so. First, as noted by Baldridge (2008) and Garrette et al. (2014), a compositional view of lexical categories can provide strong information about surrounding categories. For example, if a word has category S/NP, then it is likely that there is a primitive NP type *somewhere* else in the sentence, whether as a simple category or as part of a complex one.

Second, treating CCG categories as atomic makes it impossible to fully tag all new data, since new, rare categories may be encountered during inference. Such rare categories are not necessarily spurious; over the whole CCGbank, Hockenmaier and Steedman (2007) note that while some of the once-occurring categories "are due to noise or annotation errors, most are in fact required for certain constructions."[2] Admittedly, novel categories (*i.e.*, those not occurring in the training set) are rare in CCGbank: in the standard splits, 0.06% of word tokens in the development set and 0.04% in the test set are tagged with a category that does not occur in the training set. But since an incorrect lexical category can impair the parsability of a full sentence, it is more appropriate to consider the number of affected *sentences*, which is 0.9% for both the development and test sets.[3] Work on CCG parsers has noted their high sensitivity to supertagging accuracy (*e.g.*, Clark and Curran, 2004; Lewis et al., 2016), so such cases should not be ignored. And unlike typical classification scenarios, out-of-vocabulary lexical categories are not different in kind from in-vocabulary ones; they are composed from the same units using the same rules, suggesting that OOV categories can, in principle, be treated in a concordant manner.

---

[1]Twelve of which are for punctuation.

[2]They provide relative pronouns in pied-piping constructions and verbs which take expletive subjects as examples; we found lengthy adjunction chains to contribute as well.

[3]These proportions are even higher for out-of-domain data (Rimell and Clark, 2008).

3 Related work

While our focus in this paper is on CCG supertagging, it is worth noting that the supertagging task originates in the context of LTAG (Joshi and Srinivas, 1994; Bangalore and Joshi, 1999), which also has highly complex lexical categories. Supertagging is important for efficient parsing in such grammars as it helps narrow the search space for the parse (Clark and Curran, 2004).

Despite the complexity captured in supertags, the vast majority of existing approaches treat CCG lexical categories as atomic units for prediction, ignoring their varying complexities and structured nature. Effectively, at each time step of the input sentence, the model must decide which of a fixed set of CCG categories is the best choice. This category-classification approach is the same as for POS tagging, and indeed, existing supertagging models are very similar to (if not the same as) POS tagging models in structure.

Early work for CCG supertagging relied on maximum-entropy models with hand-specified features, a limited set of possible categories, and tag dictionaries that tracked allowed categories for frequent words based on the training data (Clark, 2002; Clark and Curran, 2004, 2007). Recent work relies heavily on word embeddings: they allow better handling of out-of-vocabulary words and decrease reliance on part-of-speech tags, where imperfect accuracy can be a detriment for the supertagger. Lewis and Steedman (2014) used externally-trained embeddings (Turian et al., 2010) combined with suffix and capitalization features in a simple feed-forward neural network as well as a CRF; they also allowed words to be tagged with categories with which they did not co-occur in the training data. Xu et al. (2015) applied the same embeddings and features in a standard Elman RNN (Elman, 1990); they later improved their model by making it bidirectional (Xu et al., 2016). Lewis et al. (2016) replaced the Elman RNNs with two-layer bidirectional LSTMs, taking advantage of the LSTM units' ability to retain information over time (Hochreiter and Schmidhuber, 1997), and incorporated a data-augmentation technique as well.

Vaswani et al. (2016) used a single-layer bidirectional LSTM but dropped all hand-specified features, removed the limit on the categories that the model could produce, used custom in-domain word embeddings, and included a language model–style LSTM over the output lexical categories that allowed the model to condition its predicted tag at time t on the previously-predicted lexical category at time $t - 1$. In addition to improving word accuracy, this latter addition drastically increased the number of tagged sentences that were parsable, even in variations that hurt word accuracy.

The current state-of-the-art result in CCG supertagging was achieved by Clark et al. (2018). Their model consisted of a two-layer bidirectional LSTM with GloVe word embeddings (Pennington et al., 2014) supplemented by the output of a character-level convolutional neural network. Their approach involved training additional "auxiliary" prediction modules on top of the same LSTM on an additional, unlabelled corpus (Chelba et al., 2014). These auxiliary modules were given an incomplete view of the input (*e.g.*, only words to the left) and trained to predict the same label that the primary prediction module predicted.

If we consider other grammars, (Kogkalidis et al., 2019) presented a type-logical grammar for Dutch and a supertagging approach that relied on primitive units. While their approach yielded improvement in word accuracy, the overall accuracy was substantially lower than with CCG supertagging; furthermore, the grammar's type system was so different that it is difficult to draw conclusions about applicability to other grammars.[4] In order to see some consideration of the composed structure of *CCG* lexical categories, we must alter our task scope somewhat. Garrette et al. (2014), following earlier work (Baldridge, 2008), applied a Bayesian model with grammar-informed priors for supertagging where only a tag dictionary and raw, unlabelled text was made available. Their model included a generative model for categories as well as the notion of *combinability*, preferring tag sequences where adjacent words could be combined via CCG rules. Similarly, work in CCG grammar induction has involved some basic consideration of how CCG categories are constructed so that that a grammar could be built using EM (Bisk and Hockenmaier, 2012) or hierarchical Dirichlet processes (Bisk and Hockenmaier, 2013). Despite these applications, consideration of CCG primitives has yet to make its way to supervised supertagging approaches; we aim to fill that gap.

---

[4]Their grammar had 5700 unique types for a corpus of 65k sentences; categories were constructed from 30 atomic types, corresponding to POS tags or phrasal categories, and 22 *non-directional* binary connectives, corresponding to dependency labels.

4 Method and model

Despite the potential advantages discussed above in Section 2, it is unclear *a priori* whether supertagging with primitive units is more or less difficult than standard, whole-category classification. While the output vocabulary becomes drastically smaller, the output sequences are longer and must be arranged correctly. One of our aims in this paper is to establish a baseline for this approach to supertagging and evaluate its difficulty as a task in comparison to the usual methods.

4.1 Linearization

Lexical categories in categorial grammars are composed of a relatively small, fixed set of primitive types (S, NP, etc.) with indications for precedence/ grouping (parentheses) and ordering (forward and backward slashes). In this paper, we approach the generation of CCG lexical categories as the prediction of a linear sequence of decomposed symbols. We use a simple linearization scheme: we split each lexical category label into tokens, using parentheses and slashes as delimiters. We keep the delimiters as units in the output sequence as well, as they crucially define the structure of the category. This linearization method yields an output vocabulary of size 38 (including parentheses and slashes); many of these are feature-typed versions of plain primitive types; *e.g.*, S_{to} and N_{num}. We refer to all units resulting from this decomposition, whether they are primitive types, slashes, or parentheses, as primitives for brevity.

It may seem difficult to try to learn to predict a sequence such as $\{(, S_{\text{dcl}}, \backslash, NP,), /, NP\}$ consistently and correctly, or to produce sequences in general that are well-formed. Any model attempting this will have to implicitly learn the rules for constructing lexical categories from primitives, such as the balancing of parentheses, or that primitive types cannot occur directly adjacent to one another and must be joined with a slash. But recent work suggests that this is not an unreasonable ask: Vinyals et al. (2015) used a similarly simple linearization scheme to convert a constituent parse tree into a sequence predictable by a linear decoder. The model did produce malformed parses on occasion, such as by forgetting to close open parentheses, but in general, it was able to perform near or above the state-of-the-art at the time, depending on how much data were used for training.

4.2 Decoding sequences of primitives

The most recent, highest-performing supertaggers are all based on bidirectional LSTM architectures. At each time step, the forward and backward LSTM outputs are combined and fed through a softmax layer to produce a distribution over categories. In order to construct a supertagger that works at the level of primitives, we propose a model that replaces the softmax prediction layer with a separate LSTM that predicts primitives in a manner similar to the decoder in RNN encoder-decoder architectures (Cho et al., 2014; Sutskever et al., 2014), or to how text is generated from neural language models.

In encoder-decoder LSTM models, an encoder LSTM is run over the input sequence. The final LSTM cell is used to initialize the decoder's LSTM cell, after which the decoder is trained to predict the output sequence. During training, the decoder receives as input the correct output for time $t - 1$, and asked to predict the output for time t. During inference, the model makes its predictions autoregressively, since the correct previous output is unknown at test time. Output sequences are padded with [START] and [STOP] symbols: the former allows the model to learn a distribution over initial output symbols, as well as providing a means to trigger the output sequence prediction process (*e.g.*, after an input sentence has been read by the encoder); the latter is how the decoder indicates its completion of the current sequence.

Standard use cases for encoder-decoder models, such as machine translation, have the property that the output sequence lengths are not easily determinable from the input sequence lengths; nor is there an easy, strictly monotonic correspondence between input and output tokens. The usual application of encoder-decoder models handles this discrepancy by mostly separating the encoding and decoding parts of the model, leaving them connected only at their ends (*i.e.*, via the copying of the encoder's hidden state to the decoder's).

A naive application of encoder-decoder models to supertagging would simply output the sequence of categories (or primitives, in our case) for a sentence, after having encoded the entire input. For supertagging, this would be less than ideal. If one were to treat the sequence of categories as the target output sequence, there would be a long path through the network from the input word to the output supertag. One could remedy this with atten-

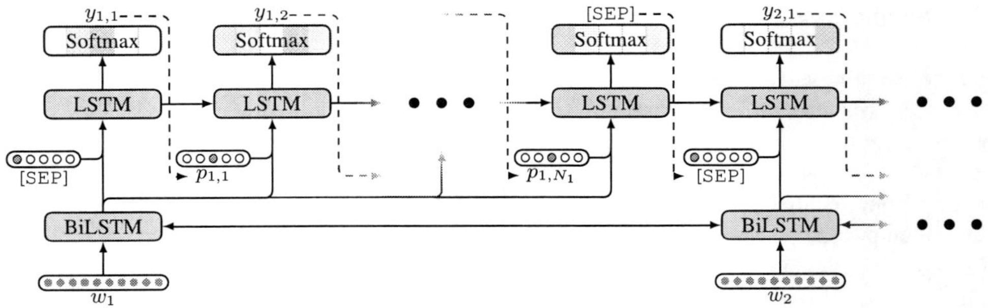

Figure 2: Our supertagging model. Where traditional models would classify an entire category for each word w_i at a time, we decode a sequence of primitives $y_{i,1}, \ldots, y_{i,N_i}$. The BiLSTM forward/backward combination layer is omitted for brevity.

tion mechanisms, but since there is a known and direct correspondence between a given encoder step and the output time steps, it is simpler to link the encoder output to the decoder directly.[5]

Our model, illustrated in Figure 2, consists of a bidirectional LSTM over the input sentence words, a feed-forward layer to combine and project the two LSTM directions, and finally by a unidirectional LSTM to produce sequences of primitives.[6] We refer to the bidirectional (base) LSTM as the encoder and the unidirectional primitive LSTM as the decoder to help differentiate the two, even though our use isn't exactly the same as in standard encoder-decoder models. Instead of initializing the decoder's cell with an encoder's final cell state, we directly use the encoder's output as inputs to the decoder, concatenated with the primitive from the previous time step.[7] During training, it is known which primitives correspond to which words, so aligning the encoder outputs to the decoder inputs is straightforward. During inference, we maintain a pointer i to select the relevant encoder output, initialized to $i = 1$. Then, whenever the decoder predicts the end of the current word's category, i is incremented so that the next decoder step gets the correct encoder output; decoding is stopped when the decoder predicts the end of the last word's category. Since one word's [STOP] symbol indicates the next word's [START] symbol, we combine the two symbols into a single [SEP] symbol, which

can be interpreted as a word boundary marker.

Importantly, we do not reset the model state between words. This enables the decoder to maintain a memory of the primitives (and, by extension, categories) previously predicted in the sentence.

5 Experimental setup

5.1 Data

As is standard, we train our model on sections 2–22 of CCGbank (Hockenmaier and Steedman, 2005), keep section 0 for development and tuning, and evaluate on section 23. As required for decoding, we decompose the categories for each word, inserting the [SEP] token at word boundaries.

To represent the input words at the lowest level of our model, we use the (frozen) 5.5B ELMo embeddings (Peters et al., 2018). Because ELMo embeddings are cased and character-based, we need very little preprocessing of the input data: we convert all "*n't*" tokens to "'*t*" and append "*n*" to the preceding token, unless it is "*can*" or "*won*"; we convert the bracket tokens to their original characters (*e.g.*, "*-LRB-*" to "(", etc.); and we replace "\/" and "*" with "/" and "*" respectively. These steps are solely to more closely match what the ELMo model saw during its training. The inputs are otherwise untouched. There is also no need for a separate token for unknown words. Comparing previous work indicates that ELMo (Clark et al., 2018) drastically outperforms GloVe (Wu et al., 2017) and even custom WSJ-trained word embeddings (Vaswani et al., 2016); we also observed this difference ourselves during early development.

5.2 Evaluation

In order to control for minor implementation differences, we implement a baseline classification-

---

[5]Our initial (non-exhaustive) tests found no benefit to adding attention to our model, instead serving only to increase memory usage and slow training down.

[6]We stick with LSTMs, as with previous work, in order to conduct a well-controlled comparison.

[7]We did experiment with priming the decoder's initial cell state; our tests found this to yield a lower word accuracy compared to including the encoder output in the decoder input, and there was no benefit to doing both.

based bidirectional LSTM supertagger. This model is the same as ours shown in Figure 2, but replaces our decoder LSTM with a softmax layer, producing one category prediction per word. All recent supertagging work has been based on this architecture, with minor variations. We refer to the baseline as **BiLSTM** and our model as **PrimDecoder**.

Since our decoder can maintain a history of previous outputs, it may be better able to produce a sequence of supertags that form a parsable sentence, even if it makes mistakes on individual words. Therefore, in addition to the usual word accuracy and parser labelled F_1, we also measure parser coverage; we use the Java version of the C&C parser (Clark et al., 2015) to parse the sentences with our predicted supertags and gold part-of-speech tags. Coverage denotes the percentage of sentences for which the parser yields a complete parse, even if the derivation is not exactly correct; it therefore serves as a measure of how well the supertagging model is learning to be syntagmatically consistent, according to the rules of the relevant grammar. Lastly, since our model has the ability to generate arbitrary tags, we additionally measure word accuracy on word tokens tagged with OOV categories. Since the parser cannot handle OOV categories, we instead give it the predicted tag from the baseline in the cases where our model generates novel tags.

5.3 Model and training details

All layers in our models other than the softmax layer use size 512. Our LSTMs use standard LSTM activations (sigmoid for the gates, tanh for the state) and we use ReLU activations (Nair and Hinton, 2010) for the layer that combines the forward and backward encoder LSTMs. ReLU layer weights are initialized according to He et al. (2015), LSTM recurrent weights according to Saxe et al. (2013), and all other weights according to Glorot and Bengio (2010). We apply variational recurrent dropout (Gal and Ghahramani, 2016) throughout our model[8], including on the embeddings, except on the encoder output that is fed to the decoder, as we found it detrimental in initial tests. For the same reason, we do not use layer normalization on the ELMo embeddings, pre-trained primitive embeddings in the decoder (standard decoders typically take pre-trained word embeddings as inputs),

attention, or scheduled sampling.

We train our models with the Adam optimizer (Kingma and Ba, 2014) for 25 epochs, halving the learning rate whenever there is no improvement in the development set loss, and keep the model weights from the epoch with the best development set accuracy. Training examples are sorted by output sequence length to yield efficient batches; the batches are subsequently processed in a semi-shuffled order, with batches being read through a shuffling buffer. We clip gradients, scaling accordingly, if the sum of gradient norms exceeds 1. During inference, we impose a maximum length on each word's predicted category; the maximum length is set to that of the longest category in the training set. Post-processing of the decoder outputs is limited to the removal of redundant parentheses.

Our models have four hyperparameters: the initial learning rate, the dropout rate on the input (*i.e.*, on the ELMo embeddings), the dropout rate on the output immediately prior to the softmax layer, and dropout rate elsewhere in the model. We tune the hyperparameters over 50 value sets sampled according to the tree-structured Parzen estimator method (Bergstra et al., 2011) as implemented in the Optuna[9] package.[10] The initial learning rate is sampled from a log-uniform distribution on $[10^{-4}, 10^{-2})$ while the dropout rates are independently sampled from a uniform distribution on $[0, 0.8)$. For each hyperparameter value set, we train the model five times with different random seeds and select the values yielding the best accuracy on the development set. We use the best values to run each model with 15 additional seeds so that we have a better estimate of the variance in model performance over random initializations. For PrimDecoder, we decode the output sequences greedily for the hyperparameter search but evaluate with beam search, with a beam width of 5.

6 Results

Table 1 summarizes our main results. Our model outperforms the baseline on all measures

The Cochran-Mantel-Haenszel (CMH) test indicates that the difference in test set word accuracy between our model and the baseline is statistically significant ($p \approx 1.6 \times 10^{-7}$); likewise for the difference in coverage ($p \approx 0$).[11] Averaging sentence

---

[8]For dropout directly between adjacent LSTM states, we use the same dropout mask not just at each time step, but for all sentences in a batch. This allows us to use recurrent dropout with the fast cuDNN LSTM implementation.

[9]https://optuna.org/

[10]We were able to execute many runs in parallel, resulting in sampling more akin to standard random sampling.

[11]For a single run, McNemar's is the usual test. Since we

Model	Development set				Test set			
	Acc	OOV	F_1	Cov	Acc	OOV	F_1	Cov
Clark et al. (2018)								
CVT	—	0	—	—	95.7	0	—	—
ELMo-based	—	0	—	—	95.8	0	—	—
BiLSTM	96.15	0	90.6	87.0	95.89	0	90.2	84.6
PrimDecoder	**96.27**	**11**	**91.3**	**96.0**	**96.00**	**5**	**90.9**	**96.2**

Table 1: Our model's word accuracy, OOV category word accuracy, parser F_1, and parser coverage on CCGbank, compared to the bidirectional LSTM classifier baseline and comparable results from the most recent previous work. All accuracies are averaged over 20 runs with different random seeds. Standard deviations range around 0.05% for word accuracy, 0.1% for F_1, 0.4% for BiLSTM coverage, and 0.2% for PrimDecoder coverage. All improvements are statistically significant with $p \ll 0.001$.

F_1 scores over the 20 runs, the Wilcoxon signed-rank test indicates statistical significance for the difference in F_1 scores ($p \approx 6.7 \times 10^{-15}$).

It is extremely rare for our model to produce malformed categories. *Over all 20 runs*, our model produces only two instances of redundant parentheses, which are automatically repaired, and seven instances of malformed categories[12], which are left as-is and therefore counted as incorrect predictions. The malformations consist entirely of missing closing parentheses or extraneous opening parentheses.

6.1 Comparison to Clark et al. (2018)

In addition to besting the baseline, our model also yields a higher word accuracy than the single-task models reported by Clark et al. (2018). The focus of their work was their novel cross-view training (CVT) approach, which allowed for efficient and effective augmentation of model performance using *unlabelled* data. They compared their approach to the alternative use of ELMo over a variety of tasks, and CCG supertagging was the only one in which CVT underperformed the incorporation of ELMo. Their result with the ELMo-based model set the state-of-the-art word accuracy for single-task CCG supertagging.

It is therefore worth briefly discussing the similarities and differences between their ELMo-based model and our baseline. Their models used two-layer LSTMs with hidden units of size 1024, projected to 512 units between/after layers; our baseline has a single layer of width 512. Where we simply include ELMo representations as inputs to our

models, they followed the recommendation of Peters et al. (2018) to include GloVe representations along with ELMo as well as to additionally provide the ELMo representations to the final output layer of the model. Since our baseline model is smaller and simpler than theirs but both are ELMo-based, it is mildly curious that our baseline outperforms their model. We expect that this difference is attributable to minor differences in implementation details.[13]

For reference, Clark et al. (2018) also reported a word accuracy of 96.0% if they trained their CVT-based model, but only if it was trained in a multi-task setting.[14] This constitutes a separate task, so the results are not directly comparable, but we note that our model achieves the same accuracy without the necessity for multi-task training, which could presumably benefit our model as well.

6.2 Novel categories

Of course, prior work as well as the baseline model cannot handle OOV categories at all, and accordingly have zero accuracies for such categories. Our model *can* generate novel categories, and can even do so correctly, though the accuracy is admittedly low, around 5% on the test set. These results indicates that our model is not merely memorizing the sequences of primitives that constitute the categories in the training set, but is learning some notion of the structure of CCG lexical categories and how subcategorical units are related among words.

Although we cannot make general claims about

---

have multiple runs, the CMH test is appropriate. The CMH test reduces to McNemar's test in the case of a single run.

[12]Which is to say, an average of 0.35 instances over a single run over the test set, which has around 55k words.

[13]For example, our decision to match the tokenization that ELMo saw during its training may have contributed to this difference.

[14]Or 96.1% with a *much* larger model, with LSTMs of width 4096.

when our model generates novel categories, it is still interesting to look at the cases where it does. We discuss some examples below where our model consistently generates novel categories, excerpting or rephrasing sentences for brevity as needed.

- In the sentence *"She was prosecuted under a law that makes it a crime to breach test security."*, the word *"makes"* has OOV category $(((S_{dcl} \backslash NP)/(S_{to} \backslash NP))/NP)/NP_{expl}$, which our model gets correct. The baseline predicts a similar (incorrect) tag where the final primitive is *NP* instead of NP_{expl}. Our model seems to pick up on contextual cues to generate the correct category; there are other such cases where our model selects the correctly typed primitive over the baseline.

- In the phrase *"Edward L. Cole, Jackson, Miss., $ 10,000 fine"*, the *"$"* has OOV category $((NP \backslash NP)/(NP \backslash NP)) /N_{num}$, modifying the word *"fine"* with category $NP \backslash NP$. Our model correctly generates the new category while the baseline incorrectly predicts $(N/N)/N_{num}$.

- In *"..., as has been the case..."*, both the baseline and our model incorrectly tag *"as"* with $((S \backslash NP) \backslash (S \backslash NP))/S_{inv}$ while the correct tag is $((S \backslash NP) \backslash (S \backslash NP))/(S_{dcl} \backslash NP)$. Then, for *"has"*, our model generates the *incorrect but novel* category $S_{inv}/(S_{pt} \backslash NP)$ in place of the correct $(S_{dcl} \backslash NP)/(S_{pt} \backslash NP)$ and in contrast to the baseline's $(S_{pss} \backslash NP)/(S_{pt} \backslash NP)$. Our model adjusted for its error and thus produced a parsable sequence.

6.3 Improvement effect analysis

Although PRIMDECODER outperforms the baseline on all fronts, there is a potential confound in determining which aspect of the model is responsible for this improvement. PRIMDECODER differs from BILSTM in two respects: the production of primitives and knowledge of prediction history. Since previous work has found that incorporating prediction history can increase both word accuracy and parser coverage (Vaswani et al., 2016), we cannot immediately attribute PRIMDECODER's higher performance to production of primitives alone.

In order to isolate these effects, we test two additional model variants. First, to examine the effect of history alone, we modify the BILSTM baseline system to include an LSTM over the lexical categories. This is similar to Vaswani et al.

	−History			+History		
	Acc	F$_1$	Cov	Acc	F$_1$	Cov
Cat	95.9	90.2	84.6	95.8	90.3	90.8
Prim	95.9	90.2	84.9	96.0	90.9	96.2

Table 2: Word accuracy, parser F$_1$, and parser coverage for the four model variants on the CCGbank test set.

(2016), but our model differs in that we feed the base LSTM outputs directly into the top "language model" LSTM rather than into a further MLP layer that combines the two LSTMs. This keeps the changes from our PRIMDECODER model minimal.

Second, to examine the effect of outputting primitives alone, we alter our model to reset the decoder's LSTM state between words, and so cannot maintain a history between words. Other than these noted changes, these two additional variants are trained in the same way as above, with the same layer sizes, same hyperparameter optimization and training procedure, and same beam width.

Combined with PRIMDECODER and BILSTM, these alterations allow us to examine all four combinations of whether the model does or doesn't have history and whether it predicts whole categories or decodes primitive sequences.

Table 2 shows the results of the four options on the CCGbank test set. On the history axis, we note a result similar to Vaswani et al. (2016): adding history to the baseline model provides useful information about past prediction history, substantially boosting parser coverage. Vaswani et al. (2016) observed a slight word accuracy decrease when doing this without scheduled sampling; since we did not use scheduled sampling to keep the comparison well-controlled, we attribute the slight decrease in word accuracy for our version to this omission.

On the other axis, we find that very little changes when allowing the model to decode primitives instead of classifying categories *if prediction history is unavailable*. Word accuracy and F$_1$ stay about the same, but there is a slight increase in parser coverage. This indicates that there is no significant detriment to supertag prediction quality when predicting primitives over categories. Although we omit the value from Table 2, the memoryless primitive decoding model can also correctly tag some words with OOV categories, though not as well as PRIMDECODER: 2% word accuracy on the development set and 0.3% on the test set. Even with a similar word accuracy to the BILSTM baseline, this model at least has the *ability* to produce new categories, an important property for a supertagger.

These results lead us to conclude that PRIMDE-CODER's outperformance of BiLSTM is due to the *conjunction* of decoding primitives and allowing the decoder to keep a memory of previous predictions. Moreover, this improvement is synergistic: the increases in word accuracy, parser F_1, and coverage are substantially greater in magnitude than the sum of the increases from the two control models. We hypothesize that our model is better able to learn associations between categories given that it has direct access to the categories' primitive units.

7 Conclusion and future work

In this paper, we have presented an alternative view to classification-based CCG supertagging where lexical categories are constructed from CCG primitives. Where CCG categories are traditionally predicted atomically, we instead found that breaking them down into their primitive types and operators provides a substantial increase in word accuracy, parser F_1, and parser coverage for English CCG supertagging. Even with a simple linearization scheme, our LSTM decoder–based model outperformed the baseline in all respects, and was also able to generate correct categories during inference that were unseen during training. Our analysis showed that there is a strong interplay between knowledge of prediction history and prediction of primitive units, with both aspects being necessary to obtain the full increases in performance that our model exhibits. We conclude that our novel consideration of CCG lexical categories as the complex units that they are is worthwhile and beneficial.

Our model demonstrates the benefit of a more careful, informed consideration of the structure of supertagging and, by extension, CCG parsing. We expect that further, more sophisticated incorporation of category structure will yield additional benefit, and are investigating such extensions in place of the straightforward linearization of the category strings we applied in this paper; this is somewhat similar to some work in LTAG supertagging (Bangalore and Joshi, 1999; Kasai et al., 2017). At the same time, other categorial grammars, such as Lambek categorial grammar, are likely to be amenable to such improvements as well, but their theoretical properties may allow for more principled methods of decomposing lexical categories, allowing the supertagger's role to be more tightly integrated in the parsing process.

Acknowledgments

We thank Elizabeth Patitsas for her helpful discussions and comments, as well as our anonymous reviewers for their questions, suggestions, and encouragement. This research was enabled in part by support provided by NSERC, SHARCNET, and Compute Canada. Training of our models was aided by the use of GNU Parallel (Tange, 2011).

References

Jason Baldridge. 2008. Weakly Supervised Supertagging with Grammar-Informed Initialization. In *Proceedings of the 22nd International Conference on Computational Linguistics (COLING 2008)*, pages 57–64, Manchester, UK. COLING 2008 Organizing Committee.

Srinivas Bangalore and Aravind K. Joshi. 1999. Supertagging: An Approach to Almost Parsing. *Computational Linguistics*, 25(2):237–265.

James S. Bergstra, Rémi Bardenet, Yoshua Bengio, and Balázs Kégl. 2011. Algorithms for Hyper-Parameter Optimization. In *Advances in Neural Information Processing Systems 24*, pages 2546–2554. Curran Associates, Inc.

Yonatan Bisk and Julia Hockenmaier. 2012. Simple robust grammar induction with combinatory categorial grammars. In *AAAI Conference on Artificial Intelligence*, pages 1643–1649.

Yonatan Bisk and Julia Hockenmaier. 2013. An HDP Model for Inducing Combinatory Categorial Grammars. *Transactions of the Association for Computational Linguistics*, 1:75–88.

Ciprian Chelba, Tomas Mikolov, Mike Schuster, Qi Ge, Thorsten Brants, Philipp Koehn, and Tony Robinson. 2014. One Billion Word Benchmark for Measuring Progress in Statistical Language Modeling. In *Proceedings of the 14th Annual Conference of the International Speech Communication Association (INTERSPEECH)*, pages 2635–2639, Singapore. International Speech Communication Association.

Kyunghyun Cho, Bart van Merrienboer, Caglar Gulcehre, Dzmitry Bahdanau, Fethi Bougares, Holger Schwenk, and Yoshua Bengio. 2014. Learning Phrase Representations using RNN Encoder–Decoder for Statistical Machine Translation. In *Proceedings of the 2014 Conference on Empirical Methods in Natural Language Processing (EMNLP)*, pages 1724–1734, Doha, Qatar. Association for Computational Linguistics.

Kevin Clark, Minh-Thang Luong, Christopher D. Manning, and Quoc Le. 2018. Semi-Supervised Sequence Modeling with Cross-View Training. In *Proceedings of the 2018 Conference on Empirical Methods in Natural Language Processing*, pages 1914–1925, Brussels, Belgium. Association for Computational Linguistics.

Stephen Clark. 2002. Supertagging for Combinatory Categorial Grammar. In *Proceedings of the Sixth International Workshop on Tree Adjoining Grammar and Related Frameworks (TAG+6)*, pages 19–24, Universitá di Venezia. Association for Computational Linguistics.

Stephen Clark and James R. Curran. 2004. The Importance of Supertagging for Wide-Coverage CCG Parsing. In *COLING 2004: Proceedings of the 20th International Conference on Computational Linguistics*, pages 282–288, Geneva, Switzerland. COLING.

Stephen Clark and James R. Curran. 2007. Wide-Coverage Efficient Statistical Parsing with CCG and Log-Linear Models. *Computational Linguistics*, 33(4):493–552.

Stephen Clark, Darren Foong, Luana Bulat, and Wenduan Xu. 2015. The Java Version of the C&C Parser Version 0.95. Technical report, University of Cambridge Computer Laboratory.

Jeffrey L. Elman. 1990. Finding Structure in Time. *Cognitive Science*, 14(2):179–211.

Yarin Gal and Zoubin Ghahramani. 2016. A Theoretically Grounded Application of Dropout in Recurrent Neural Networks. In *Advances in Neural Information Processing Systems 29*, pages 1019–1027. Curran Associates, Inc.

Dan Garrette, Chris Dyer, Jason Baldridge, and Noah A. Smith. 2014. Weakly-Supervised Bayesian Learning of a CCG Supertagger. In *Proceedings of the Eighteenth Conference on Computational Natural Language Learning*, pages 141–150, Ann Arbor, Michigan. Association for Computational Linguistics.

Xavier Glorot and Yoshua Bengio. 2010. Understanding the difficulty of training deep feedforward neural networks. In *Proceedings of the Thirteenth International Conference on Artificial Intelligence and Statistics*, volume 9 of *Proceedings of Machine Learning Research*, pages 249–256, Chia Laguna Resort, Sardinia, Italy. PMLR.

Kaiming He, Xiangyu Zhang, Shaoqing Ren, and Jian Sun. 2015. Delving Deep into Rectifiers: Surpassing Human-Level Performance on ImageNet Classification. In *2015 IEEE International Conference on Computer Vision (ICCV)*, pages 1026–1034.

Sepp Hochreiter and Jürgen Schmidhuber. 1997. Long Short-Term Memory. *Neural Computation*, 9(8):1735–1780.

Julia Hockenmaier and Mark Steedman. 2005. *CCGbank LDC2005T13*. Linguistic Data Consortium, Philadelphia, PA, USA.

Julia Hockenmaier and Mark Steedman. 2007. CCGbank: A Corpus of CCG Derivations and Dependency Structures Extracted from the Penn Treebank. *Computational Linguistics*, 33(3):355–396.

Aravind K. Joshi and B. Srinivas. 1994. Disambiguation of Super Parts of Speech (or Supertags): Almost Parsing. In *COLING 1994 Volume 1: The 15th International Conference on Computational Linguistics*, pages 154–160.

Jungo Kasai, Bob Frank, Tom McCoy, Owen Rambow, and Alexis Nasr. 2017. TAG Parsing with Neural Networks and Vector Representations of Supertags. In *Proceedings of the 2017 Conference on Empirical Methods in Natural Language Processing*, pages 1713–1723, Copenhagen, Denmark. Association for Computational Linguistics.

Diederik P. Kingma and Jimmy Ba. 2014. Adam: A Method for Stochastic Optimization. In *Proceedings of the 3rd International Conference for Learning Representations*, San Diego, USA.

Konstantinos Kogkalidis, Michael Moortgat, and Tejaswini Deoskar. 2019. Constructive Type-Logical Supertagging With Self-Attention Networks. In *Proceedings of the 4th Workshop on Representation Learning for NLP (RepL4NLP-2019)*, pages 113–123, Florence, Italy. Association for Computational Linguistics.

Mike Lewis, Kenton Lee, and Luke Zettlemoyer. 2016. LSTM CCG Parsing. In *Proceedings of the 2016 Conference of the North American Chapter of the Association for Computational Linguistics: Human Language Technologies*, pages 221–231, San Diego, USA. Association for Computational Linguistics.

Mike Lewis and Mark Steedman. 2014. Improved CCG Parsing with Semi-supervised Supertagging. *Transactions of the Association for Computational Linguistics*, 2:327–338.

Vinod Nair and Geoffrey E. Hinton. 2010. Rectified Linear Units Improve Restricted Boltzmann Machines. In *Proceedings of the 27th International Conference on Machine Learning (ICML-10)*, pages 807–814, Haifa, Israel. Omnipress.

Jeffrey Pennington, Richard Socher, and Christopher Manning. 2014. GloVE: Global Vectors for Word Representation. In *Proceedings of the 2014 Conference on Empirical Methods in Natural Language Processing (EMNLP)*, pages 1532–1543, Doha, Qatar. Association for Computational Linguistics.

Matthew Peters, Mark Neumann, Mohit Iyyer, Matt Gardner, Christopher Clark, Kenton Lee, and Luke Zettlemoyer. 2018. Deep Contextualized Word Representations. In *Proceedings of the 2018 Conference of the North American Chapter of the Association for Computational Linguistics: Human Language Technologies, Volume 1 (Long Papers)*, pages 2227–2237, New Orleans, Louisiana. Association for Computational Linguistics.

Barbara Plank, Anders Søgaard, and Yoav Goldberg. 2016. Multilingual Part-of-Speech Tagging with Bidirectional Long Short-Term Memory Models and Auxiliary Loss. In *Proceedings of the 54th Annual Meeting of the Association for Computational Linguistics (Volume 2: Short Papers)*, pages 412–418, Berlin, Germany. Association for Computational Linguistics.

Laura Rimell and Stephen Clark. 2008. Adapting a Lexicalized-Grammar Parser to Contrasting Domains. In *Proceedings of the 2008 Conference on Empirical Methods in Natural Language Processing*, pages 475–484, Honolulu, Hawaii. Association for Computational Linguistics.

Andrew M. Saxe, James L. McClelland, and Surya Ganguli. 2013. Exact solutions to the nonlinear dynamics of learning in deep linear neural networks. In *Proceedings of the 2nd International Conference on Learning Representations*, Banff, Canada.

Ilya Sutskever, Oriol Vinyals, and Quoc V Le. 2014. Sequence to Sequence Learning with Neural Networks. In *Advances in Neural Information Processing Systems 27*, pages 3104–3112. Curran Associates, Inc.

Ole Tange. 2011. GNU parallel - the command-line power tool. *;login: The USENIX Magazine*, 36(1):42–47.

Ann Taylor, Mitchell Marcus, and Beatrice Santorini. 2003. The Penn Treebank: An Overview. In Anne Abeillé, editor, *Treebanks: Building and Using Parsed Corpora*, Text, Speech and Language Technology, pages 5–22. Springer Netherlands, Dordrecht.

Joseph Turian, Lev-Arie Ratinov, and Yoshua Bengio. 2010. Word Representations: A Simple and General Method for Semi-Supervised Learning. In *Proceedings of the 48th Annual Meeting of the Association for Computational Linguistics*, pages 384–394, Uppsala, Sweden. Association for Computational Linguistics.

Ashish Vaswani, Yonatan Bisk, Kenji Sagae, and Ryan Musa. 2016. Supertagging With LSTMs. In *Proceedings of the 2016 Conference of the North American Chapter of the Association for Computational Linguistics: Human Language Technologies*, pages 232–237, San Diego, California. Association for Computational Linguistics.

Oriol Vinyals, Łukasz Kaiser, Terry Koo, Slav Petrov, Ilya Sutskever, and Geoffrey Hinton. 2015. Grammar as a Foreign Language. In *Advances in Neural Information Processing Systems 28*, pages 2773–2781. Curran Associates, Inc.

Huijia Wu, Jiajun Zhang, and Chengqing Zong. 2017. A Dynamic Window Neural Network for CCG Supertagging. In *AAAI Conference on Artificial Intelligence*, pages 3337–3343.

Wenduan Xu, Michael Auli, and Stephen Clark. 2015. CCG Supertagging with a Recurrent Neural Network. In *Proceedings of the 53rd Annual Meeting of the Association for Computational Linguistics and the 7th International Joint Conference on Natural Language Processing (Volume 2: Short Papers)*, pages 250–255, Beijing, China. Association for Computational Linguistics.

Wenduan Xu, Michael Auli, and Stephen Clark. 2016. Expected F-Measure Training for Shift-Reduce Parsing with Recurrent Neural Networks. In *Proceedings of the 2016 Conference of the North American Chapter of the Association for Computational Linguistics: Human Language Technologies*, pages 210–220, San Diego, California. Association for Computational Linguistics.

What's in a Name? Are BERT Named Entity Representations just as Good for any other Name?

Sriram Balasubramanian[†]   Naman Jain[†]   Gaurav Jindal[†]
Abhijeet Awasthi   Sunita Sarawagi
Indian Institute of Technology, Bombay
{sriramb,namanjain,gauravj,awasthi,sunita}@cse.iitb.ac.in

Abstract

We evaluate named entity representations of BERT-based NLP models by investigating their robustness to replacements from the same typed class in the input. We highlight that on several tasks while such perturbations are natural, state of the art trained models are surprisingly brittle. The brittleness continues even with the recent entity-aware BERT models. We also try to discern the cause of this non-robustness, considering factors such as tokenization and frequency of occurrence. Then we provide a simple method that ensembles predictions from multiple replacements while jointly modeling the uncertainty of type annotations and label predictions. Experiments on three NLP tasks show that our method enhances robustness and increases accuracy on both natural and adversarial datasets.

1   Introduction

Contextual word embeddings from heavily pre-trained language models (Peters et al., 2018; Devlin et al., 2018) now form the basis of many NLP tasks. While they have lead to improved accuracy for most tasks, there are mounting concerns on how well these embeddings encapsulate syntactic and semantic constructs such as synonyms, misspellings, and knowledge representations. Indeed, it has been shown that even BERT based models are not robust to synonym swaps or spelling mistakes in a sentence (Jin et al., 2019; Hsieh et al., 2019; Sun et al., 2019). In this work, we investigate how well these contextual representations fare for named entities.

Designing robust representations of named entities is challenging due to the sheer variety of named entities. Named entities diversify with language, geographical location, time of history, and even with the fine types. Adding to this the varying

______
† equal contribution, sorted alphabetically by last name

length of such entities combined with out of vocabulary names, the complexity only increases.

We quantify how well current systems understand named entities by studying their robustness to substitutions of name mentions in a sentence with other names within an entity class. The entity class within which we seek such robustness is task-dependent and easy for humans to provide. For example, we may require a natural language inference model to be robust to the replacement of company names within the input sentence pairs. In Table 1 we show a sentence pair which contains mentions of a company name `Facebook`. When we replace that mention with other company names like `Microsoft` or `Google`, a robust model should continue to make the same prediction. Likewise, we may require a co-reference resolution model to be robust to replacements of person names in a passage, and a grammar error correction model to be robust to replacement of person names of same gender or country names. A good language representation should be able to generalize well to such perturbations and not deviate from its output upon such perturbations.

The contributions of this work are three-fold. First, we investigate the robustness of trained NLP models using a generic algorithm that we develop. We empirically demonstrate a lack of robustness of state of the art BERT-based models for different user-specified typed classes spanning three NLP tasks: natural language inference (NLI), coreference resolution (CoRef), and Grammar Error Correction (GEC). The lack of robustness is specifically of concern for an entity-focused task like CoRef, where 85% of test sentences have change in their predictions with a single person name change.

Second, we try to seek explanations for such lack of robustness, by observing performance vs. frequency of named entities occurring in the fine-tuning dataset or based on the count of tokens

Proceedings of the 5th Workshop on Representation Learning for NLP (RepL4NLP-2020), pages 205–214
July 9, 2020. ©2020 Association for Computational Linguistics

<table>
<tr><td>

Sentence 1: Magner , who is 54 and known as Marge , has been the consumer group 's chief operating officer since April 2002 , and sits on ~~Facebook~~ Microsoft 's management committee
Sentence 2: She has been the consumer unit 's chief operating officer since April 2002 , and sits ~~Facebook~~ Microsoft 's management committee.
Gold: 1 ; **Prediction:** Original: 1; Perturbed: 0

Sentence 1: The workers accuse ~~Goldman~~ Novell of " reverse age discrimination " because of a change in retirement benefits in 1997 .
Sentence 2: ~~Goldman~~ Novell was sued when it changed its retirement benefits in 1997 .
Gold: 0 ; **Prediction:** Original: 0; Perturbed: 1

</td></tr>
</table>

Table 1: Examples on paraphrase detection task – Replacement of an entity

in a named entity. We also explored if BERT's wordpiece-level masking was particularly unfavorable to entities by switching to Span-BERT, the recent span based masking model. While overall accuracy improved for all datasets with Span-BERT, we found no change in the robustness of the model.

Finally, we develop a simple approach that ensembles predictions from multiple replacements (RESEMBLE) while modeling the uncertainty of type annotations and label predictions. Our approach not only improves performance on adversarial datasets but also on the original datasets, and achieves higher stability on all the tasks.

2 Evaluating Robustness to Named-Entity Replacements

We study the robustness of BERT-based NLP models w.r.t. type-specific named-entity substitutions, for tasks like NLI, GEC and CoRef. Algorithm 1 describes our method of probing NLP models for lack of robustness. Let V be a dictionary of candidate named entities of a given type c, and D denote a dataset consisting of sentence-label pairs $(\mathbf{x}, y)$. Let G be a model fine-tuned on a pre-trained BERT. For each sentence $(\mathbf{x}, y) \in D$, we identify the mentions of named-entities of the type c in $\mathbf{x}^1$. We obtain a perturbed sentence $\mathbf{x}_m$ by replacing all mentions of a distinct name in $\mathbf{x}$ by a random entry from V. We repeat this process B times where B is a budget (we used 50), with replacement of names. Over the B perturbations, the sentence with the lowest accuracy is added to the set D_{Worst} and the highest accuracy added to the set D_{Best}. A lower variance in model's performance across the datasets $\{D, D_{\text{Worst}}, D_{\text{Best}}\}$ is indicative of higher robust-

---

Algorithm 1: Probing a model using named-entity substitutions

---

Data: D(dataset) , V(names), M(metric), B(budget)
Result: D_{worst}, D_{best} (datasets on which the model performs worst and best)
for $(x, y) \in D$ **do**
  min_score $= \infty$, max_score $= -\infty$;
  $N \leftarrow \text{RandomSelection}(V, B)$;
  for $n \in N$ **do**
    $x' \leftarrow \text{Replace}(x, n)$;   // Details in text for each task
    score $\leftarrow M(G(x'), y)$;
    if score $<$ min_score **then**
      min_score $\leftarrow$ score, $x_{\text{worst}} \leftarrow x'$
    end
    if score $>$ max_score **then**
      max_score $\leftarrow$ score, $x_{\text{best}} \leftarrow x'$
    end
  end
  $D_{\text{worst}} \leftarrow D_{\text{worst}} + (x_{\text{worst}}, y)$;
  $D_{\text{best}} \leftarrow D_{\text{best}} + (x_{\text{best}}, y)$;
end

---

ness and vice-versa. We also measure stability as the fraction of sentences in D whose predictions stay unchanged within the budget sized replacements.

We use the above method to evaluate the robustness of state-of-the-art BERT based models. We evaluate NLI with organization name replacements, GEC with person and country name replacements, and CoRef with person name replacements. In Table 3 we report accuracy on the original, worst, and best case perturbations of the input and stability for the four task-entity combinations. We discuss task details and results next.

---

[1] We pre-filtered using a named entity tagger in the spaCy library, and made manual corrections so that all tagged entity mentions are correct in D.

Task: GEC; **Perturbed Entity**: Person
Text: One day ~~Penny~~ Bujalski discovered it and it **go** to tell it to his queen .
Original Prediction: One day Penny discovered it and **went** to tell it to his queen .
Perturbed Prediction: One day Bujalski discovered it and to tell it to his queen.
Text: the two boys heard that he was planing to steal some money and kill people so the boys start their adventure on stopping ~~Abigale~~ Injuin Joe .
Original Prediction: The two boys heard that he was planning to steal some money and kill people so the boys started their adventure by stopping **Abigale** .
Perturbed Prediction: The two boys heard that he was planning to steal some money and kill people so the boys started their adventure by stopping **Joe** .

Task: GEC; **Perturbed Entity**: Country
Text: There are countries , such as ~~Greece~~ Oman or ~~Bulgaria~~ Venezuela , in which the econmoy **relies** merely on tourism .
Original Prediction: There are countries , such as Greece or Bulgaria , in which the econmoy **relies** merely on tourism .
Perturbed Prediction: There are countries , such as Oman or Venezuela , in which the econmoy **rely** merely on tourism .
Text: I am 20 years old **,** living in Port - Said , ~~Egypt~~ China .
Original Prediction: I am 20 years old **and** living in Port - Said , Egypt .
Perturbed Prediction: I am 20 years old **,** living in Port - Said , China .

Task: CoRef; **Perturbed Entity**: Person
Text: And ~~Chris Hill~~ Sam Rusnock our ambassador was in China a few days ago. he made the point and Secretary Rice made the point yesterday to the Chinese Foreign minister , we want to see China use its influence. Speaker Newt Gingrich the former speaker Republican weighed in on this debate in this way. [truncated] Well uh with all due respect to Speaker Gingrich we are on a course which has a reasonable chance of success.
Original Predicted Cluster: [“Chris Hill our ambassador”,”he”]
Perturbed Predicted Cluster: [“Sam Rusnock our ambassador”,”he”, ”Speaker Gingrich”]
Text: ~~Arianna Huffington~~ Sydnie Rabaut uh in this lengthy piece this morning, Judy Miller is quoted excuse me as saying [truncated]. Do you buy this notion that she doesn’t recall who this other source was? No of course not Howie. In fact I think this is the major unanswered question.
Original Predicted Cluster:[”Arianna Huffington”, ”you”, ”I”]
Perturbed Predicted Cluster: [ ]

Table 2: Lack of robustness of GEC and CoRef model with respect to person and country names

	NLI F_1	GEC $F_{0.5}$		CoRef F_1
Dataset	ORG	PER	COUN	PER
Original	84.82	50.93	47.87	76.47
Worst	79.90	36.51	32.12	60.91
Best	90.03	58.32	51.47	87.85
Stability	86.8%	75%	63.4%	12.86%

Table 3: Adversarial Evaluation of BERT on different tasks

2.1 Natural Language Inference (NLI)

Task Paraphrase detection is a binary classification task on whether two sentences are paraphrases of each other. We work on the paraphrasing task of the GLUE dataset (Wang et al., 2018). The standard dataset split consists of 4077 training sentence pairs and 1726 testing pairs. We use the BERT-base model fine-tuned on the training dataset. The model takes as input the concatenated sentence pairs and predicts a binary output. The metric used for this task is F_1 score on the binary output.

Attack details We measure robustness over the organization concept class. As the replacement dictionary V we used organization names from Fortune 500 companies. We filter out sentence pairs consisting of organization name mention in each sentence of the pair and get 218 sentence pairs. We use spaCy (Honnibal, 2016) for tagging the sentences followed by manual inspection of matched entities so that in the 218 filtered sentences all entity mentions are correctly identified.

Results Observe in Table 3 almost a 10% swing in F-score between D_{Worst}, D_{Best} just by replacing organization names in test instances. The perturbation dictionary consisted of Fortune 500 companies, and were not particularly obscure either. As the examples in Table 1 show some of these replacements do not span rare names (Facebook to Microsoft or Goldman to Novell)

2.2 Grammatical error correction (GEC)

Task Grammatical error correction is a sequence prediction task, given an incorrect sentence as input we have to predict the grammatically correct output. We use the LOCNESS corpus (Granger, 1998) comprising of incorrect and correct parallel English essays. The standard dataset split consists of 34,308 incorrect-correct sentence pairs for training and 4,384 pairs for testing. We use the publicly available parallel edit model from (Awasthi et al.,

2019). It uses a BERT model for predicting the edits at every token on the input and applies those edits to compute the final output. We only use a single iteration of the model for ease of evaluation. The performance is measured using $F_{0.5}$ score based on M2 files (Bryant et al., 2017).

Attack details We measure robustness on two concept classes: person names and country names. From the test set, 328 sentences mentioned person names and 82 mentioned country names. For person names, we perform gender-specific replacements. The person name dictionary was created as follows: we start with a large dictionary of 4018 female first names, 3437 male first names and 151670 last names and remove names encountered in the training data. We then generate about 250 names from these sets by combining first names and last names. For countries we use 58 non-frequent country names.

Results The gap in accuracy between the best and worst-case perturbations is almost 20% for both person name and country name replacements. Moreover, we find that 25% of the sentences change prediction on changing person names and more than 35% sentences vary prediction of country names! Table 2 shows some examples. Notice how changing the country from Greece to Oman and Bulgaria to Venezuela changes the edit predictions five tokens away in the sentence.

2.3 Coreference Resolution (CoRef)

Task Coreference resolution refers to the problem of finding all expressions that refer to the same entity in a text. We work on the standard OntoNotes dataset from the CoNLL-2012 shared task on coreference resolution (Pradhan et al., 2012). Each document represents one instance and has a series of sentences within it. The standard split consists of 2,802 training documents and 348 testing documents. We use the BERT base model fine-tuned on the training dataset from (Joshi et al., 2019b). The model predicts top-k spans for a document and then computes antecedent scores for them and thereby builds clusters for coreference. Since documents in OntoNotes contain many clusters while we replace only mentions of a single name in the long document, to better highlight differences, we measure F score for only the gold clusters with the replaced entity.

Attack details We measure the robustness with respect to person names. We filter out documents containing a person name based on gold annotations in the OntoNotes corpus, and get 210 documents. Replacement vocabulary V was made in similar way as mentioned for GEC using the same male, female and last name dictionaries. We also ensure that the name replacements do not alter the coreferences. Therefore, we replace every instance of each name occurring in the document with our randomly sampled adversarial name, taking care that first(or last) names are replaced with adversarial first(or last) names. In case of any ambiguity, we replace the name with the last name. Also the replacements are gender specific.

Results We found the worst stability for CoRef and only 13% of the sentences preserved predictions on named-entity replacements. Also, the gap between the worst and best case perturbations is almost 30 F_1 points. As seen from the truncated document examples in the second-last row of Table 2, replacing the name `Chris Hill` to `Sam Rusnock` makes the model mispredict the original cluster, as it predicts another name `Speaker Gingrich` as co-referent to `Sam Rusnock`. Even in second example changing the name `Arianna Huffington` to `Sydnie Rabau` causes model to miss the its entire cluster! We also found that on an average, predictions of model differ by two clusters per sentence after name perturbation. For one document almost 17 clusters were affected by a single entity swap. The non-robustness on CoRef is especially surprising since it is principally a task about named entities. Our experiments were on the widely used OntoNotes dataset with person name mentions. Such varying performance should be a cause of concern for benchmarking CoRef models. Perhaps, the dataset needs to be augmented with variants arising out of named-entity replacements and stability should be a required performance metric, in addition to accuracy on the original sentence.

Another interesting observation across tasks is that the accuracy on the original D is enhanced after moving to D_{Best} — that is, just substituting names in a given instance with more 'favorable' names can lead to substantial gains. We will exploit this observation to enhance base accuracy and improve the robustness of NLP models in Section 4.

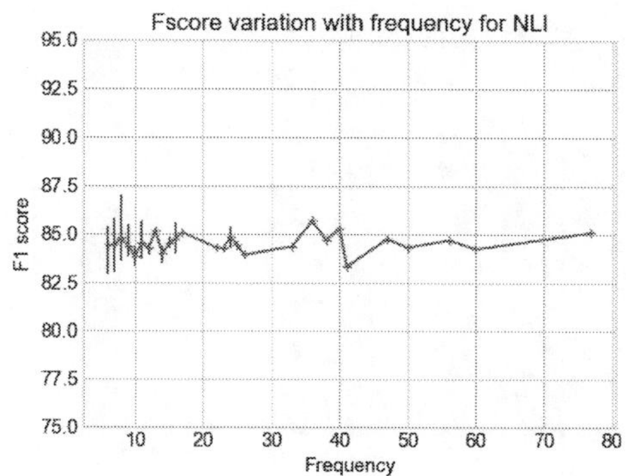

Figure 1: Variation of NLI model's performance with frequency of named entity in training dataset. The green lines depict variance across performance of names of a given frequency

3   Causes of Non-Robustness

We then sought to investigate reasons for such lack of stability. We first attempted to see if the poor accuracy of certain names can be explained by their frequency of occurrence in the training dataset. In Figure 1 we plot a graph of the frequency of a named-entity in the training corpus against the F-score on the NLI task. As we can see there is no strong correlation of frequency with the performance of a named entity, in fact, an organization name appearing in only four sentence pairs (`Goldman`) performed better than `Microsoft` which was present in over 30 sentence pairs. `Facebook` which is not even present in the training set performs better than `Microsoft` or `Google`. This is likely due to the biases learned during the massive pre-training that BERT-based models enjoy.

Our next guess was to see if the number of tokens in BERT's word-piece tokenization of named entity causes any significant impact on accuracy. Sequence labeling models like PIE (Awasthi et al., 2019) for GEC are most likely to be susceptible to that effect. In Figure 2 we show accuracy against the number of tokens in a named entity for GEC. We compared performance across three classes – 1 token length entities or two token length entities or three or more token length entities. We created budget sized copies of the original dataset and compare performance across three variants – (Original, Best, and Worst) but found no significant difference in accuracy with the number of tokens. However, we did observe some anecdotal evidence

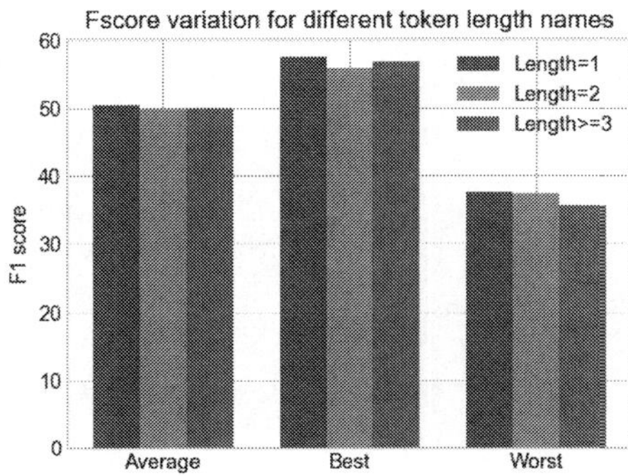

Figure 2: Variation of F_1 scores for GEC model with different token length perturbation.

of specific nuisance tokens arising out of the word piece model on out of vocabulary names. For example consider the person name `Tobey` that gets tokenized as `[To, ##bey]` or `Injuin` which is tokenized as `[In, ##juin]`. The first token of the names are "To" or "In", both frequent prepositions, which perhaps BERT finds difficult to disambiguate. As we can see from the second example in Table 2 – `Injuin` confuses the given model and the model even deletes the name probably since "In" proposition is not required there. Another artifact could be memorized correlations between names (e.g. `Obama` and `President`) that tasks like CoRef could exploit. Recent work (Poerner et al., 2019) has infact shown that BERT based models use surface form of entities for relational reasoning.

	NLI (ORG) F_1	CoRef (PER) F_1
Original	86.80	76.71
Worst	82.7	62.37
Best	90.2	86.76
Stability	89.9%	16.19%

Table 4: Adversarial Evaluation of Span-BERT on different tasks

Finally, we explore if BERT's single token masking model is unfavorable to robust entity representations by comparing with a language model pre-trained by masking spans covering multiple tokens. Specifically, we use Span-BERT (Joshi et al., 2019a), which is trained with masked language modeling on spans instead of tokens. We tried to compare the performance on NLI and CoRef[2] in

<hr>

[2]We were unable to train Span-BERT for GEC, since in

comparison with BERT. The results can be found in Table 4. We were surprised that Span-BERT does not provide any better robustness, although it does provide consistent higher accuracy on all tasks. Various metrics such as – the difference between worst and best accuracy, stability are both very similar for BERT and Span-BERT.

4 Enhancing Robustness

We propose a simple ensembling with replacements approach (referred to as RESEMBLE) that does not require any retraining and can work with any existing pre-trained language model. We assume a type annotator T that marks mentions of entities of the type c for which robustness needs to enhanced. The type-annotator might be noisy. We identify a small set M of entities of type c on which the model provides high accuracy on a validation set. We call these the list of canonical entities.

Given any input $\mathbf{x}$, we invoke the task-specific model G to obtain predicted labels $\hat{\mathbf{y}}$ and the type annotator T to obtain type annotations $\hat{\mathbf{z}}$. If $\hat{\mathbf{z}}$ denotes that a named entity of type c is present in one or more spans of $\mathbf{x}$, we generate new sentences $\mathbf{x}_m$ by replacing the named entities with canonical named entities $m \in M$. The model G when applied to $\mathbf{x}_m$ generates prediction $\hat{\mathbf{y}}_m$.

Let the true labels of $\mathbf{x}$ and $\mathbf{x}_m$ be $\mathbf{y}$ and $\mathbf{y}_m$ respectively, and the true type of $\mathbf{x}$ be $\mathbf{z}$. If the type annotator correctly identified the spans corresponding to concept class c (i.e., $\mathbf{z} = \hat{\mathbf{z}}$), $\mathbf{y}$ and all $\mathbf{y}_m$s have to agree as per our requirement of robustness. We use this to define a revised distribution over true $\mathbf{y}$ from the individual predictions as follows:

$$P_R(\mathbf{y}|\mathbf{x}, \hat{\mathbf{z}}) \propto (1 - P(\mathbf{z} = \hat{\mathbf{z}}|\mathbf{x}))P(\mathbf{y}|\mathbf{x})$$

$$+ P(\mathbf{z} = \hat{\mathbf{z}}|\mathbf{x}) \left(P(\mathbf{y}|\mathbf{x}) \prod_m P(\mathbf{y}|\mathbf{x}_m) \right)^{\frac{1}{m+1}} \quad (1)$$

The above is an annotator confidence weighted average of two terms: The first half calculates the probability of $\mathbf{y}$ from the default model G when the type annotator may be wrong and the $\mathbf{y}_m$ predictions should be ignored. The second half calculates the ensembled agreement probability when the type annotator is correct. We calculate that as a geometric mean of the predictions from the different replacements. In the above equation, the ensembled

<hr>

released Span-BERT checkpoints were not compatible with the GEC model probability is under the simplifying assumption that all entity replacements have the same number of tokens. During implementation, we remove this assumption, and implement a more detailed span-level agreement for variable-length entities.

An important requirement for the above expression is that the probabilities provided by the different models express true uncertainty of predictions, that is, they be well-calibrated. Unfortunately, modern neural networks tend to be uncalibrated. To calibrate the probabilities, we use a popular method called temperature scaling (Guo et al., 2017) where probabilities are raised by an exponent, which is the inverse of the temperature. Temperature scaling flattens the probability distribution over output classes thus reduces the confidence until it is correctly calibrated. The expression is as follows:

$$P_T(y|\mathbf{x}) = \frac{P(y|\mathbf{x})^{\frac{1}{T}}}{\sum_{y'} P(y'|\mathbf{x})^{\frac{1}{T}}}$$

where y denotes a scalar prediction. For two of our tasks (GEC and CoRef), the output from our BERT-based models is a product of probabilities from multiple positions. We apply the same temperature scale to each prediction. Thus, our final expression becomes:

$$P_R(\mathbf{y}|\mathbf{x}, \hat{\mathbf{z}}) \propto (1 - P(\mathbf{z} = \hat{\mathbf{z}}|\mathbf{x}))P_T(\mathbf{y}|\mathbf{x})$$
$$+ P(\mathbf{z} = \hat{\mathbf{z}}|\mathbf{x}) \left(P_T(\mathbf{y}|\mathbf{x}) \prod_m P(\mathbf{y}|\mathbf{x}_m) \right)^{\frac{1}{m+1}}$$

$$(2)$$

The temperature hyper-parameter T is fixed from a validation dataset. Note we do not apply temperature scaling to the predictions from the canonical entries.

4.1 Empirical Results

For each task, we will describe the defense mechanisms used, with the description of the replacement list, and replacement strategies. The calibration hyper-parameters used for the defense methods are temperatures $T = 2$ across all tasks. The canonical dictionary M for NLI comprises of `Microsoft`, `Nasdaq` and `IBM`. For GEC, due to the huge size of the GEC corpus we pick the most common English first names and combine them with common English last names. We use three male names (`John, James Brown, Robert Johnson`) and three female names (`Patricia, Mary Jones, Jennifer Brown`) for replacement. If gender is ambiguous, we use 1 male name and 2 female names (`John, Mary Jones, Jennifer Brown`). For CoRef, we used the top 3 frequent person names from the training dataset for our replacement list namely – `George Bush, Bill Clinton, Ehud Barak`. We also present results when we restrict the cannonical dictionary M to only the first name in the above described lists.

We show results with RESEMBLE in Table 5. We perform defense on four datasets – `Original, Best, Worst, Random Replacement`. For random replacement, we constructed 10 new datasets from the original dataset with its names replaced with randomly selected names, and then evaluate the performance of our models on these datasets. We present the mean and standard deviation of the F scores across these newly constructed datasets. For best and worst we evaluate performance on datasets generated from Algo. 1. First observe that accuracy of even the original test dataset improves with our simple replacement ensembling while reducing the variance. For example, for GEC F score increases from 50.93 to 51.81. The variance has also reduced as seen for the random replacement datasets. The adversarial accuracy improves significantly — for CoRef we see a jump of D_{Worst} from 60.91 to 68.31 and for GEC the gains are even higher. The difference between the best and worst accuracy reduces drastically. Although for D_{Best} accuracy drops with RESEMBLE, the overall gains across the three dataset variants are much higher. Further a single canonical entry $M = 1$ is almost as effective as larger ensembles of $M = 3$. This implies that at test-time, we have to deploy the model on at most two instances to enjoy significantly higher robustness. This shows that replacement with canonical entities while accounting for uncertainty of entity identification is a viable alternative to enhance robustness.

5 Related Work

Study of BERT Representations Jin et al. (2019); Hsieh et al. (2019) study robustness of state of the art BERT fine-tuned models on classification, entailment, and machine translation tasks with respect to synonym replacements. The former used a black box scenario while the latter used input gradients and attention magnitudes to

Dataset	NLI(ORG) F_1			GEC(PER) $F_{0.5}$			CoRef(PER) F_1		
	Original	RESEMBLE		Original	RESEMBLE		Original	RESEMBLE	
		M=1	M=3		M=1	M=3		M=1	M=3
Original	84.80	85.16	85.16	50.93	51.81	51.53	76.47	76.87	76.71
Worst	79.90	82.71	82.71	36.51	47.09	46.75	60.91	68.31	69.43
Best	90.03	86.91	86.63	58.32	55.38	55.38	87.85	82.6	82.18
Random Replacement	85.53 (0.54)	85.48 (0.50)	85.50 (0.40)	49.96 (1.05)	51.47 (0.70)	52.03 (0.66)	76.37 (1.04)	76.78 (0.75)	76.87 (0.81)

Table 5: Adversarial Evaluation of BERT on different tasks comparing the accuracy on the original model against our algorithm with a canonical dictionary of size (M) 1 or 3. For Random Replacement dataset, mean across the ten artificial datasets along with standard deviation in brackets is presented

find probable candidate replacements. Sun et al. (2019) applied an adversarial mis-spelling attack to BERT using gradient-based saliencies. Poerner et al. (2019) show that BERT uses the surface form of words for relational reasoning (guessing person with an Italian sounding name speaks Italian). Zhang et al. (2019a) generated adversarial sentence pairs for paraphrase detection by swapping the order of named entities in two sentences which was enough to fool BERT. Joshi et al. (2019a) introduced Span-BERT that is trained on masked language modelling on spans instead of tokens. Zhang et al. (2019b) developed ERNIE model for entity linking which combines named entity embeddings from knowledge graph with BERT.

Other Robustness Studies in NLP Techniques for generating adversarial examples to study robustness of NLP models have seen a lot of enthusiasm in recent years. These approaches can be loosely categorized into three types – character-level (Ebrahimi et al., 2018b,a) or word-level or sentence-level (Zhao et al., 2018; Iyyer et al., 2018; Ribeiro et al., 2018). Our work is most related to word-level attacks which we elaborate on. Liang et al. (2018) proposed word insertion, deletion, or replacement using gradient magnitudes for classification tasks but requires human effort to ensure the sensibility of the replacements. Samanta and Mehta (2017) used synonym replacements along with the gradient sign method for choosing the worst synonym replacement. Alzantot et al. (2018) provides a population-based genetic algorithm for synonym attacks for sentiment classification and textual entailment in a black-box setting. Ren et al. (2019) developed a greedy algorithm for synonym swaps using weighted gradient based word saliencies, for sentiment classification and entailment.

In this work, we also perform word-level attacks but our focus is robustness to named entity replacements. The closest work to ours is (Prabhakaran et al., 2019) that checks the sensitivity of models with respect to named entities but they only consider sentiment or toxicity classification. Our work covers more interesting structured prediction tasks such as coreference resolution and grammatical error correction.

Defenses in NLP Most approaches (Cheng et al., 2018; Jia and Liang, 2017) for defenses in NLP have focused on augmenting training datasets with adversarial instances. Pruthi et al. (2019) proposed a word recognition model along with backoff strategies for robustness against misspellings. Zhou et al. (2019) used an adversarial detection cum replacement strategy. We did not consider data augmentation methods because that would significantly increase the training time for models like GEC.

There has also been a trend in usage of certified robustness approaches (Ko et al., 2019; Jia et al., 2019; Huang et al., 2019; Shi et al., 2020) which provide guarantees on the minimum performance of models. The main technique so far is to propagate interval bounds around input word embeddings and has been applied for robustness to synonyms change. Synonyms are expected to have similar embeddings, but interval bounds are unlikely to work for entities within a large concept class. We are not aware of any prior work that enhances robustness with canonical replacements like ours in the context of an existing language model.

6 Conclusions and Future Work

In this work we show that state of the art BERT-based models are surprisingly brittle to named entity replacements. We propose RESEMBLE, a simple ensembling approach to increase robustness while also improving nominal accuracy. The general paradigm of enhancing robustness via ensembles on guided instance perturbations is a promising direction and needs to be explored for other tasks too.

Acknowledgement We thank the anonymous reviewers for their constructive feedback on this work. This research was partly sponsored by IBM AI Horizon Networks - IIT Bombay initiative and partly by a Google India AI/ML Research Award. Abhijeet is supported by Google PhD Fellowship in Machine Learning.

References

Moustafa Alzantot, Yash Sharma, Ahmed Elgohary, Bo-Jhang Ho, Mani Srivastava, and Kai-Wei Chang. 2018. Generating natural language adversarial examples. In *Proceedings of the 2018 Conference on Empirical Methods in Natural Language Processing*.

Abhijeet Awasthi, Sunita Sarawagi, Rasna Goyal, Sabyasachi Ghosh, and Vihari Piratla. 2019. Parallel iterative edit models for local sequence transduction. In *Proceedings of the 2019 Conference on Empirical Methods in Natural Language Processing and the 9th International Joint Conference on Natural Language Processing (EMNLP-IJCNLP)*.

Christopher Bryant, Mariano Felice, and Ted Briscoe. 2017. Automatic annotation and evaluation of error types for grammatical error correction. In *Proceedings of the 55th Annual Meeting of the Association for Computational Linguistics (Volume 1: Long Papers)*.

Yong Cheng, Zhaopeng Tu, Fandong Meng, Junjie Zhai, and Yang Liu. 2018. Towards robust neural machine translation. In *Proceedings of the 56th Association for Computational Linguistics (Volume 1: Long Papers)*.

Jacob Devlin, Ming-Wei Chang, Kenton Lee, and Kristina Toutanova. 2018. Bert: Pre-training of deep bidirectional transformers for language understanding. *arXiv preprint arXiv:1810.04805*.

Javid Ebrahimi, Daniel Lowd, and Dejing Dou. 2018a. On adversari al examples for character-level neural machine translation. *International Conference on Computational Linguistics (COLING)*.

Javid Ebrahimi, Anyi Rao, Daniel Lowd, and Dejing Dou. 2018b. Hotflip: White-box adversarial examples for nlp. *Association for Computational Linguistics (ACL)*.

S. Granger. 1998. The computer learner corpus: A versatile new source of data for sla research. *Learner English on Computer. Addison Wesley Longman : London New York, 3-18*.

Chuan Guo, Geoff Pleiss, Yu Sun, and Kilian Q. Weinberger. 2017. On calibration of modern neural networks. In *Proceedings of the 34th International Conference on Machine Learning, ICML 2017, Sydney, NSW, Australia, 6-11 August 2017*, pages 1321–1330.

M Honnibal. 2016. spacy: Industrial-strength natural language processing in python.

Yu-Lun Hsieh, Minhao Cheng, Da-Cheng Juan, Wei Wei, Wen-Lian Hsu, and Cho-Jui Hsieh. 2019. On the robustness of self-attentive models.

Po-Sen Huang, Robert Stanforth, Johannes Welbl, Chris Dyer, Dani Yogatama, Sven Gowal, Krishnamurthy Dvijotham, and Pushmeet Kohli. 2019. Achieving verified robustness to symbol substitutions via interval bound propagation. In *Proceedings of the 2019 Conference on Empirical Methods in Natural Language Processing (EMNLP)*.

Mohit Iyyer, John Wieting, Kevin Gimpel, and Luke Zettlemoyer. 2018. Adversarial example generation with syntactically controlled paraphrase networks. In *Proceedings of NAACL*.

Robin Jia and Percy Liang. 2017. Adversarial examples for evaluating reading comprehension systems. In *Proceedings of the 2017 Conference on Empirical Methods in Natural Language Processing*.

Robin Jia, Aditi Raghunathan, Kerem Göksel, and Percy Liang. 2019. Certified robustness to adversarial word substitutions. In *Proceedings of the 2019 Conference on Empirical Methods in Natural Language Processing (EMNLP)*.

Di Jin, Zhijing Jin, Joey Tianyi Zhou, and Peter Szolovits. 2019. Is bert really robust? natural language attack on text classification and entailment. *arXiv preprint arXiv:1907.11932*.

Mandar Joshi, Danqi Chen, Yinhan Liu, Daniel S. Weld, Luke Zettlemoyer, and Omer Levy. 2019a. SpanBERT: Improving pre-training by representing and predicting spans. *arXiv preprint arXiv:1907.10529*.

Mandar Joshi, Omer Levy, Luke Zettlemoyer, and Daniel Weld. 2019b. BERT for coreference resolution: Baselines and analysis. In *Proceedings of the 2019 Conference on Empirical Methods in Natural Language Processing and the 9th International Joint Conference on Natural Language Processing (EMNLP-IJCNLP)*.

Ching-Yun Ko, Zhaoyang Lyu, Lily Weng, Luca Daniel, Ngai Wong, and Dahua Lin. 2019. POPQORN: Quantifying robustness of recurrent neural networks. In *Proceedings of the 36th International Conference on Machine Learning*.

Bin Liang, Hongcheng Li, Miaoqiang Su, Pan Bian, Xirong Li, and Wenchang Shi. 2018. Deep text classification can be fooled. *International Joint Conference on Artificial Intelligence, IJCAI 2018,*.

Matthew E Peters, Mark Neumann, Mohit Iyyer, Matt Gardner, Christopher Clark, Kenton Lee, and Luke Zettlemoyer. 2018. Deep contextualized word representations. *arXiv preprint arXiv:1802.05365*.

Nina Poerner, Ulli Waltinger, and Hinrich Schütze. 2019. Bert is not a knowledge base (yet): Factual knowledge vs. name-based reasoning in unsupervised qa.

Vinodkumar Prabhakaran, Ben Hutchinson, and Margaret Mitchell. 2019. Perturbation sensitivity analysis to detect unintended model biases. *EMNLP*.

Sameer Pradhan, Alessandro Moschitti, Nianwen Xue, Olga Uryupina, and Yuchen Zhang. 2012. CoNLL-2012 shared task: Modeling multilingual unrestricted coreference in OntoNotes. In *Joint Conference on EMNLP and CoNLL - Shared Task*.

Danish Pruthi, Bhuwan Dhingra, and Zachary C Lipton. 2019. Combating adversarial misspellings with robust word recognition.

Shuhuai Ren, Yihe Deng, Kun He, and Wanxiang Che. 2019. Generating natural language adversarial examples through probability weighted word saliency.

Marco Tulio Ribeiro, Sameer Singh, and Carlos Guestrin. 2018. Semantically equivalent adversarial rules for debugging NLP models. In *Proceedings of the 56th Annual Meeting of the Association for Computational Linguistics (Volume 1: Long Papers)*.

Suranjana Samanta and Sameep Mehta. 2017. Towards crafting text adversarial samples. *CoRR, abs/1707.02812.,*.

Zhouxing Shi, Huan Zhang, Kai-Wei Chang, Minlie Huang, and Cho-Jui Hsieh. 2020. Robustness verification for transformers. In *International Conference on Learning Representations*.

Lichao Sun, Kazuma Hashimoto, Wenpeng Yin, Akari Asai, Jia Li, Philip Yu, and Caiming Xiong. 2019. Adv-bert: Bert is not robust on misspellings! generating nature adversarial samples on bert. *arXiv preprint arXiv:2003.04985*.

Alex Wang, Amanpreet Singh, Julian Michael, Felix Hill, Omer Levy, and Samuel Bowman. 2018. GLUE: A multi-task benchmark and analysis platform for natural language understanding. In *Proceedings of the 2018 EMNLP Workshop BlackboxNLP: Analyzing and Interpreting Neural Networks for NLP*.

Yuan Zhang, Jason Baldridge, and Luheng He. 2019a. PAWS: Paraphrase adversaries from word scrambling. In *Proceedings of the 2019 Conference of the North American Chapter of the Association for Computational Linguistics*.

Zhengyan Zhang, Xu Han, Zhiyuan Liu, Xin Jiang, Maosong Sun, and Qun Liu. 2019b. ERNIE: Enhanced language representation with informative entities. In *Proceedings of ACL 2019*.

Zhengli Zhao, Dheeru Dua, and Sameer Singh. 2018. Generating natural adversarial examples. In *International Conference on Learning Representations*.

Yichao Zhou, Jyun-Yu Jiang, Kai-Wei Chang, and Wei Wang. 2019. Learning to discriminate perturbations for blocking adversarial attacks in text classification. In *Proceedings of the 2019 Conference on Empirical Methods in Natural Language Processing (EMNLP)*.